Kakuriyo
Bed & Breakfast for Spirits

Art by
Waco Ioka

Original Story by Midori Yuma
Character Design by Laruha

CONTENTS

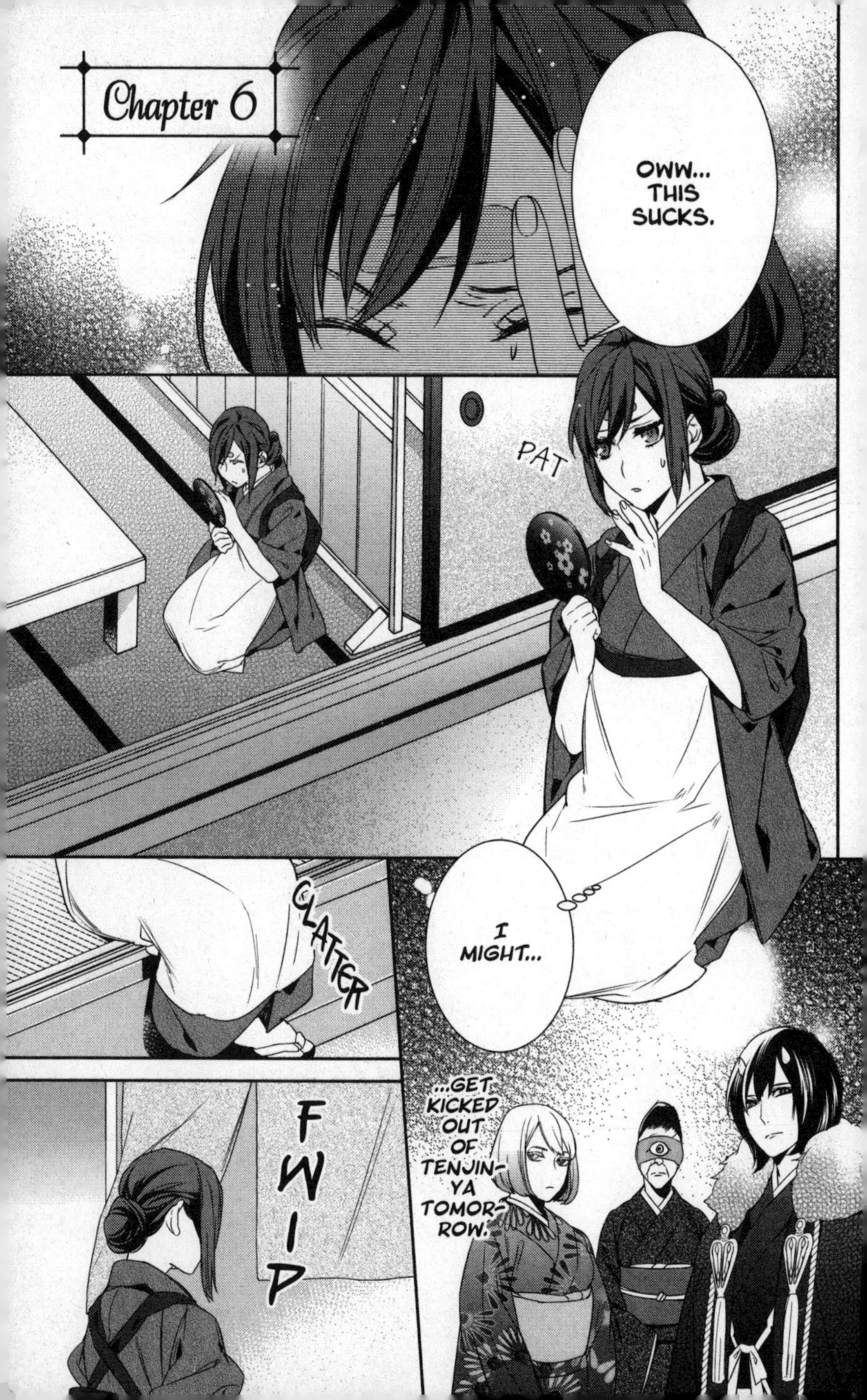
Chapter 6
OWW... THIS SUCKS.
PAT
I MIGHT...
...GET KICKED OUT OF TENJIN-YA TOMORROW.
CLATTER
FWIP

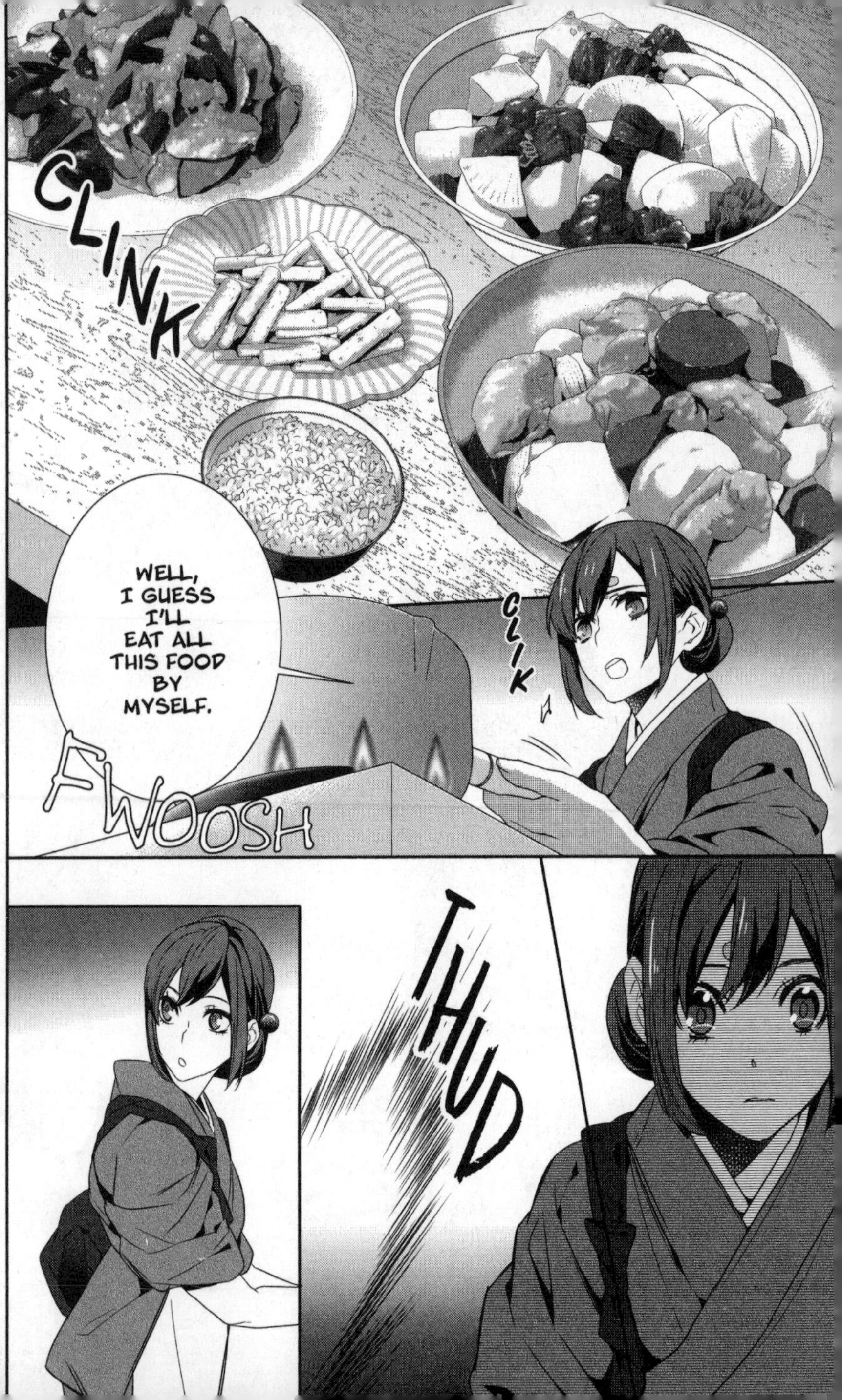
CLINK
CLIK
WELL, I GUESS I'LL EAT ALL THIS FOOD BY MYSELF.
FWOOSH
THUD

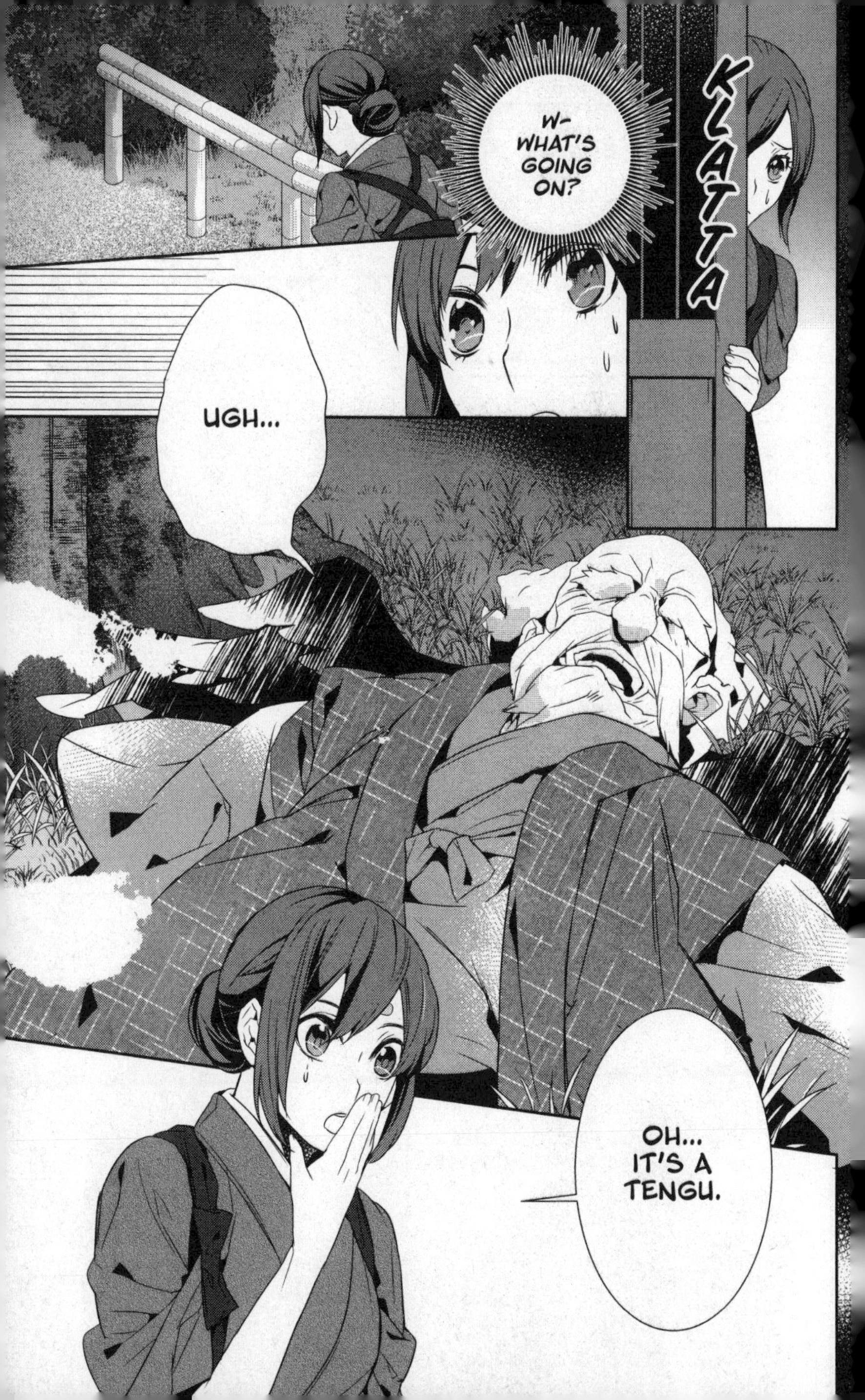
KLATTA
W-WHAT'S GOING ON?
UGH...
OH... IT'S A TENGU.

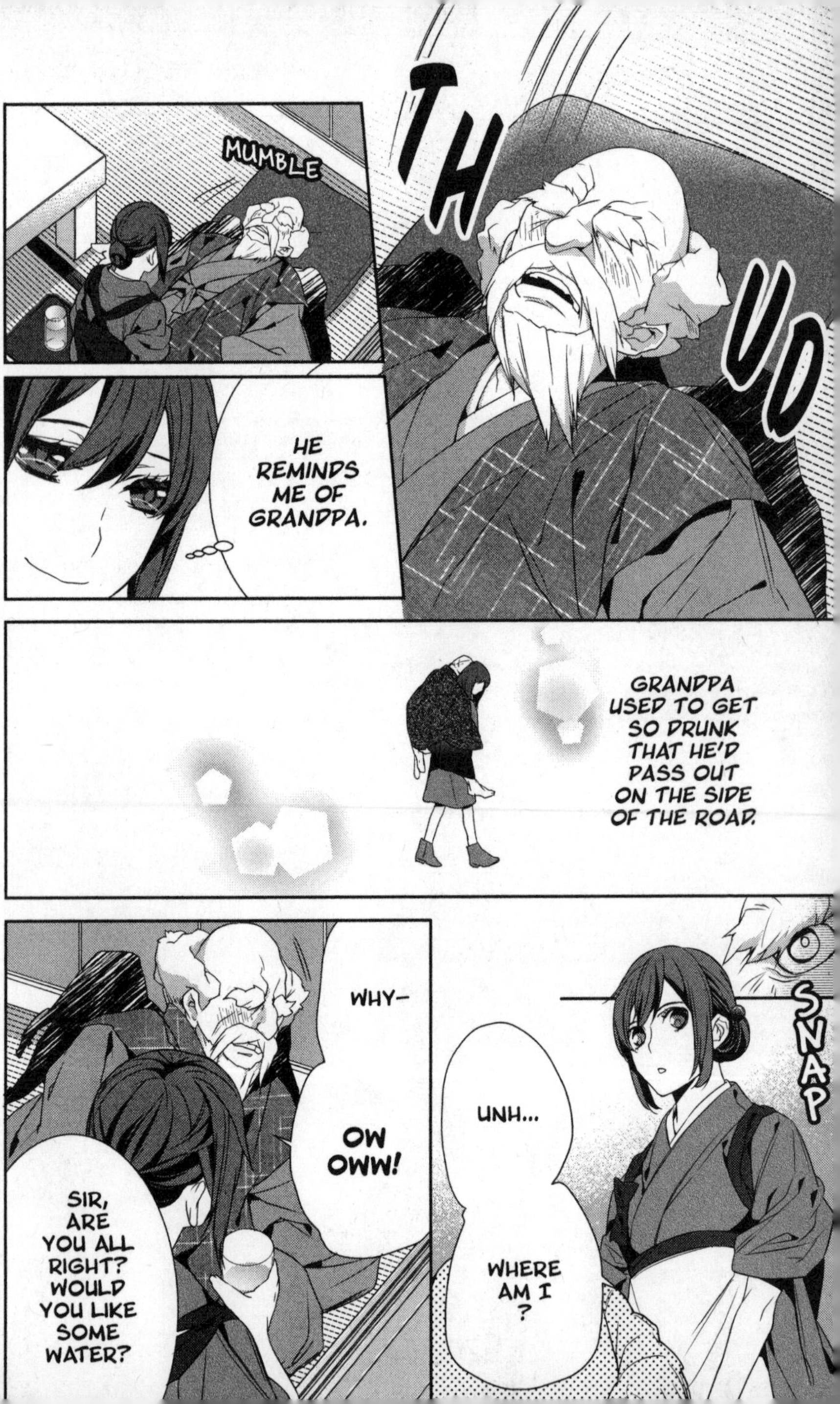
THUD
MUMBLE
HE REMINDS ME OF GRANDPA.
GRANDPA USED TO GET SO DRUNK THAT HE'D PASS OUT ON THE SIDE OF THE ROAD.
SNAP
UNH...
WHERE AM I ?
WHY-
OW OWW!
SIR, ARE YOU ALL RIGHT? WOULD YOU LIKE SOME WATER?

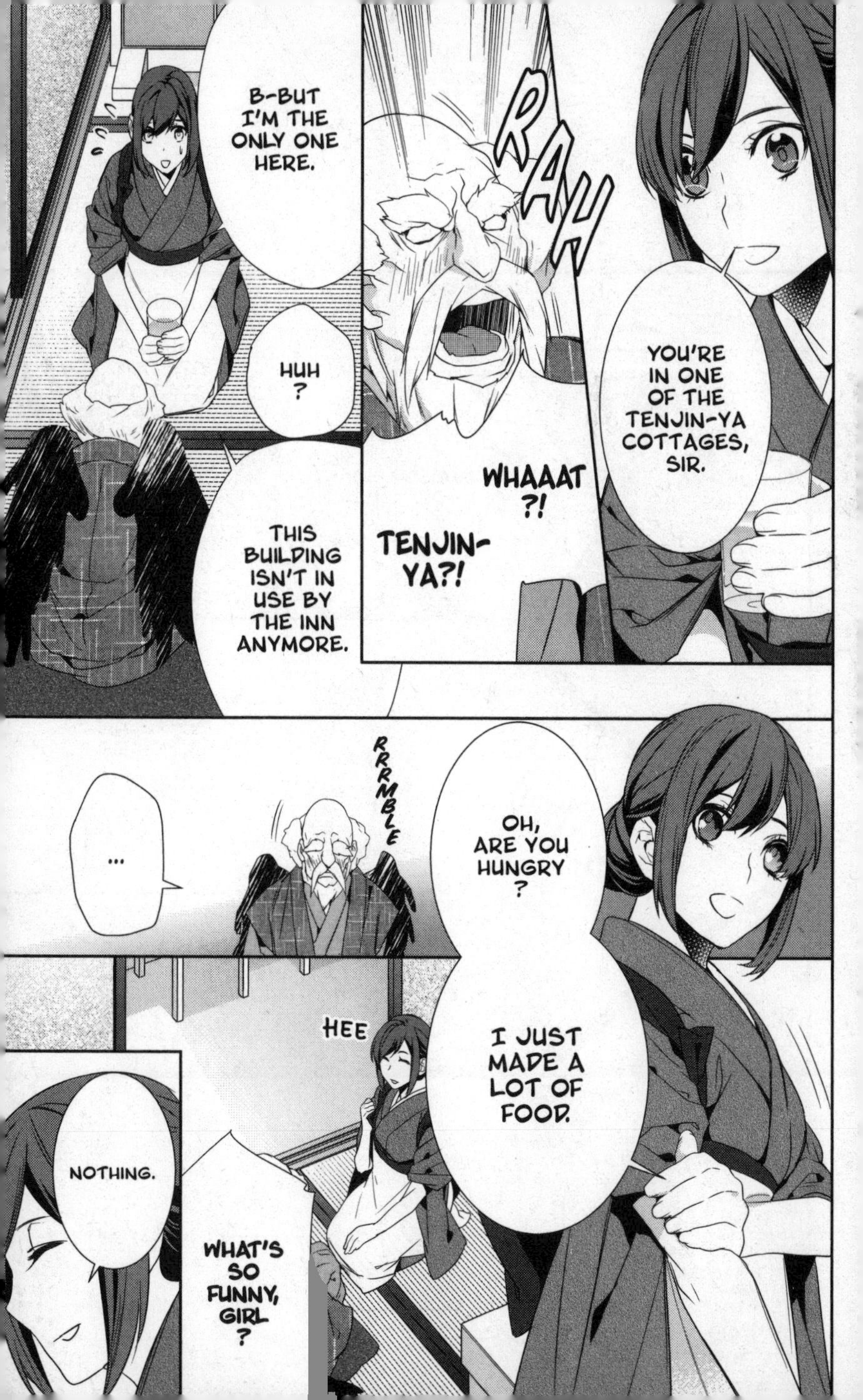
YOU'RE IN ONE OF THE TENJIN-YA COTTAGES, SIR.
RAH
WHAAAT?!
TENJIN-YA?!
B-BUT I'M THE ONLY ONE HERE.
HUH?
THIS BUILDING ISN'T IN USE BY THE INN ANYMORE.
OH, ARE YOU HUNGRY?
RRRMBLE
...
I JUST MADE A LOT OF FOOD.
HEE
WHAT'S SO FUNNY, GIRL?
NOTHING.

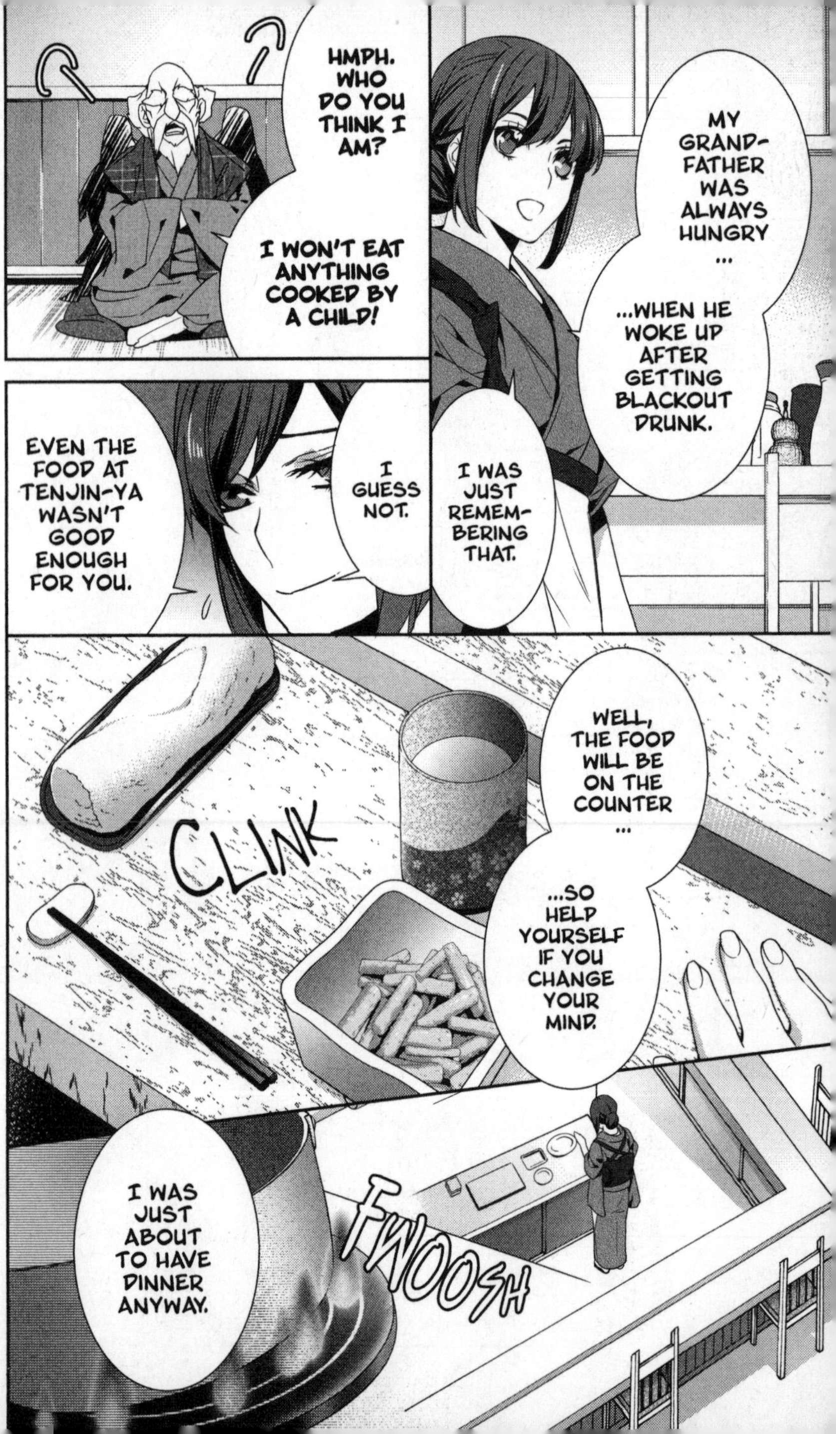
MY GRANDFATHER WAS ALWAYS HUNGRY...
...WHEN HE WOKE UP AFTER GETTING BLACKOUT DRUNK.
HMPH. WHO DO YOU THINK I AM?
I WON'T EAT ANYTHING COOKED BY A CHILD!
I WAS JUST REMEMBERING THAT.
I GUESS NOT.
EVEN THE FOOD AT TENJIN-YA WASN'T GOOD ENOUGH FOR YOU.
WELL, THE FOOD WILL BE ON THE COUNTER...
...SO HELP YOURSELF IF YOU CHANGE YOUR MIND.
CLINK
FWOOSH
I WAS JUST ABOUT TO HAVE DINNER ANYWAY.

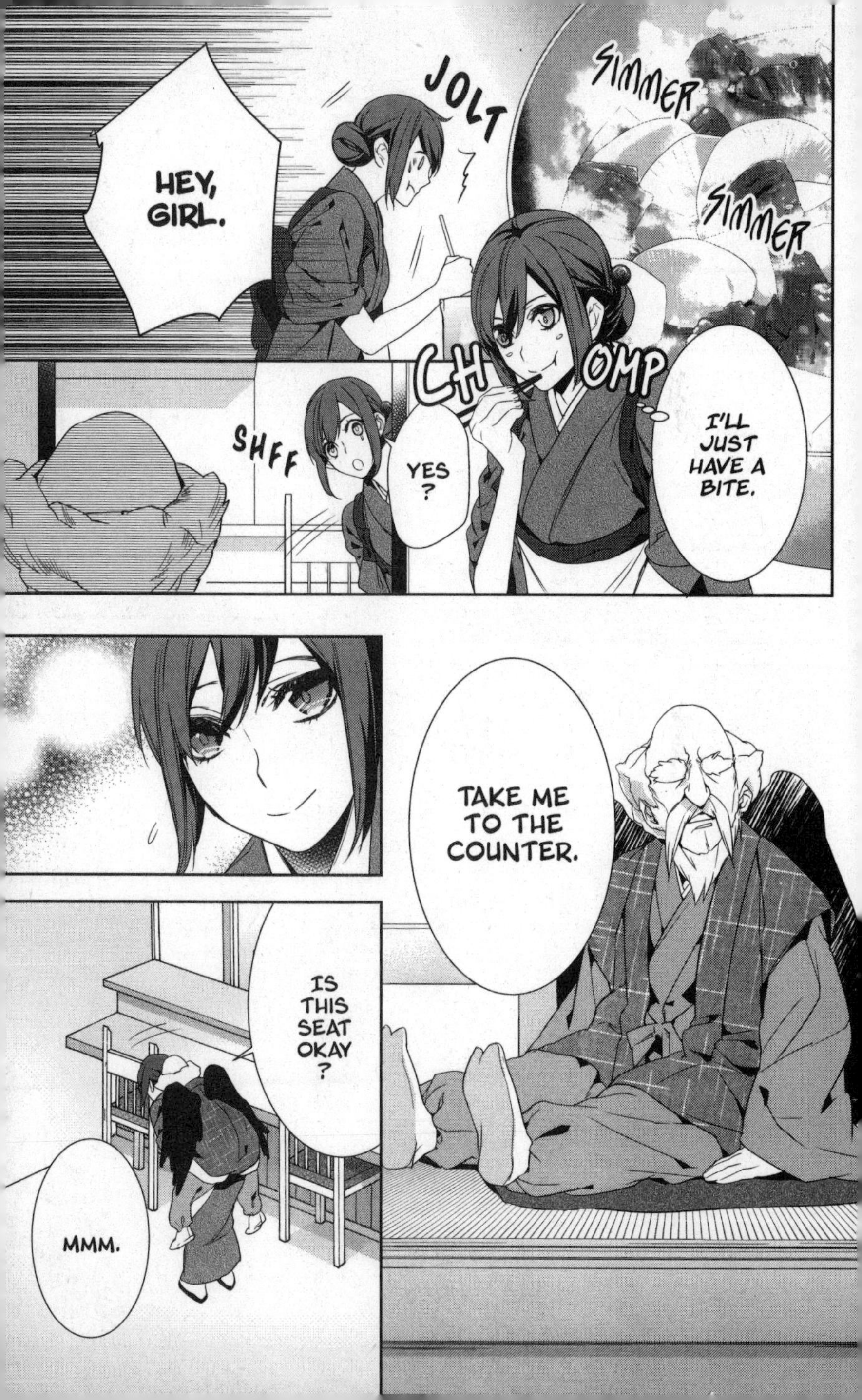
SIMMER
SIMMER
CHOMP
I'LL JUST HAVE A BITE.
HEY, GIRL.
JOLT
SHFF
YES?
TAKE ME TO THE COUNTER.
IS THIS SEAT OKAY?
MMM.

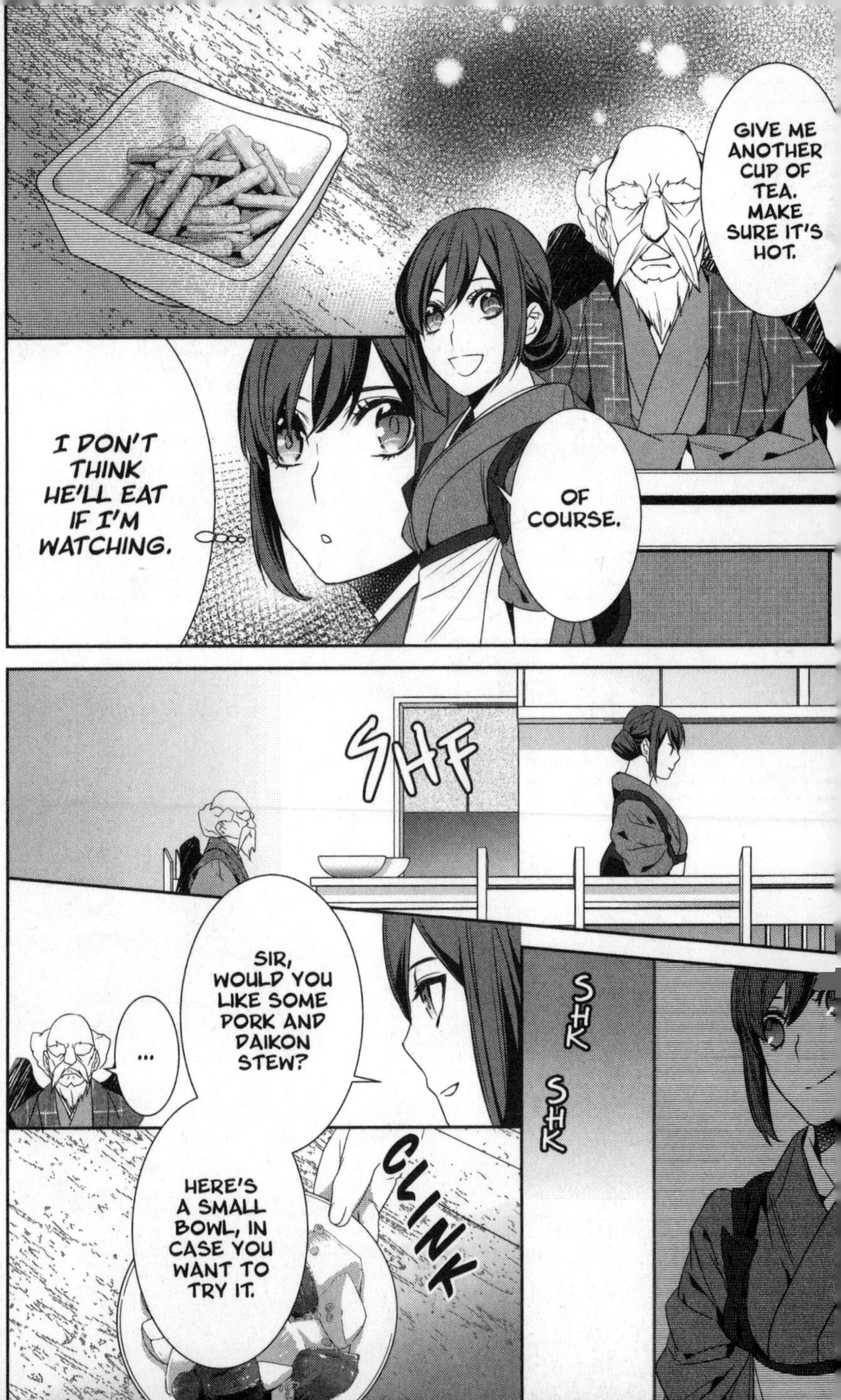

GIVE ME ANOTHER CUP OF TEA. MAKE SURE IT'S HOT.
OF COURSE.
I DON'T THINK HE'LL EAT IF I'M WATCHING.
SHF
SHK SHK
SIR, WOULD YOU LIKE SOME PORK AND DAIKON STEW?
...
HERE'S A SMALL BOWL, IN CASE YOU WANT TO TRY IT.
CLINK

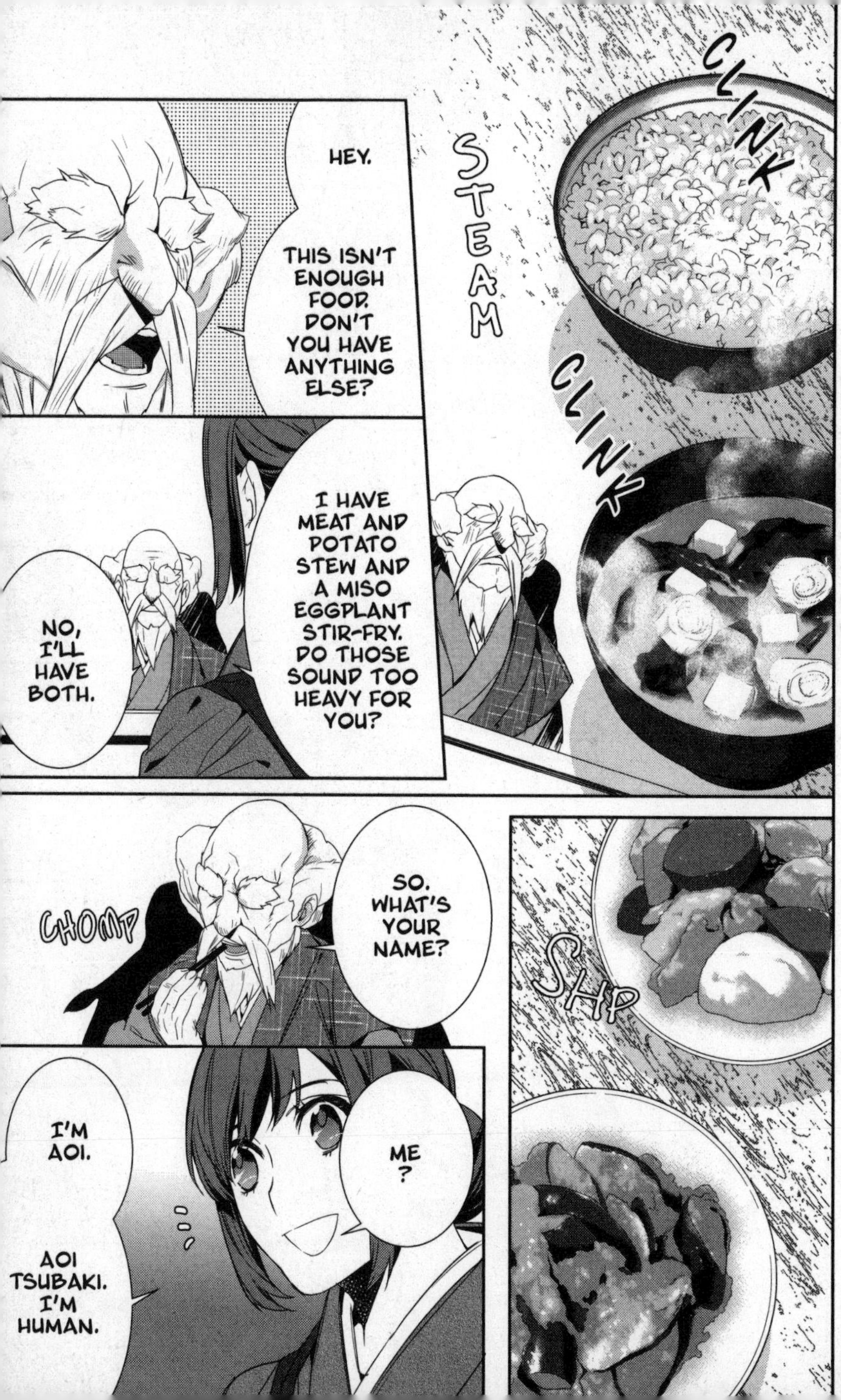
CLINK
STEAM
CLINK
HEY.
THIS ISN'T ENOUGH FOOD. DON'T YOU HAVE ANYTHING ELSE?
I HAVE MEAT AND POTATO STEW AND A MISO EGGPLANT STIR-FRY. DO THOSE SOUND TOO HEAVY FOR YOU?
NO, I'LL HAVE BOTH.
SHP
SO. WHAT'S YOUR NAME?
CHOMP
ME?
I'M AOI.
AOI TSUBAKI. I'M HUMAN.

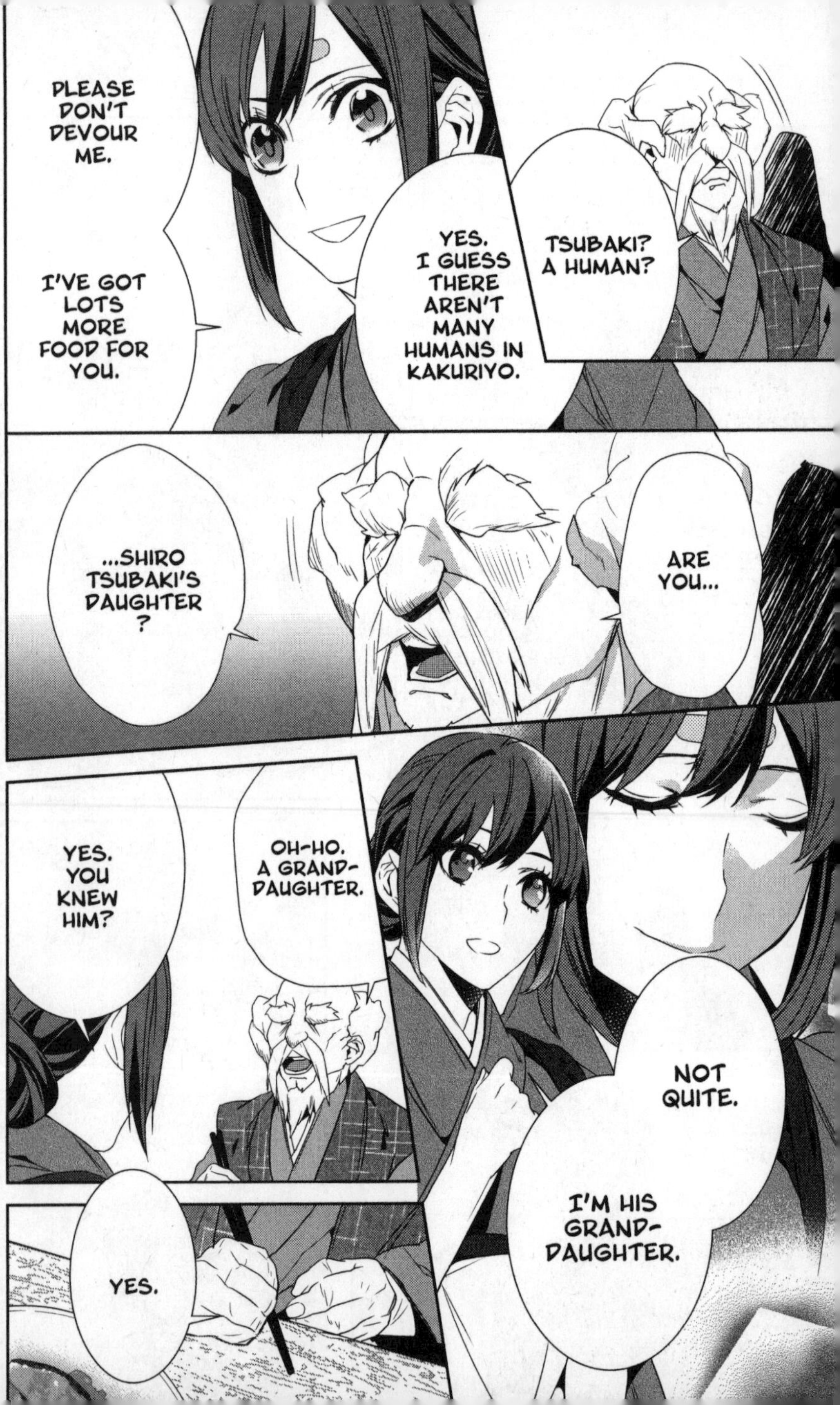
TSUBAKI? A HUMAN?
YES. I GUESS THERE AREN'T MANY HUMANS IN KAKURIYO.
PLEASE DON'T DEVOUR ME.
I'VE GOT LOTS MORE FOOD FOR YOU.
ARE YOU...
...SHIRO TSUBAKI'S DAUGHTER ?
NOT QUITE.
I'M HIS GRAND-DAUGHTER.
OH-HO. A GRAND-DAUGHTER.
YES. YOU KNEW HIM?
YES.

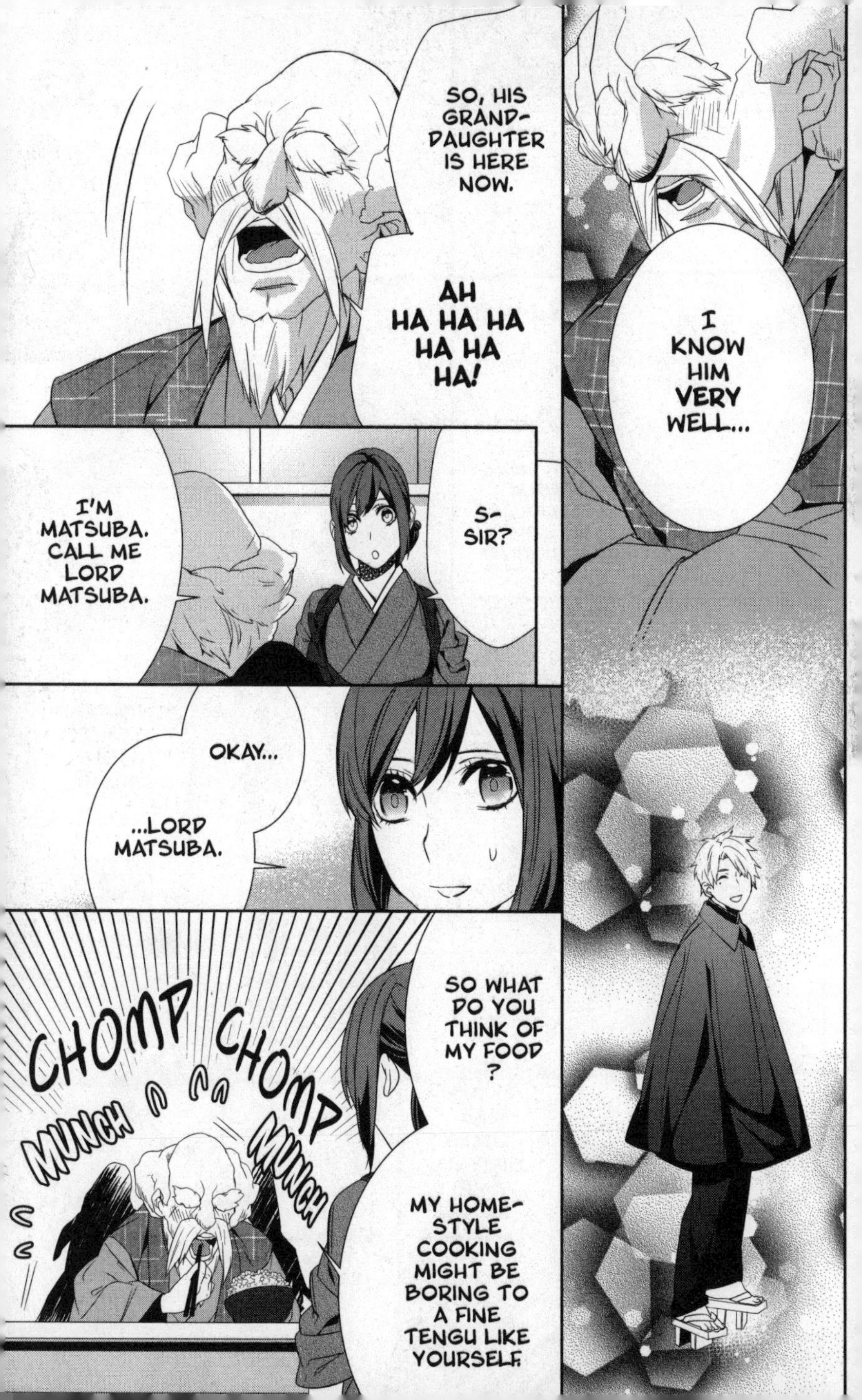
I KNOW HIM VERY WELL...
SO, HIS GRAND-DAUGHTER IS HERE NOW.
AH HA HA HA HA HA HA!
S-SIR?
I'M MATSUBA. CALL ME LORD MATSUBA.
OKAY...
...LORD MATSUBA.
SO WHAT DO YOU THINK OF MY FOOD?
MY HOME-STYLE COOKING MIGHT BE BORING TO A FINE TENGU LIKE YOURSELF.
CHOMP CHOMP
MUNCH MUNCH

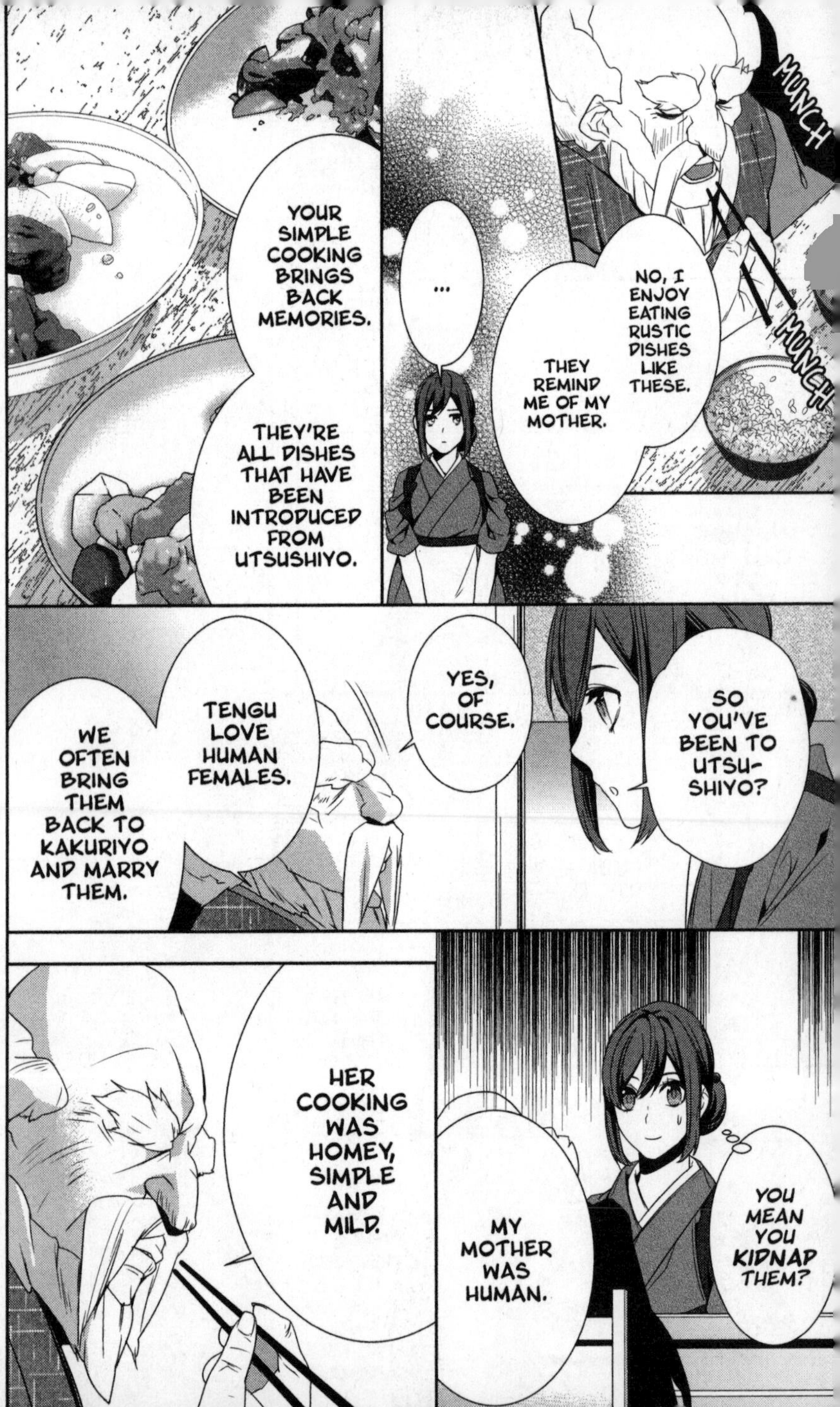
MUNCH
NO, I ENJOY EATING RUSTIC DISHES LIKE THESE.
THEY REMIND ME OF MY MOTHER.
MUNCH
...
YOUR SIMPLE COOKING BRINGS BACK MEMORIES.
THEY'RE ALL DISHES THAT HAVE BEEN INTRODUCED FROM UTSUSHIYO.
SO YOU'VE BEEN TO UTSU-SHIYO?
YES, OF COURSE.
TENGU LOVE HUMAN FEMALES.
WE OFTEN BRING THEM BACK TO KAKURIYO AND MARRY THEM.
YOU MEAN YOU KIDNAP THEM?
MY MOTHER WAS HUMAN.
HER COOKING WAS HOMEY, SIMPLE AND MILD.

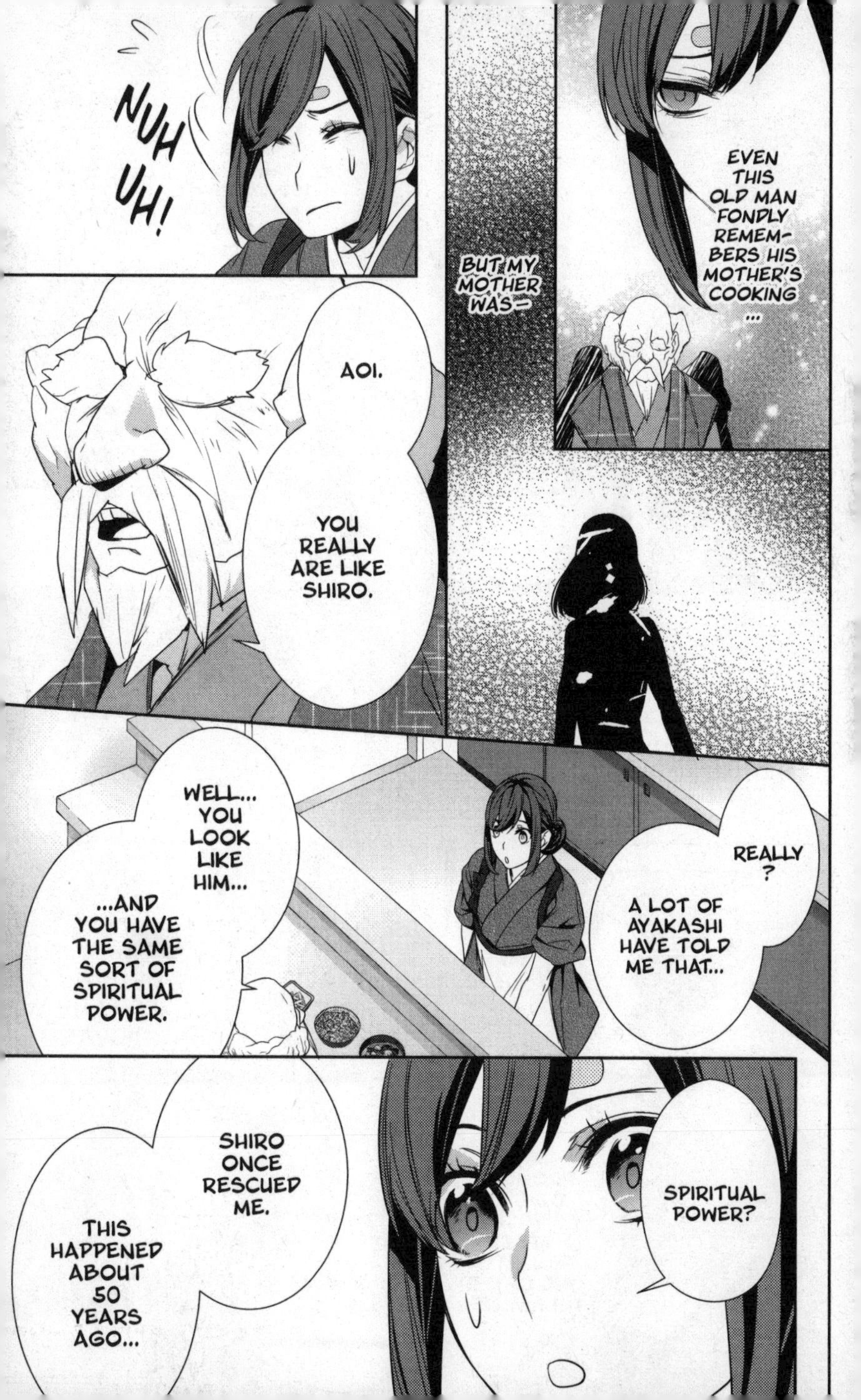
EVEN THIS OLD MAN FONDLY REMEMBERS HIS MOTHER'S COOKING ...
BUT MY MOTHER WAS—
NUH UH!
AOI.
YOU REALLY ARE LIKE SHIRO.
REALLY?
A LOT OF AYAKASHI HAVE TOLD ME THAT...
WELL... YOU LOOK LIKE HIM...
...AND YOU HAVE THE SAME SORT OF SPIRITUAL POWER.
SPIRITUAL POWER?
SHIRO ONCE RESCUED ME.
THIS HAPPENED ABOUT 50 YEARS AGO...

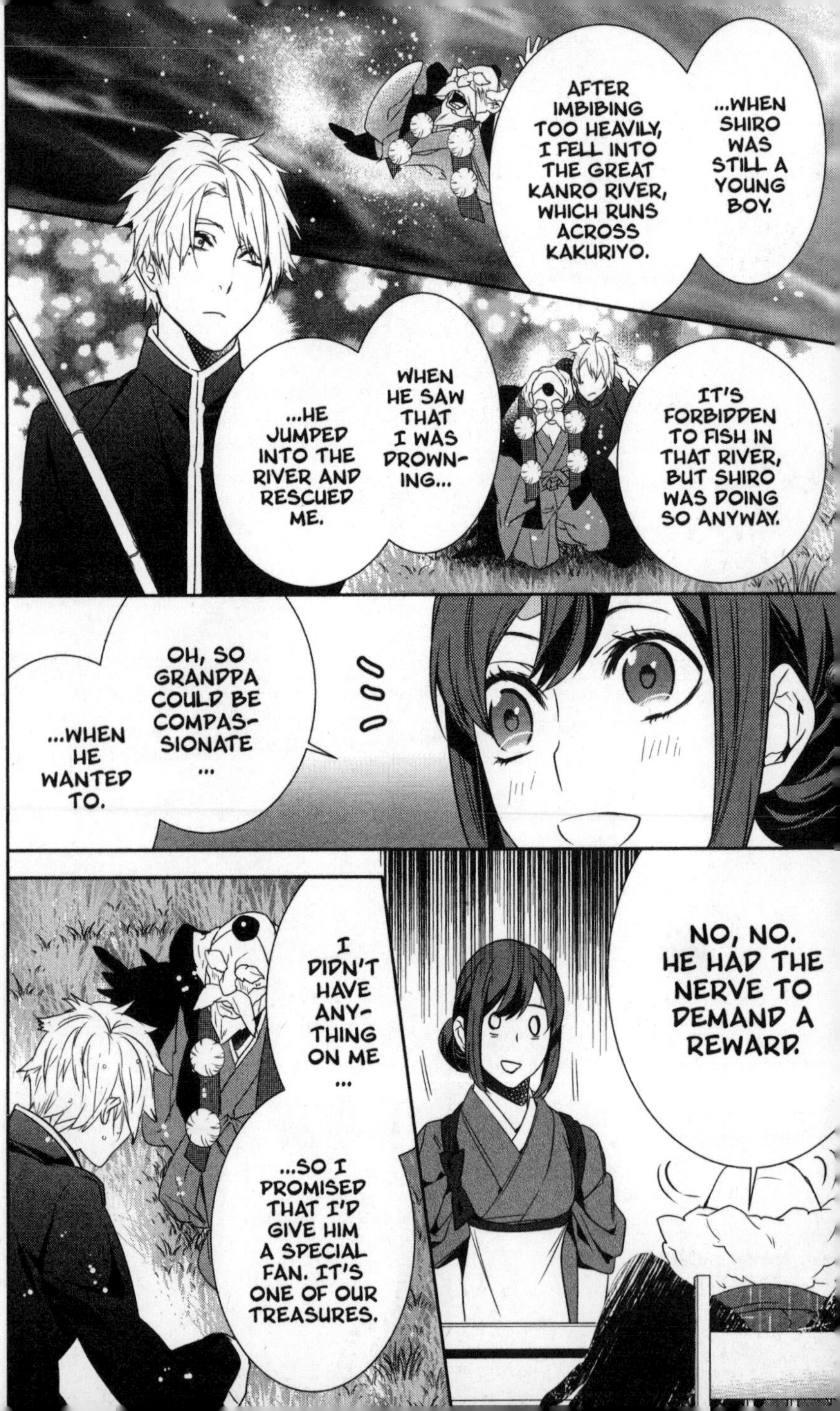
...WHEN SHIRO WAS STILL A YOUNG BOY.
AFTER IMBIBING TOO HEAVILY, I FELL INTO THE GREAT KANRO RIVER, WHICH RUNS ACROSS KAKURIYO.
IT'S FORBIDDEN TO FISH IN THAT RIVER, BUT SHIRO WAS DOING SO ANYWAY.
WHEN HE SAW THAT I WAS DROWNING...
...HE JUMPED INTO THE RIVER AND RESCUED ME.
OH, SO GRANDPA COULD BE COMPASSIONATE...
...WHEN HE WANTED TO.
NO, NO. HE HAD THE NERVE TO DEMAND A REWARD.
I DIDN'T HAVE ANYTHING ON ME...
...SO I PROMISED THAT I'D GIVE HIM A SPECIAL FAN. IT'S ONE OF OUR TREASURES.

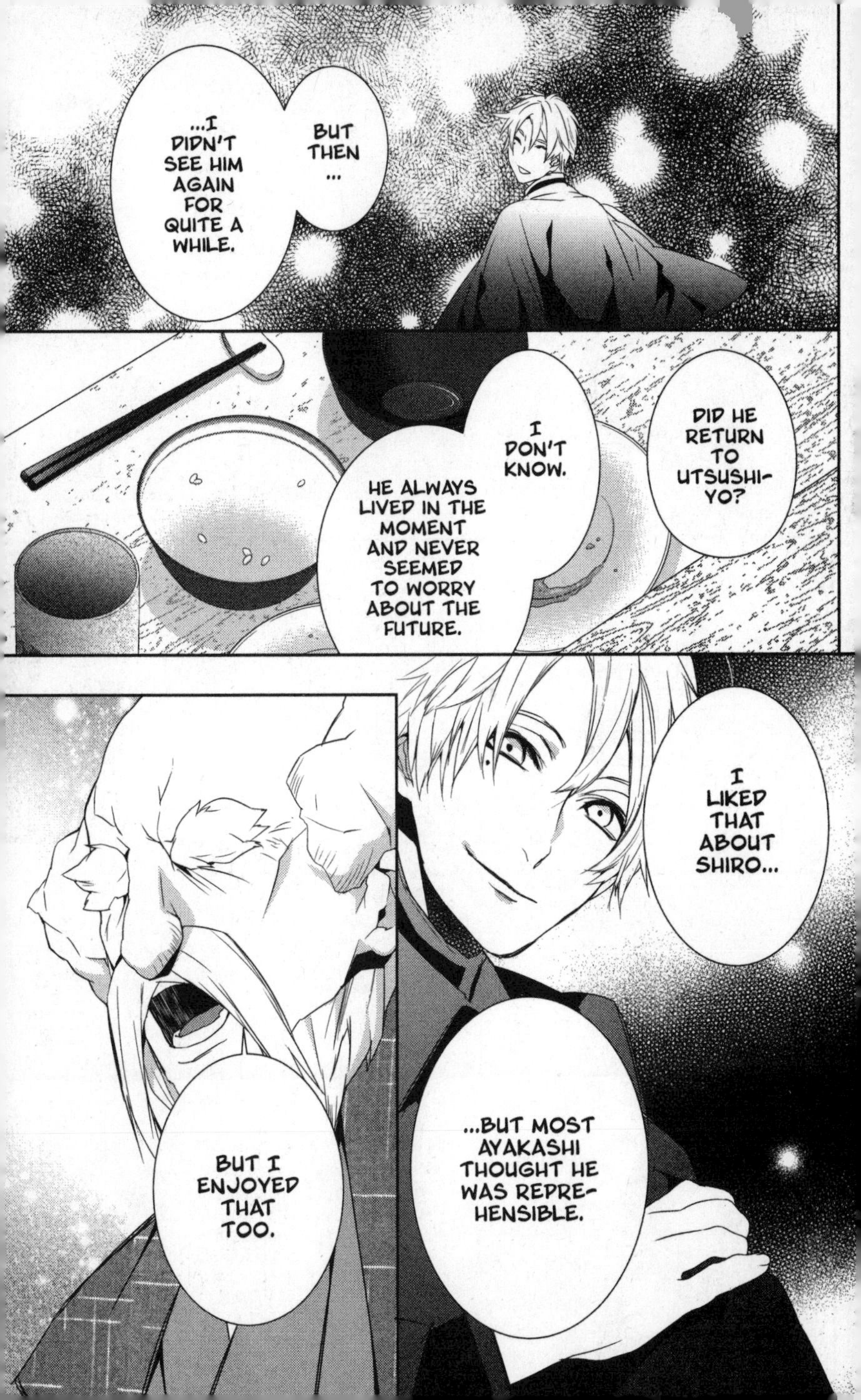
BUT THEN ...
...I DIDN'T SEE HIM AGAIN FOR QUITE A WHILE.
DID HE RETURN TO UTSUSHI-YO?
I DON'T KNOW.
HE ALWAYS LIVED IN THE MOMENT AND NEVER SEEMED TO WORRY ABOUT THE FUTURE.
I LIKED THAT ABOUT SHIRO...
...BUT MOST AYAKASHI THOUGHT HE WAS REPRE-HENSIBLE.
BUT I ENJOYED THAT TOO.

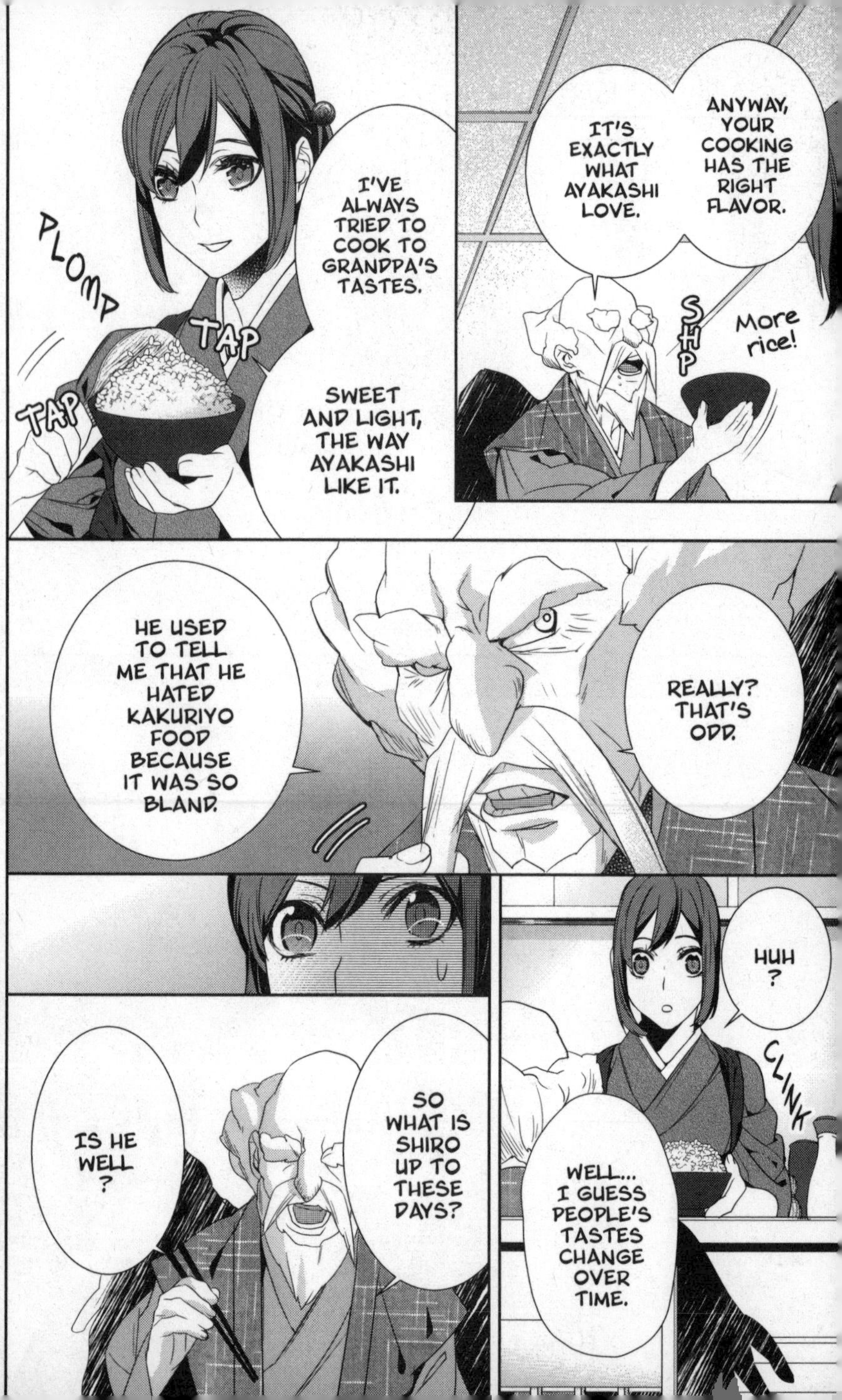
ANYWAY, YOUR COOKING HAS THE RIGHT FLAVOR.
IT'S EXACTLY WHAT AYAKASHI LOVE.
SHP
More rice!
I'VE ALWAYS TRIED TO COOK TO GRANDPA'S TASTES.
PLOMP
TAP
TAP
SWEET AND LIGHT, THE WAY AYAKASHI LIKE IT.
REALLY? THAT'S ODD.
HE USED TO TELL ME THAT HE HATED KAKURIYO FOOD BECAUSE IT WAS SO BLAND.
HUH?
CLINK
WELL... I GUESS PEOPLE'S TASTES CHANGE OVER TIME.
SO WHAT IS SHIRO UP TO THESE DAYS?
IS HE WELL?

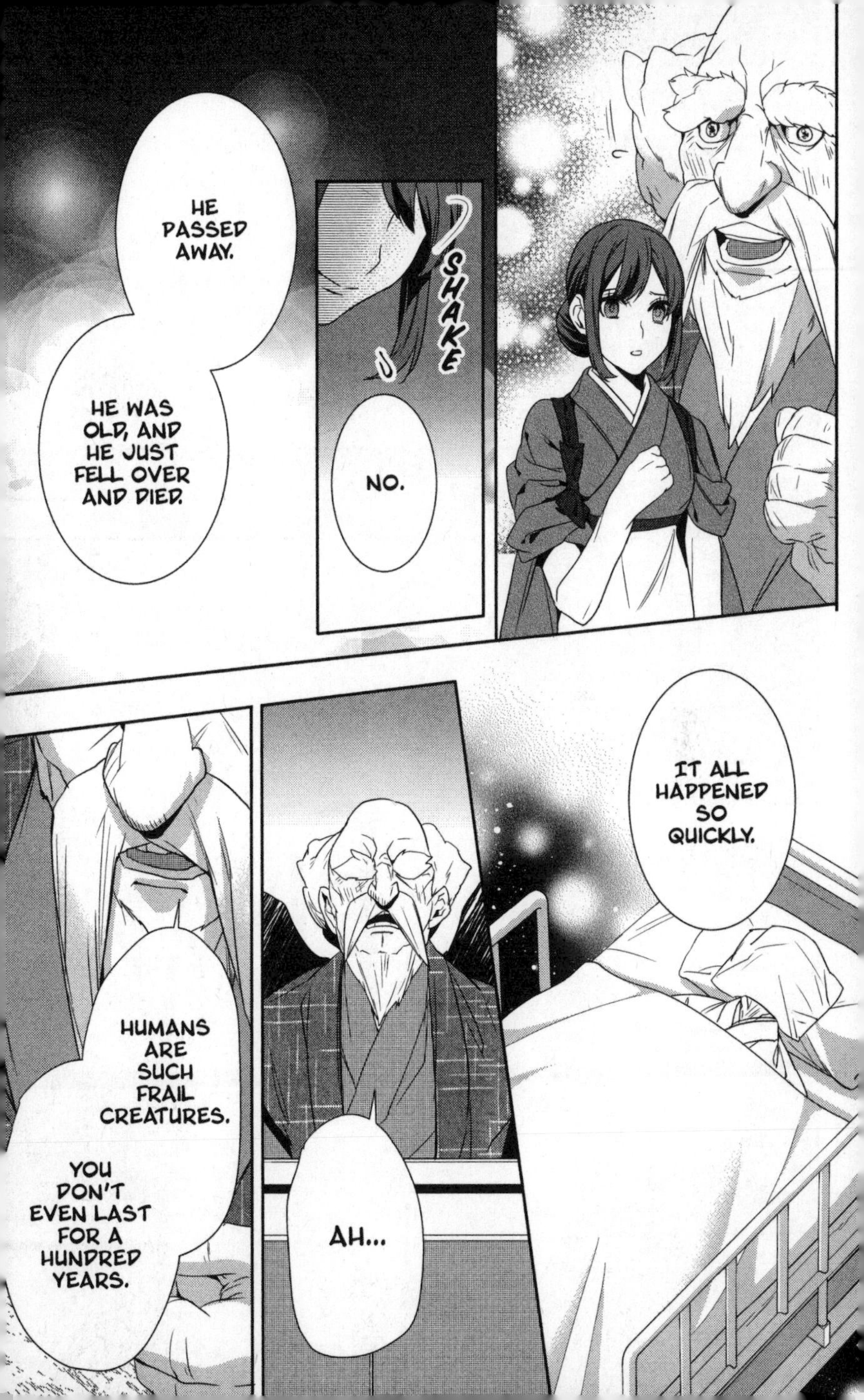
SHAKE
NO.
HE PASSED AWAY.
HE WAS OLD, AND HE JUST FELL OVER AND DIED.
IT ALL HAPPENED SO QUICKLY.
AH...
HUMANS ARE SUCH FRAIL CREATURES.
YOU DON'T EVEN LAST FOR A HUNDRED YEARS.

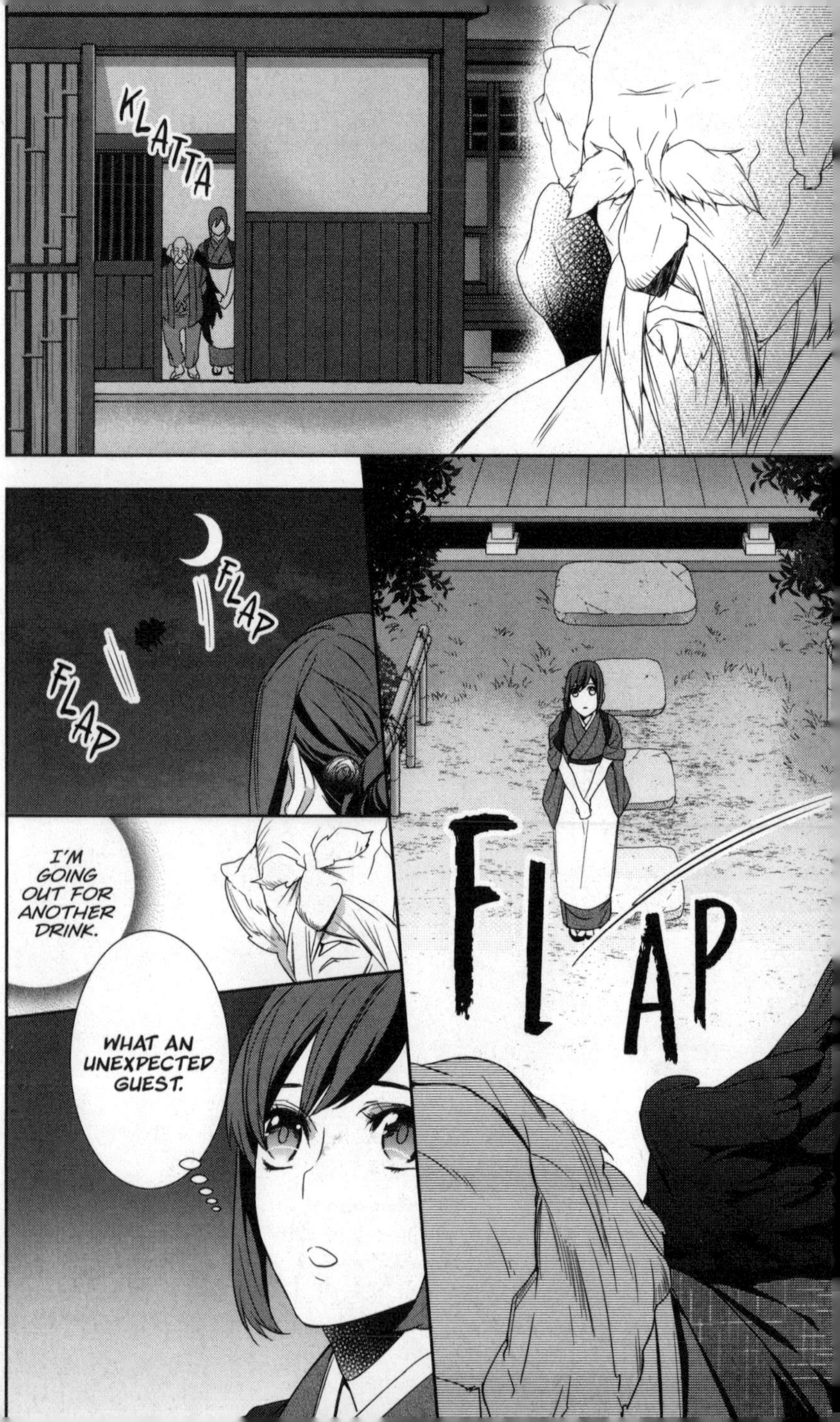
KLATTA
FLAP
FLAP
FLAP
I'M GOING OUT FOR ANOTHER DRINK.
WHAT AN UNEXPECTED GUEST.

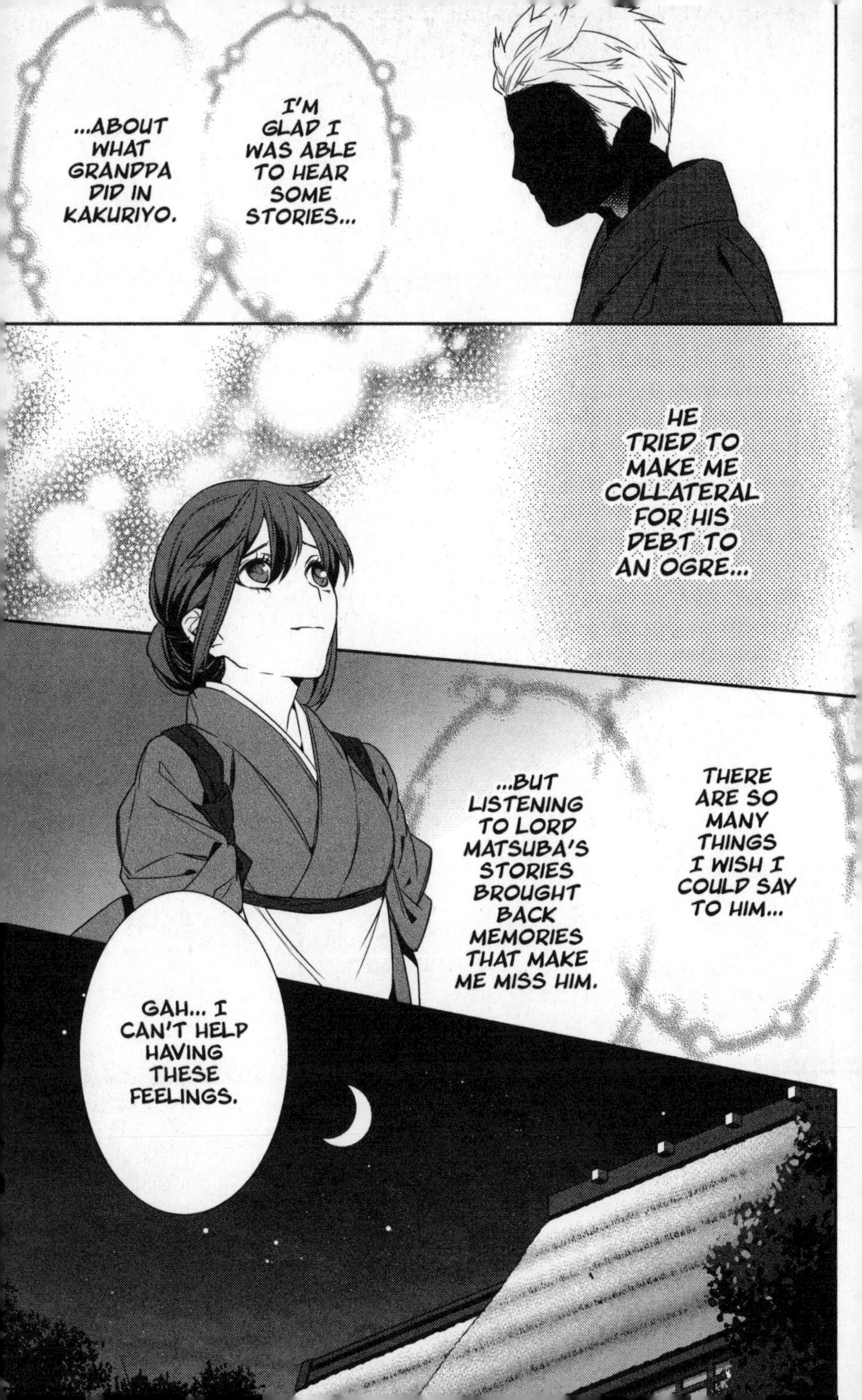
I'M GLAD I WAS ABLE TO HEAR SOME STORIES...
...ABOUT WHAT GRANDPA DID IN KAKURIYO.
HE TRIED TO MAKE ME COLLATERAL FOR HIS DEBT TO AN OGRE...
THERE ARE SO MANY THINGS I WISH I COULD SAY TO HIM...
...BUT LISTENING TO LORD MATSUBA'S STORIES BROUGHT BACK MEMORIES THAT MAKE ME MISS HIM.
GAH... I CAN'T HELP HAVING THESE FEELINGS.

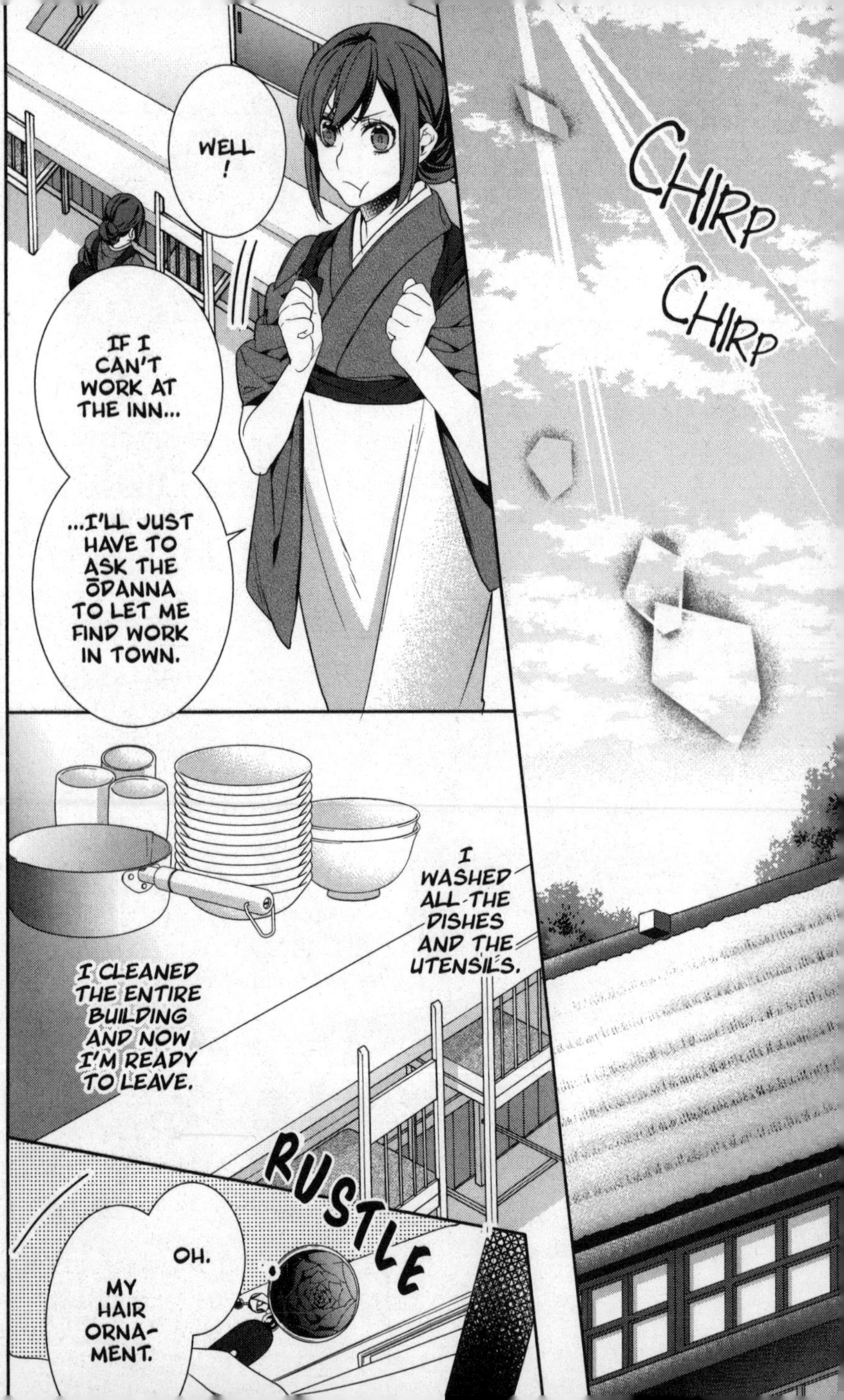
CHIRP CHIRP
WELL!
IF I CAN'T WORK AT THE INN...
...I'LL JUST HAVE TO ASK THE ŌDANNA TO LET ME FIND WORK IN TOWN.
I WASHED ALL THE DISHES AND THE UTENSILS.
I CLEANED THE ENTIRE BUILDING AND NOW I'M READY TO LEAVE.
RUSTLE
OH.
MY HAIR ORNA-MENT.

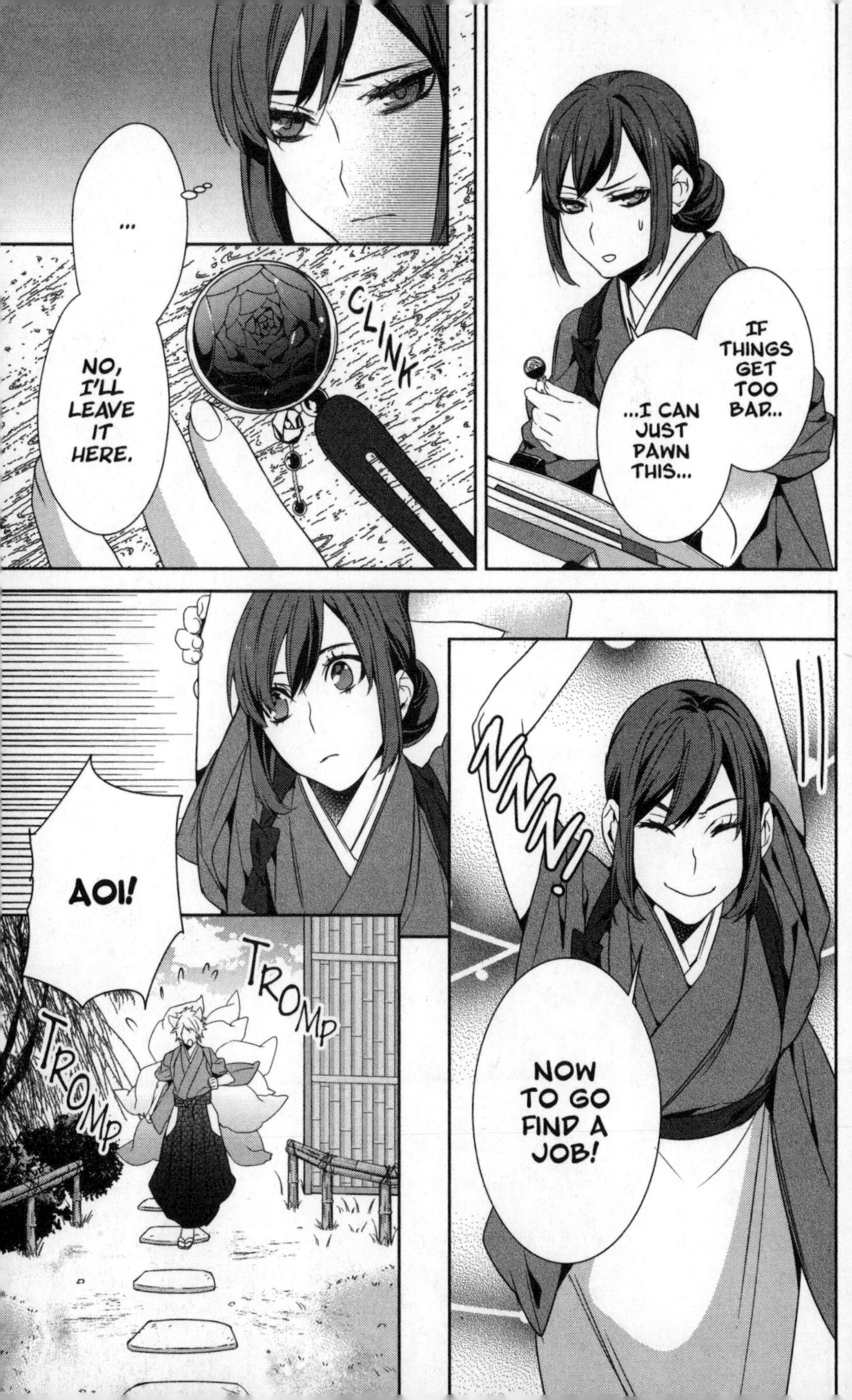

IF THINGS GET TOO BAD...
...I CAN JUST PAWN THIS...
...
CLINK
NO, I'LL LEAVE IT HERE.
NNNN!
NOW TO GO FIND A JOB!
AOI!
TROMP
TROMP

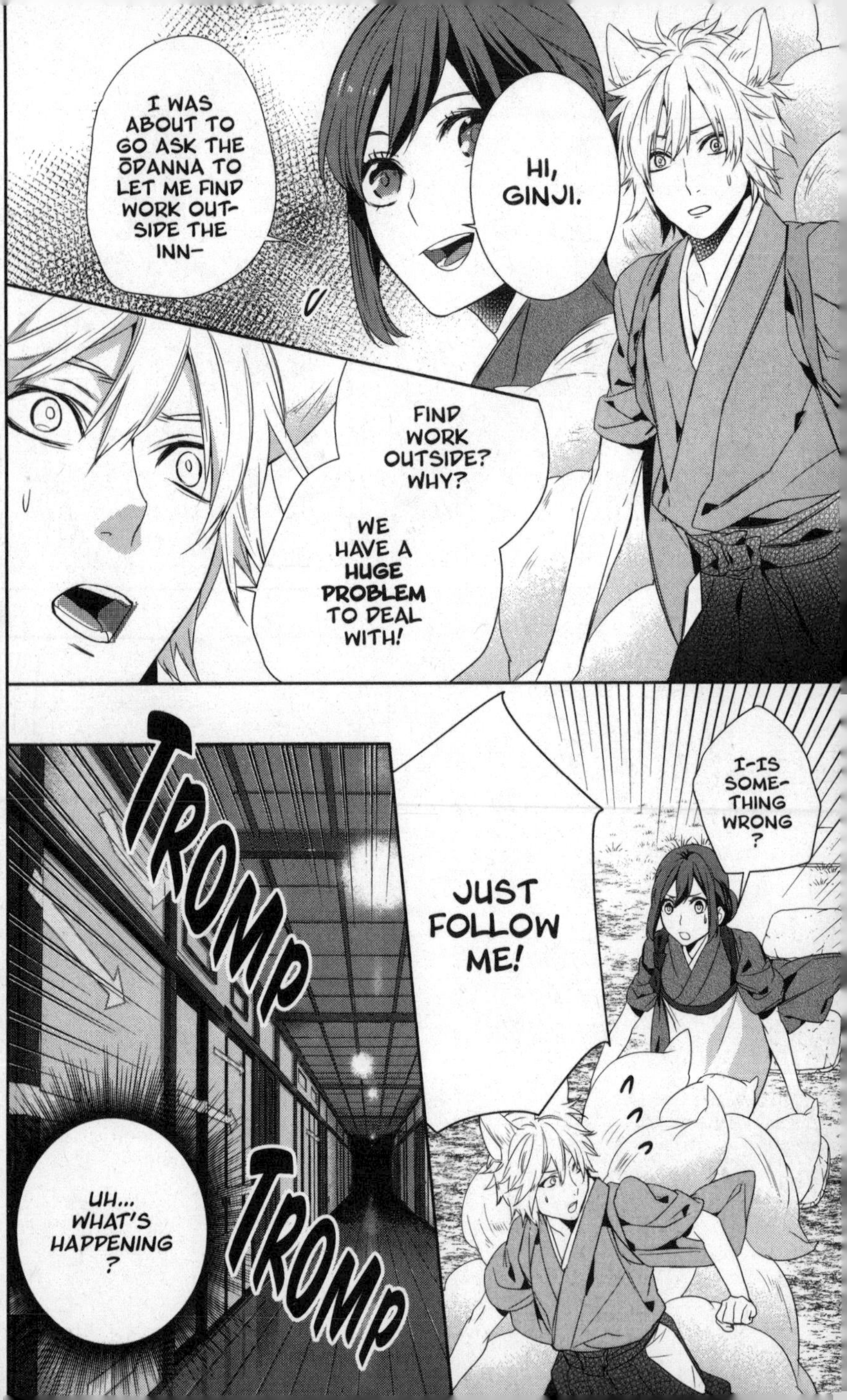
HI, GINJI.
I WAS ABOUT TO GO ASK THE ŌDANNA TO LET ME FIND WORK OUT-SIDE THE INN—
FIND WORK OUTSIDE? WHY?
WE HAVE A HUGE PROBLEM TO DEAL WITH!
I-IS SOME-THING WRONG?
JUST FOLLOW ME!
TROMP
TROMP
UH... WHAT'S HAPPENING?

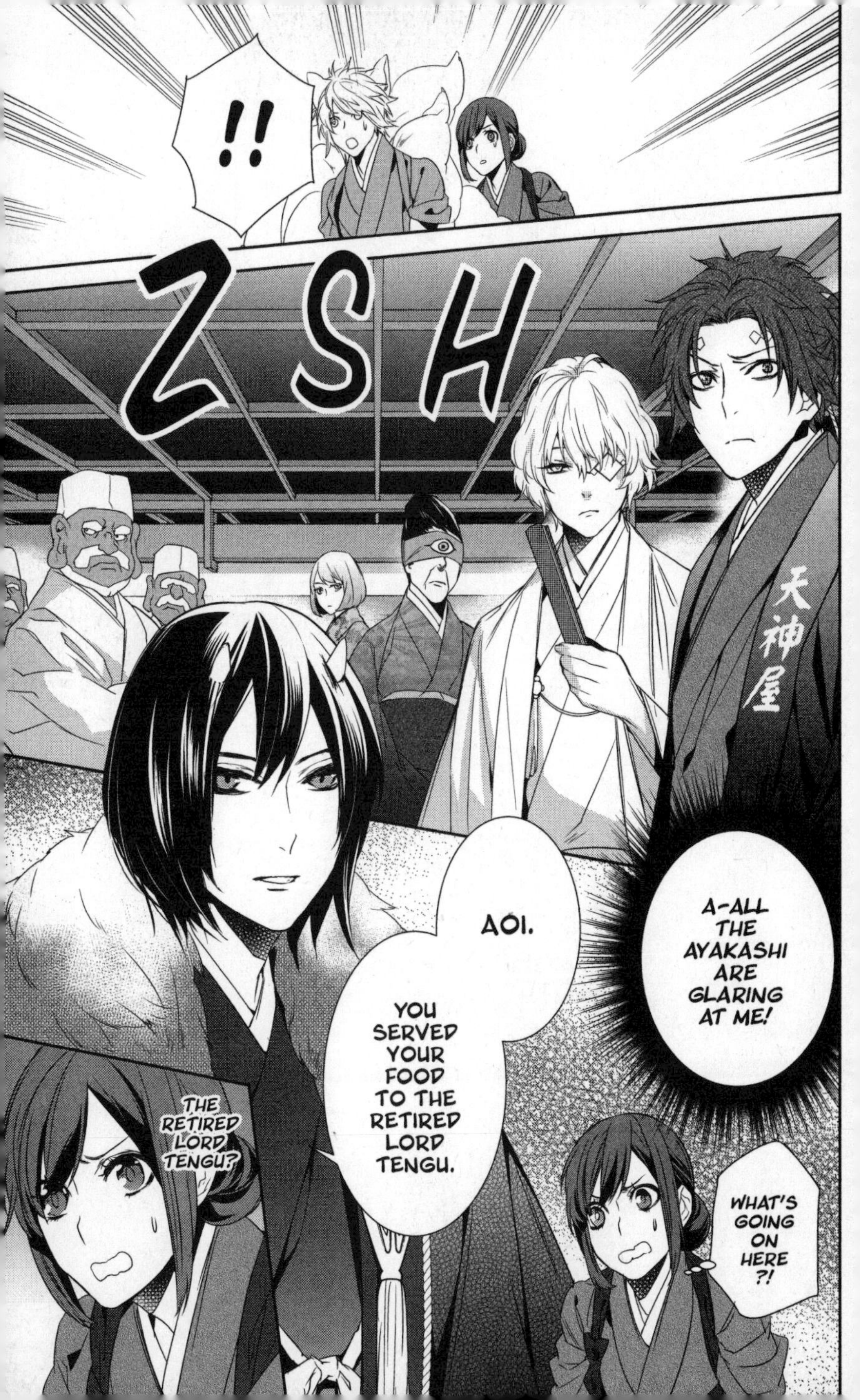
!!
ZSH
天神屋
A-ALL THE AYAKASHI ARE GLARING AT ME!
AOI.
YOU SERVED YOUR FOOD TO THE RETIRED LORD TENGU.
WHAT'S GOING ON HERE?!
THE RETIRED LORD TENGU?

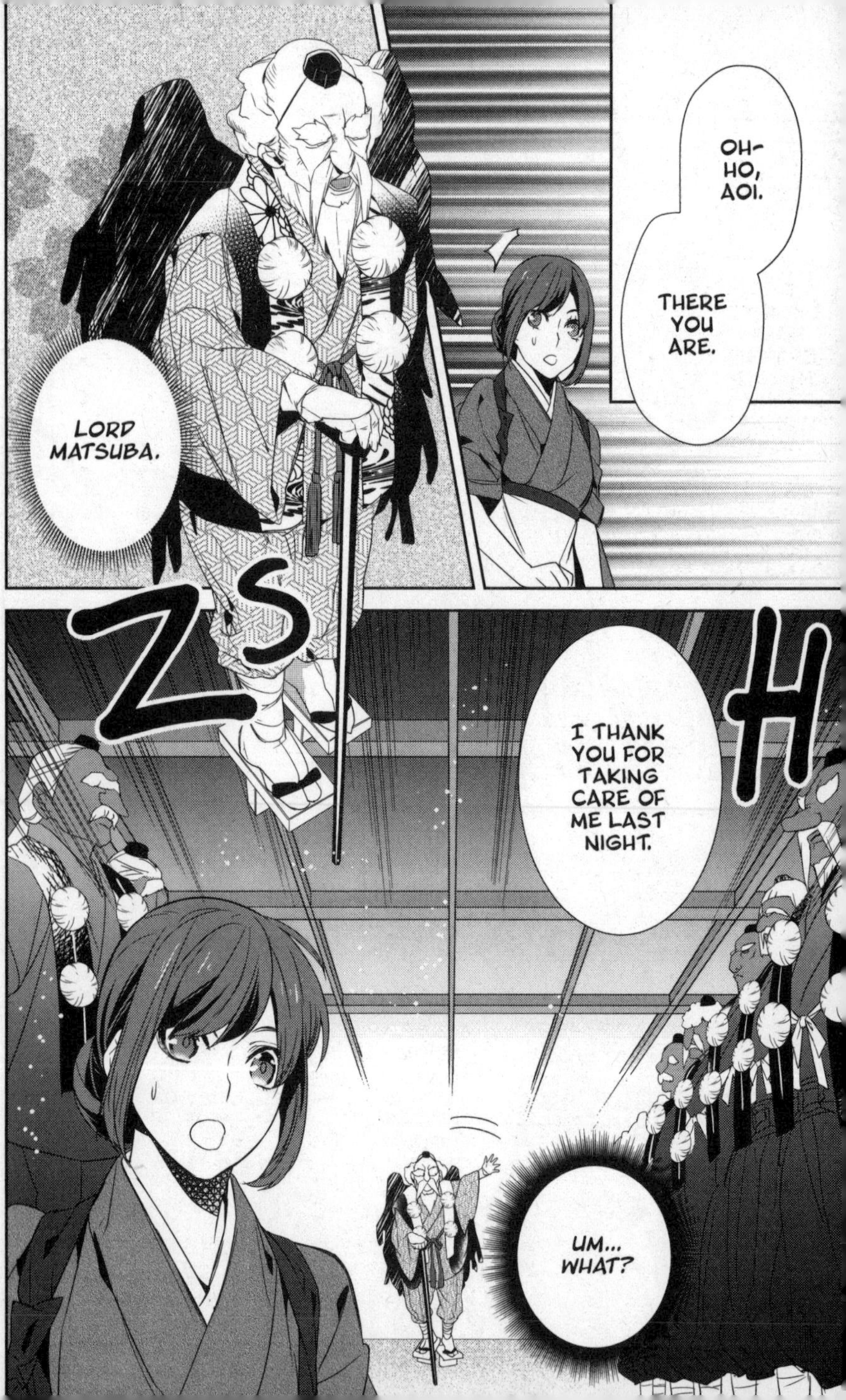
OH-HO, AOI.
THERE YOU ARE.
LORD MATSUBA.
ZSH
I THANK YOU FOR TAKING CARE OF ME LAST NIGHT.
UM... WHAT?

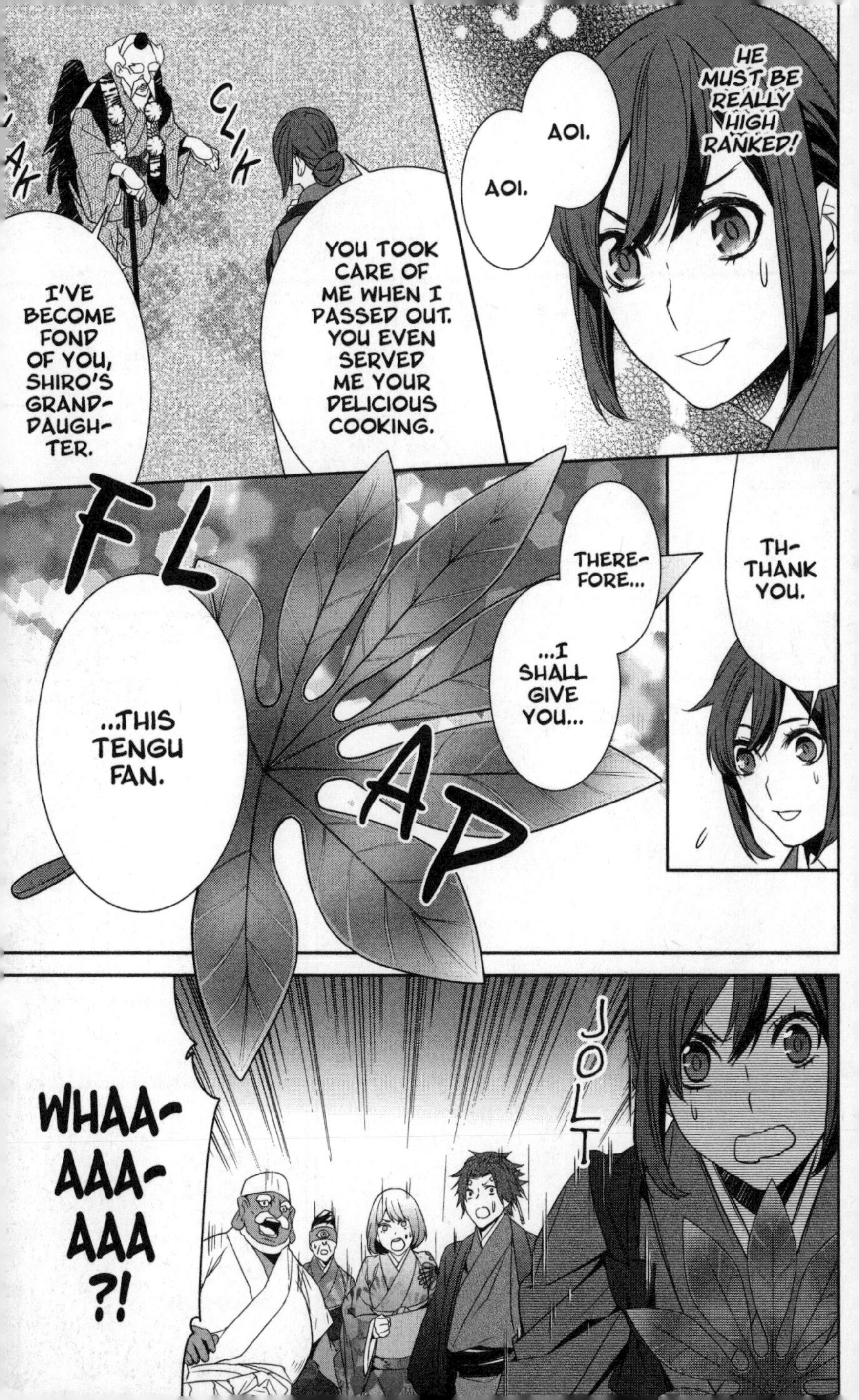
HE MUST BE REALLY HIGH RANKED!
AOI.
AOI.
CLIK
AK
YOU TOOK CARE OF ME WHEN I PASSED OUT. YOU EVEN SERVED ME YOUR DELICIOUS COOKING.
I'VE BECOME FOND OF YOU, SHIRO'S GRAND-DAUGH-TER.
TH-THANK YOU.
THERE-FORE...
...I SHALL GIVE YOU...
FLAP
...THIS TENGU FAN.
JOLT
WHAA-AAA-AAA?!

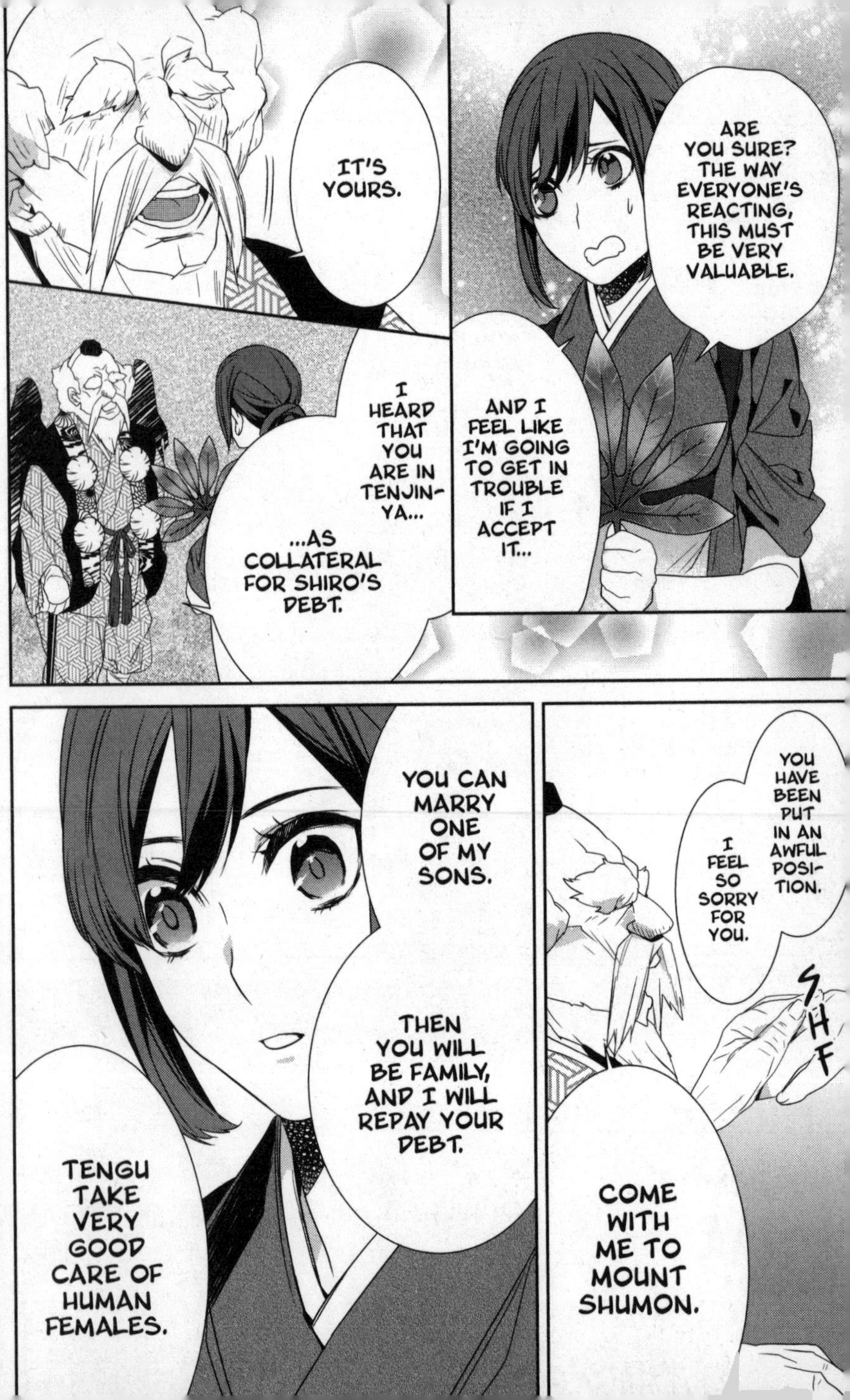
ARE YOU SURE? THE WAY EVERYONE'S REACTING, THIS MUST BE VERY VALUABLE.
AND I FEEL LIKE I'M GOING TO GET IN TROUBLE IF I ACCEPT IT...
IT'S YOURS.
I HEARD THAT YOU ARE IN TENJIN-YA...
...AS COLLATERAL FOR SHIRO'S DEBT.
YOU HAVE BEEN PUT IN AN AWFUL POSITION.
I FEEL SO SORRY FOR YOU.
SHF
COME WITH ME TO MOUNT SHUMON.
YOU CAN MARRY ONE OF MY SONS.
THEN YOU WILL BE FAMILY, AND I WILL REPAY YOUR DEBT.
TENGU TAKE VERY GOOD CARE OF HUMAN FEMALES.

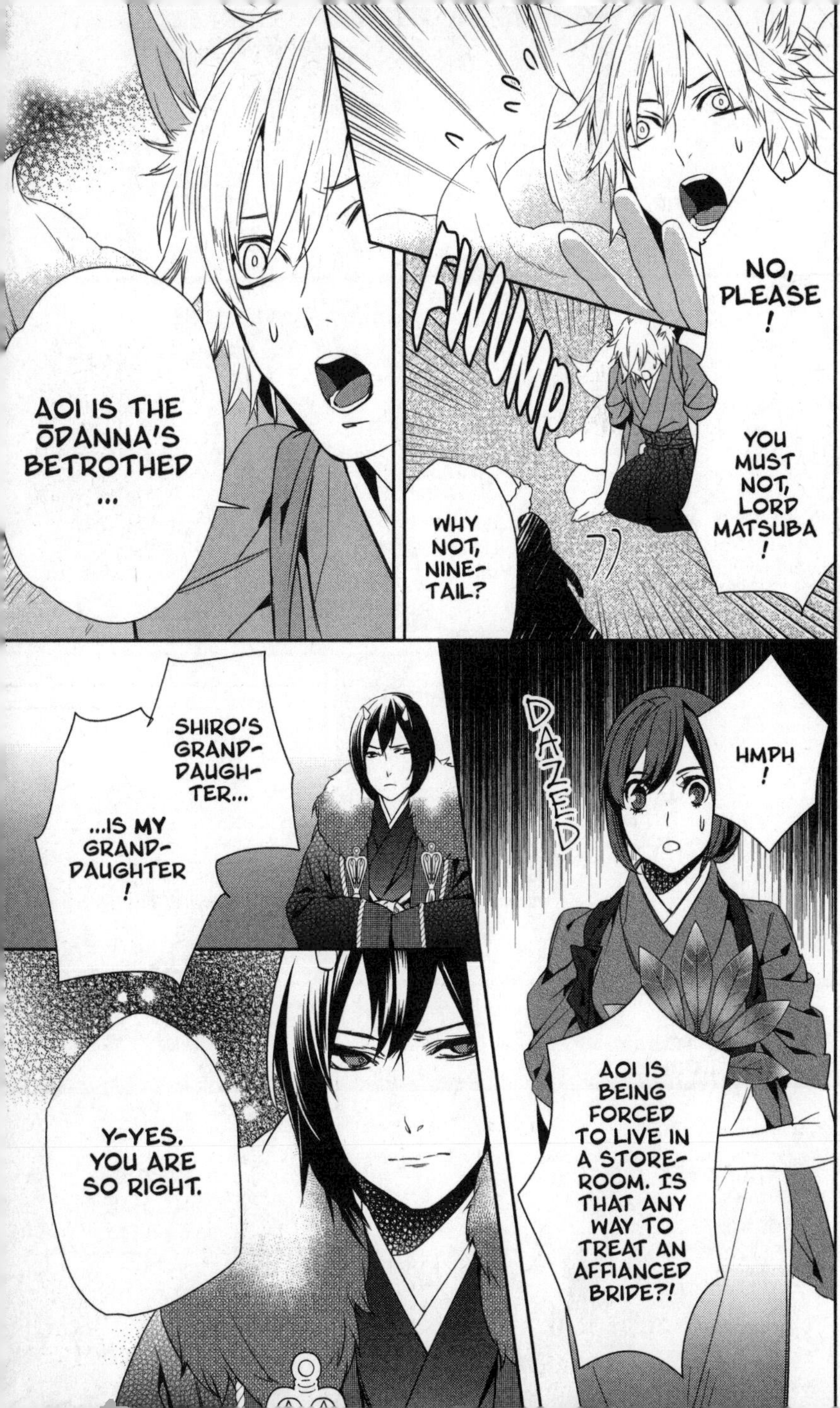
NO, PLEASE!
FWUMP
YOU MUST NOT, LORD MATSUBA!
WHY NOT, NINE-TAIL?
AOI IS THE ŌDANNA'S BETROTHED...
DAZED
HMPH!
AOI IS BEING FORCED TO LIVE IN A STOREROOM. IS THAT ANY WAY TO TREAT AN AFFIANCED BRIDE?!
SHIRO'S GRANDDAUGHTER...
...IS MY GRANDDAUGHTER!
Y-YES. YOU ARE SO RIGHT.

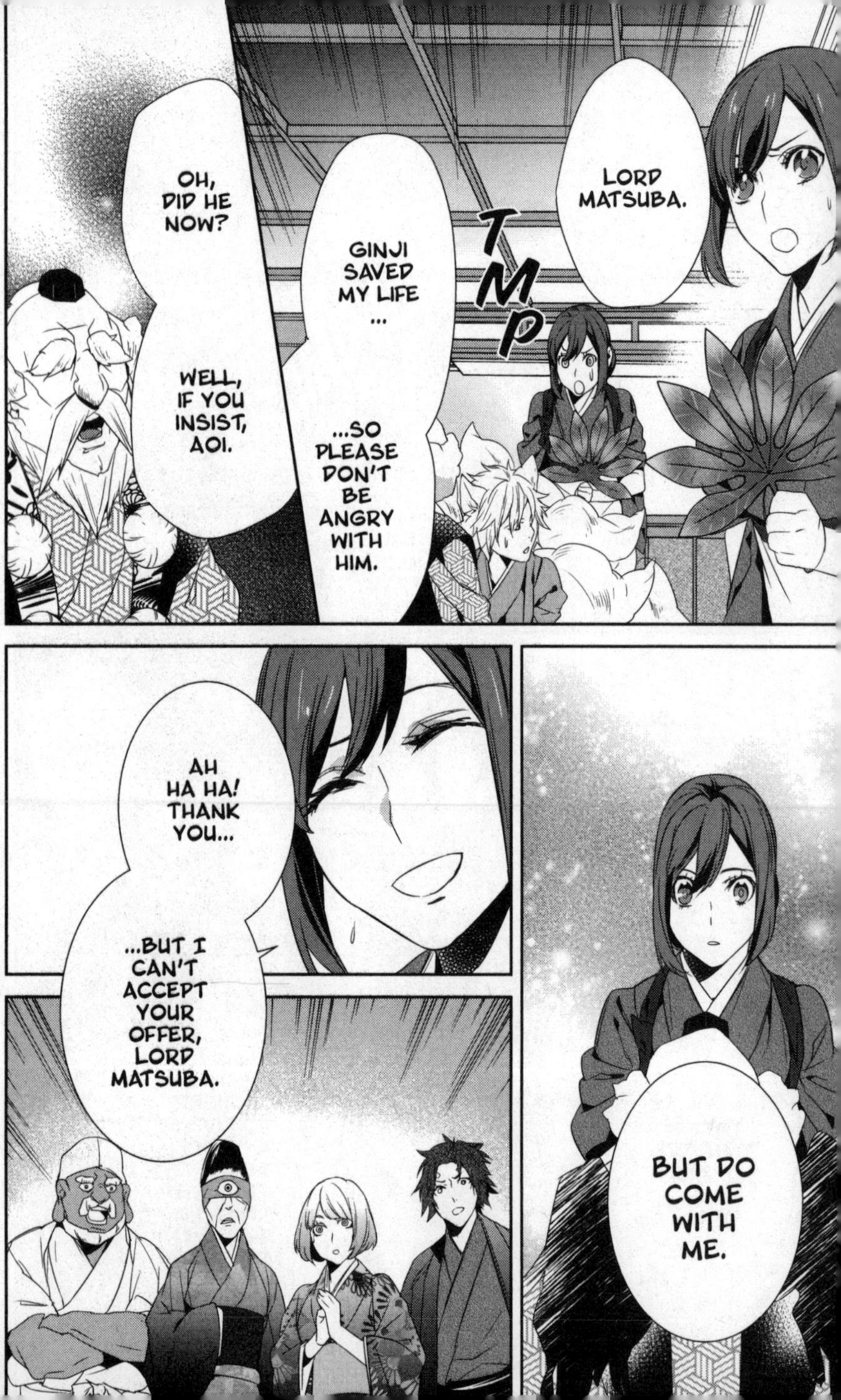
LORD MATSUBA.
TMP
GINJI SAVED MY LIFE ...
...SO PLEASE DON'T BE ANGRY WITH HIM.
OH, DID HE NOW?
WELL, IF YOU INSIST, AOI.
AH HA HA! THANK YOU...
...BUT I CAN'T ACCEPT YOUR OFFER, LORD MATSUBA.
BUT DO COME WITH ME.

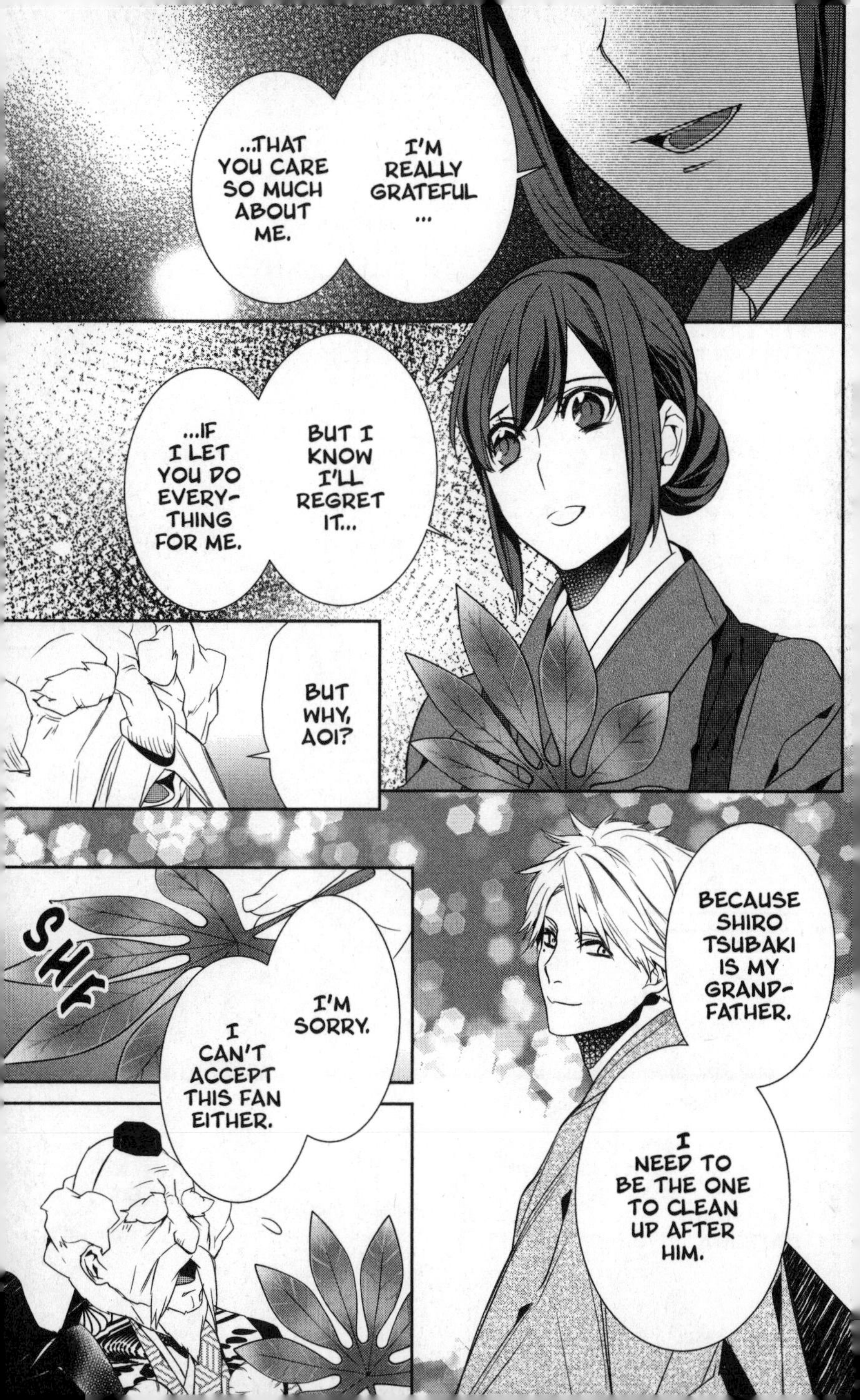
I'M REALLY GRATEFUL...
...THAT YOU CARE SO MUCH ABOUT ME.
BUT I KNOW I'LL REGRET IT...
...IF I LET YOU DO EVERYTHING FOR ME.
BUT WHY, AOI?
BECAUSE SHIRO TSUBAKI IS MY GRANDFATHER.
I NEED TO BE THE ONE TO CLEAN UP AFTER HIM.
SHF
I'M SORRY.
I CAN'T ACCEPT THIS FAN EITHER.

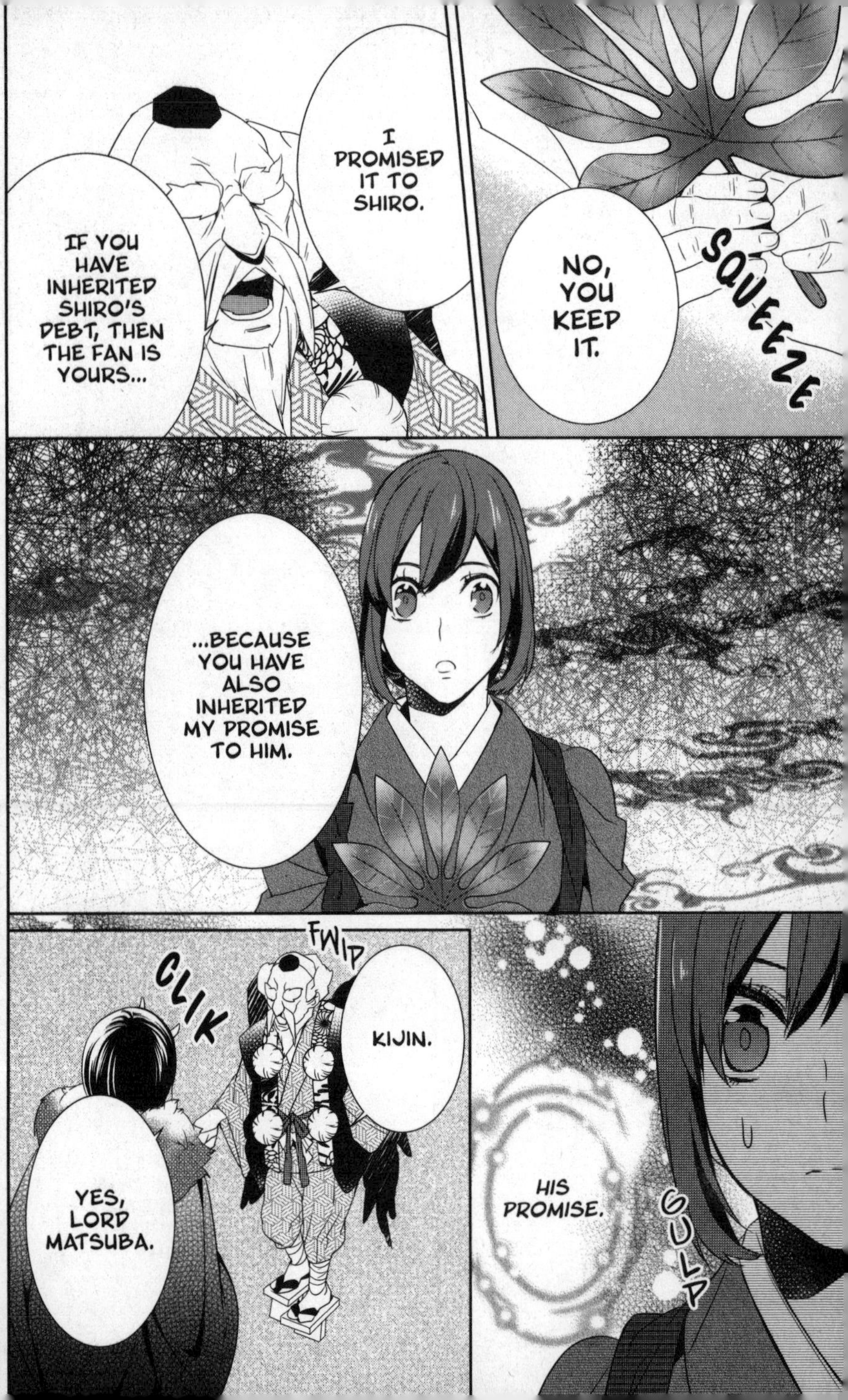
SQUEEZE
NO, YOU KEEP IT.
I PROMISED IT TO SHIRO.
IF YOU HAVE INHERITED SHIRO'S DEBT, THEN THE FAN IS YOURS...
...BECAUSE YOU HAVE ALSO INHERITED MY PROMISE TO HIM.
HIS PROMISE.
GULP
FWIP
KIJIN.
CLIK
YES, LORD MATSUBA.

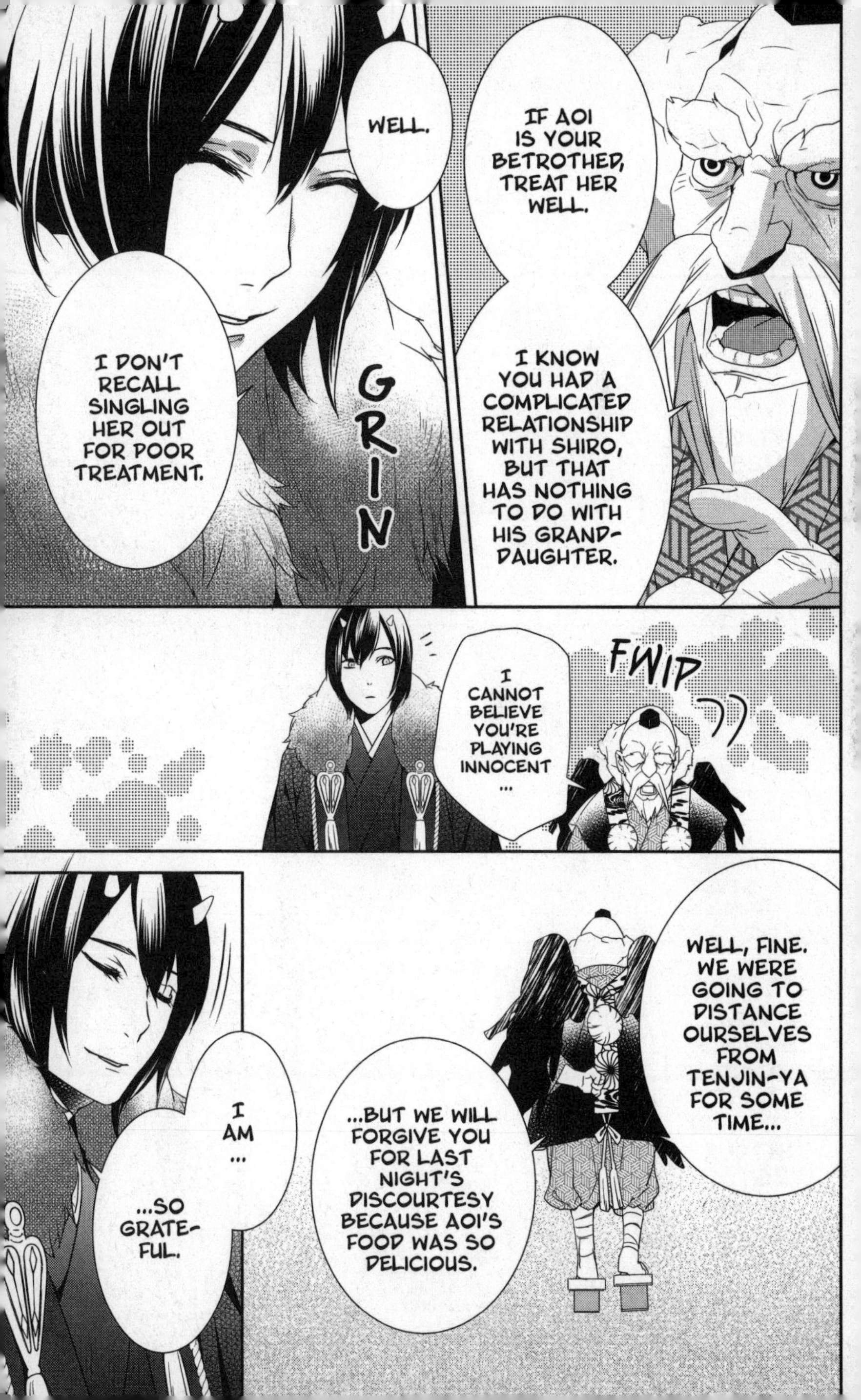
IF AOI IS YOUR BETROTHED, TREAT HER WELL.
I KNOW YOU HAD A COMPLICATED RELATIONSHIP WITH SHIRO, BUT THAT HAS NOTHING TO DO WITH HIS GRAND-DAUGHTER.
WELL.
I DON'T RECALL SINGLING HER OUT FOR POOR TREATMENT.
GRIN
FWIP
I CANNOT BELIEVE YOU'RE PLAYING INNOCENT...
WELL, FINE. WE WERE GOING TO DISTANCE OURSELVES FROM TENJIN-YA FOR SOME TIME...
...BUT WE WILL FORGIVE YOU FOR LAST NIGHT'S DISCOURTESY BECAUSE AOI'S FOOD WAS SO DELICIOUS.
I AM...
...SO GRATE-FUL.

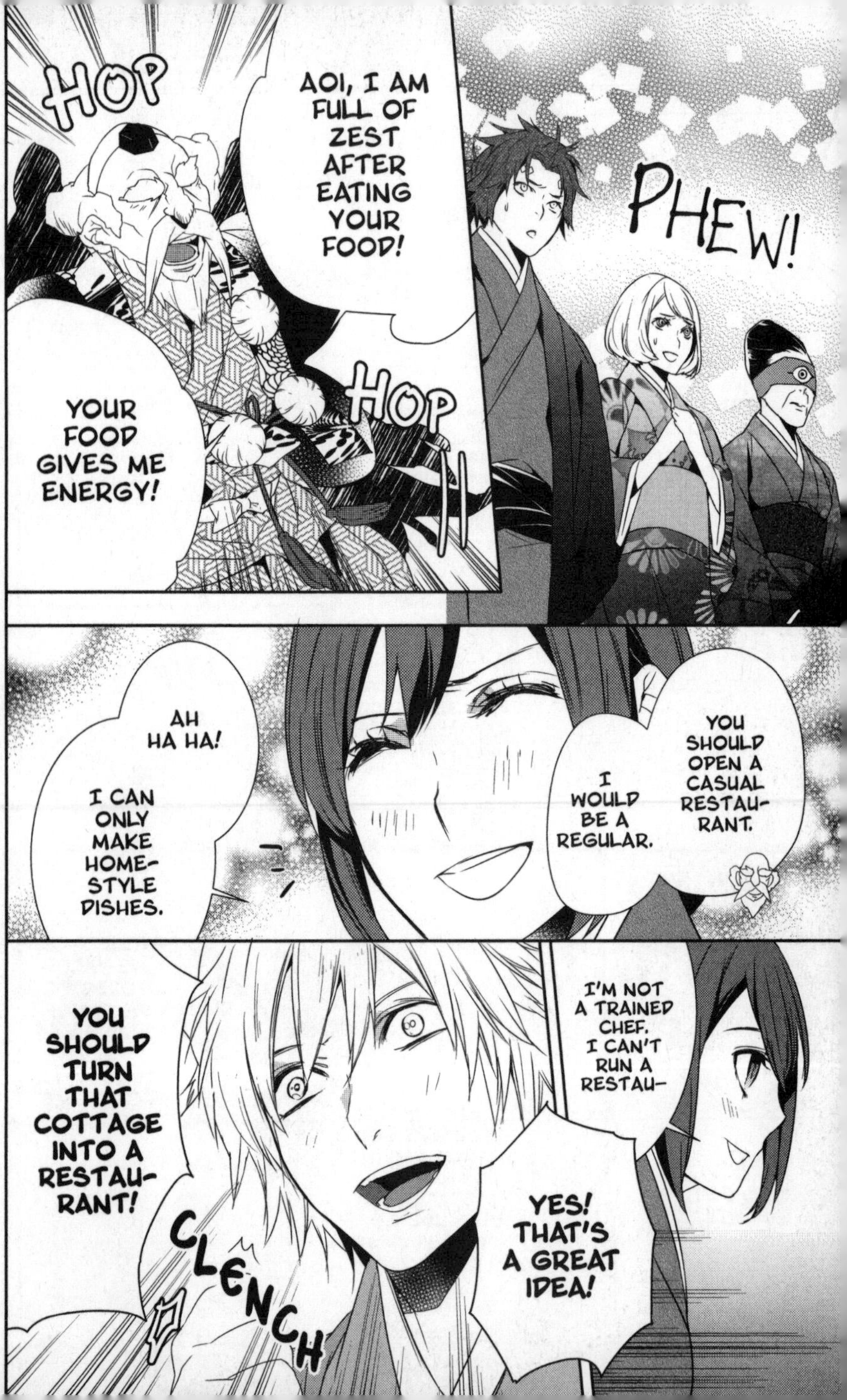
PHEW!
AOI, I AM FULL OF ZEST AFTER EATING YOUR FOOD!
HOP
HOP
YOUR FOOD GIVES ME ENERGY!
YOU SHOULD OPEN A CASUAL RESTAU-RANT.
I WOULD BE A REGULAR.
AH HA HA!
I CAN ONLY MAKE HOME-STYLE DISHES.
I'M NOT A TRAINED CHEF. I CAN'T RUN A RESTAU-
YOU SHOULD TURN THAT COTTAGE INTO A RESTAU-RANT!
YES! THAT'S A GREAT IDEA!
CLENCH

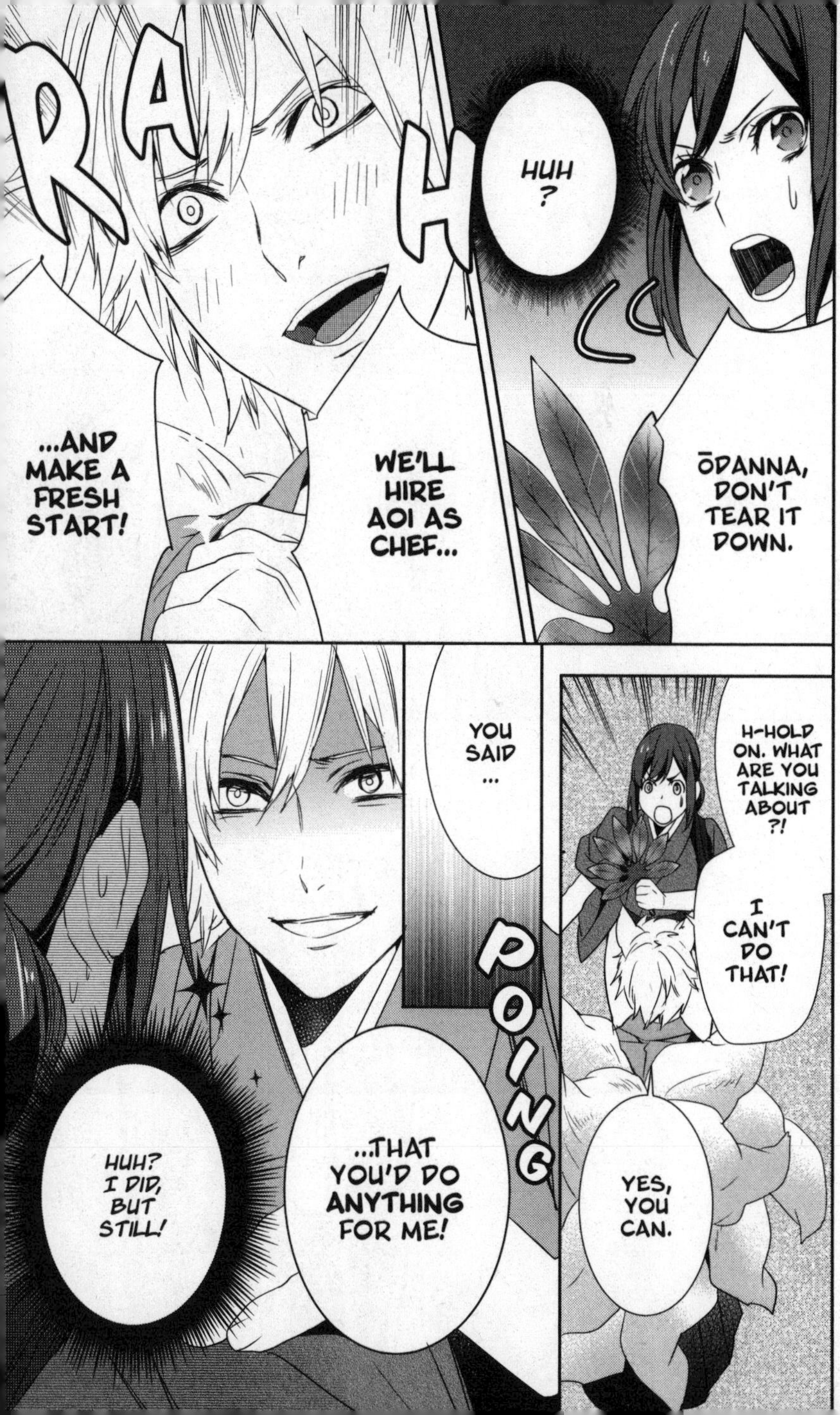
HUH ?
ŌDANNA, DON'T TEAR IT DOWN.
RAH
WE'LL HIRE AOI AS CHEF...
...AND MAKE A FRESH START!
H-HOLD ON. WHAT ARE YOU TALKING ABOUT ?!
I CAN'T DO THAT!
YES, YOU CAN.
YOU SAID ...
...THAT YOU'D DO ANYTHING FOR ME!
POING
HUH? I DID, BUT STILL!

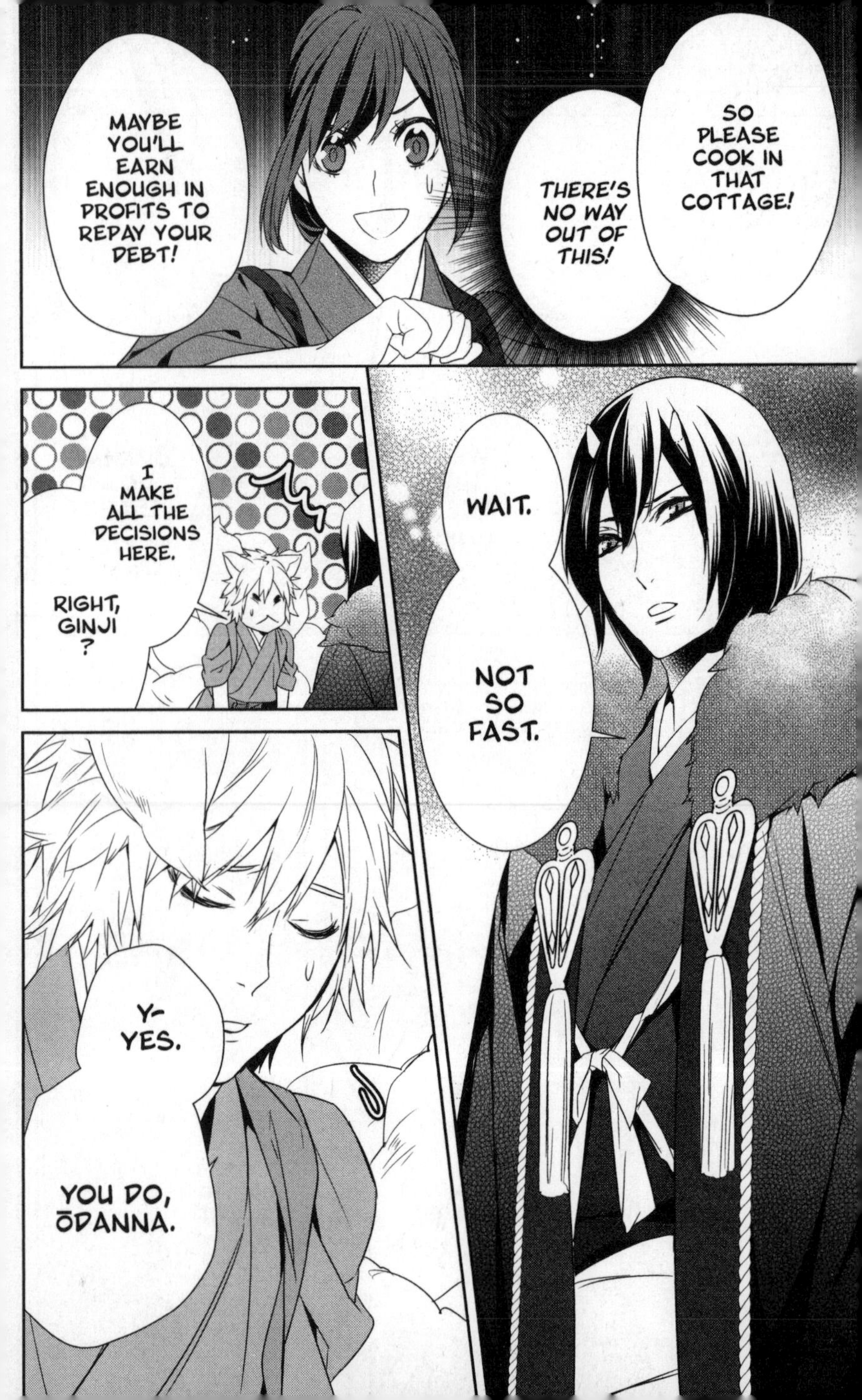
SO PLEASE COOK IN THAT COTTAGE!
THERE'S NO WAY OUT OF THIS!
MAYBE YOU'LL EARN ENOUGH IN PROFITS TO REPAY YOUR DEBT!
WAIT.
NOT SO FAST.
I MAKE ALL THE DECISIONS HERE.
RIGHT, GINJI?
Y-YES.
YOU DO, ŌDANNA.

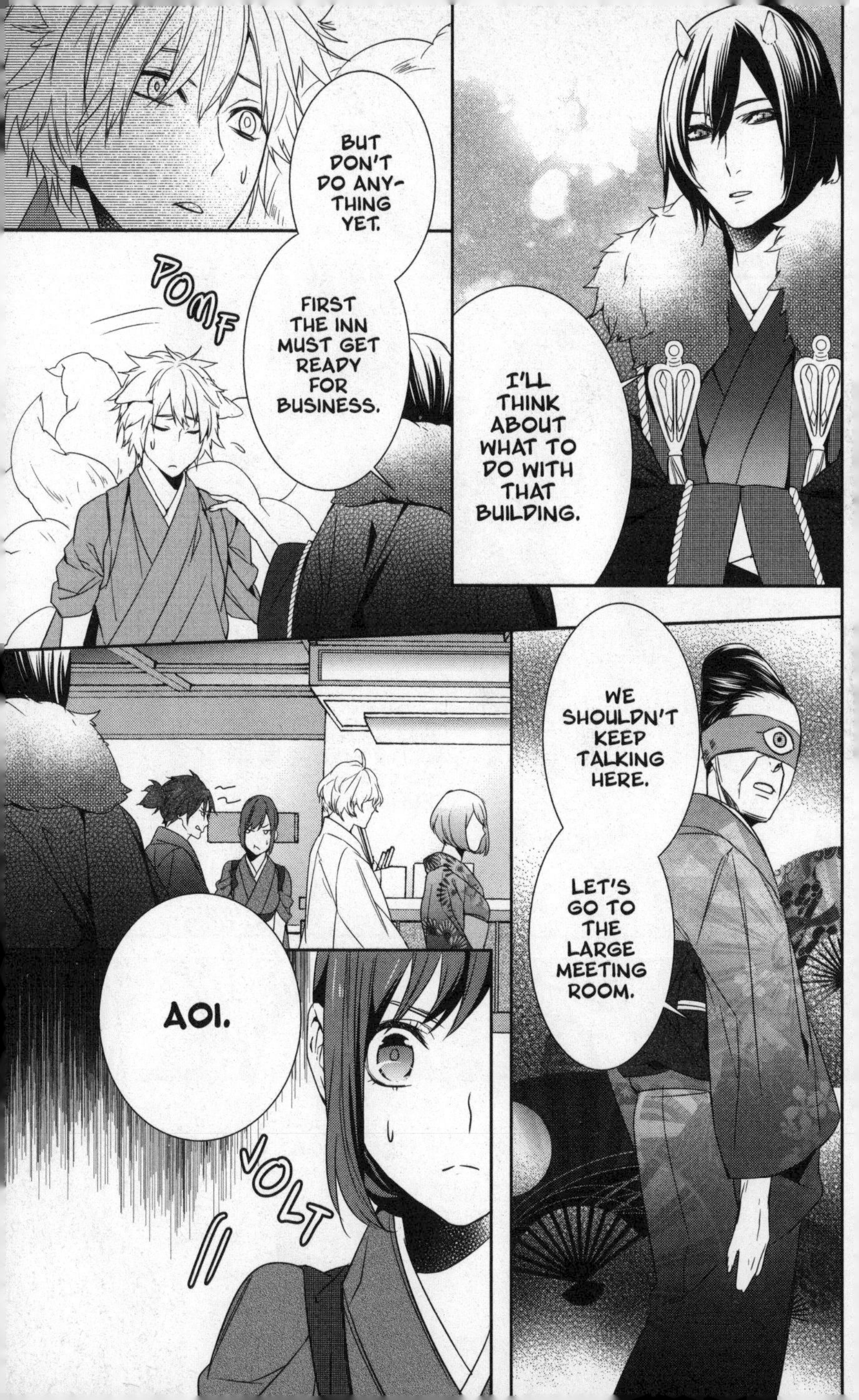
I'LL THINK ABOUT WHAT TO DO WITH THAT BUILDING.
BUT DON'T DO ANY-THING YET.
FIRST THE INN MUST GET READY FOR BUSINESS.
POMF
WE SHOULDN'T KEEP TALKING HERE.
LET'S GO TO THE LARGE MEETING ROOM.
AOI.
JOLT

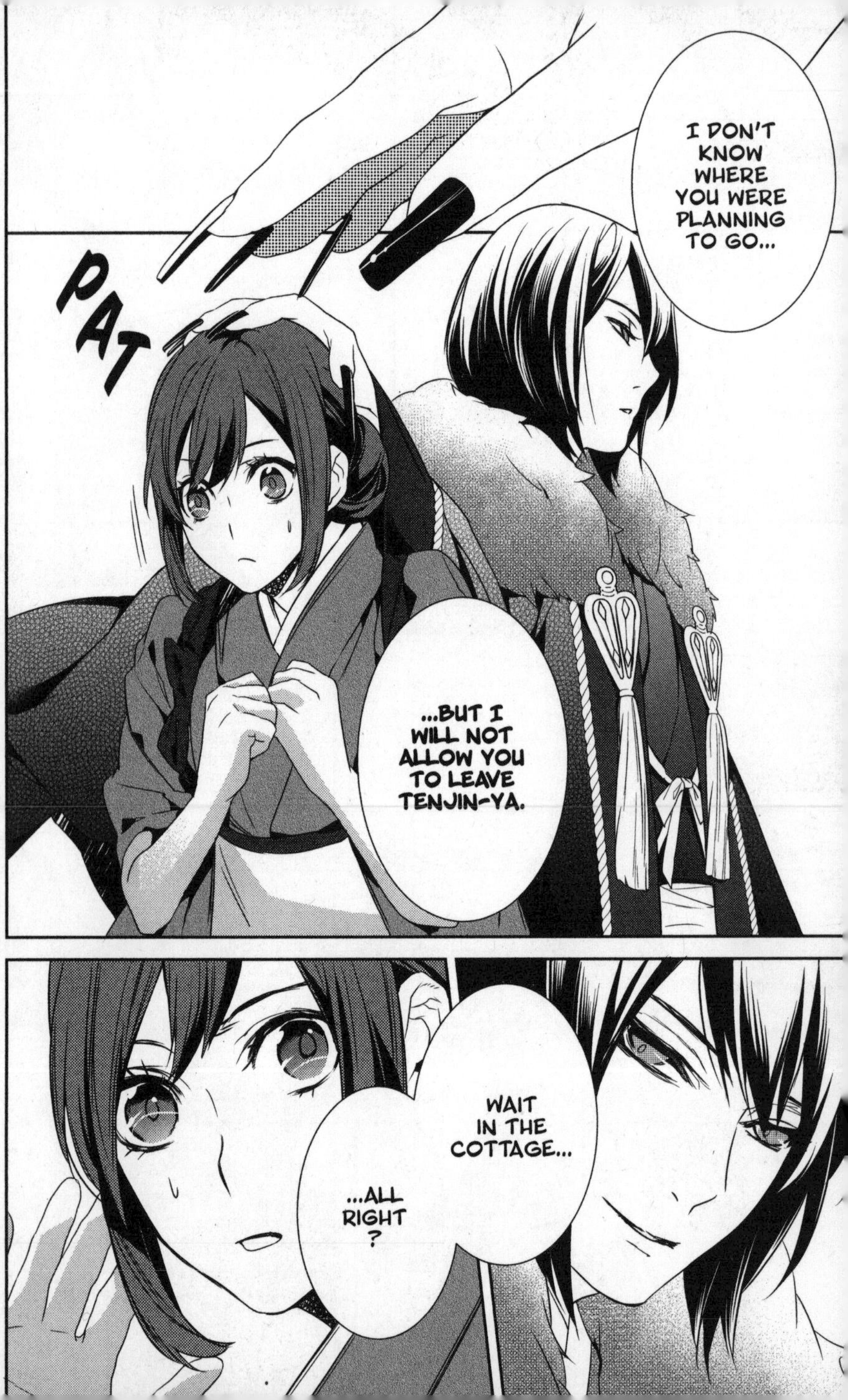
I DON'T KNOW WHERE YOU WERE PLANNING TO GO...
PAT
...BUT I WILL NOT ALLOW YOU TO LEAVE TENJIN-YA.
WAIT IN THE COTTAGE...
...ALL RIGHT?

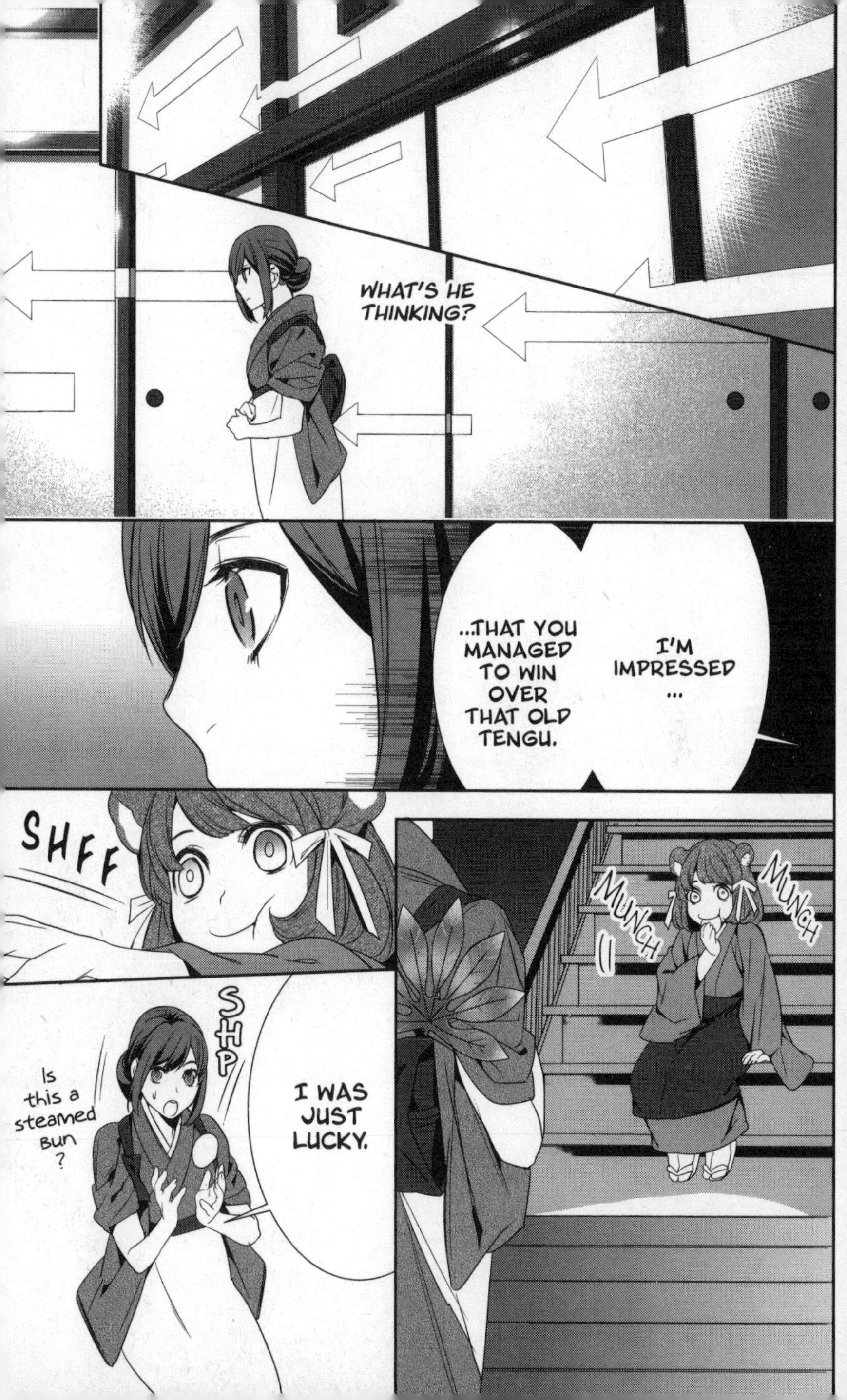
WHAT'S HE THINKING?
I'M IMPRESSED...
...THAT YOU MANAGED TO WIN OVER THAT OLD TENGU.
MUNCH
MUNCH
SHFF
SHP
I WAS JUST LUCKY.
Is this a steamed bun?

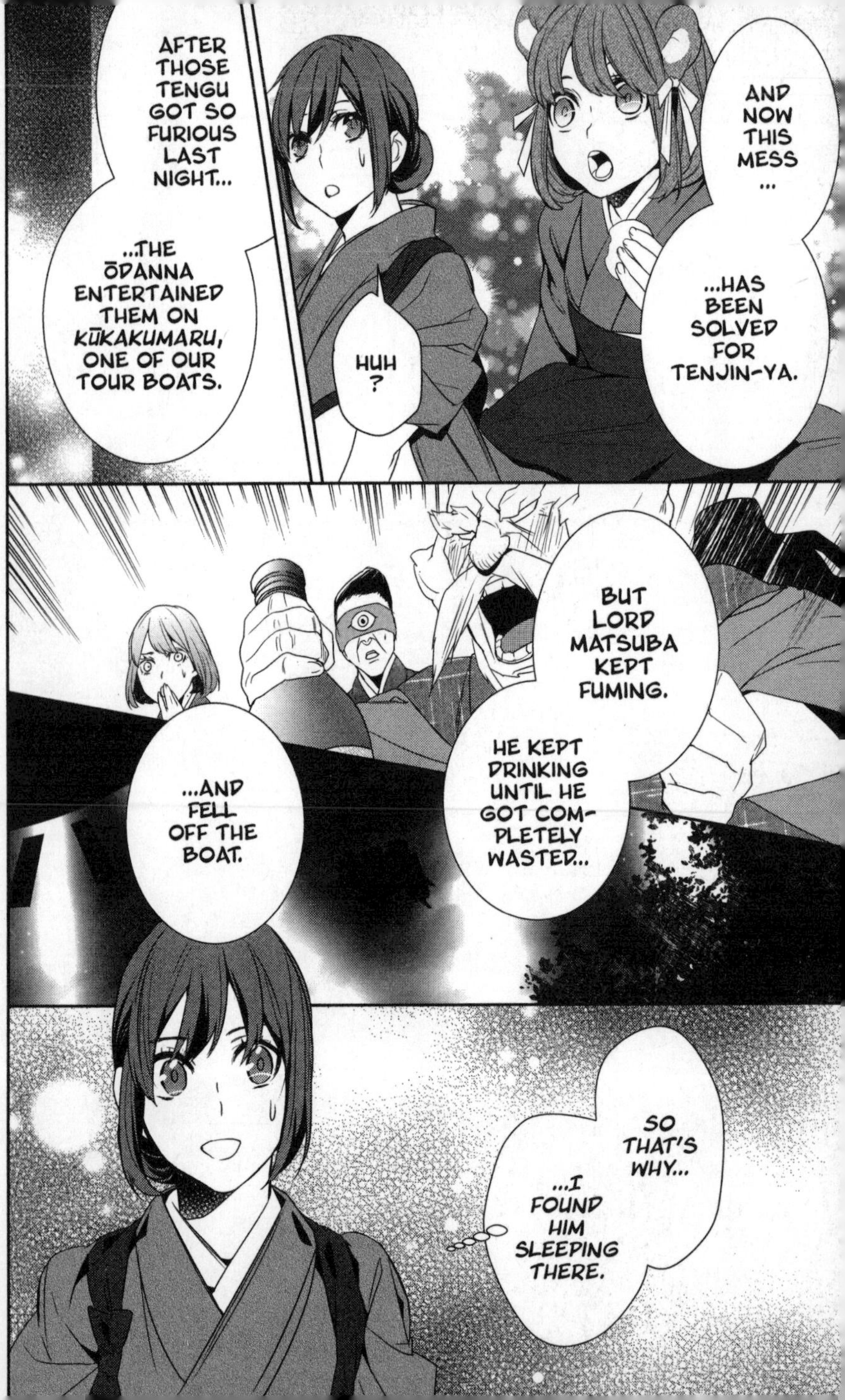
AND NOW THIS MESS...
...HAS BEEN SOLVED FOR TENJIN-YA.
HUH?
AFTER THOSE TENGU GOT SO FURIOUS LAST NIGHT...
...THE ŌDANNA ENTERTAINED THEM ON KŪKAKUMARU, ONE OF OUR TOUR BOATS.
BUT LORD MATSUBA KEPT FUMING.
HE KEPT DRINKING UNTIL HE GOT COMPLETELY WASTED...
...AND FELL OFF THE BOAT.
SO THAT'S WHY...
...I FOUND HIM SLEEPING THERE.

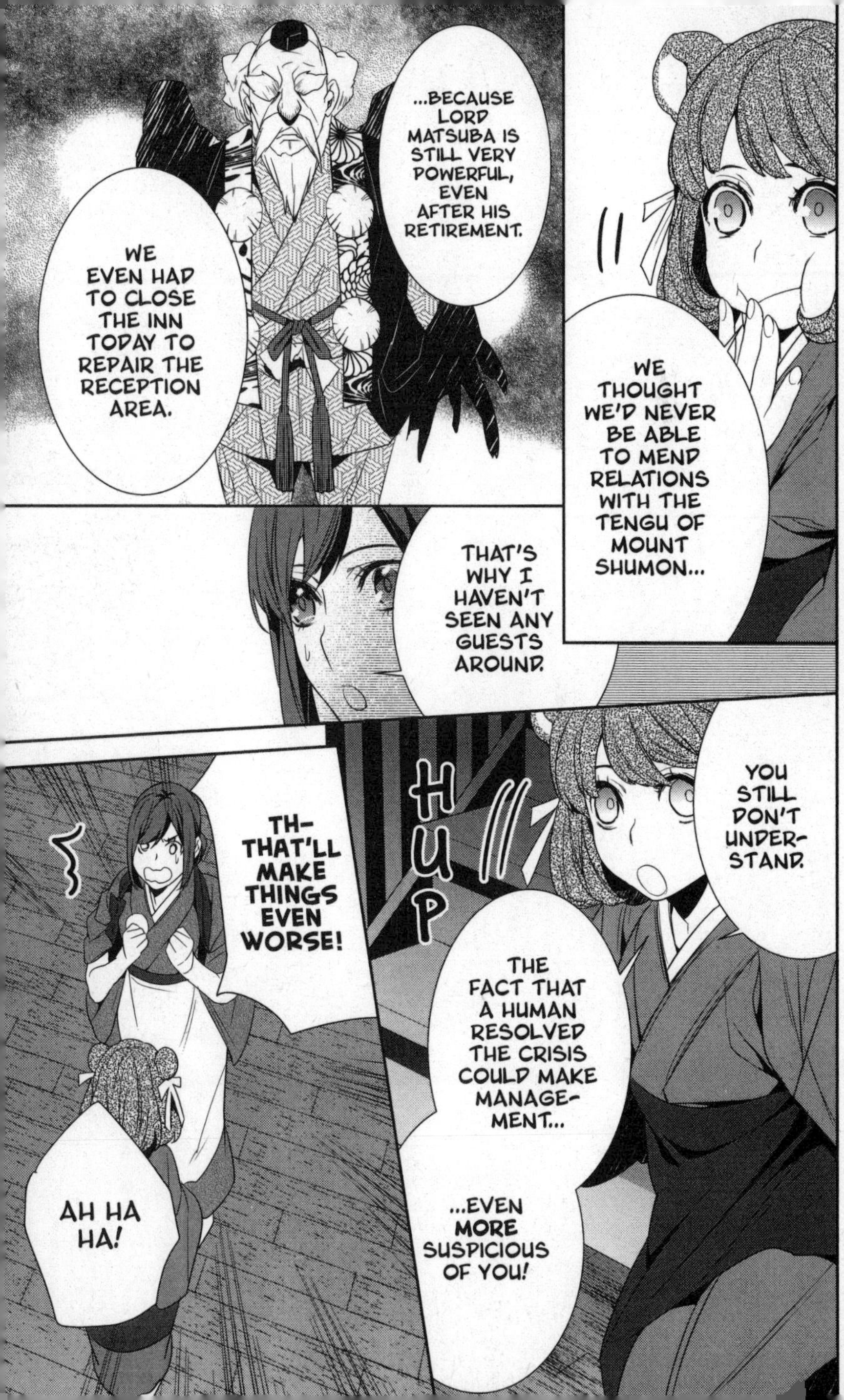
WE THOUGHT WE'D NEVER BE ABLE TO MEND RELATIONS WITH THE TENGU OF MOUNT SHUMON...
...BECAUSE LORD MATSUBA IS STILL VERY POWERFUL, EVEN AFTER HIS RETIREMENT.
WE EVEN HAD TO CLOSE THE INN TODAY TO REPAIR THE RECEPTION AREA.
THAT'S WHY I HAVEN'T SEEN ANY GUESTS AROUND.
HUP
YOU STILL DON'T UNDER-STAND.
THE FACT THAT A HUMAN RESOLVED THE CRISIS COULD MAKE MANAGE-MENT...
...EVEN MORE SUSPICIOUS OF YOU!
TH-THAT'LL MAKE THINGS EVEN WORSE!
AH HA HA!

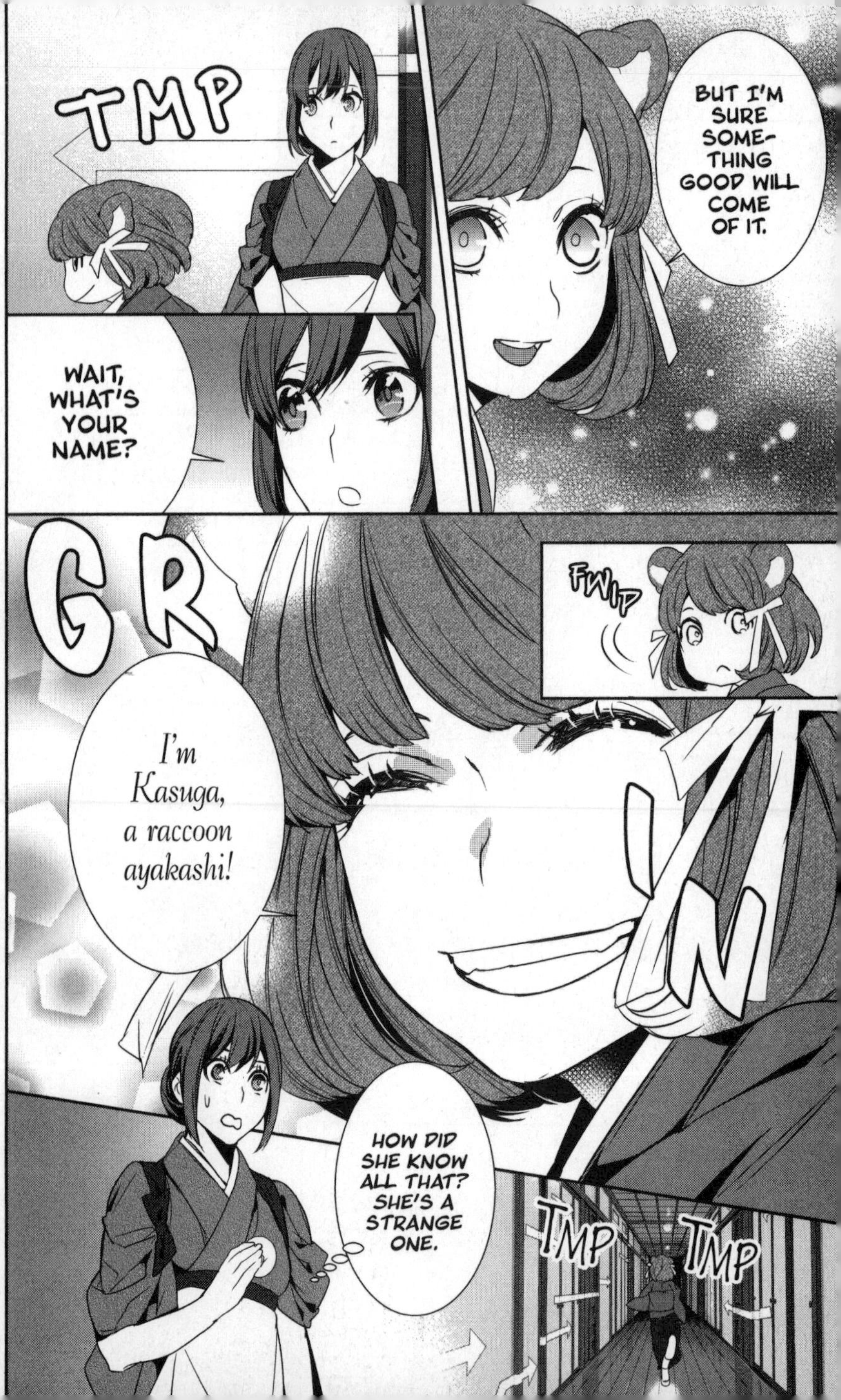

BUT I'M SURE SOMETHING GOOD WILL COME OF IT.
TMP
WAIT, WHAT'S YOUR NAME?
FWIP
GR
I'm Kasuga, a raccoon ayakashi!
IN
TMP TMP
HOW DID SHE KNOW ALL THAT? SHE'S A STRANGE ONE.

Kakuriyo
Bed & Breakfast
for Spirits

Kakuriyo
Bed & Breakfast
for Spirits

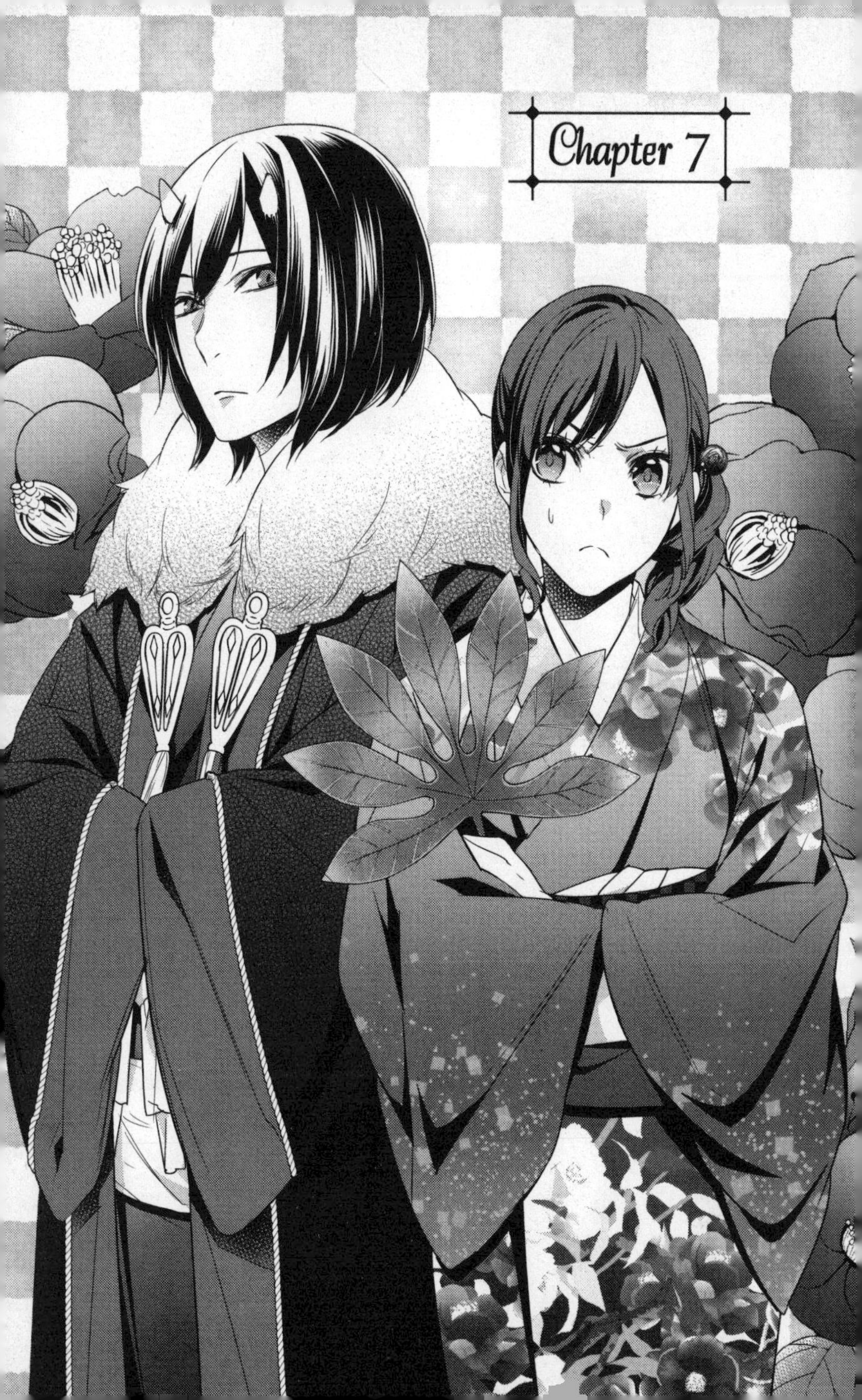
Chapter 7

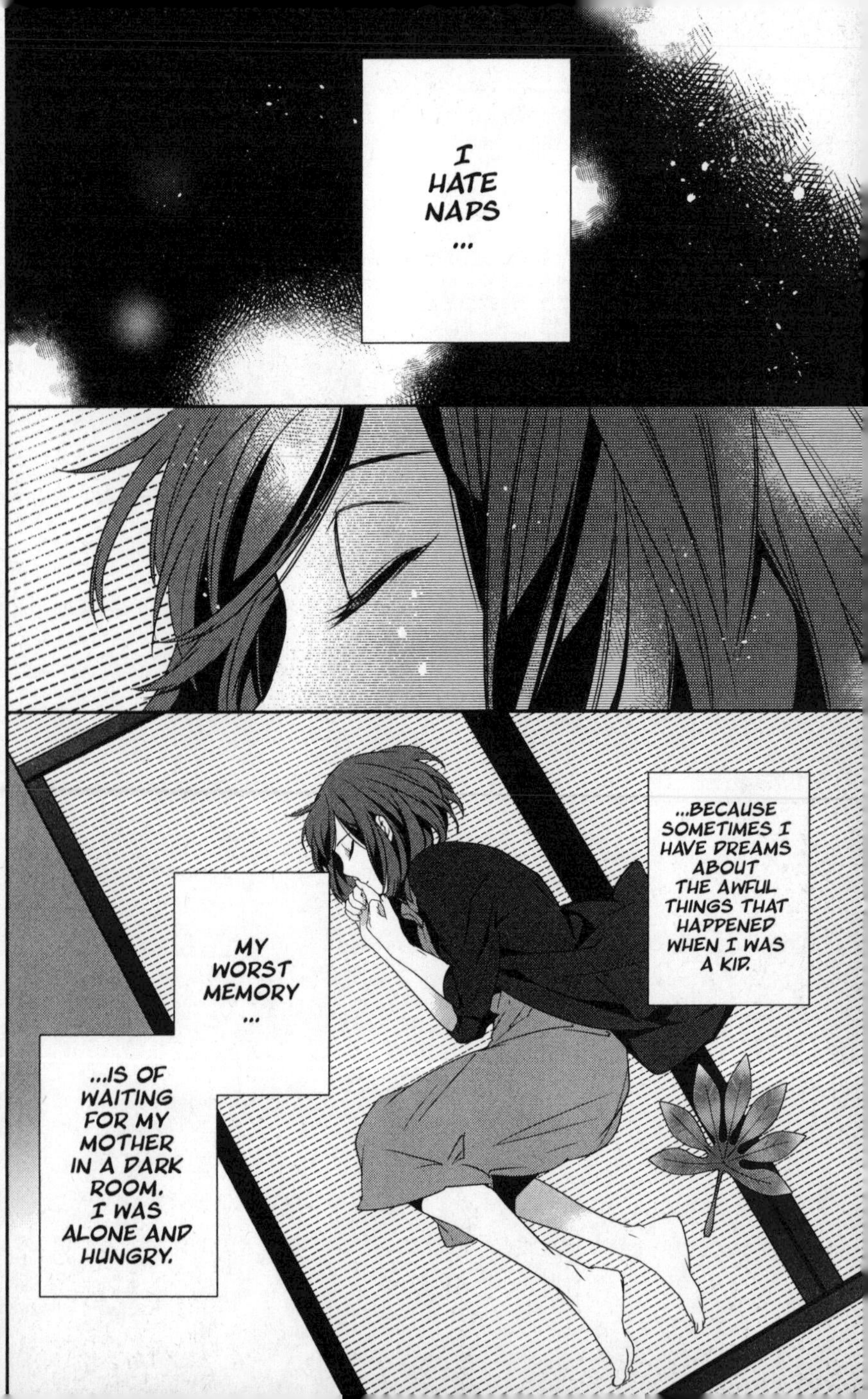
I HATE NAPS ...
...BECAUSE SOMETIMES I HAVE DREAMS ABOUT THE AWFUL THINGS THAT HAPPENED WHEN I WAS A KID.
MY WORST MEMORY ...
...IS OF WAITING FOR MY MOTHER IN A DARK ROOM. I WAS ALONE AND HUNGRY.

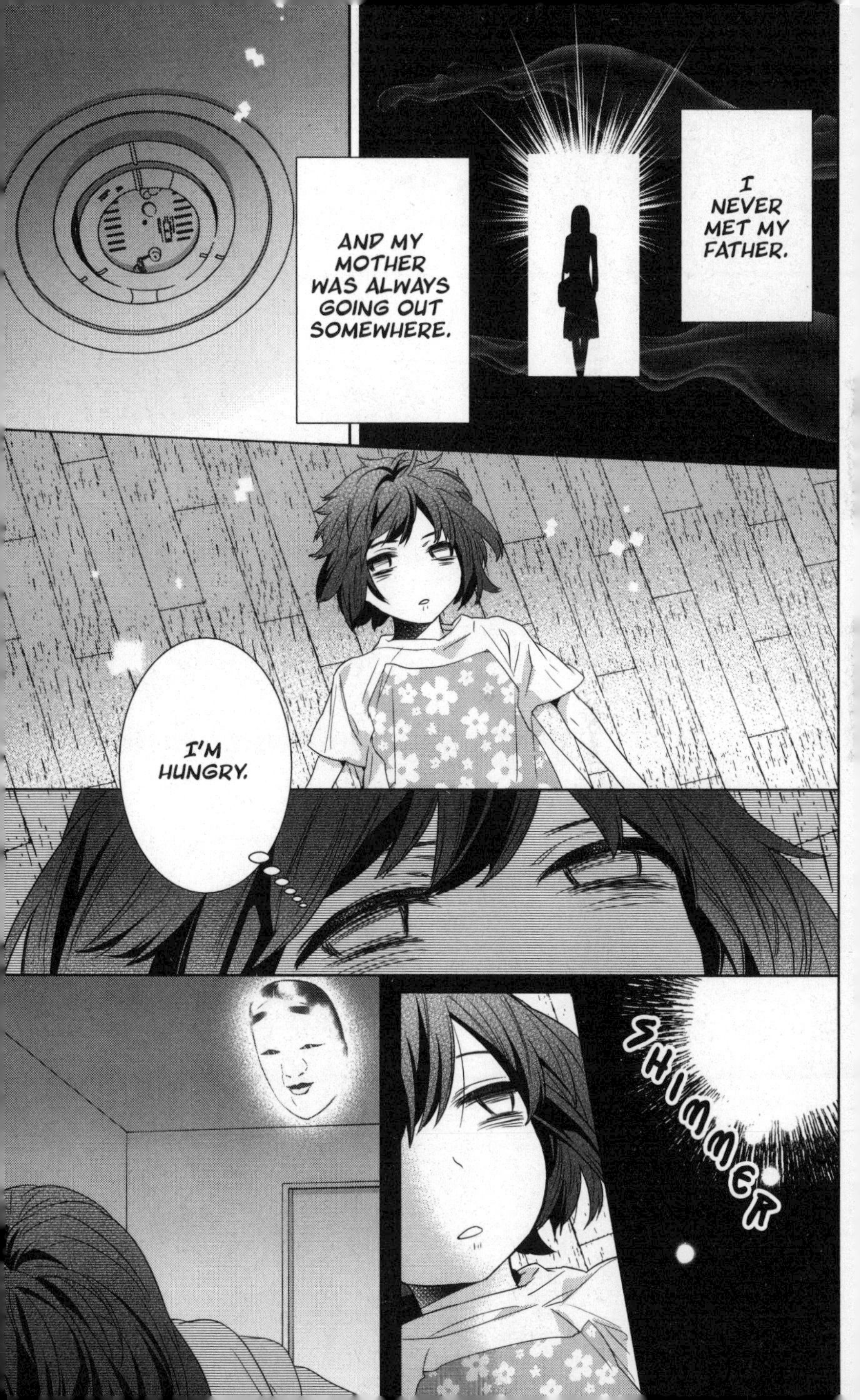
I NEVER MET MY FATHER.
AND MY MOTHER WAS ALWAYS GOING OUT SOMEWHERE.
I'M HUNGRY.
SHIMMER

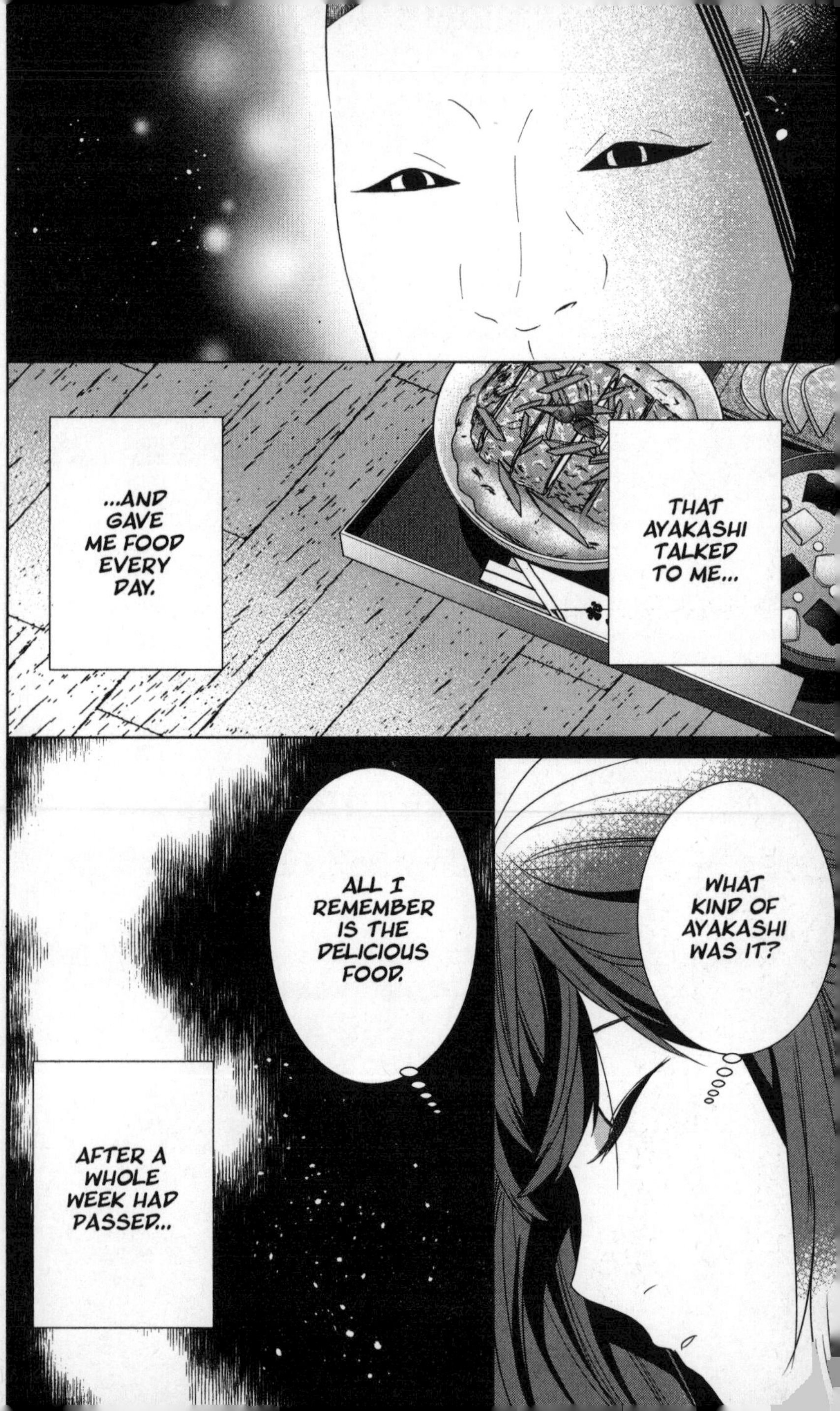
THAT AYAKASHI TALKED TO ME...
...AND GAVE ME FOOD EVERY DAY.
WHAT KIND OF AYAKASHI WAS IT?
ALL I REMEMBER IS THE DELICIOUS FOOD.
AFTER A WHOLE WEEK HAD PASSED...

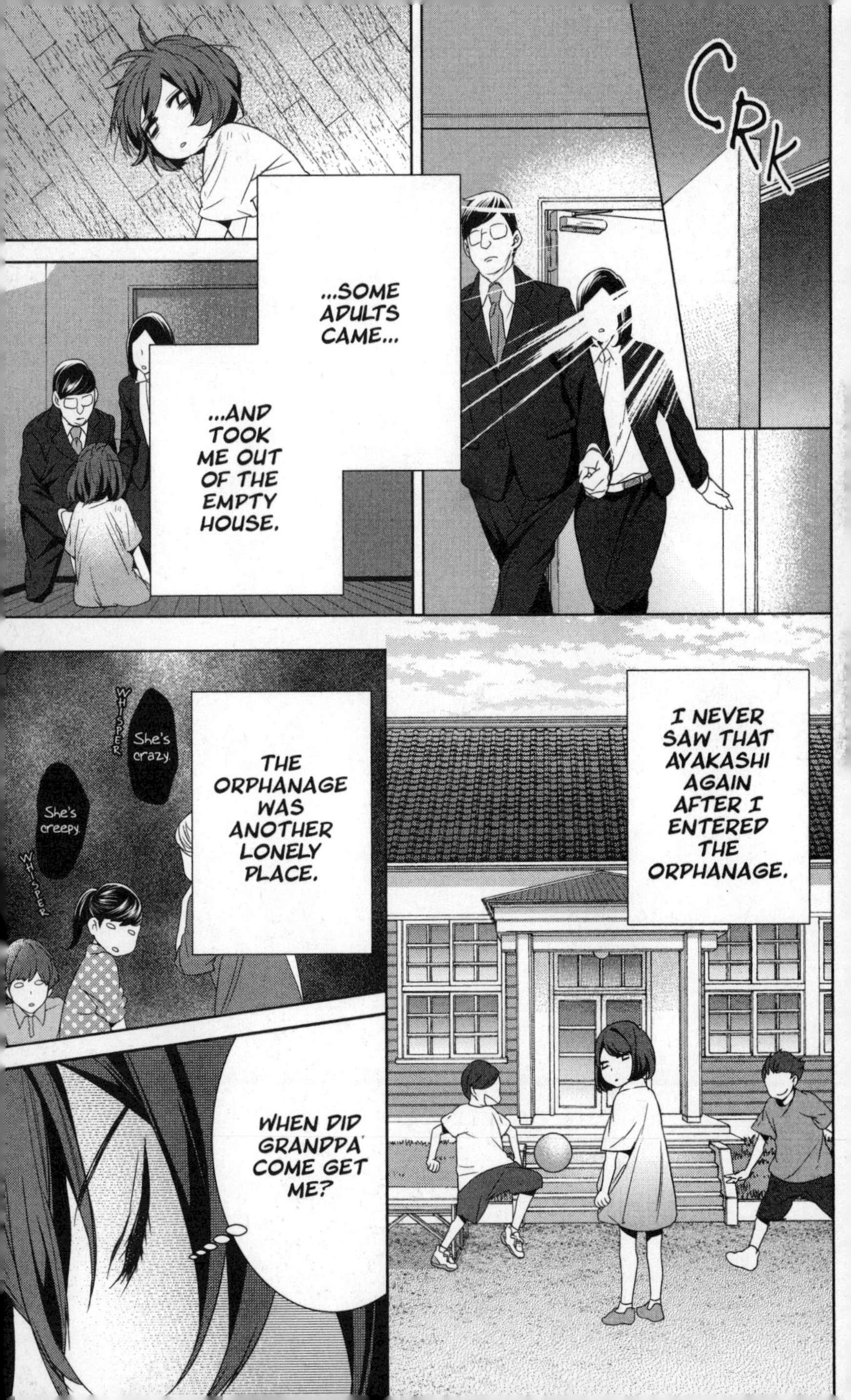
CRK
...SOME ADULTS CAME...
...AND TOOK ME OUT OF THE EMPTY HOUSE.
I NEVER SAW THAT AYAKASHI AGAIN AFTER I ENTERED THE ORPHANAGE.
THE ORPHANAGE WAS ANOTHER LONELY PLACE.
WHISPER
She's crazy.
She's creepy.
WHISPER
WHEN DID GRANDPA COME GET ME?

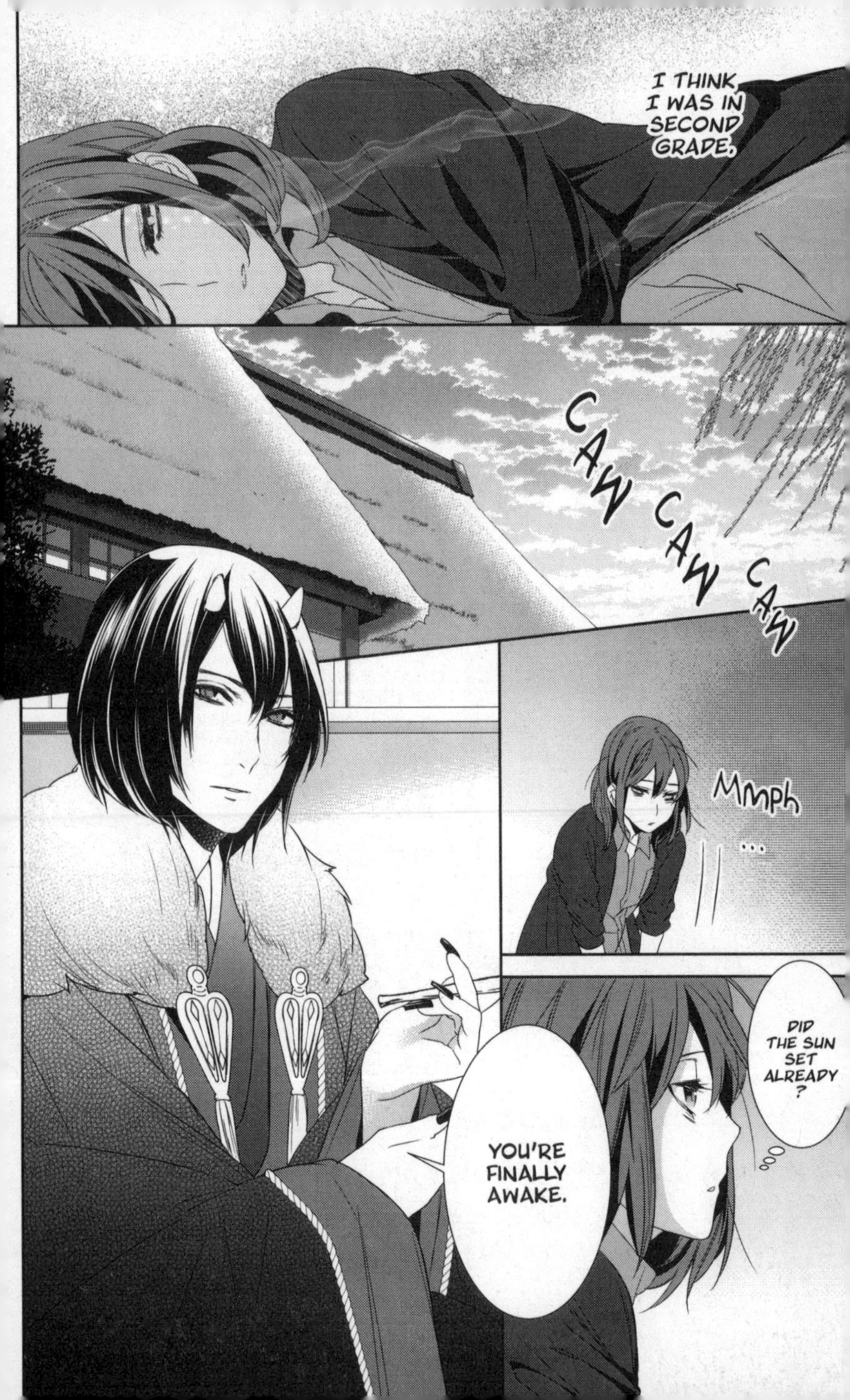
I THINK I WAS IN SECOND GRADE.
CAW CAW CAW
Mmph
...
DID THE SUN SET ALREADY?
YOU'RE FINALLY AWAKE.

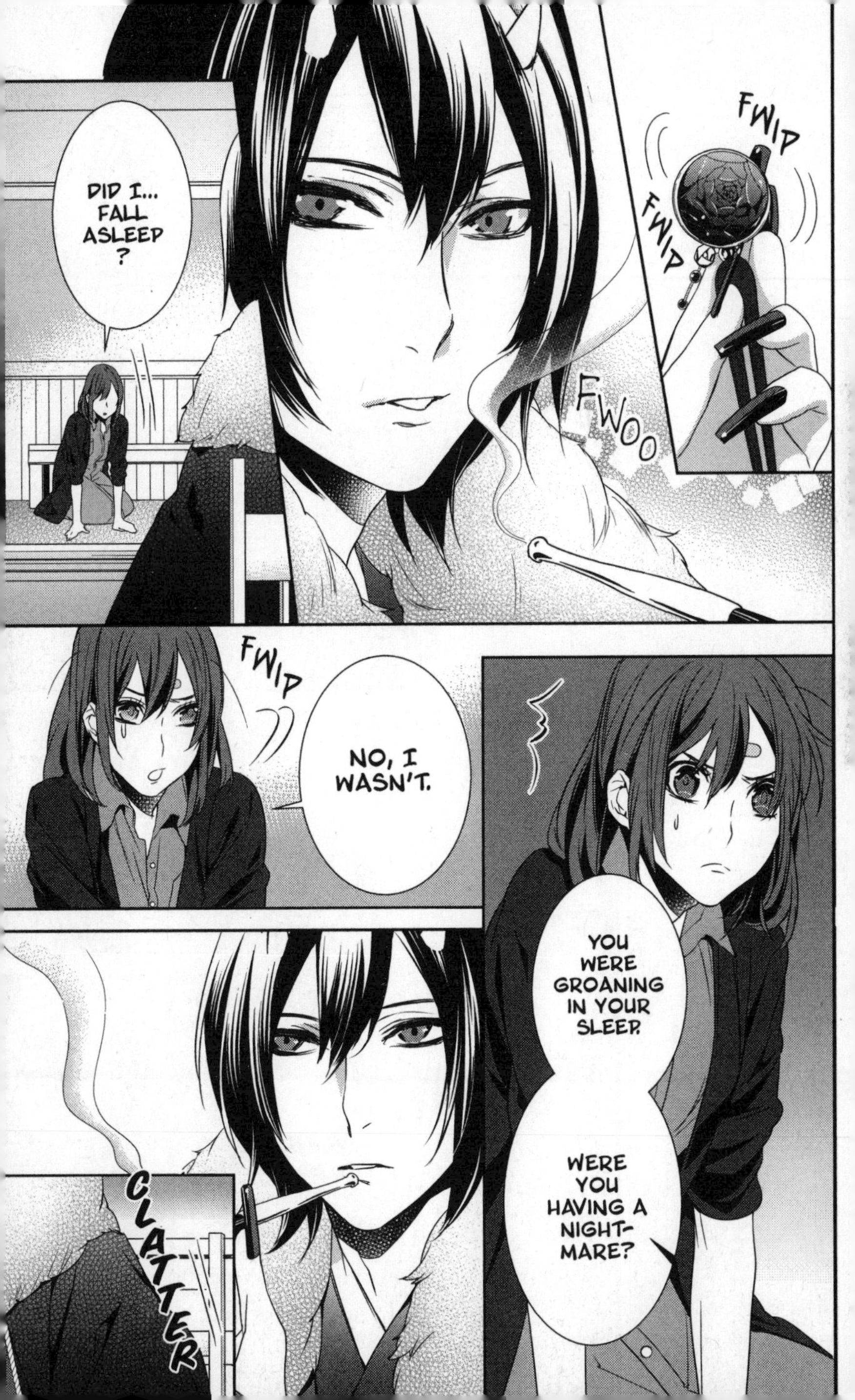
FWIP
FWIP
FWOO
DID I... FALL ASLEEP?
YOU WERE GROANING IN YOUR SLEEP.
WERE YOU HAVING A NIGHT-MARE?
FWIP
NO, I WASN'T.
CLATTER

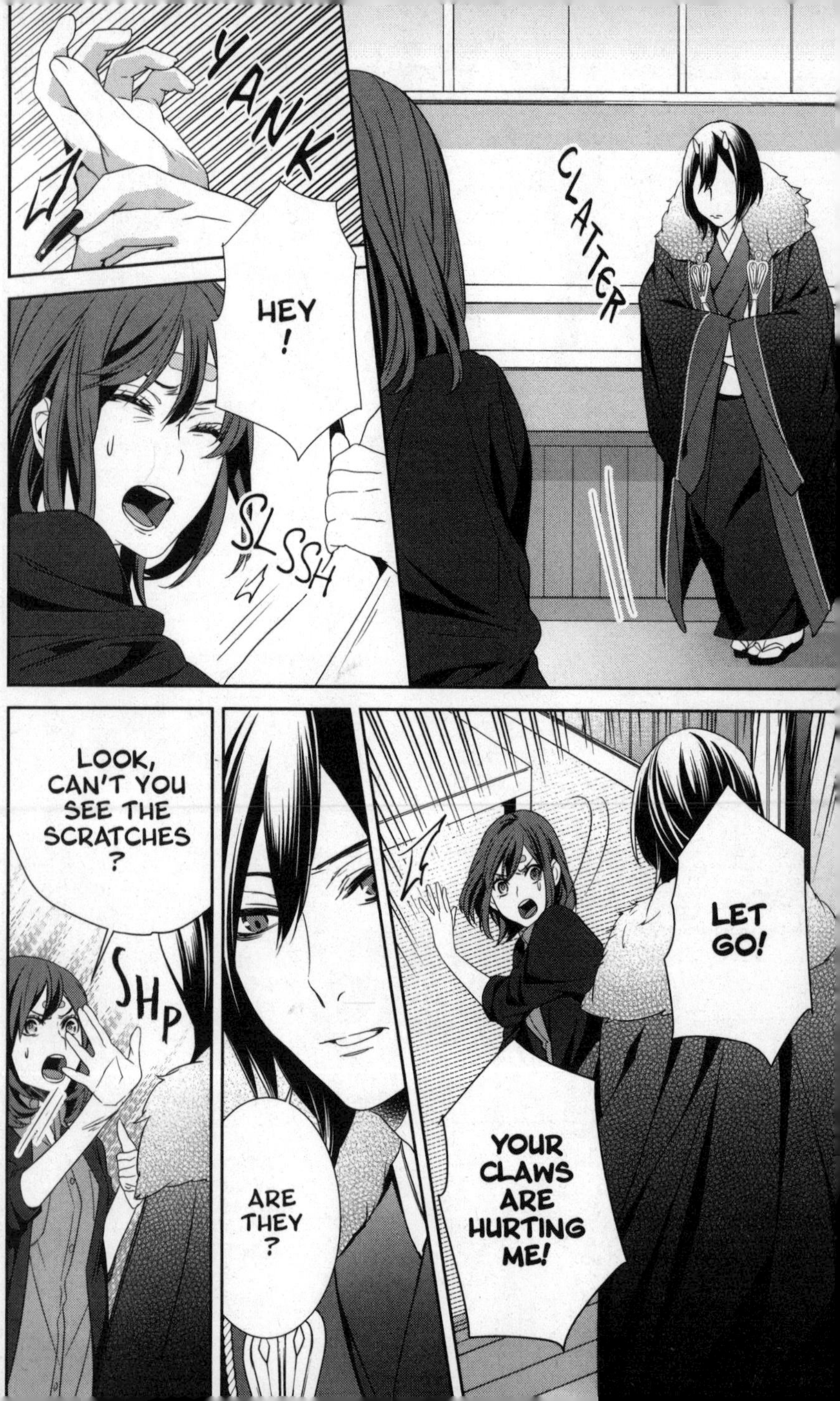
CLATTER
YANK
HEY!
SLSSH
LET GO!
YOUR CLAWS ARE HURTING ME!
ARE THEY?
LOOK, CAN'T YOU SEE THE SCRATCHES?
SHP

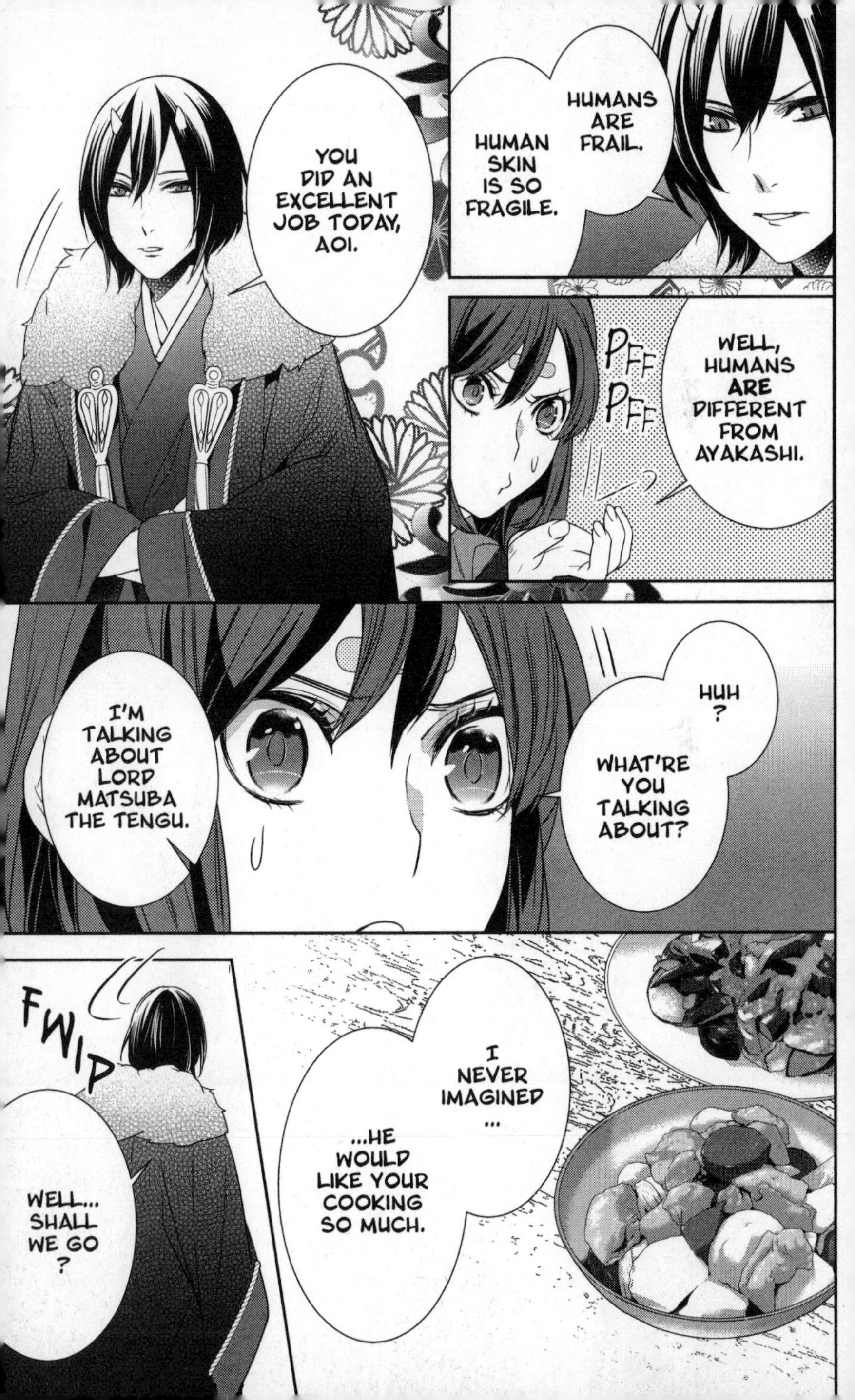
HUMANS ARE FRAIL. HUMAN SKIN IS SO FRAGILE.
PFF PFF
WELL, HUMANS **ARE** DIFFERENT FROM AYAKASHI.
YOU DID AN EXCELLENT JOB TODAY, AOI.
HUH? WHAT'RE YOU TALKING ABOUT?
I'M TALKING ABOUT LORD MATSUBA THE TENGU.
I NEVER IMAGINED... ...HE WOULD LIKE YOUR COOKING SO MUCH.
FWIP
WELL... SHALL WE GO?

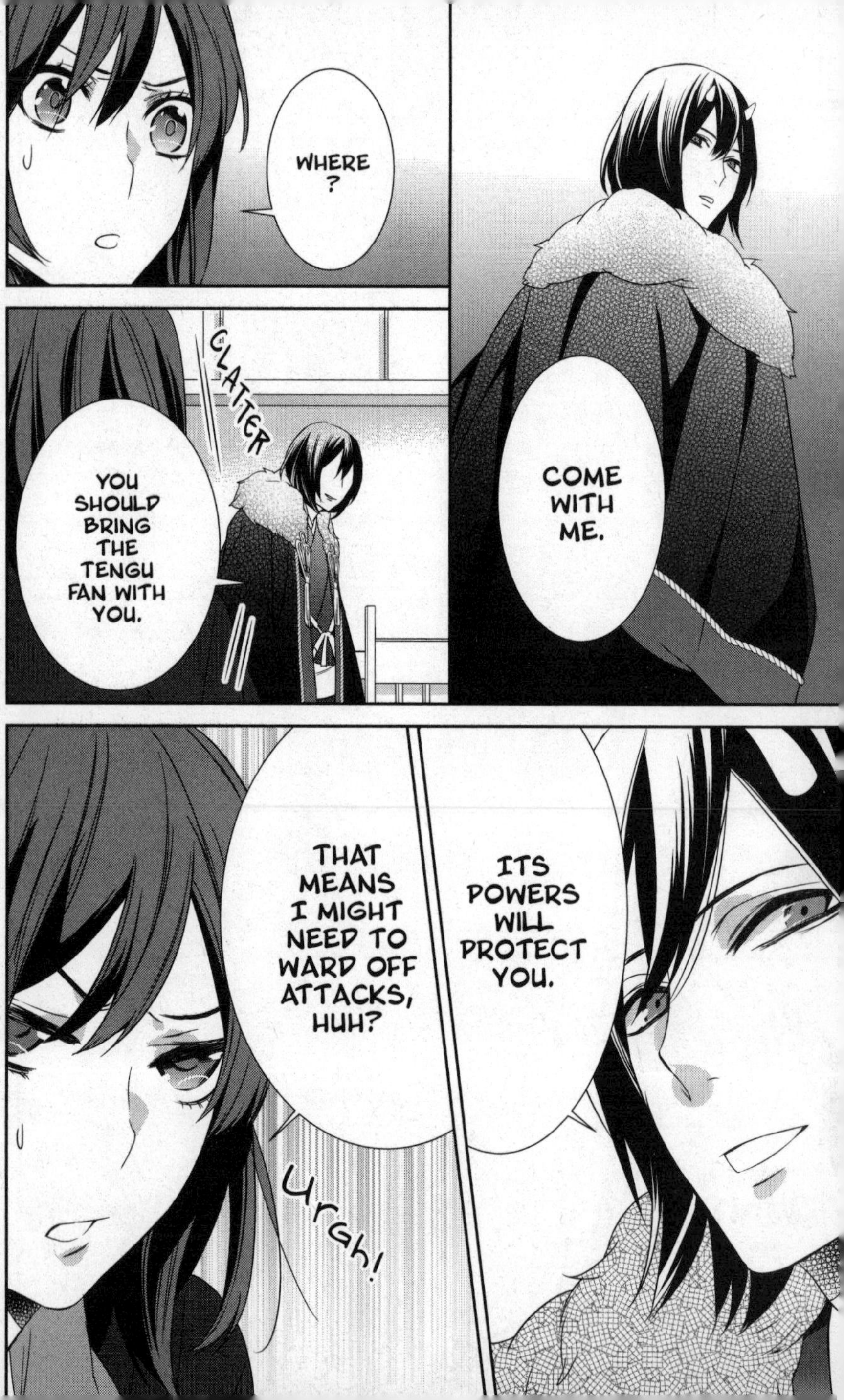
COME WITH ME.
WHERE?
CLATTER
YOU SHOULD BRING THE TENGU FAN WITH YOU.
ITS POWERS WILL PROTECT YOU.
THAT MEANS I MIGHT NEED TO WARD OFF ATTACKS, HUH?
Urgh!

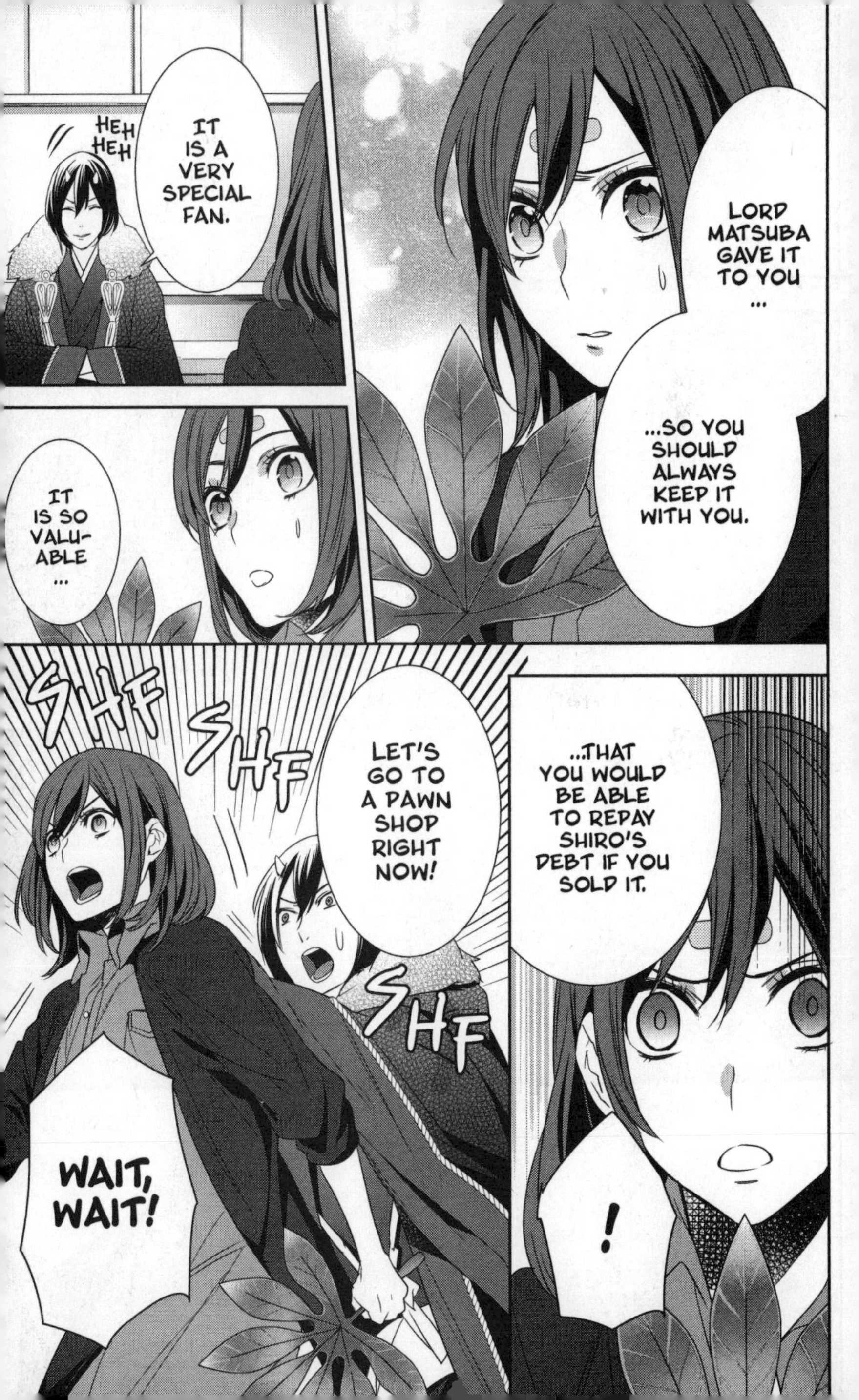
LORD MATSUBA GAVE IT TO YOU ...
...SO YOU SHOULD ALWAYS KEEP IT WITH YOU.
HEH HEH
IT IS A VERY SPECIAL FAN.
IT IS SO VALUABLE ...
...THAT YOU WOULD BE ABLE TO REPAY SHIRO'S DEBT IF YOU SOLD IT.
!
SHF SHF
LET'S GO TO A PAWN SHOP RIGHT NOW!
SHF
WAIT, WAIT!

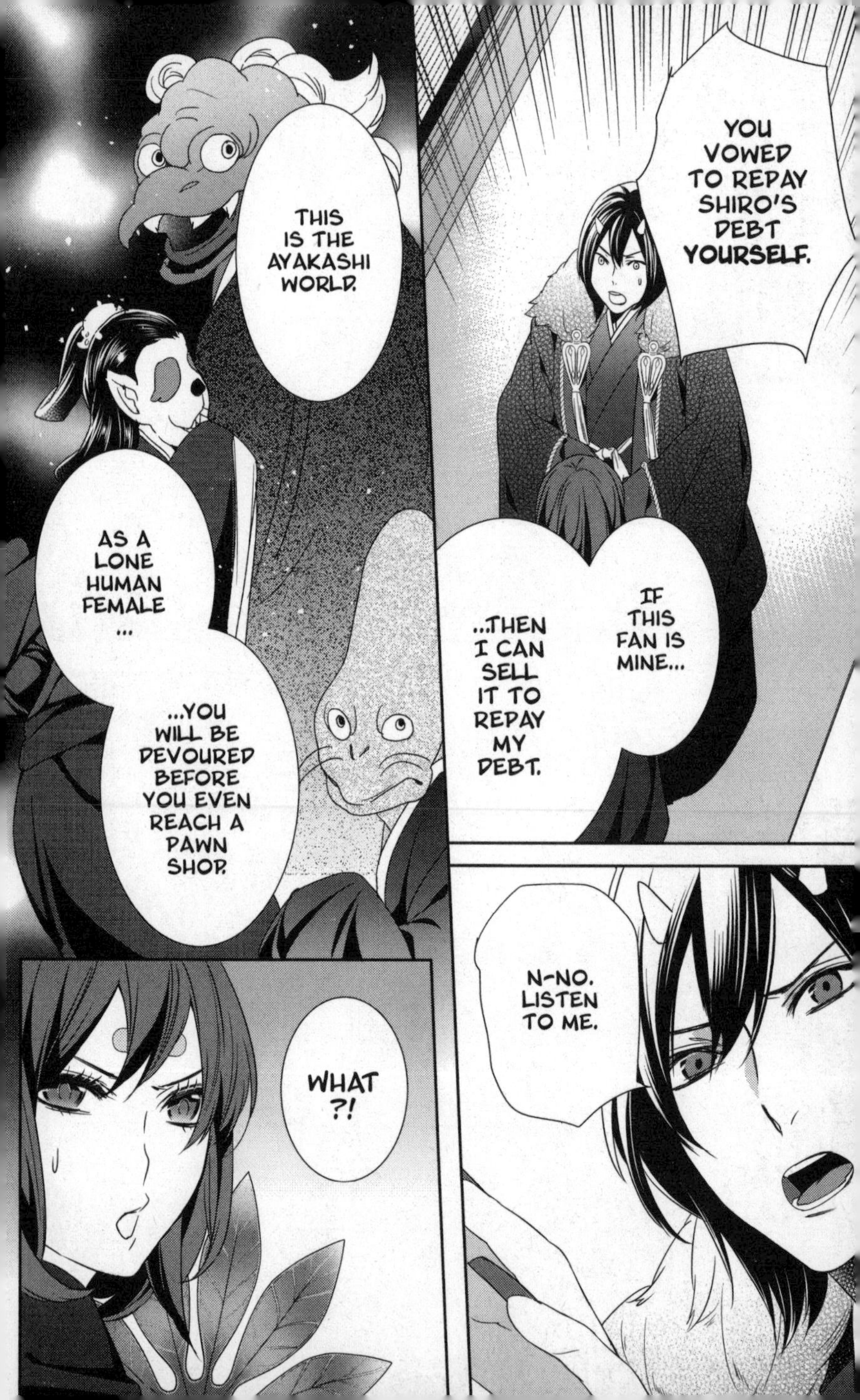
YOU VOWED TO REPAY SHIRO'S DEBT YOURSELF.
IF THIS FAN IS MINE...
...THEN I CAN SELL IT TO REPAY MY DEBT.
THIS IS THE AYAKASHI WORLD.
AS A LONE HUMAN FEMALE...
...YOU WILL BE DEVOURED BEFORE YOU EVEN REACH A PAWN SHOP.
N-NO. LISTEN TO ME.
WHAT?!

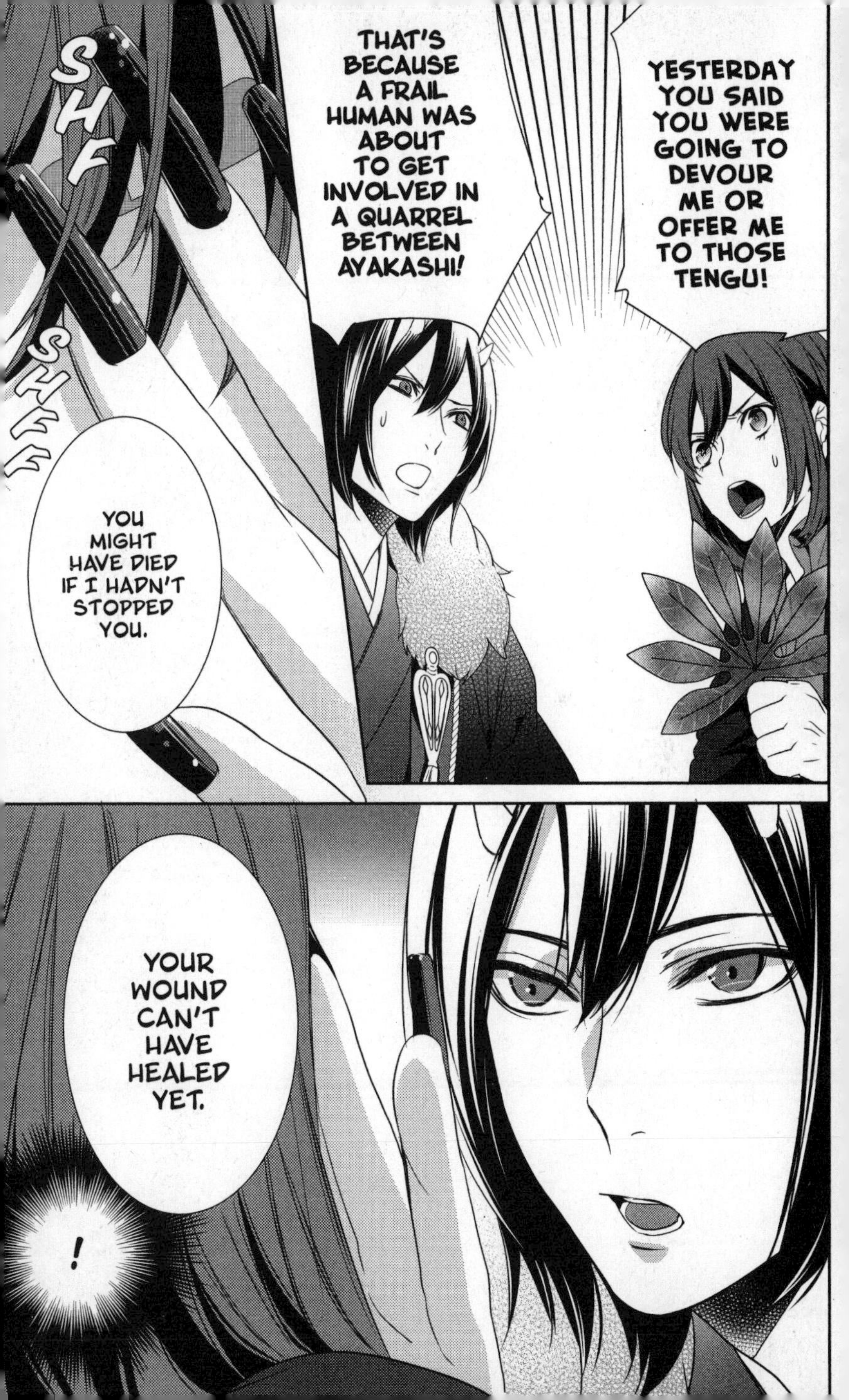
YESTERDAY YOU SAID YOU WERE GOING TO DEVOUR ME OR OFFER ME TO THOSE TENGU!
THAT'S BECAUSE A FRAIL HUMAN WAS ABOUT TO GET INVOLVED IN A QUARREL BETWEEN AYAKASHI!
SHF
SHFF
YOU MIGHT HAVE DIED IF I HADN'T STOPPED YOU.
YOUR WOUND CAN'T HAVE HEALED YET.
!

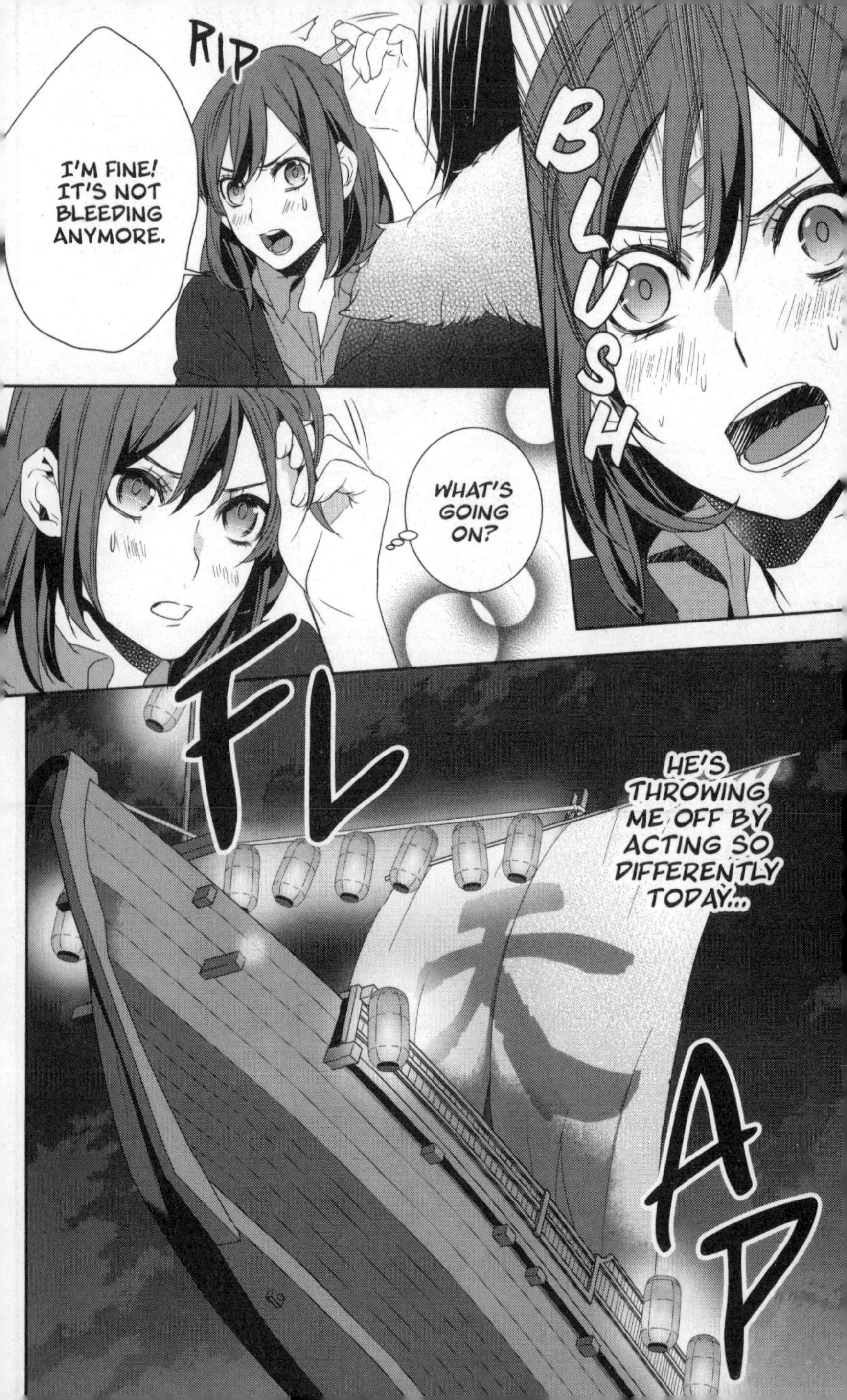
BLUSH
RIP
I'M FINE! IT'S NOT BLEEDING ANYMORE.
WHAT'S GOING ON?
HE'S THROWING ME OFF BY ACTING SO DIFFERENTLY TODAY...
FLAP

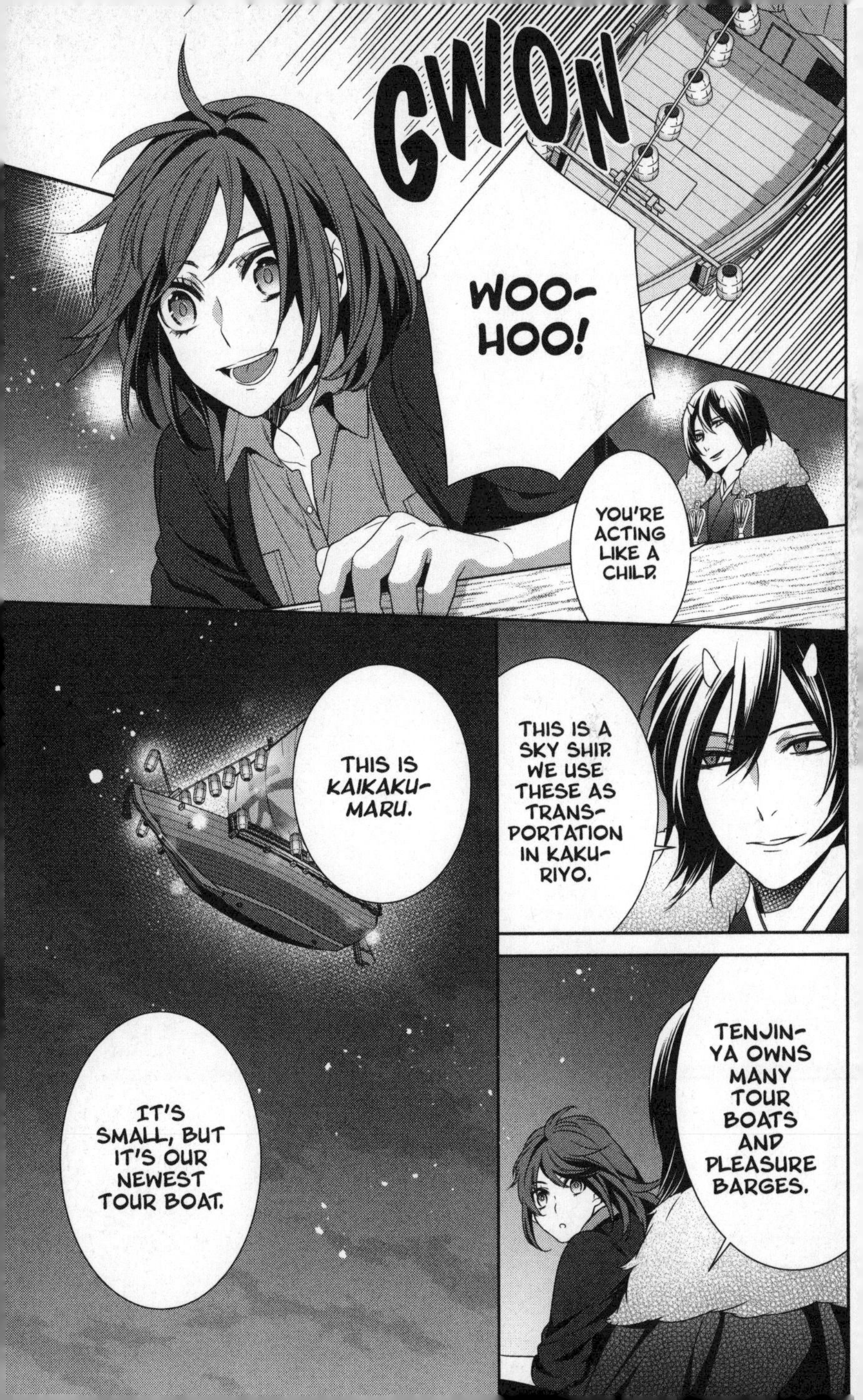
GWON
WOO-HOO!
YOU'RE ACTING LIKE A CHILD.
THIS IS A SKY SHIP. WE USE THESE AS TRANSPORTATION IN KAKURIYO.
TENJIN-YA OWNS MANY TOUR BOATS AND PLEASURE BARGES.
THIS IS KAIKAKU-MARU.
IT'S SMALL, BUT IT'S OUR NEWEST TOUR BOAT.

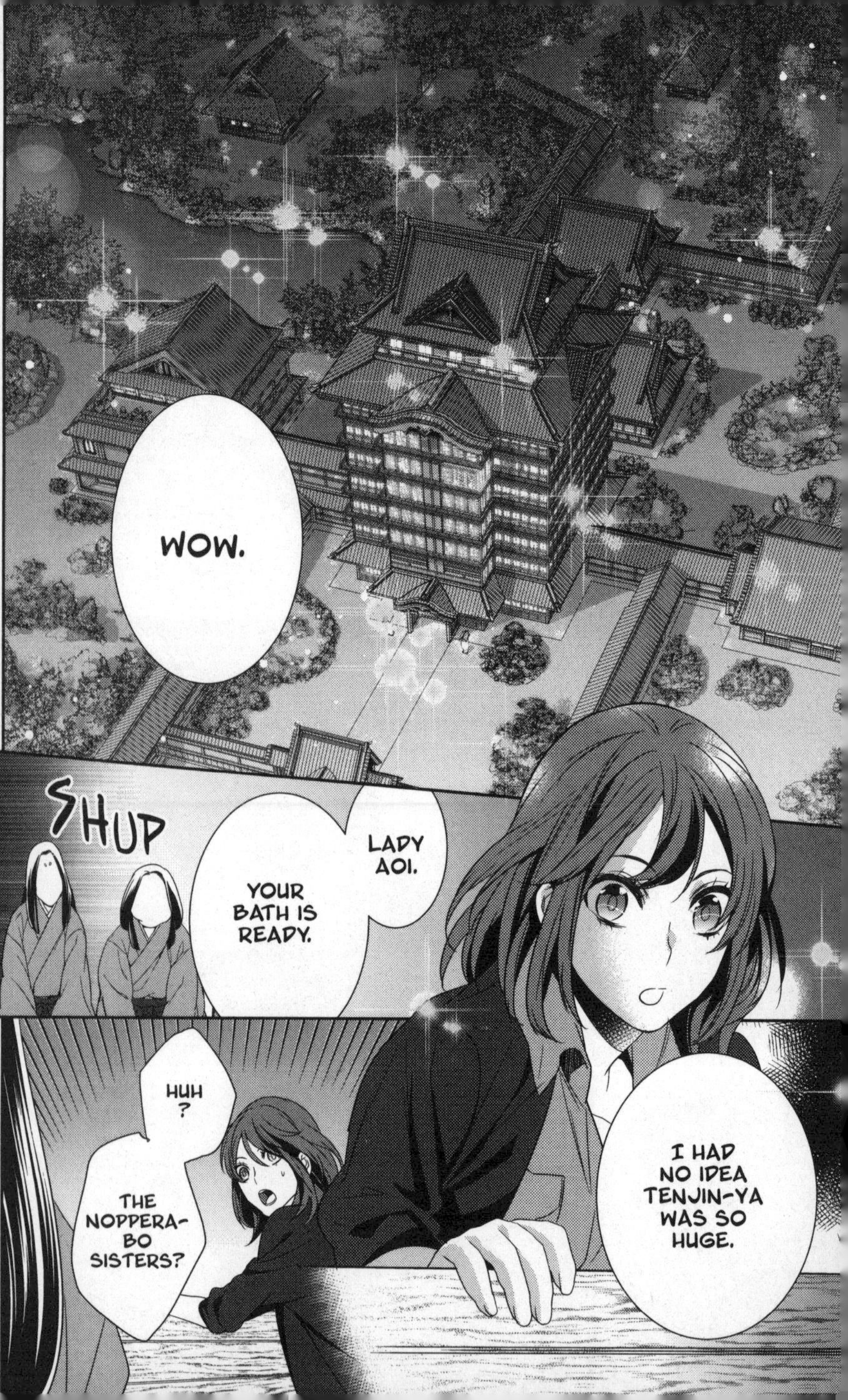
WOW.
LADY AOI.
YOUR BATH IS READY.
SHUP
I HAD NO IDEA TENJIN-YA WAS SO HUGE.
HUH?
THE NOPPERA-BO SISTERS?

Kakuriyo
Bed & Breakfast
for Spirits

Kakuriyo

Bed & Breakfast for Spirits

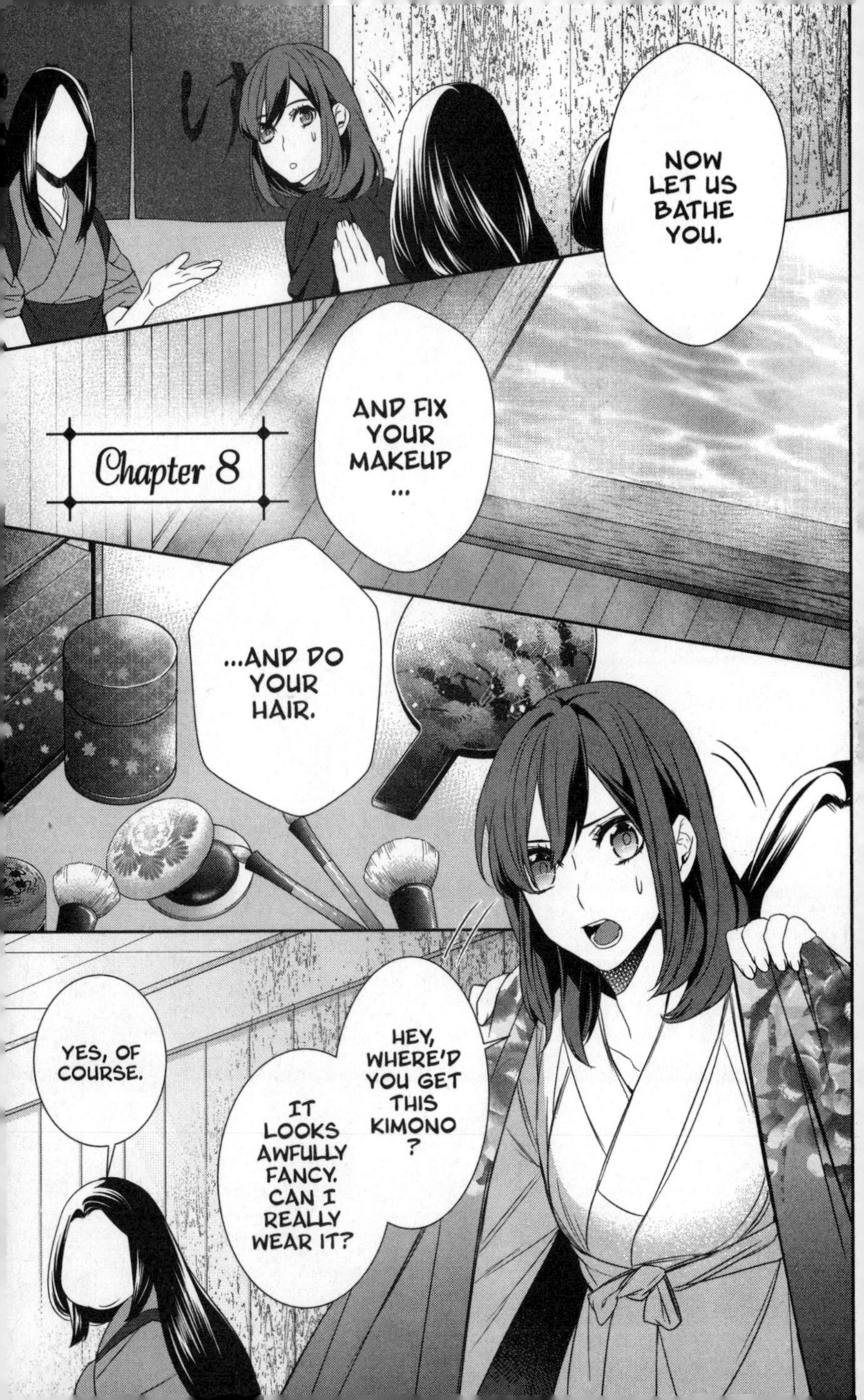
NOW LET US BATHE YOU.
AND FIX YOUR MAKEUP ...
Chapter 8
...AND DO YOUR HAIR.
HEY, WHERE'D YOU GET THIS KIMONO?
IT LOOKS AWFULLY FANCY. CAN I REALLY WEAR IT?
YES, OF COURSE.

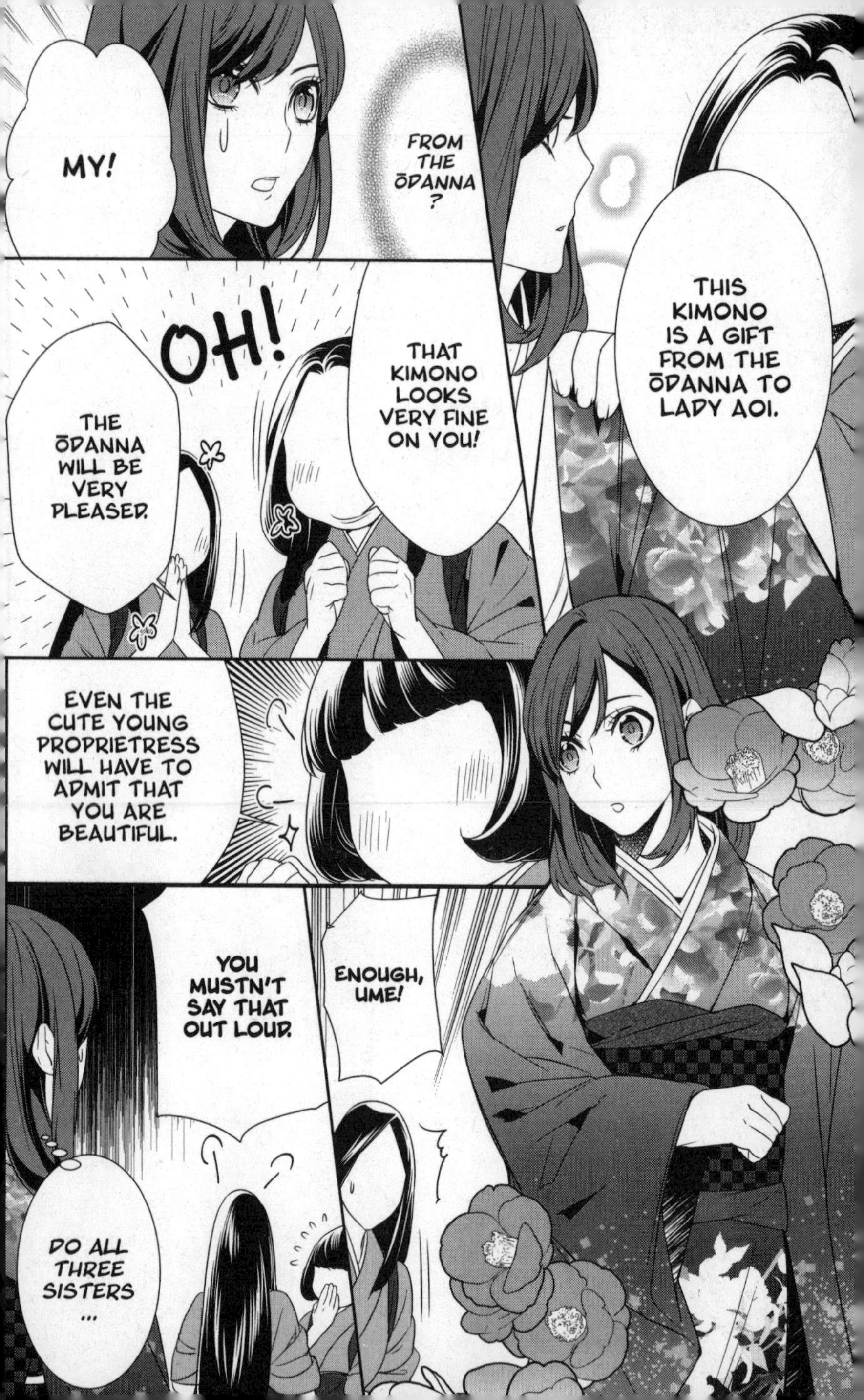
THIS KIMONO IS A GIFT FROM THE ŌDANNA TO LADY AOI.
FROM THE ŌDANNA?
MY!
OH!
THAT KIMONO LOOKS VERY FINE ON YOU!
THE ŌDANNA WILL BE VERY PLEASED.
EVEN THE CUTE YOUNG PROPRIETRESS WILL HAVE TO ADMIT THAT YOU ARE BEAUTIFUL.
ENOUGH, UME!
YOU MUSTN'T SAY THAT OUT LOUD.
DO ALL THREE SISTERS ...

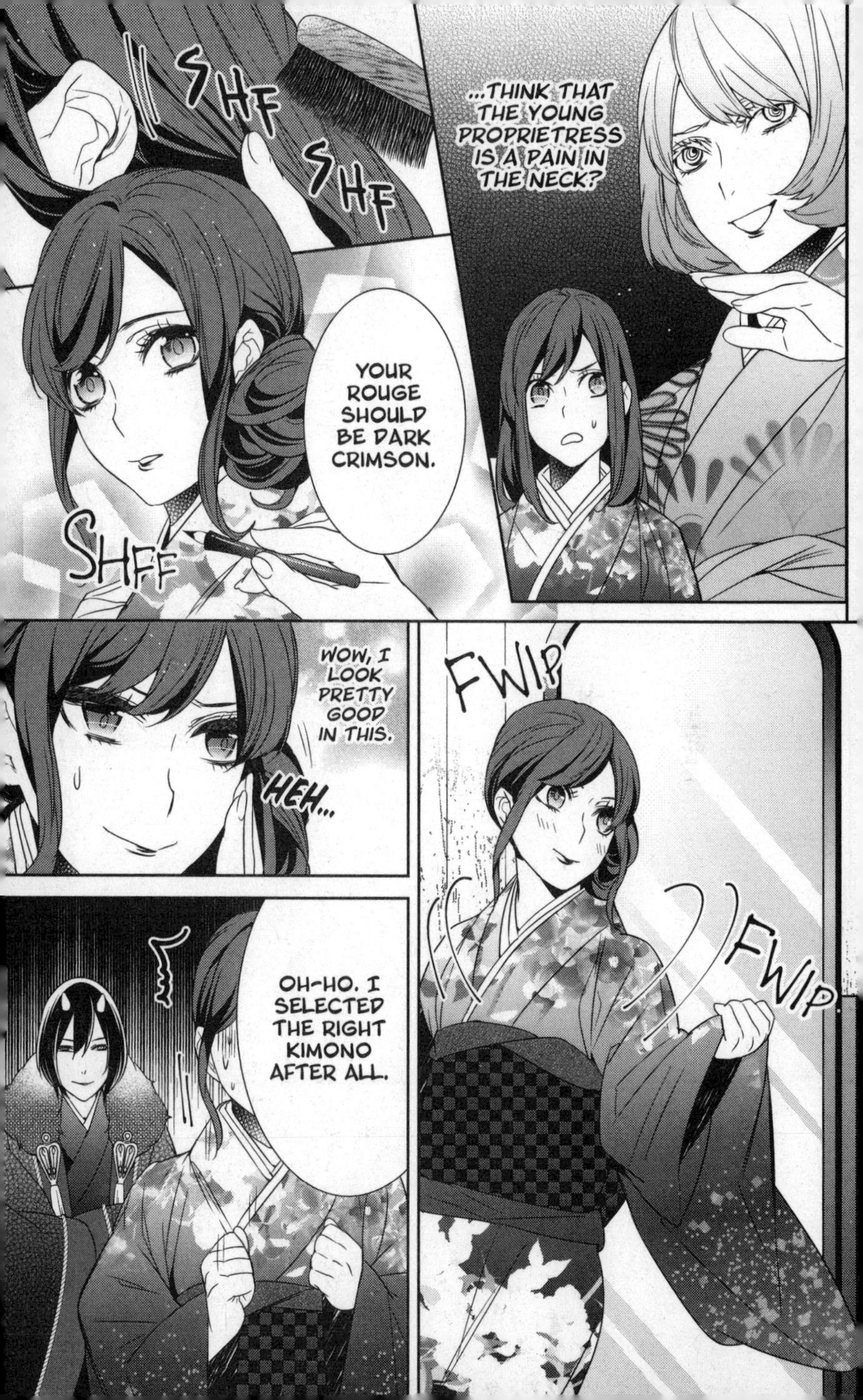
...THINK THAT THE YOUNG PROPRIETRESS IS A PAIN IN THE NECK?
SHF
SHF
YOUR ROUGE SHOULD BE DARK CRIMSON.
SHFF
FWIP
FWIP
WOW, I LOOK PRETTY GOOD IN THIS.
HEH...
OH-HO. I SELECTED THE RIGHT KIMONO AFTER ALL.

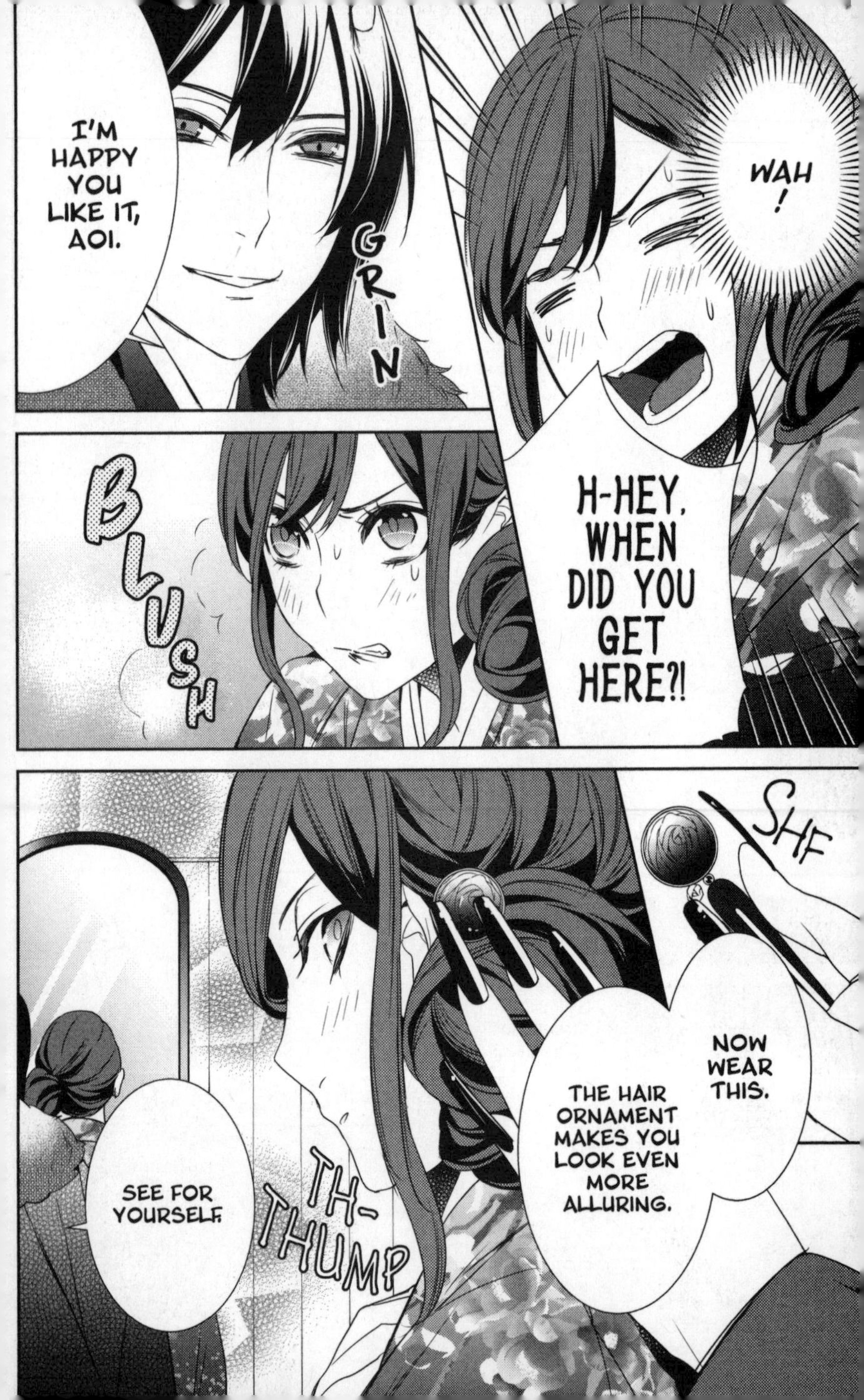
WAH!
H-HEY, WHEN DID YOU GET HERE?!
I'M HAPPY YOU LIKE IT, AOI.
GRIN
BLUSH
SHF
NOW WEAR THIS.
THE HAIR ORNAMENT MAKES YOU LOOK EVEN MORE ALLURING.
TH-THUMP
SEE FOR YOURSELF.

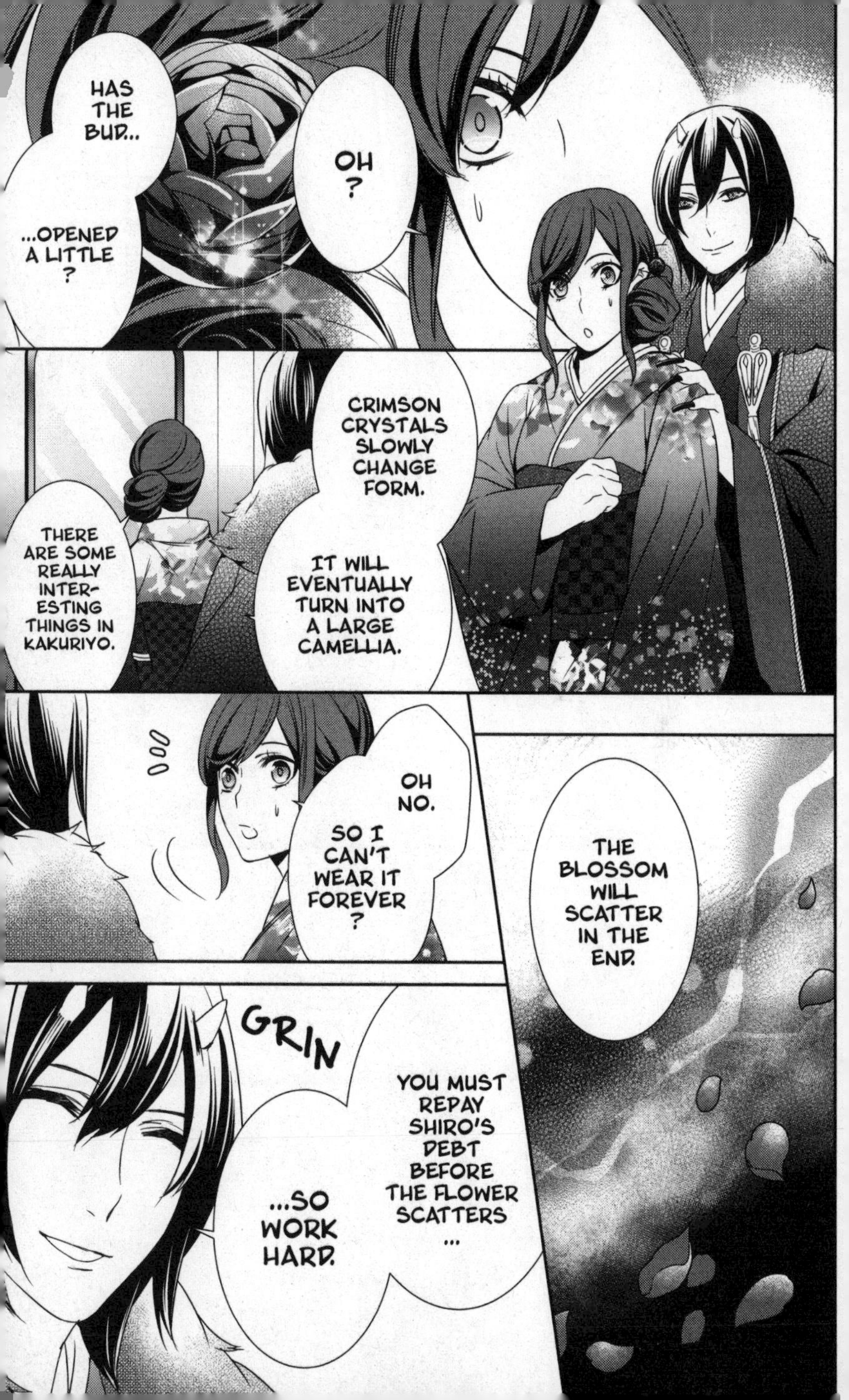
OH?
HAS THE BUD...
...OPENED A LITTLE?
CRIMSON CRYSTALS SLOWLY CHANGE FORM.
IT WILL EVENTUALLY TURN INTO A LARGE CAMELLIA.
THERE ARE SOME REALLY INTERESTING THINGS IN KAKURIYO.
THE BLOSSOM WILL SCATTER IN THE END.
OH NO.
SO I CAN'T WEAR IT FOREVER?
GRIN
YOU MUST REPAY SHIRO'S DEBT BEFORE THE FLOWER SCATTERS...
...SO WORK HARD.

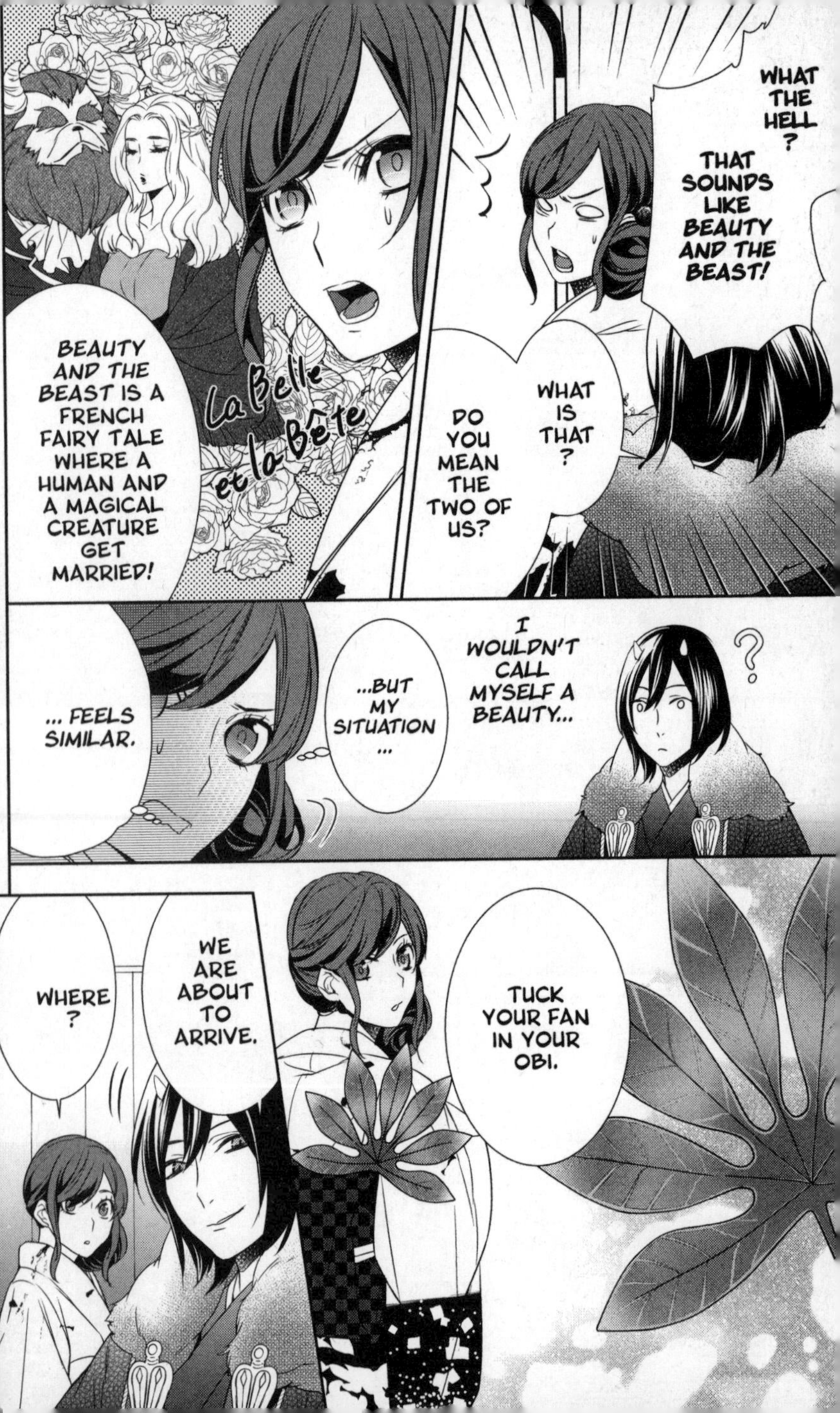

WHAT THE HELL?
THAT SOUNDS LIKE BEAUTY AND THE BEAST!
WHAT IS THAT?
DO YOU MEAN THE TWO OF US?
BEAUTY AND THE BEAST IS A FRENCH FAIRY TALE WHERE A HUMAN AND A MAGICAL CREATURE GET MARRIED!
La Belle et la Bête
I WOULDN'T CALL MYSELF A BEAUTY...
...BUT MY SITUATION...
... FEELS SIMILAR.
TUCK YOUR FAN IN YOUR OBI.
WE ARE ABOUT TO ARRIVE.
WHERE?

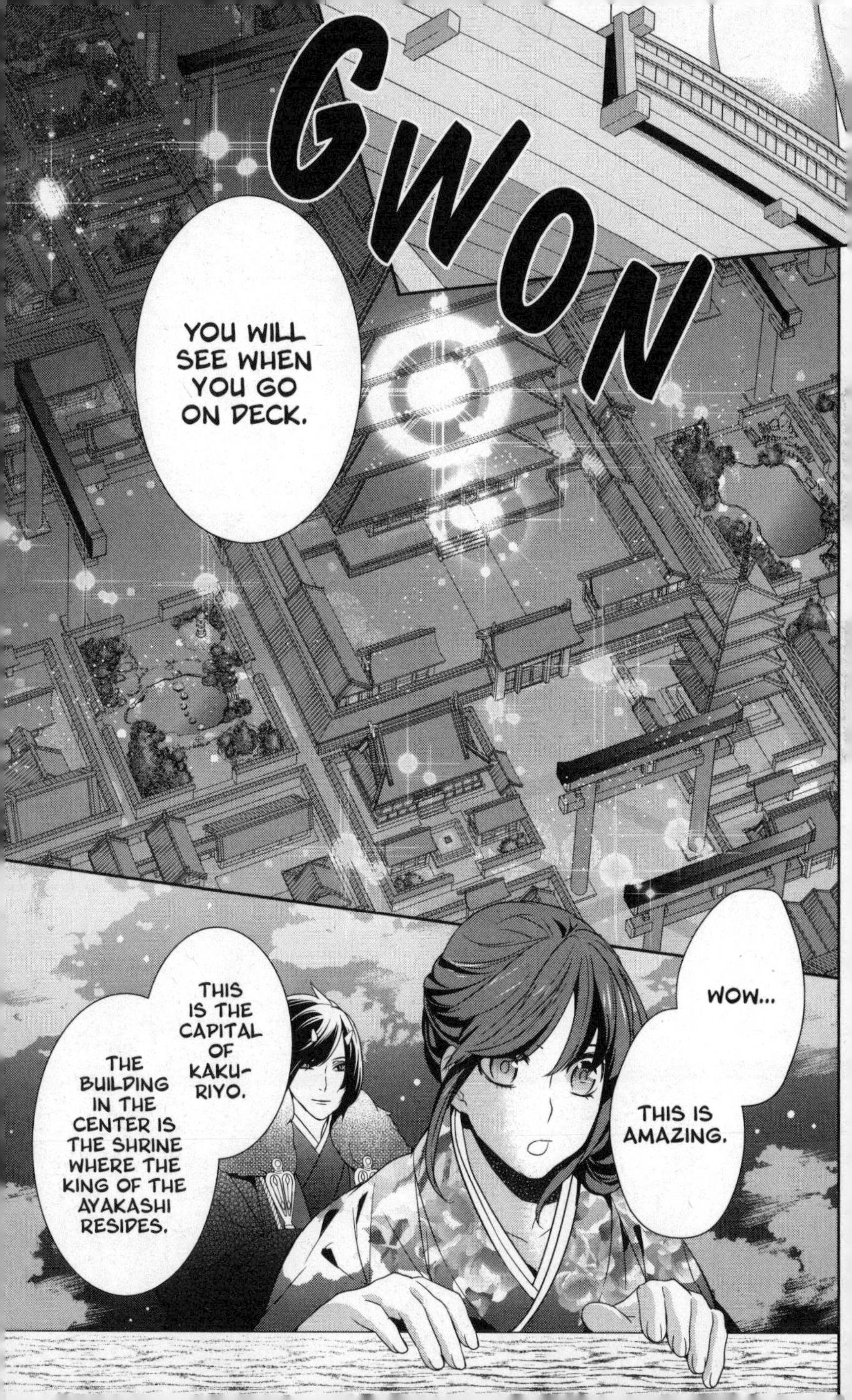
GWON
YOU WILL SEE WHEN YOU GO ON DECK.
WOW...
THIS IS AMAZING.
THIS IS THE CAPITAL OF KAKURIYO.
THE BUILDING IN THE CENTER IS THE SHRINE WHERE THE KING OF THE AYAKASHI RESIDES.

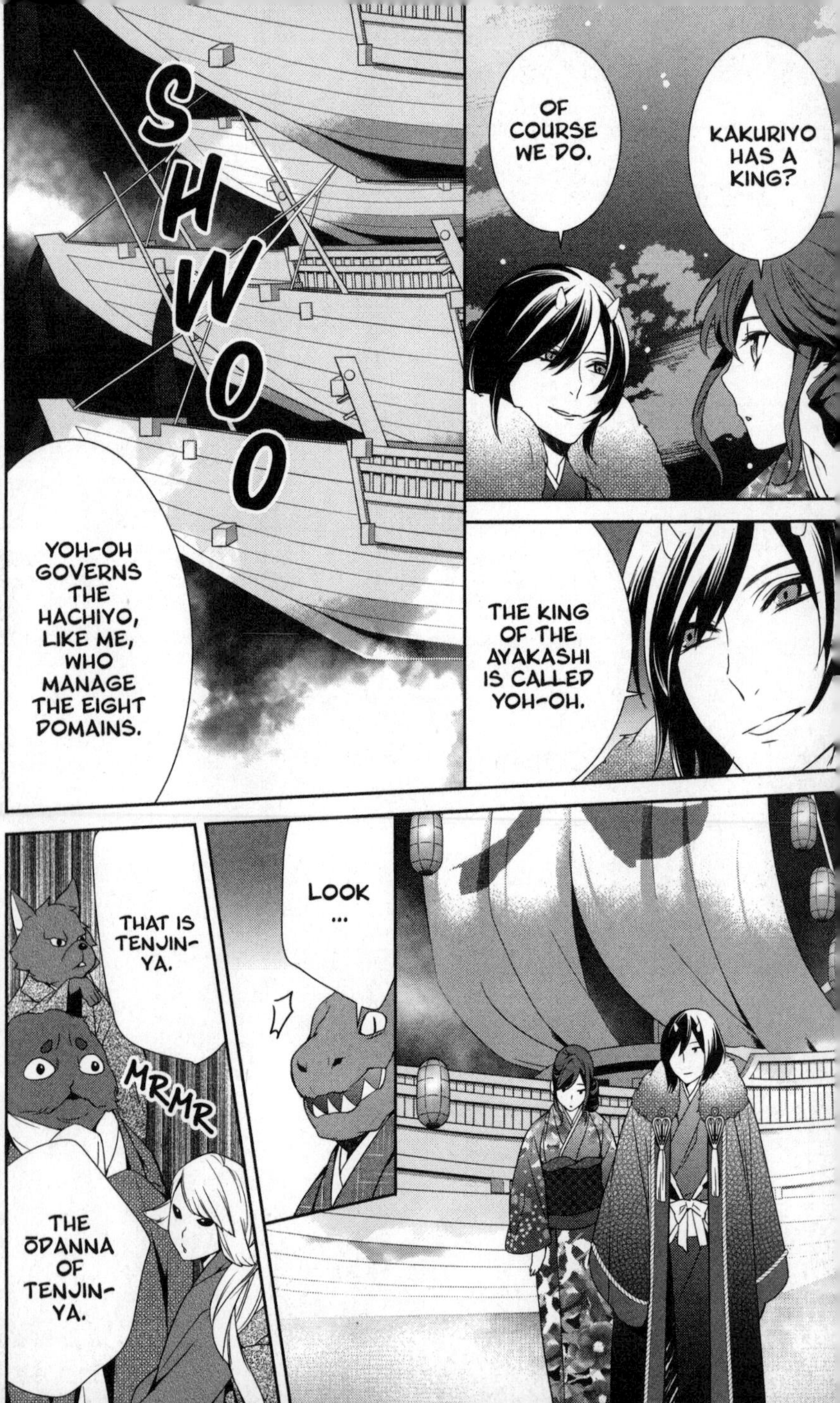

KAKURIYO HAS A KING?
OF COURSE WE DO.
THE KING OF THE AYAKASHI IS CALLED YOH-OH.
SHWOO
YOH-OH GOVERNS THE HACHIYO, LIKE ME, WHO MANAGE THE EIGHT DOMAINS.
LOOK ...
THAT IS TENJIN-YA.
MRMR
THE ŌDANNA OF TENJIN-YA.

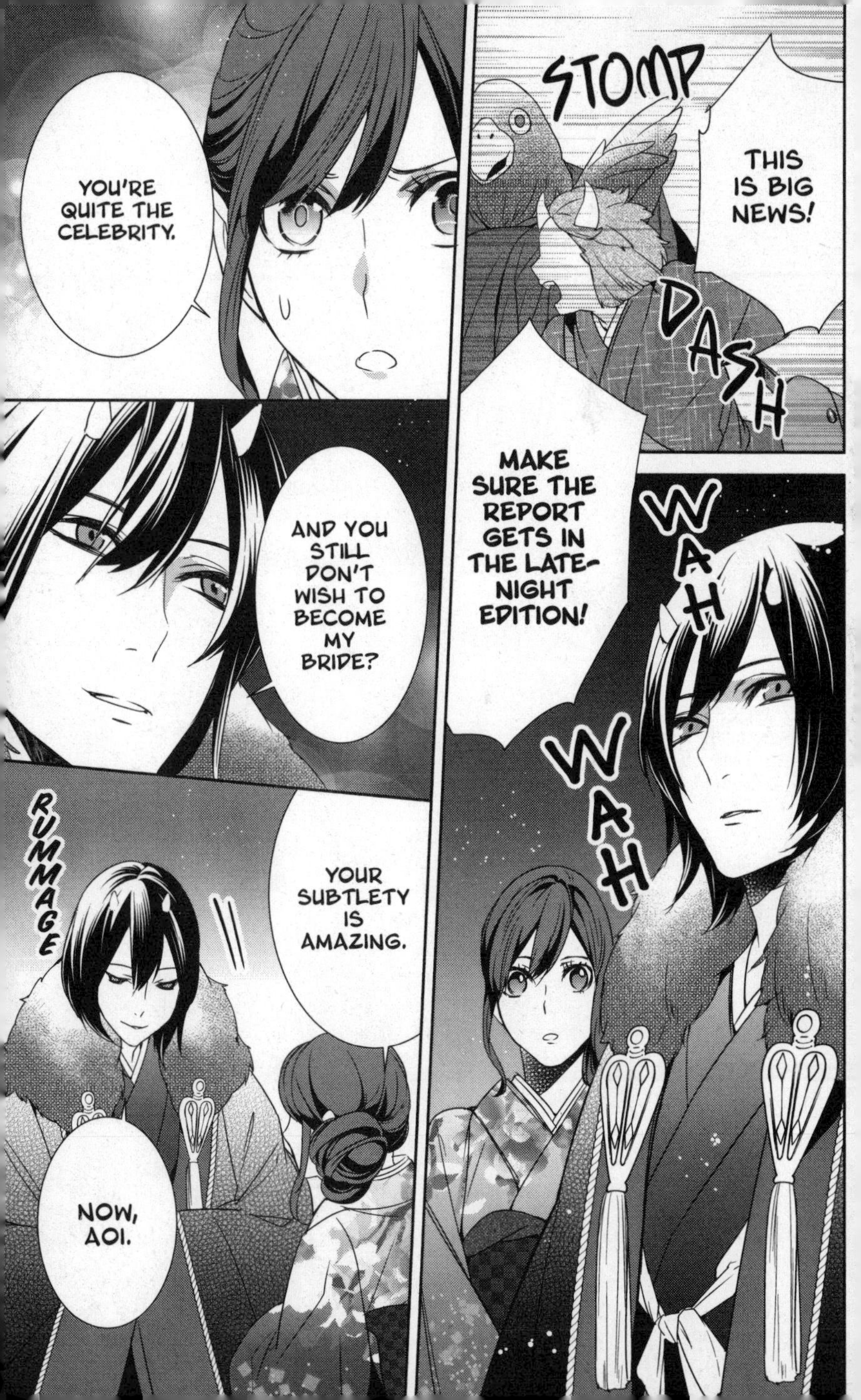
STOMP
THIS IS BIG NEWS!
DASH
MAKE SURE THE REPORT GETS IN THE LATE-NIGHT EDITION!
WAH WAH
YOU'RE QUITE THE CELEBRITY.
AND YOU STILL DON'T WISH TO BECOME MY BRIDE?
YOUR SUBTLETY IS AMAZING.
RUMMAGE
NOW, AOI.

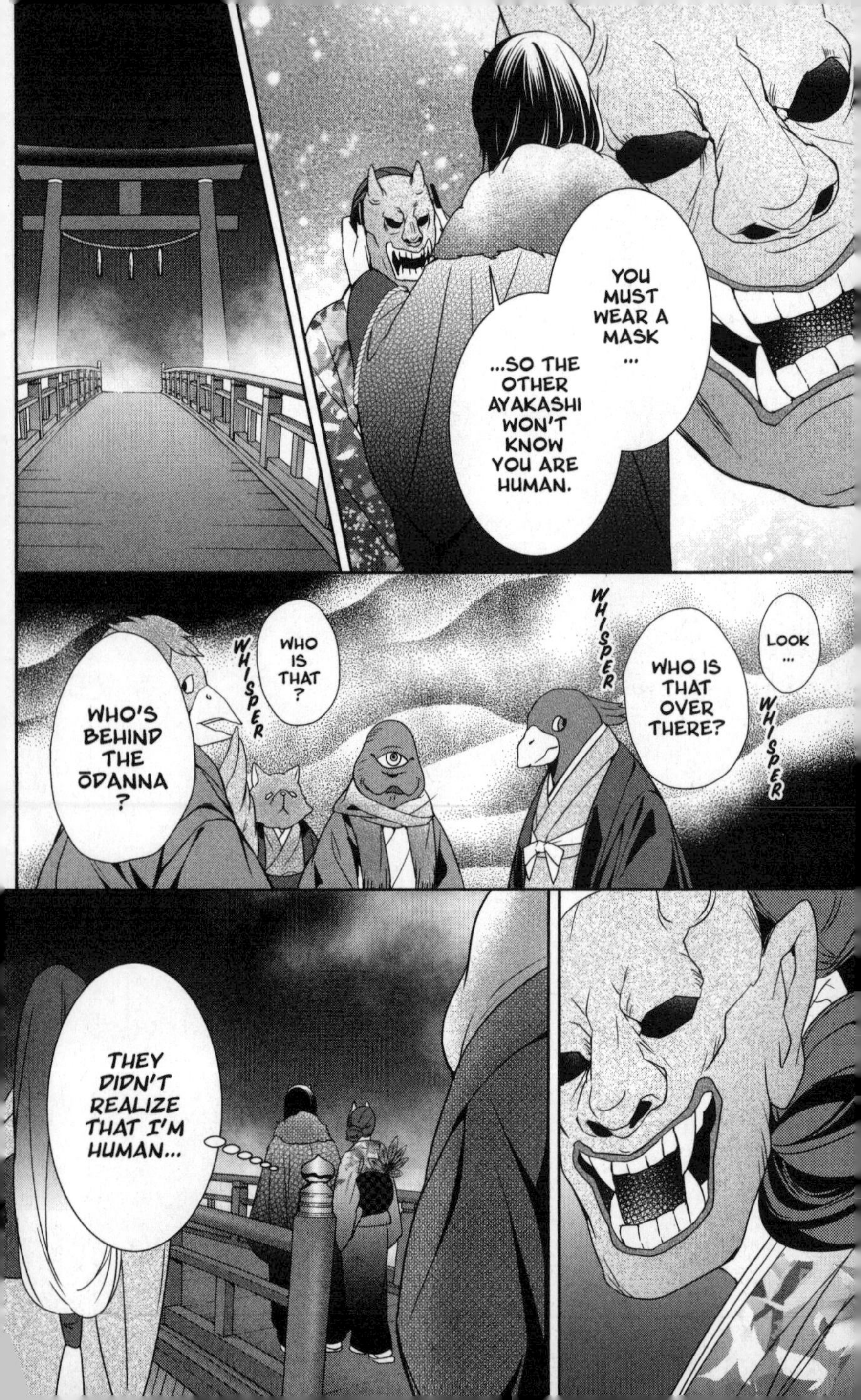
YOU MUST WEAR A MASK...
...SO THE OTHER AYAKASHI WON'T KNOW YOU ARE HUMAN.
LOOK...
WHISPER
WHO IS THAT OVER THERE?
WHISPER
WHO IS THAT?
WHISPER
WHO'S BEHIND THE ŌDANNA?
THEY DIDN'T REALIZE THAT I'M HUMAN...

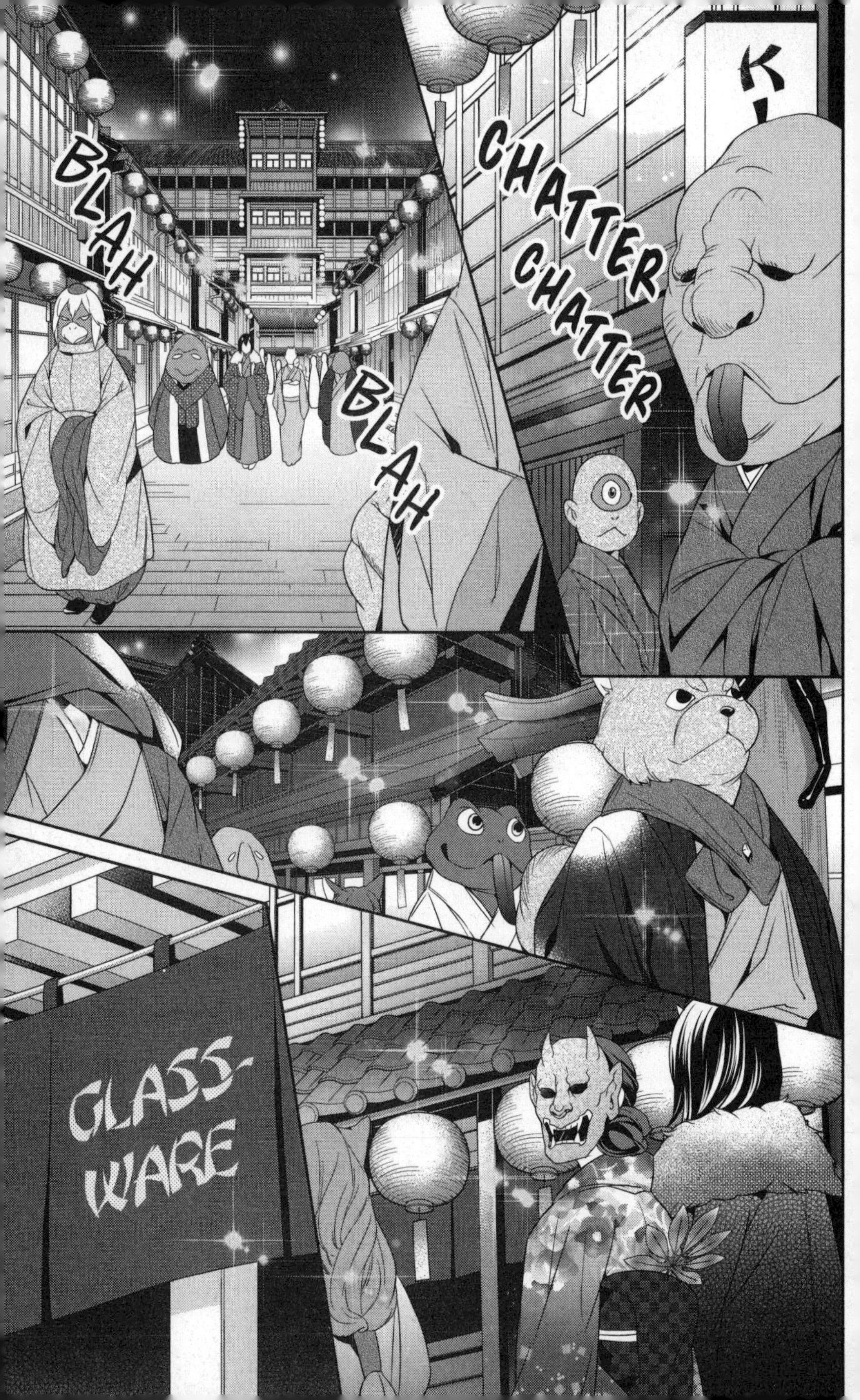
K
CHATTER CHATTER
BLAH
BLAH
GLASS-WARE

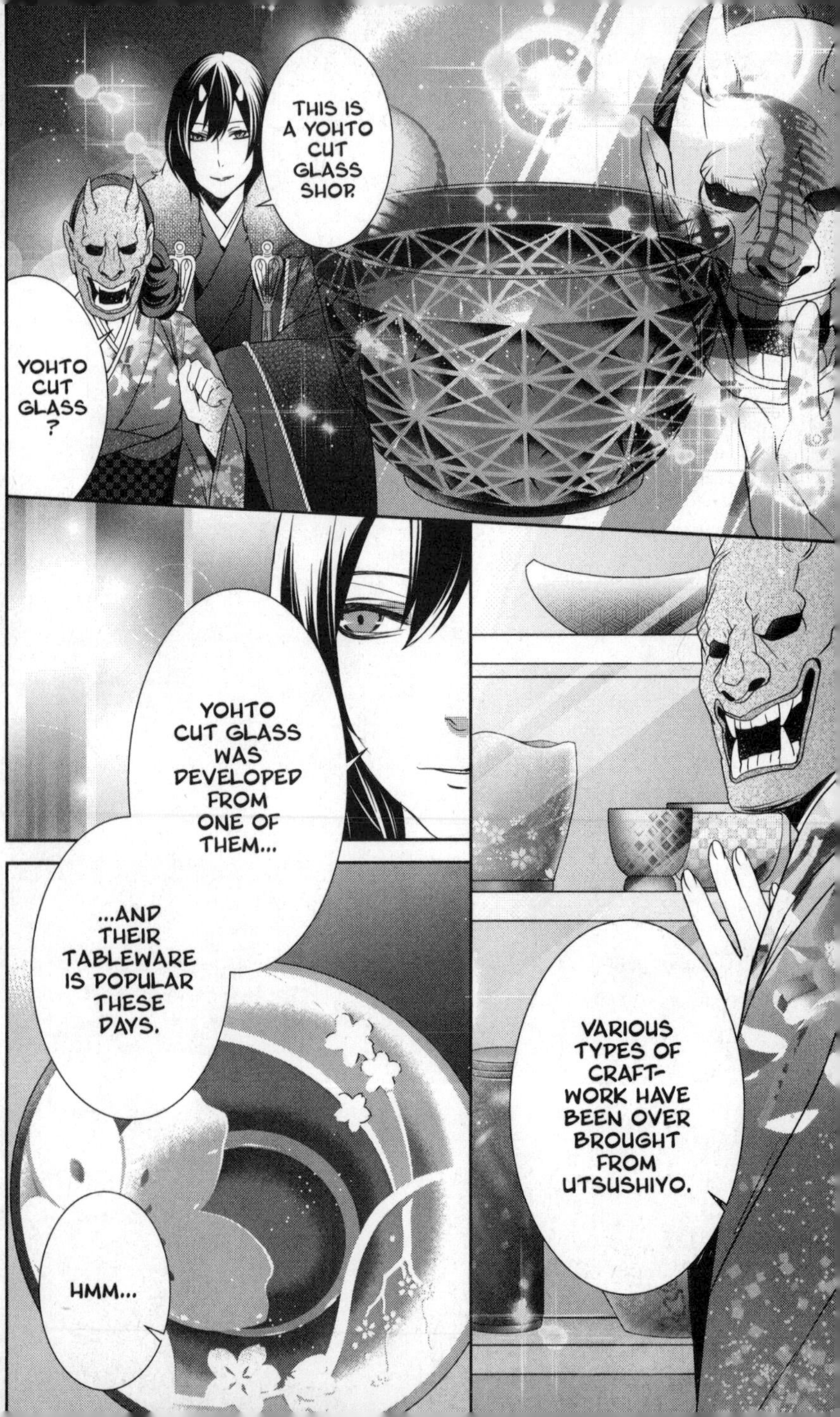
THIS IS A YOHTO CUT GLASS SHOP.
YOHTO CUT GLASS ?
VARIOUS TYPES OF CRAFT-WORK HAVE BEEN OVER BROUGHT FROM UTSUSHIYO.
YOHTO CUT GLASS WAS DEVELOPED FROM ONE OF THEM...
...AND THEIR TABLEWARE IS POPULAR THESE DAYS.
HMM...

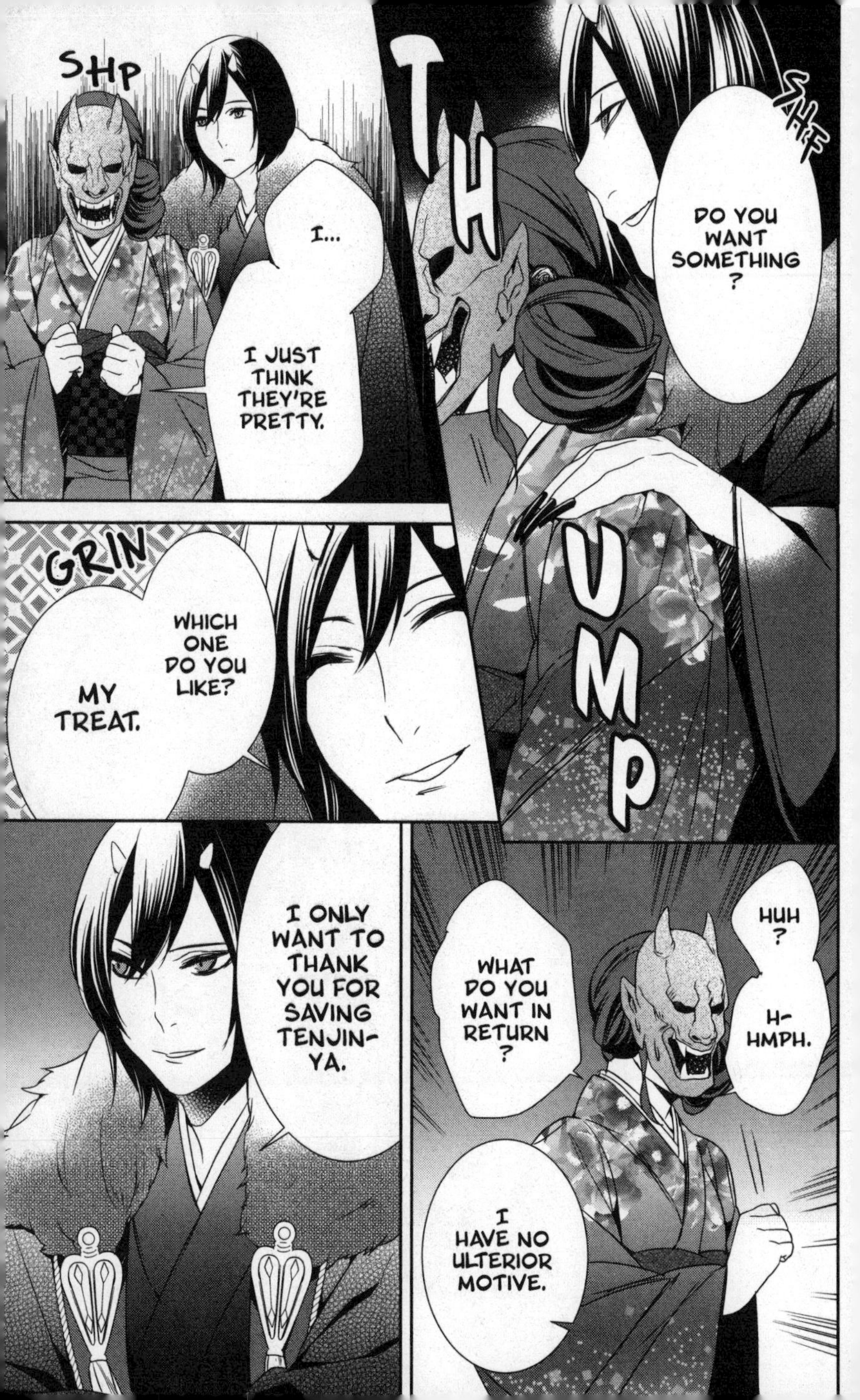
THUMP
SHF
DO YOU WANT SOMETHING?
SHP
I...
I JUST THINK THEY'RE PRETTY.
GRIN
WHICH ONE DO YOU LIKE?
MY TREAT.
HUH?
WHAT DO YOU WANT IN RETURN?
H-HMPH.
I HAVE NO ULTERIOR MOTIVE.
I ONLY WANT TO THANK YOU FOR SAVING TENJIN-YA.

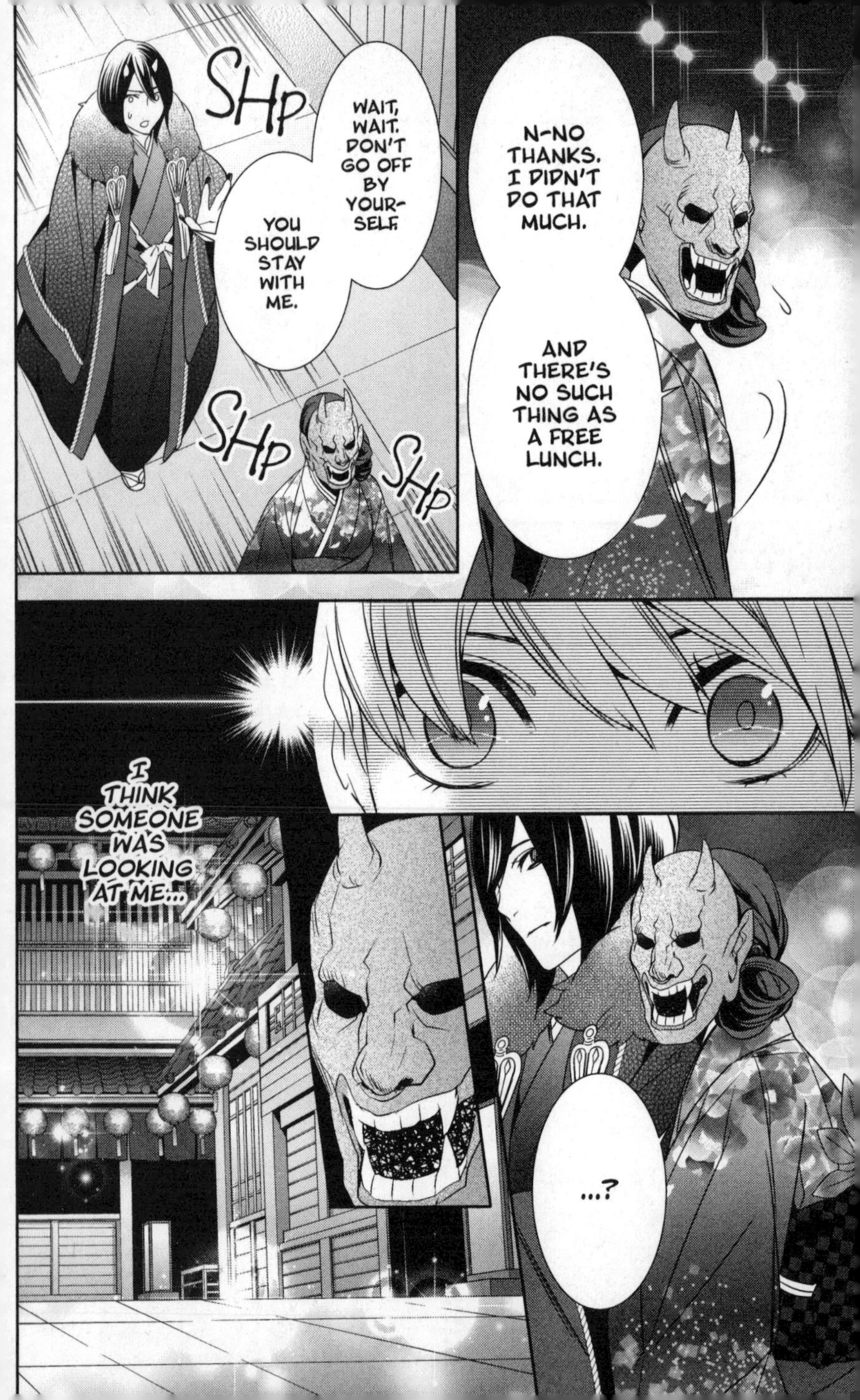
N-NO THANKS. I DIDN'T DO THAT MUCH.
AND THERE'S NO SUCH THING AS A FREE LUNCH.
WAIT, WAIT. DON'T GO OFF BY YOURSELF.
SHp
YOU SHOULD STAY WITH ME.
SHp
SHp
I THINK SOMEONE WAS LOOKING AT ME...
...?

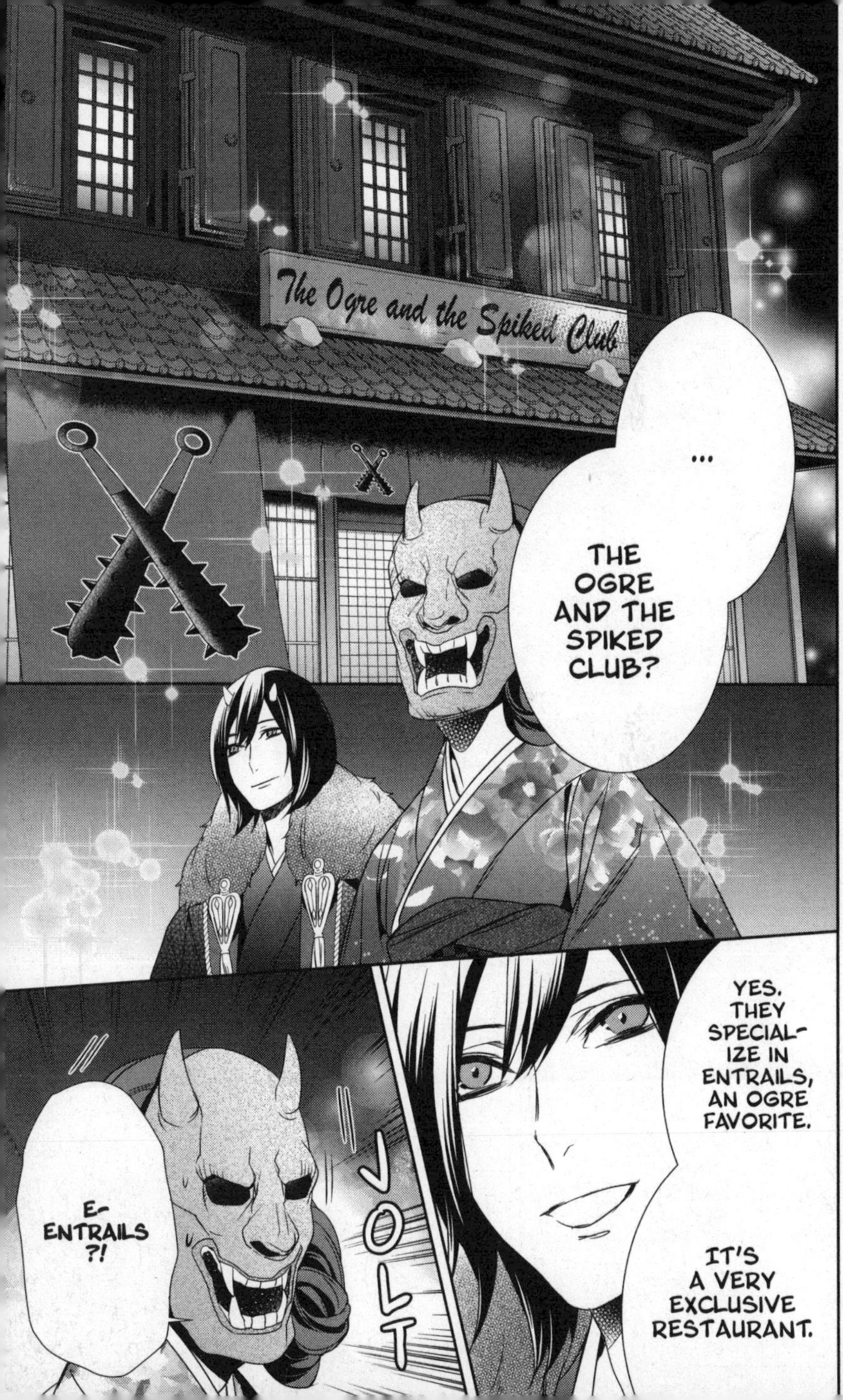
The Ogre and the Spiked Club
...
THE OGRE AND THE SPIKED CLUB?
YES. THEY SPECIAL-IZE IN ENTRAILS, AN OGRE FAVORITE.
IT'S A VERY EXCLUSIVE RESTAURANT.
JOLT
E-ENTRAILS?!

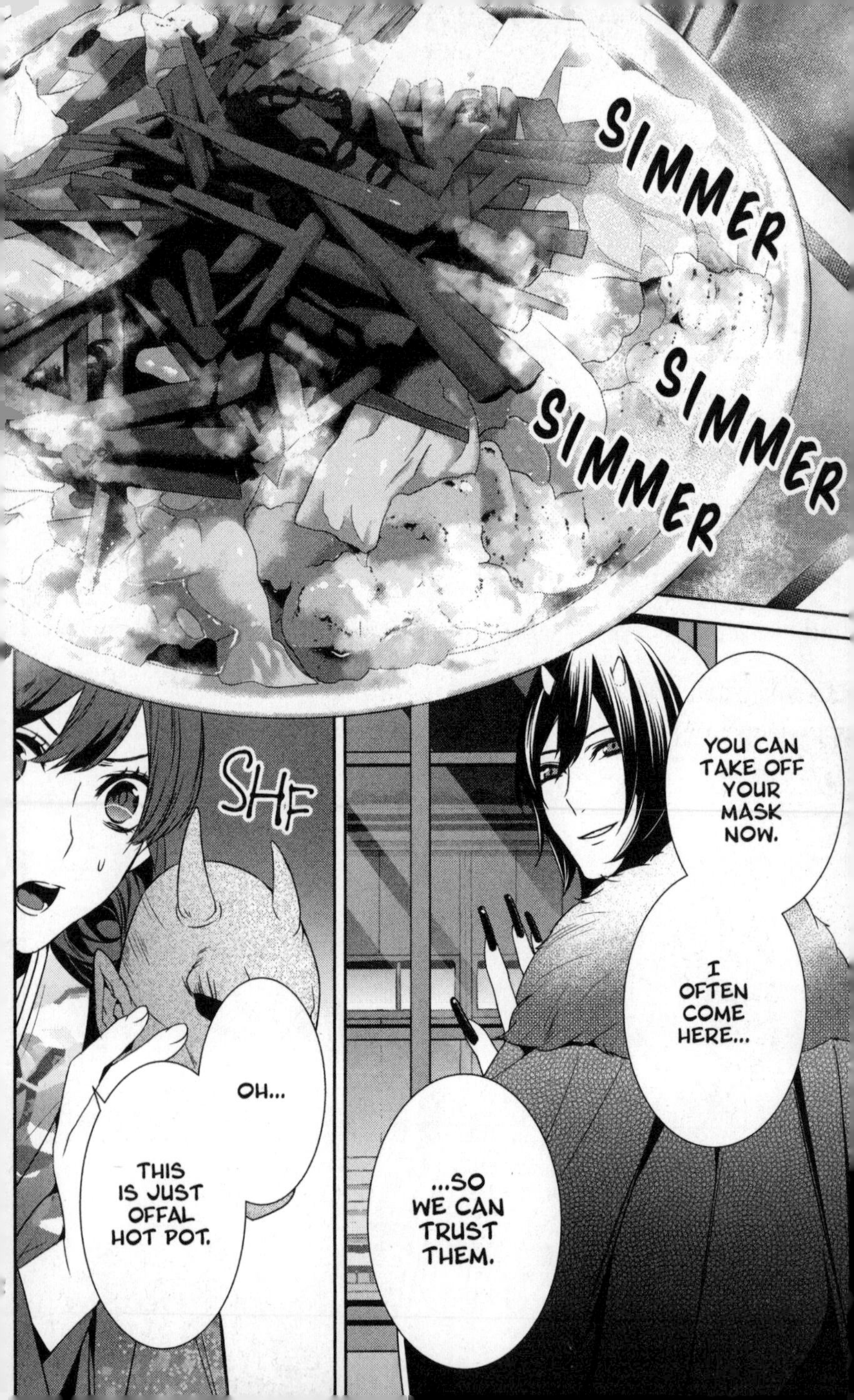
SIMMER
SIMMER
SIMMER
YOU CAN TAKE OFF YOUR MASK NOW.
I OFTEN COME HERE...
...SO WE CAN TRUST THEM.
SHF
OH...
THIS IS JUST OFFAL HOT POT.

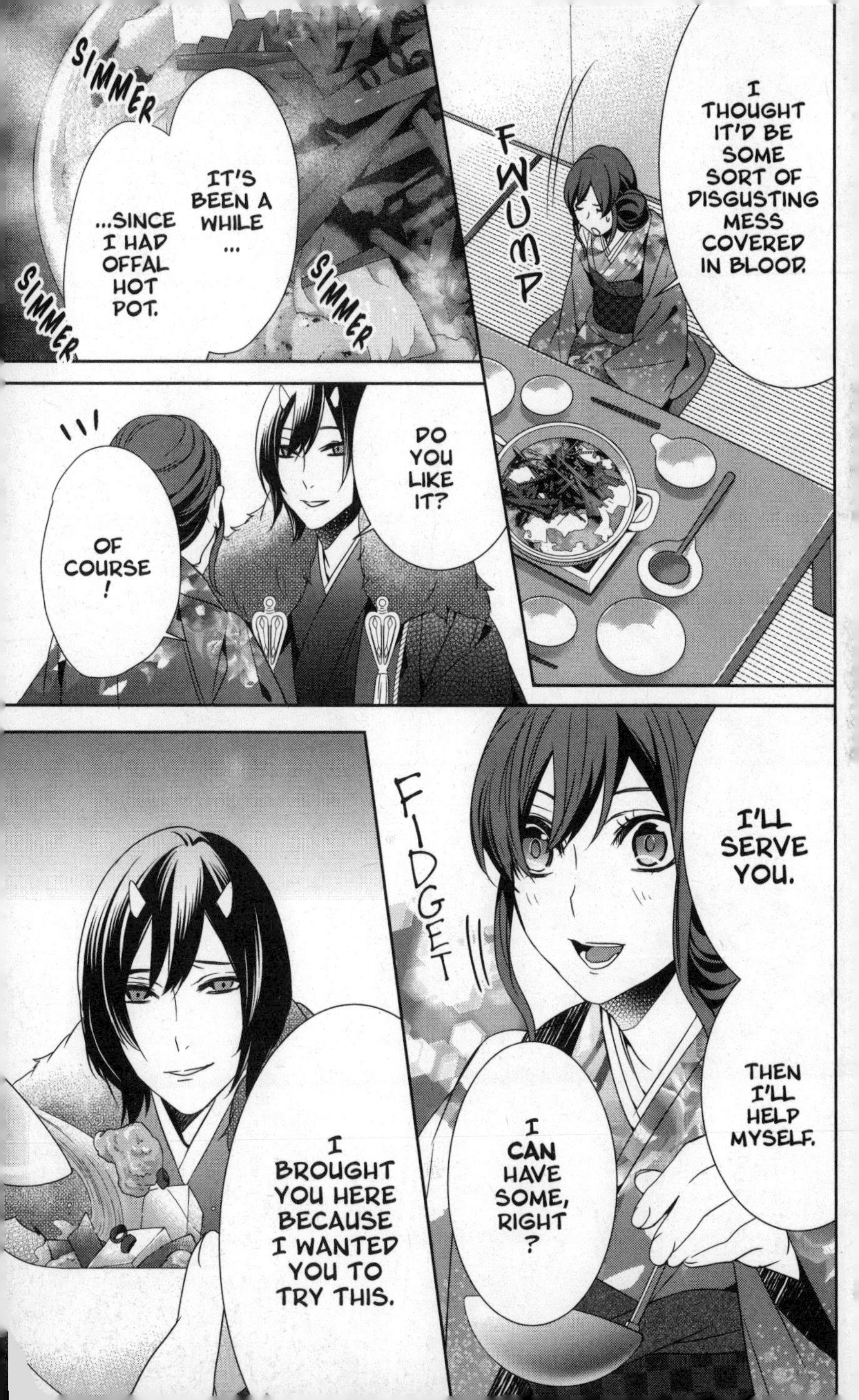
I THOUGHT IT'D BE SOME SORT OF DISGUSTING MESS COVERED IN BLOOD.
FWUMP
SIMMER
IT'S BEEN A WHILE...
...SINCE I HAD OFFAL HOT POT.
SIMMER
SIMMER
DO YOU LIKE IT?
OF COURSE!
I'LL SERVE YOU.
FIDGET
THEN I'LL HELP MYSELF.
I CAN HAVE SOME, RIGHT?
I BROUGHT YOU HERE BECAUSE I WANTED YOU TO TRY THIS.

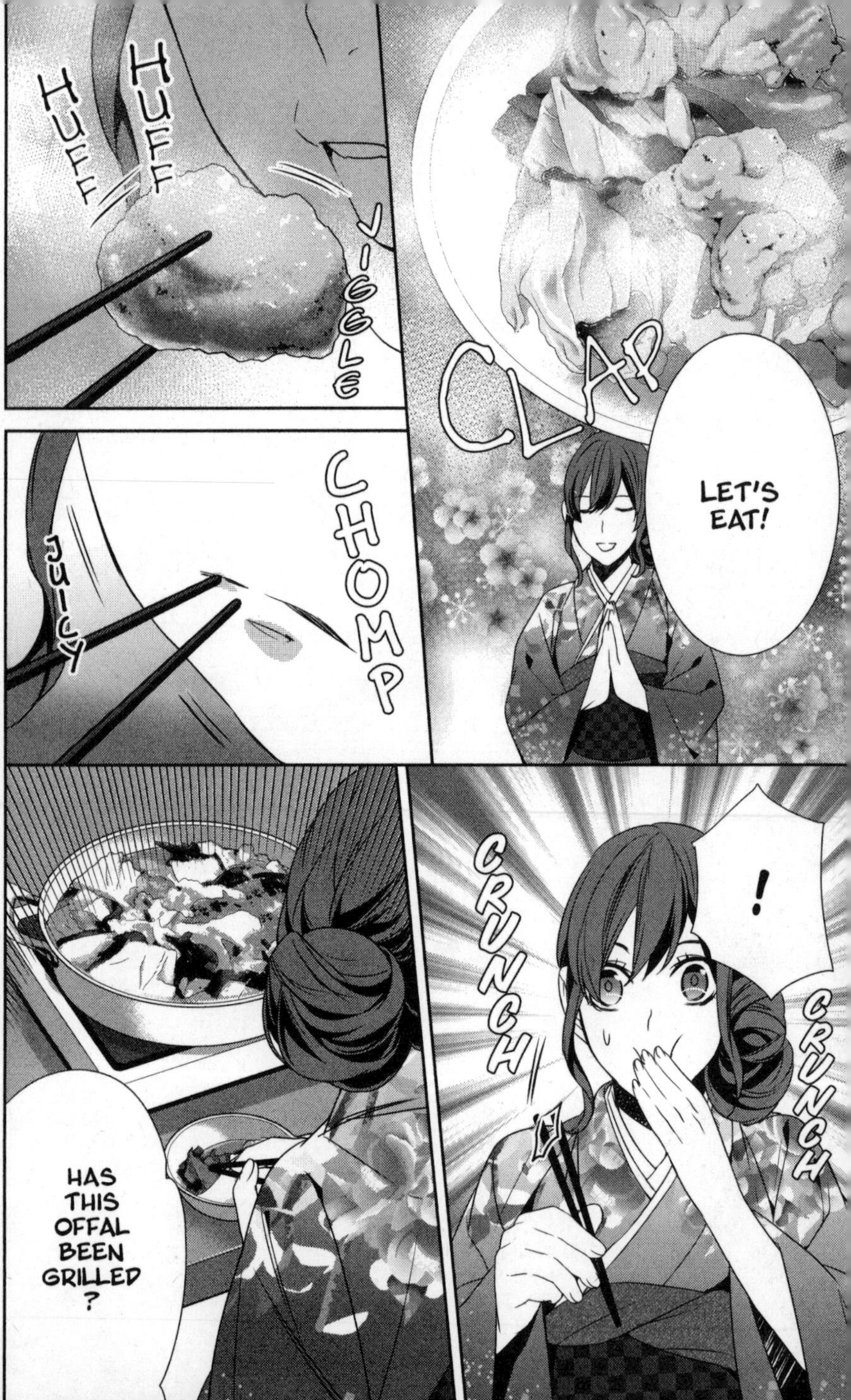
CLAP
LET'S EAT!
HUFF HUFF
JIGGLE
CHOMP
JUICY
!
CRUNCH CRUNCH
HAS THIS OFFAL BEEN GRILLED?

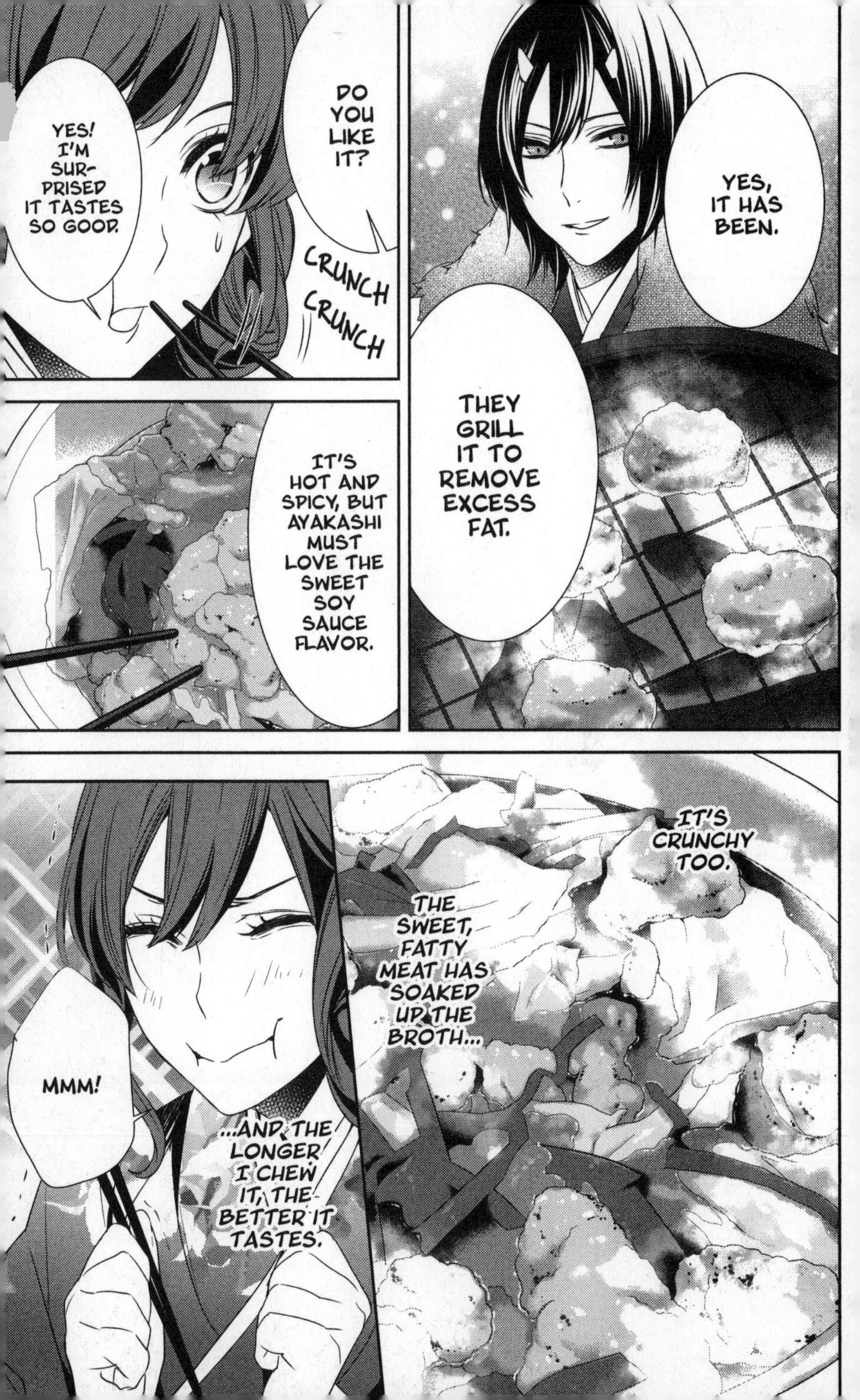
YES, IT HAS BEEN.
THEY GRILL IT TO REMOVE EXCESS FAT.
DO YOU LIKE IT?
YES! I'M SUR-PRISED IT TASTES SO GOOD.
CRUNCH CRUNCH
IT'S HOT AND SPICY, BUT AYAKASHI MUST LOVE THE SWEET SOY SAUCE FLAVOR.
IT'S CRUNCHY TOO.
THE SWEET, FATTY MEAT HAS SOAKED UP THE BROTH...
...AND THE LONGER I CHEW IT, THE BETTER IT TASTES.
MMM!

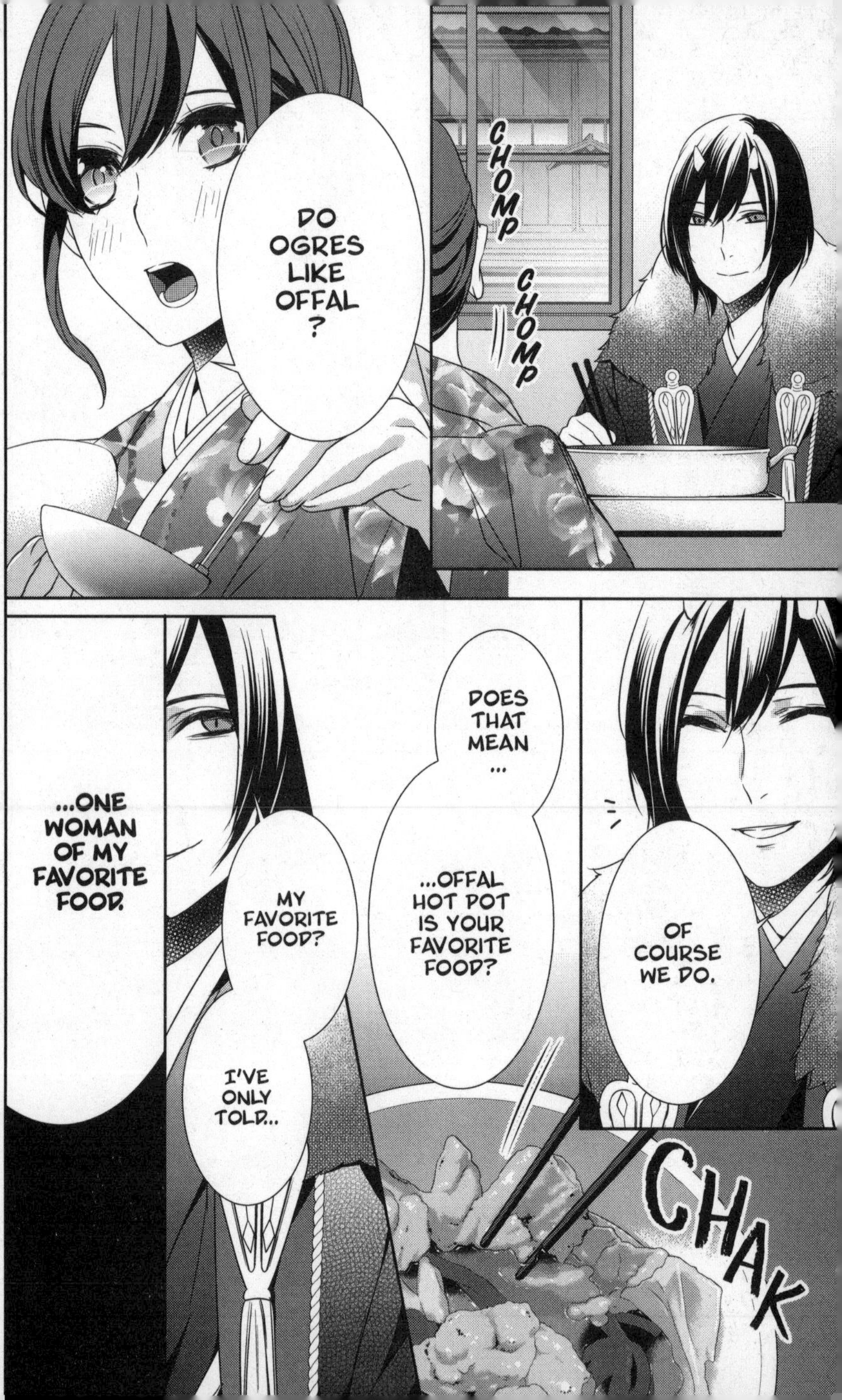
CHOMP CHOMP
DO OGRES LIKE OFFAL?
OF COURSE WE DO.
DOES THAT MEAN...
...OFFAL HOT POT IS YOUR FAVORITE FOOD?
CHAK
MY FAVORITE FOOD?
I'VE ONLY TOLD...
...ONE WOMAN OF MY FAVORITE FOOD.

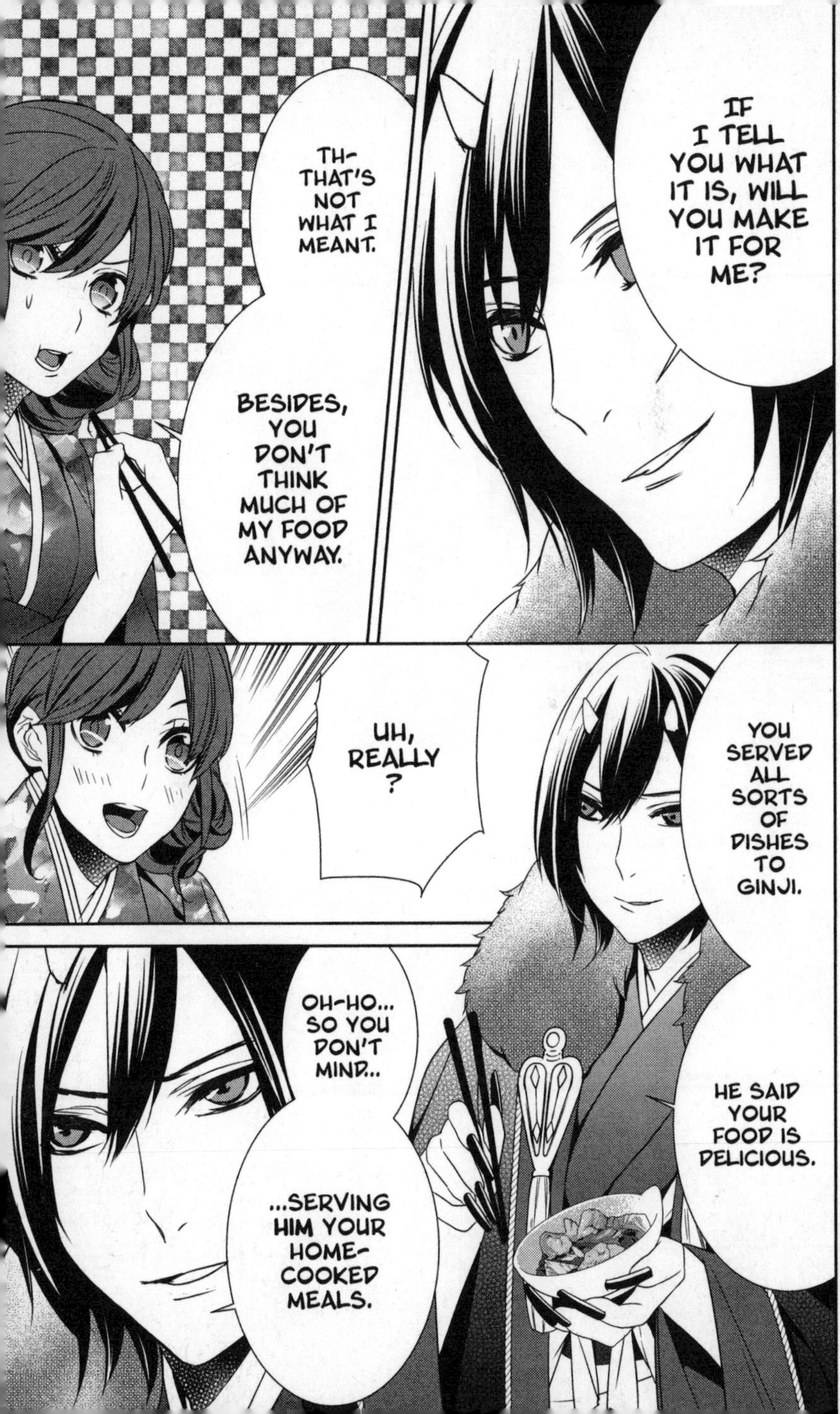
IF I TELL YOU WHAT IT IS, WILL YOU MAKE IT FOR ME?
TH-THAT'S NOT WHAT I MEANT.
BESIDES, YOU DON'T THINK MUCH OF MY FOOD ANYWAY.
YOU SERVED ALL SORTS OF DISHES TO GINJI.
HE SAID YOUR FOOD IS DELICIOUS.
UH, REALLY?
OH-HO... SO YOU DON'T MIND...
...SERVING HIM YOUR HOME-COOKED MEALS.

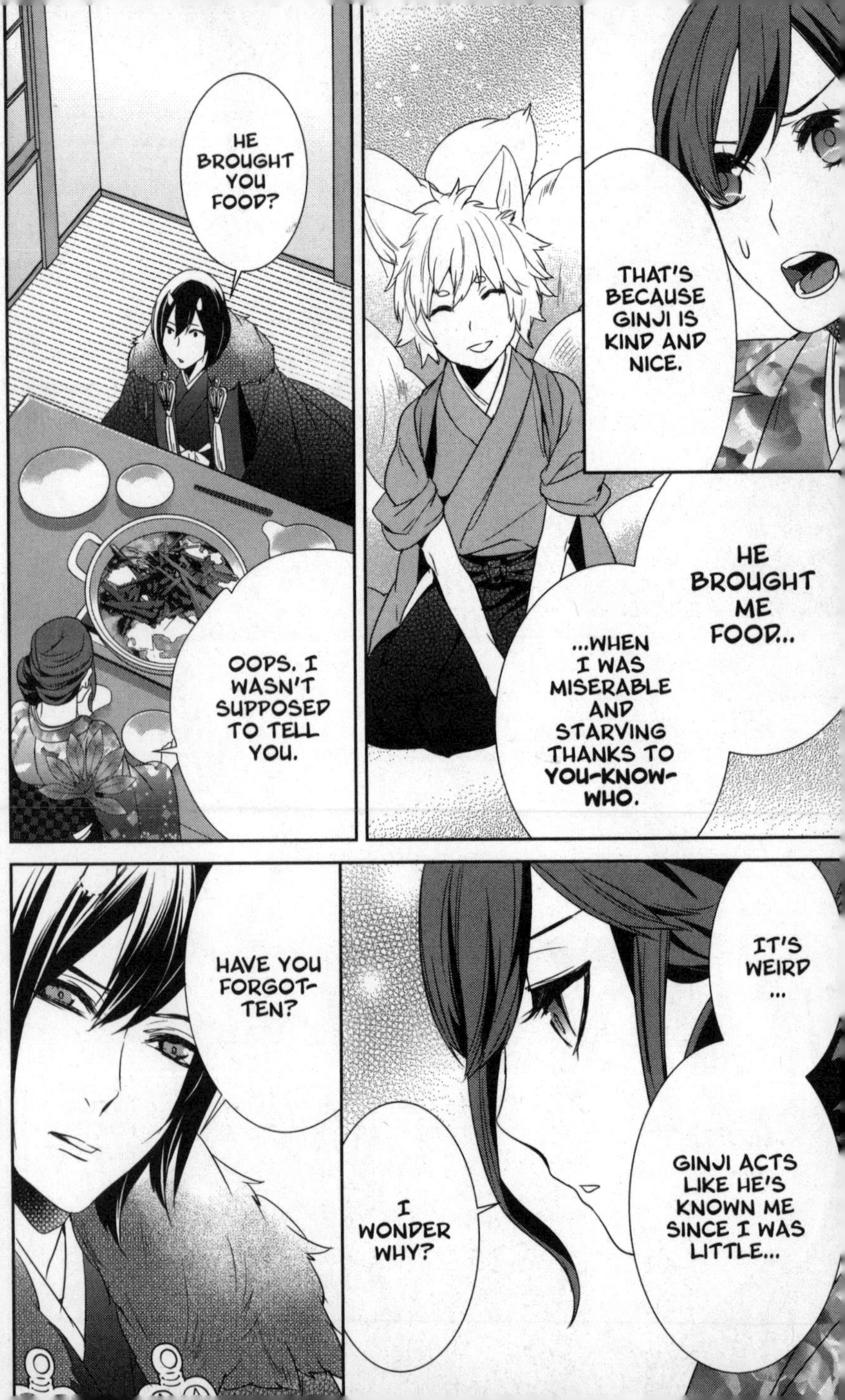
THAT'S BECAUSE GINJI IS KIND AND NICE.
HE BROUGHT ME FOOD...
...WHEN I WAS MISERABLE AND STARVING THANKS TO YOU-KNOW-WHO.
HE BROUGHT YOU FOOD?
OOPS. I WASN'T SUPPOSED TO TELL YOU.
IT'S WEIRD...
GINJI ACTS LIKE HE'S KNOWN ME SINCE I WAS LITTLE...
I WONDER WHY?
HAVE YOU FORGOT-TEN?

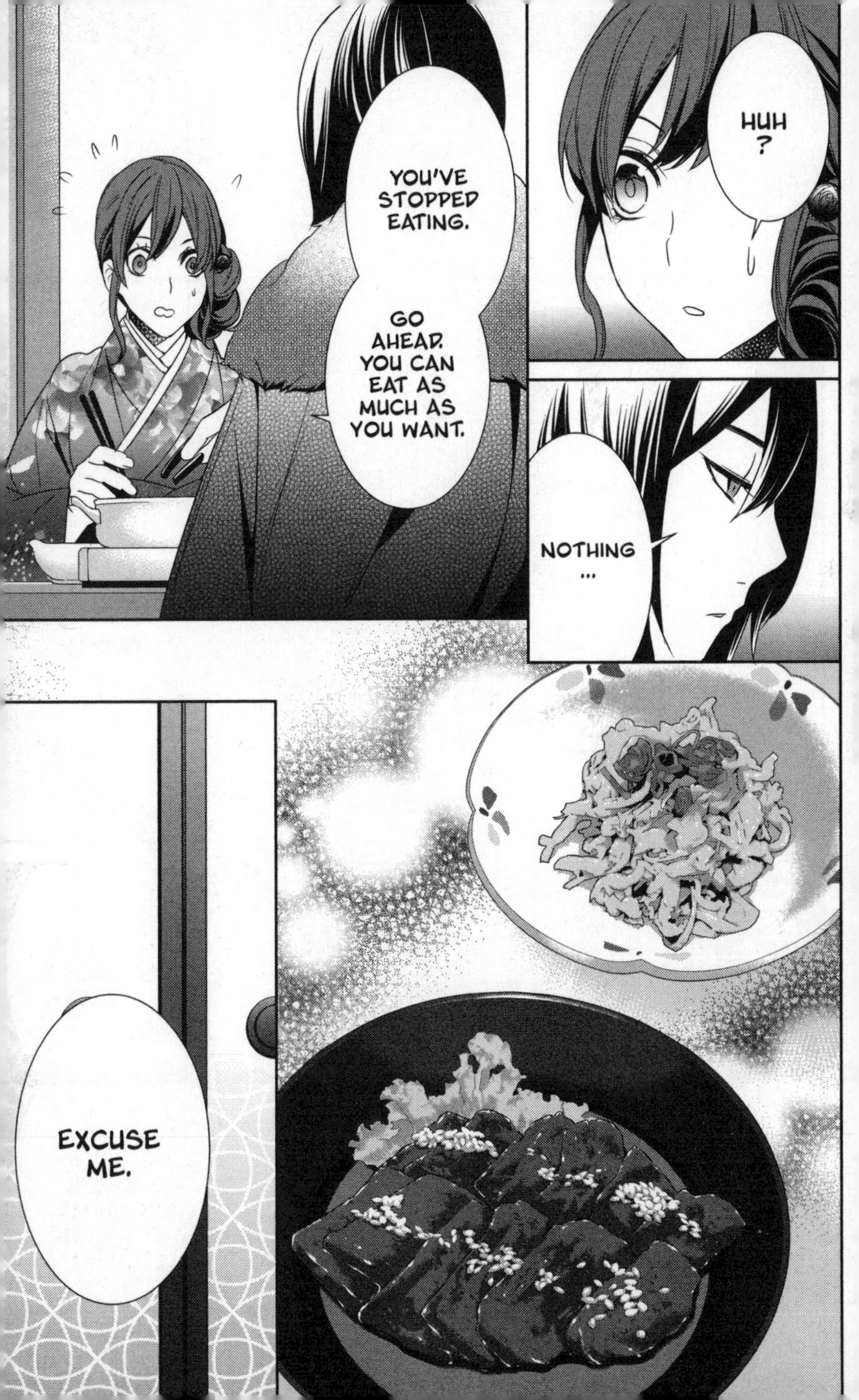
HUH?
NOTHING...
YOU'VE STOPPED EATING.
GO AHEAD. YOU CAN EAT AS MUCH AS YOU WANT.
EXCUSE ME.

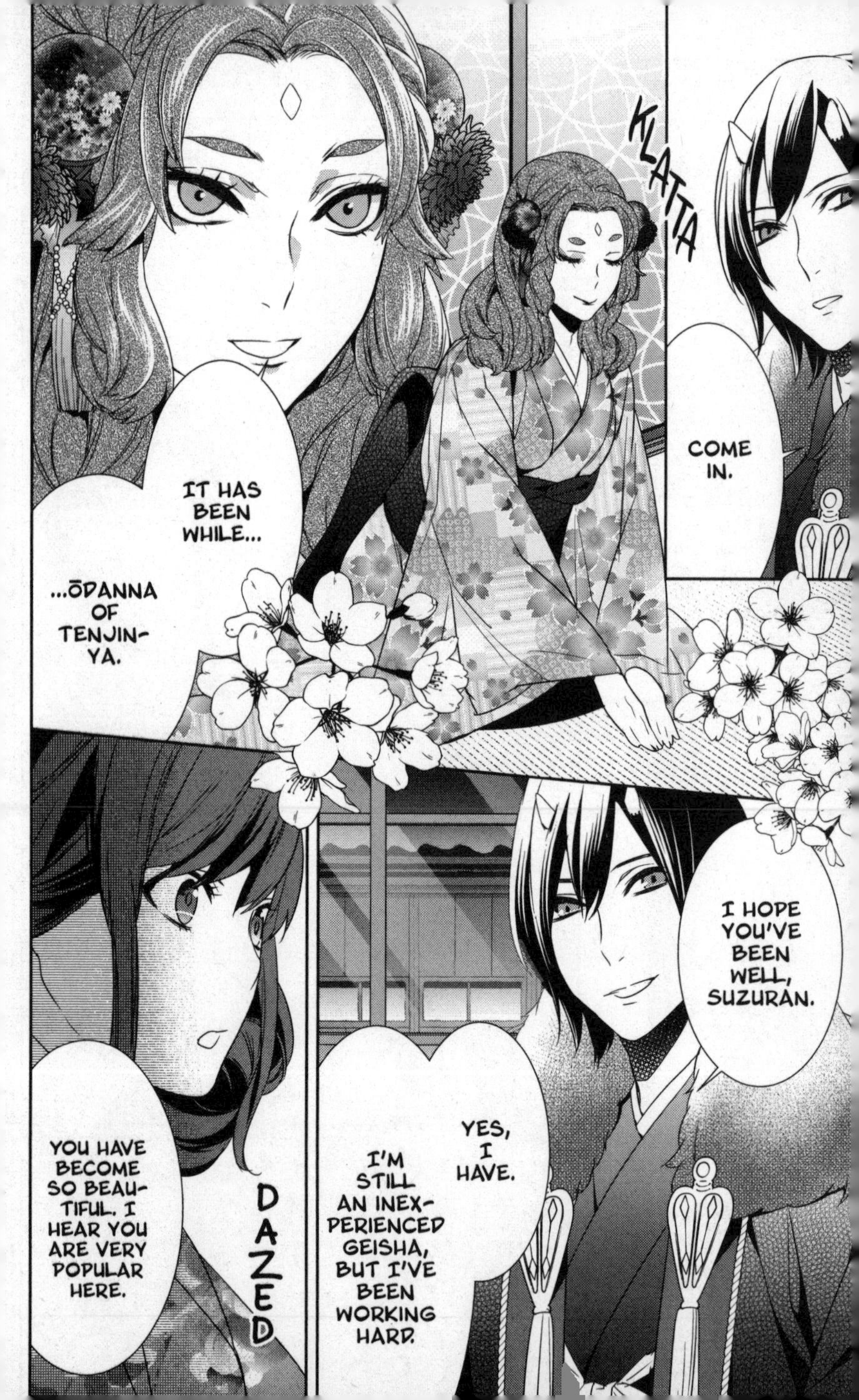
COME IN.
KLATTA
IT HAS BEEN WHILE...
...ŌDANNA OF TENJIN-YA.
I HOPE YOU'VE BEEN WELL, SUZURAN.
YES, I HAVE.
I'M STILL AN INEXPERIENCED GEISHA, BUT I'VE BEEN WORKING HARD.
YOU HAVE BECOME SO BEAUTIFUL. I HEAR YOU ARE VERY POPULAR HERE.
DAZED

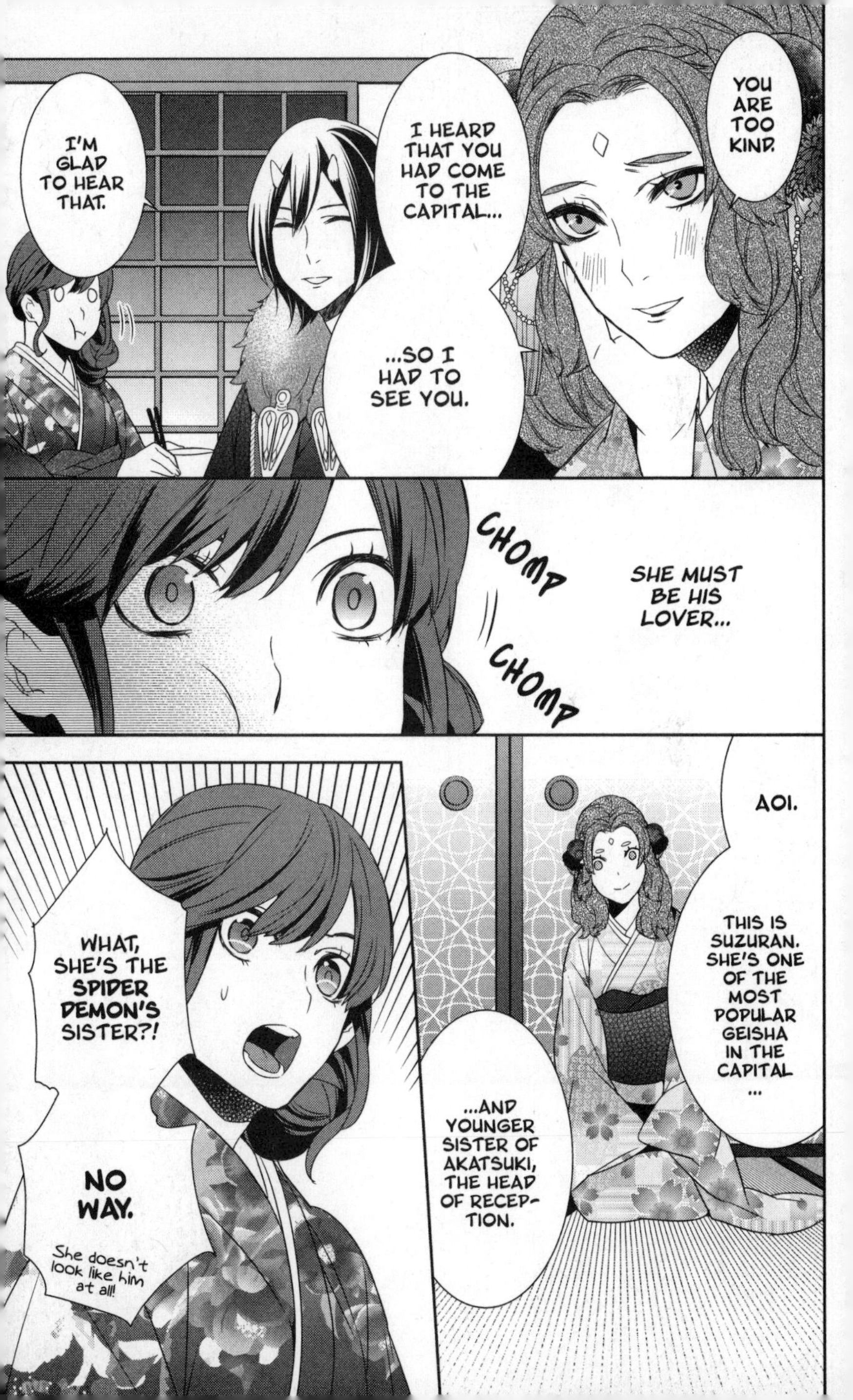
YOU ARE TOO KIND.
I HEARD THAT YOU HAD COME TO THE CAPITAL...
...SO I HAD TO SEE YOU.
I'M GLAD TO HEAR THAT.
SHE MUST BE HIS LOVER...
CHOMP
CHOMP
AOI.
THIS IS SUZURAN. SHE'S ONE OF THE MOST POPULAR GEISHA IN THE CAPITAL ...
...AND YOUNGER SISTER OF AKATSUKI, THE HEAD OF RECEP-TION.
WHAT, SHE'S THE SPIDER DEMON'S SISTER?!
NO WAY.
She doesn't look like him at all!

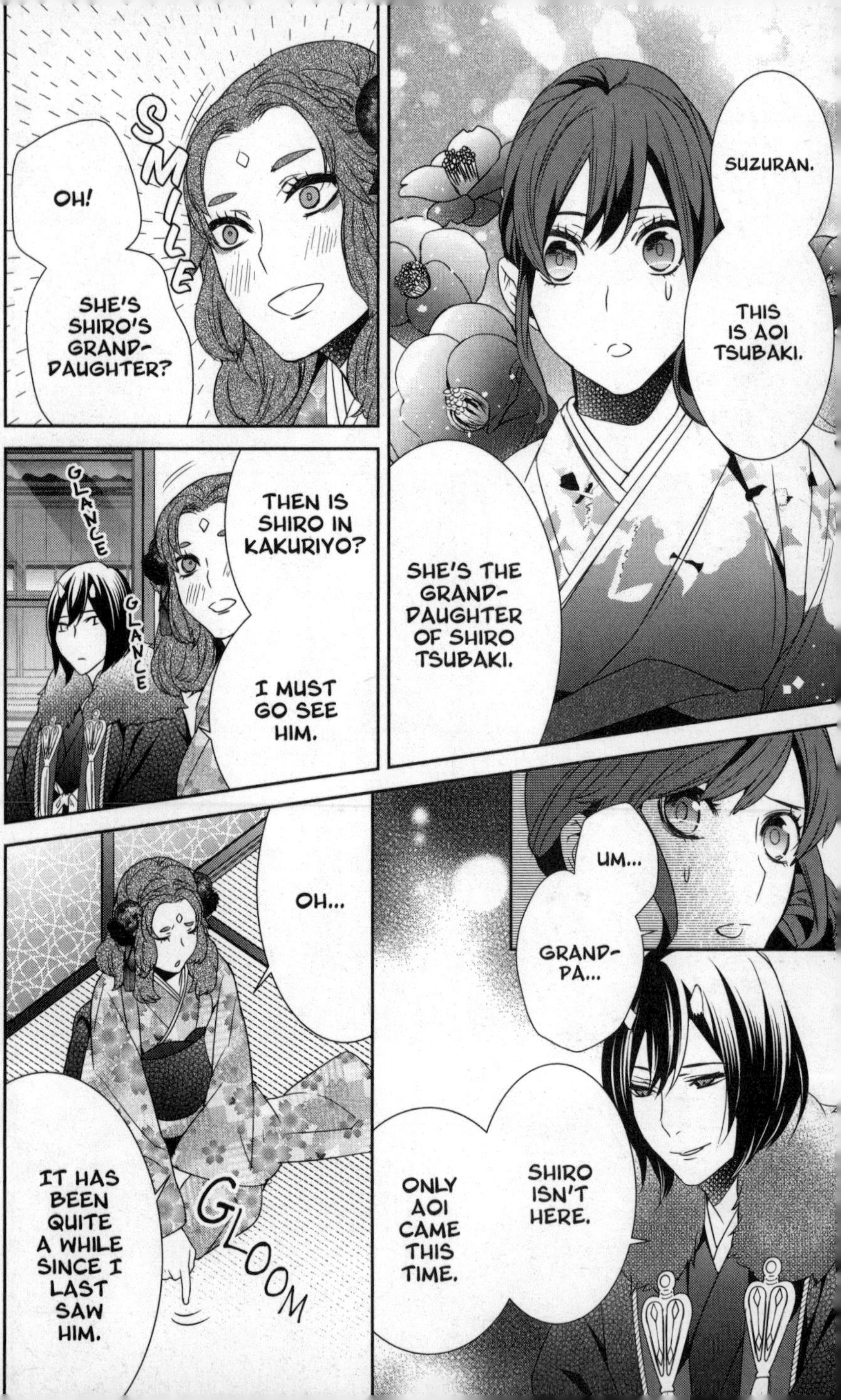
SUZURAN.
THIS IS AOI TSUBAKI.
SHE'S THE GRANDDAUGHTER OF SHIRO TSUBAKI.
SMILE
OH!
SHE'S SHIRO'S GRANDDAUGHTER?
GLANCE
GLANCE
THEN IS SHIRO IN KAKURIYO?
I MUST GO SEE HIM.
UM...
GRANDPA...
SHIRO ISN'T HERE.
ONLY AOI CAME THIS TIME.
OH...
GLOOM
IT HAS BEEN QUITE A WHILE SINCE I LAST SAW HIM.

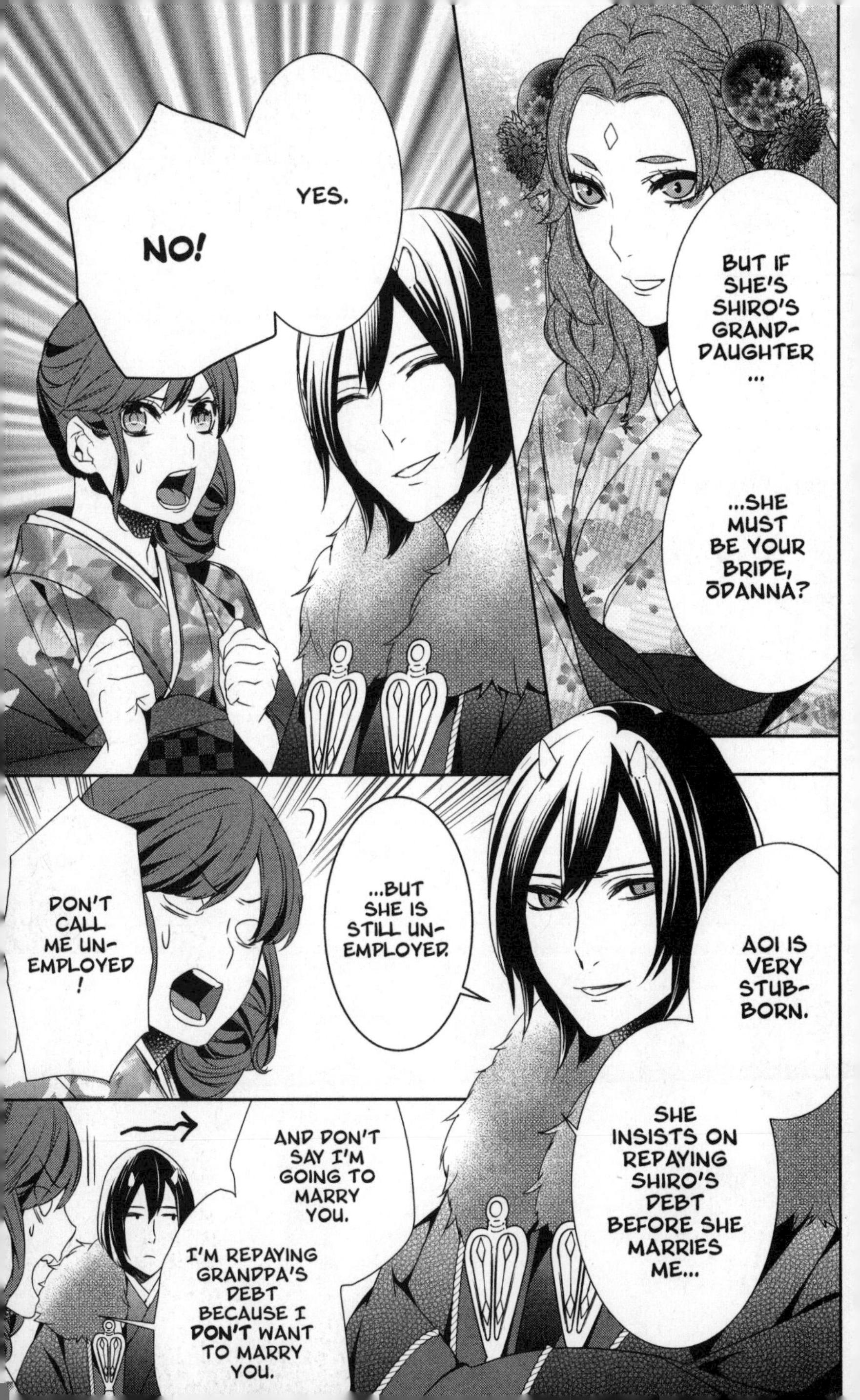
BUT IF SHE'S SHIRO'S GRANDDAUGHTER...
...SHE MUST BE YOUR BRIDE, ŌDANNA?
YES.
NO!
AOI IS VERY STUBBORN.
SHE INSISTS ON REPAYING SHIRO'S DEBT BEFORE SHE MARRIES ME...
...BUT SHE IS STILL UNEMPLOYED.
DON'T CALL ME UNEMPLOYED!
AND DON'T SAY I'M GOING TO MARRY YOU.
I'M REPAYING GRANDPA'S DEBT BECAUSE I **DON'T** WANT TO MARRY YOU.

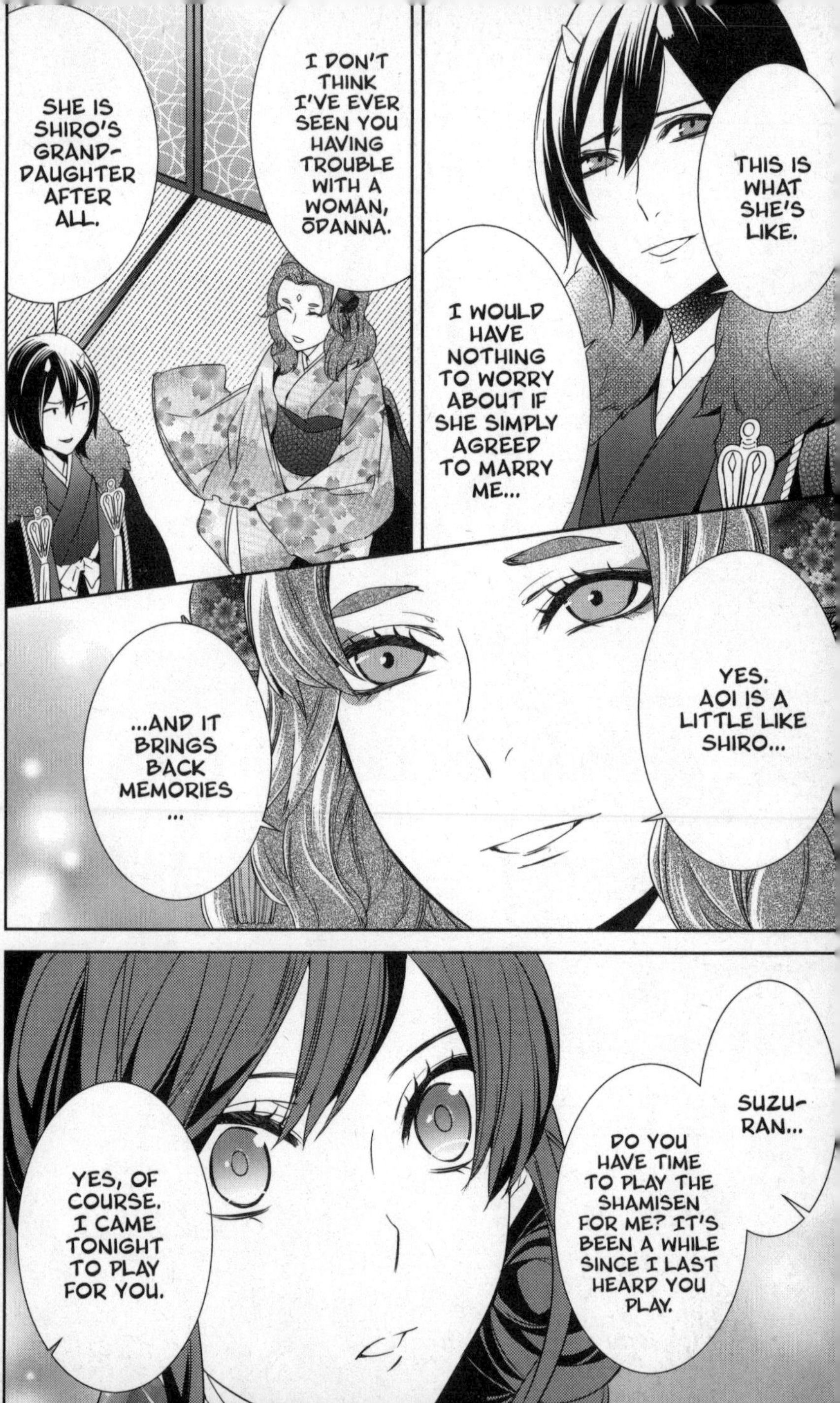
THIS IS WHAT SHE'S LIKE.
I WOULD HAVE NOTHING TO WORRY ABOUT IF SHE SIMPLY AGREED TO MARRY ME...
I DON'T THINK I'VE EVER SEEN YOU HAVING TROUBLE WITH A WOMAN, ŌDANNA.
SHE IS SHIRO'S GRAND-DAUGHTER AFTER ALL.
YES. AOI IS A LITTLE LIKE SHIRO...
...AND IT BRINGS BACK MEMORIES...
SUZU-RAN...
DO YOU HAVE TIME TO PLAY THE SHAMISEN FOR ME? IT'S BEEN A WHILE SINCE I LAST HEARD YOU PLAY.
YES, OF COURSE. I CAME TONIGHT TO PLAY FOR YOU.

Kakuriyo
Bed & Breakfast
for Spirits

Kakuriyo
Bed & Breakfast
for Spirits

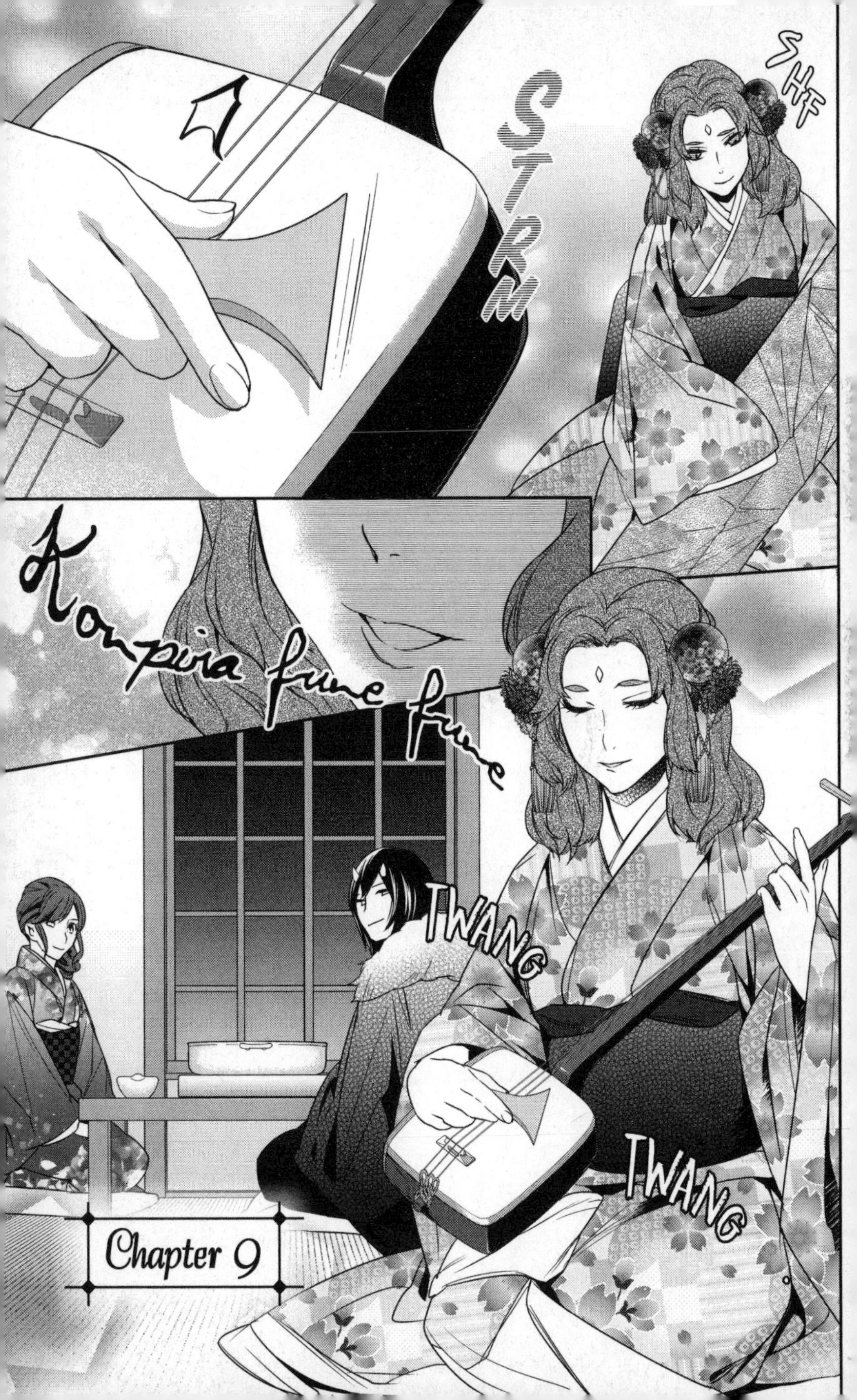
SHF
STRM
Kompira fune fune
TWANG
TWANG
Chapter 9

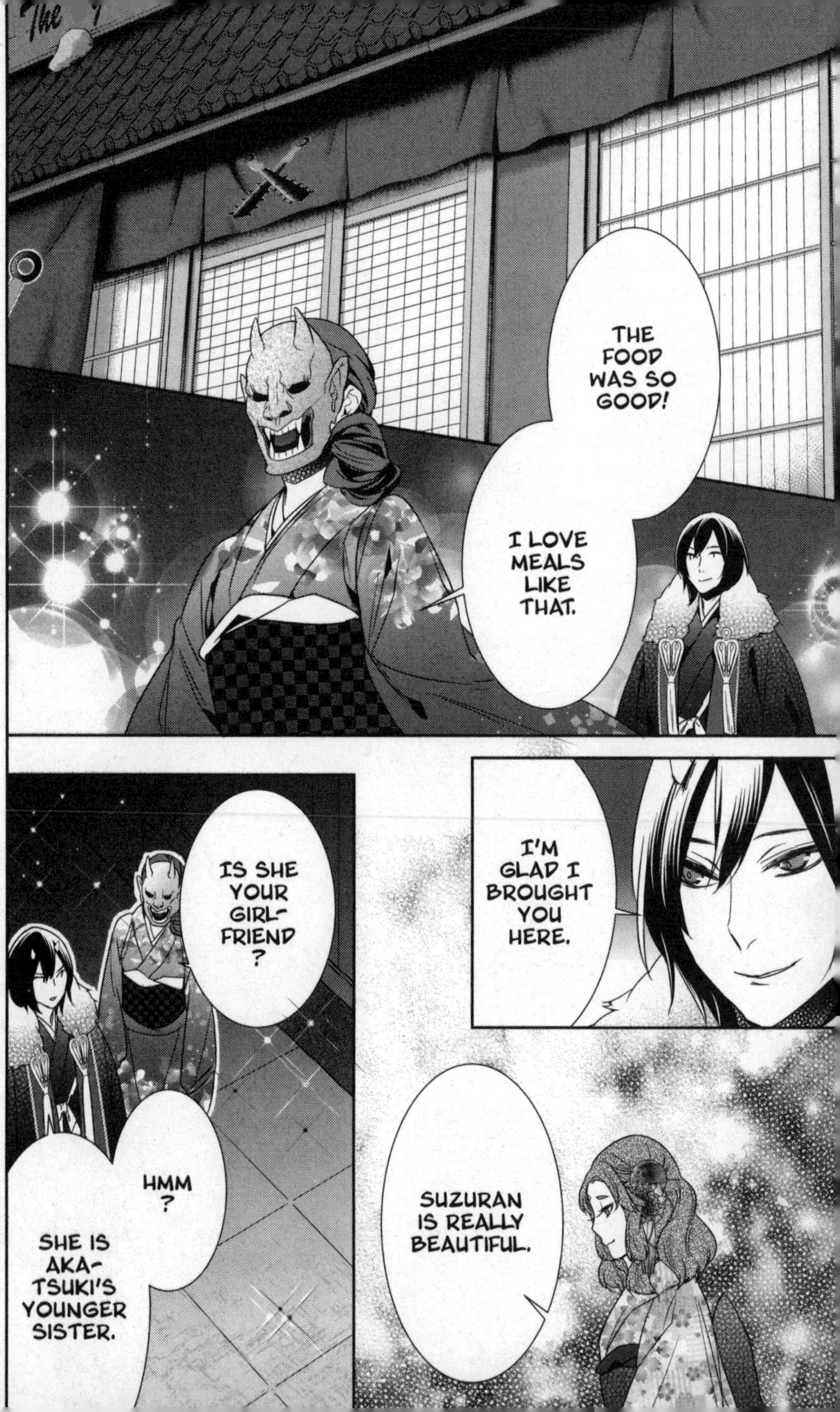
THE FOOD WAS SO GOOD!
I LOVE MEALS LIKE THAT.
I'M GLAD I BROUGHT YOU HERE.
IS SHE YOUR GIRL-FRIEND?
SUZURAN IS REALLY BEAUTIFUL.
HMM?
SHE IS AKA-TSUKI'S YOUNGER SISTER.

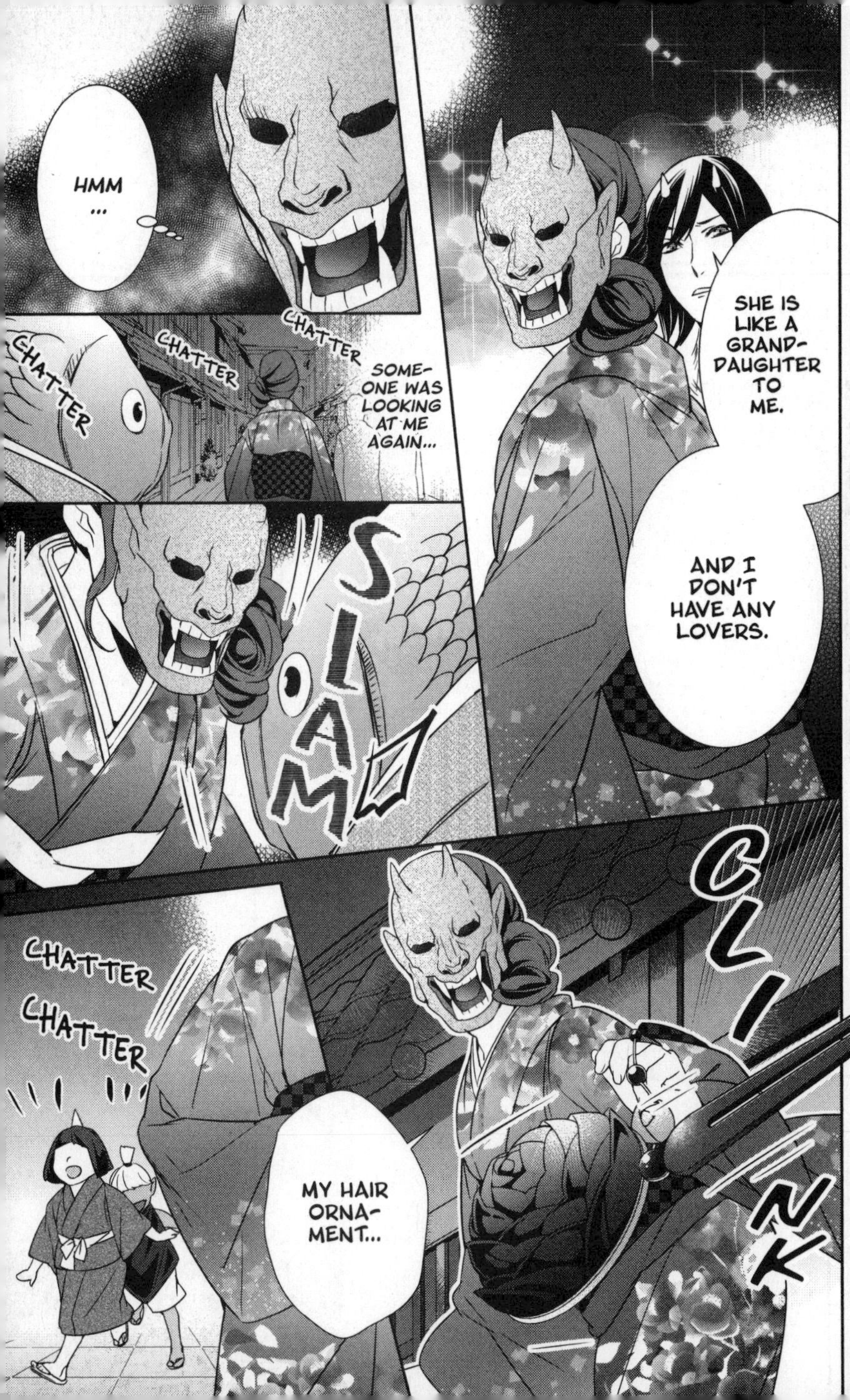
SHE IS LIKE A GRAND-DAUGHTER TO ME.
AND I DON'T HAVE ANY LOVERS.
HMM ...
CHATTER
CHATTER
CHATTER
SOME-ONE WAS LOOKING AT ME AGAIN...
SLAM
CLINK
CHATTER
CHATTER
MY HAIR ORNA-MENT...

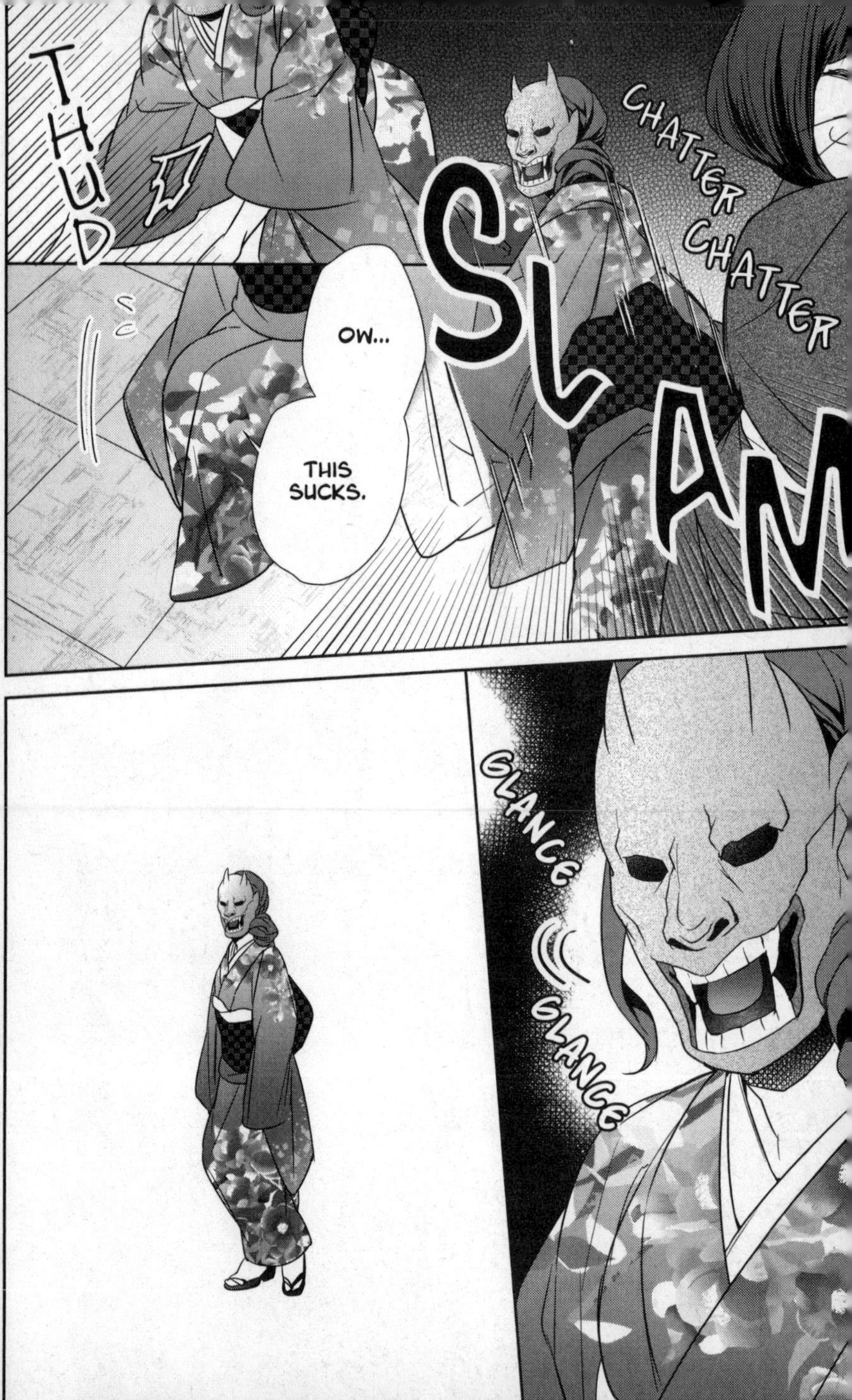
CHATTER CHATTER
SLAM
THUD
OW...
THIS SUCKS.
GLANCE GLANCE

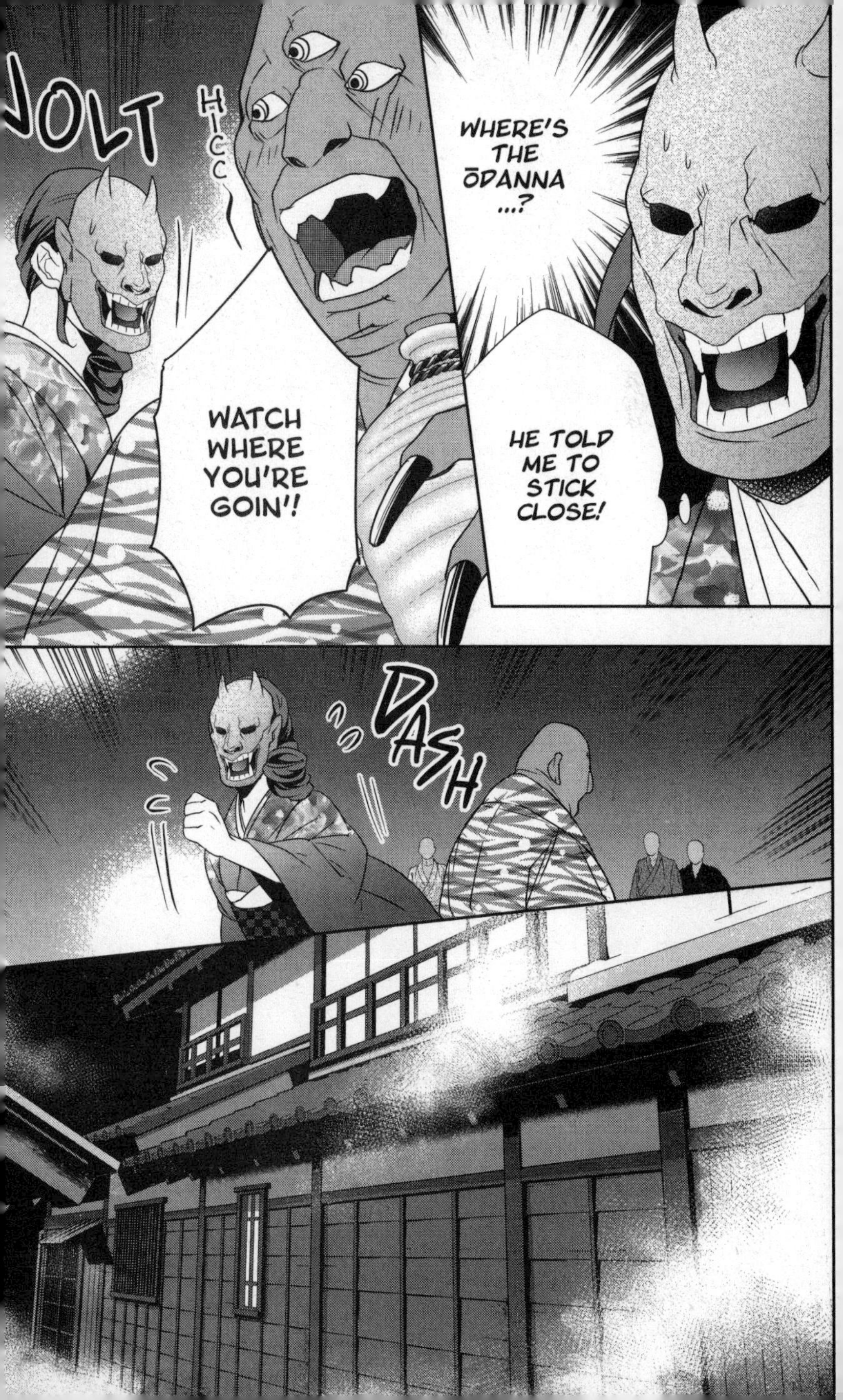
WHERE'S THE ŌDANNA ...?
HE TOLD ME TO STICK CLOSE!
JOLT
HICC
WATCH WHERE YOU'RE GOIN'!
DASH

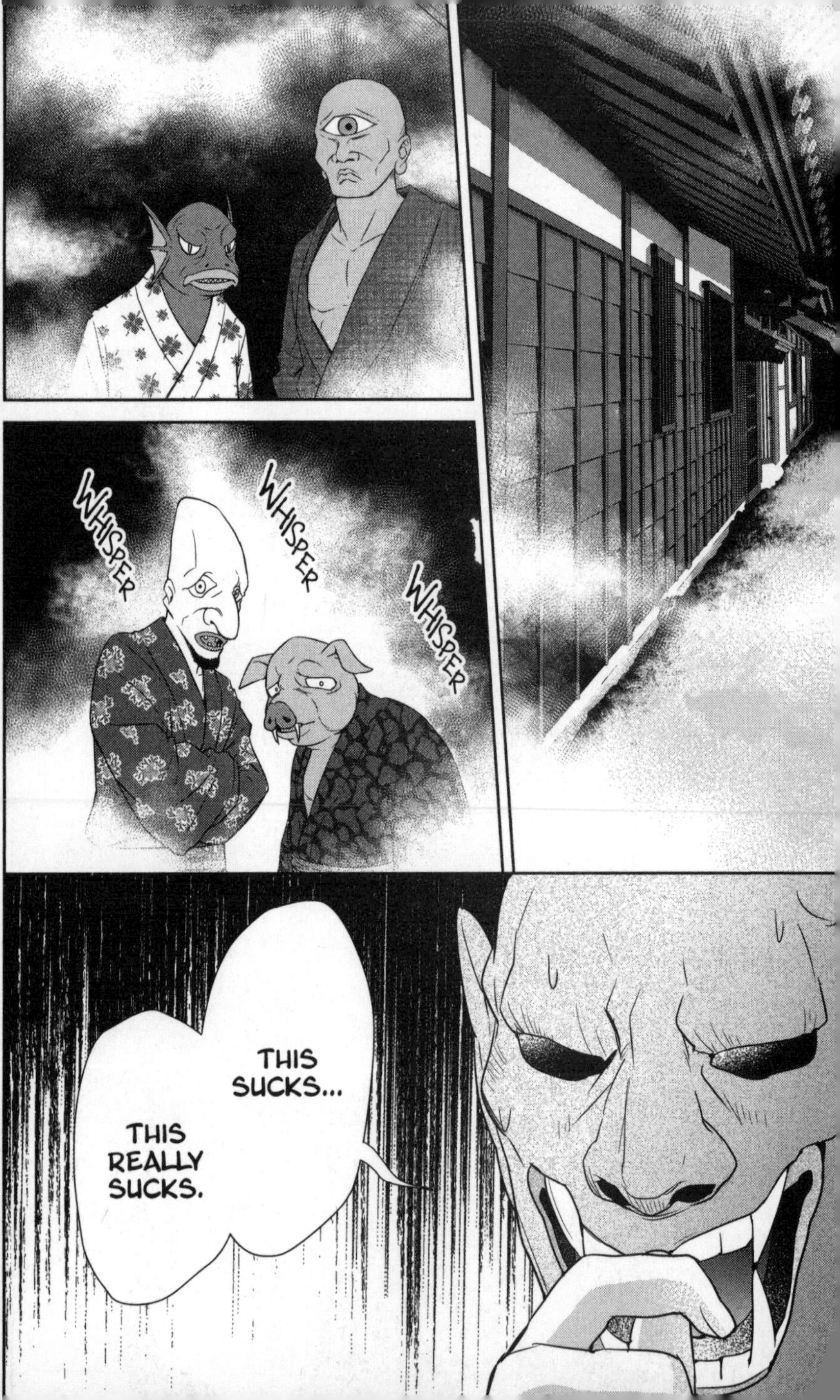
WHISPER
WHISPER
WHISPER
THIS SUCKS...
THIS REALLY SUCKS.

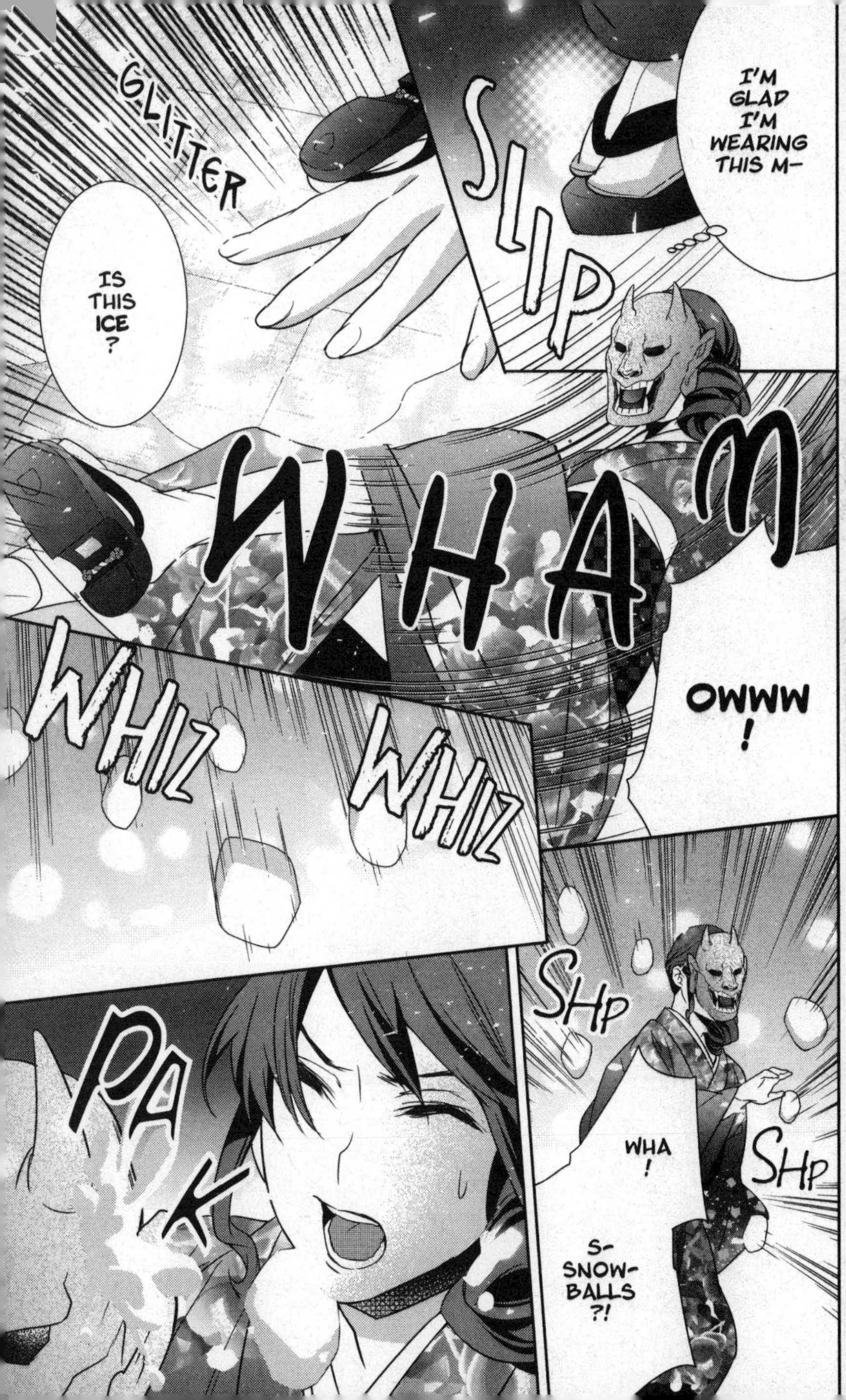

I'M GLAD I'M WEARING THIS M-
SLIP
GLITTER
IS THIS ICE?
WHAM
OWWW!
WHIZ
WHIZ
SHP
WHA!
SHP
S-SNOWBALLS?!
PAK

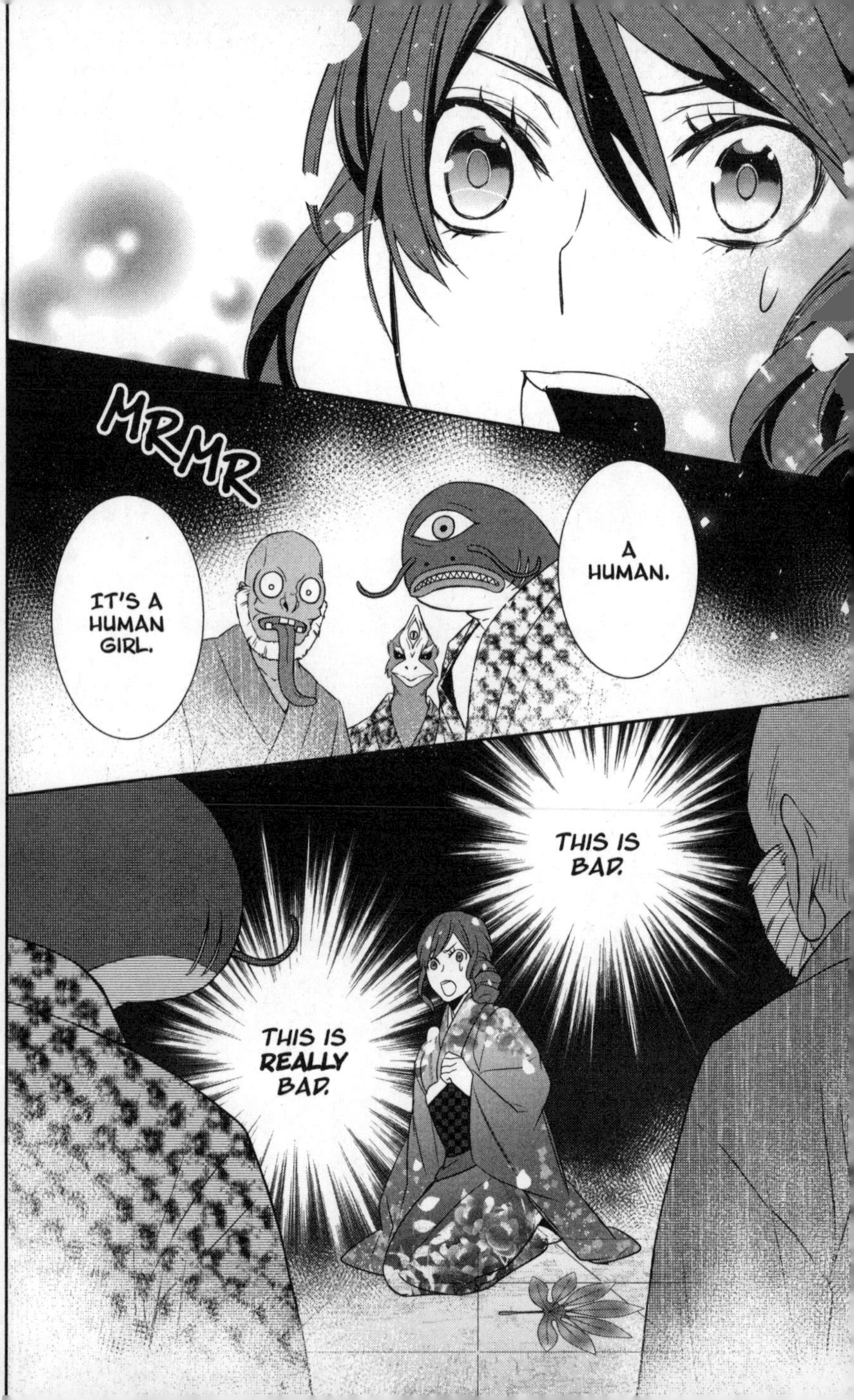
A HUMAN.
MRMR
IT'S A HUMAN GIRL.
THIS IS BAD.
THIS IS REALLY BAD.

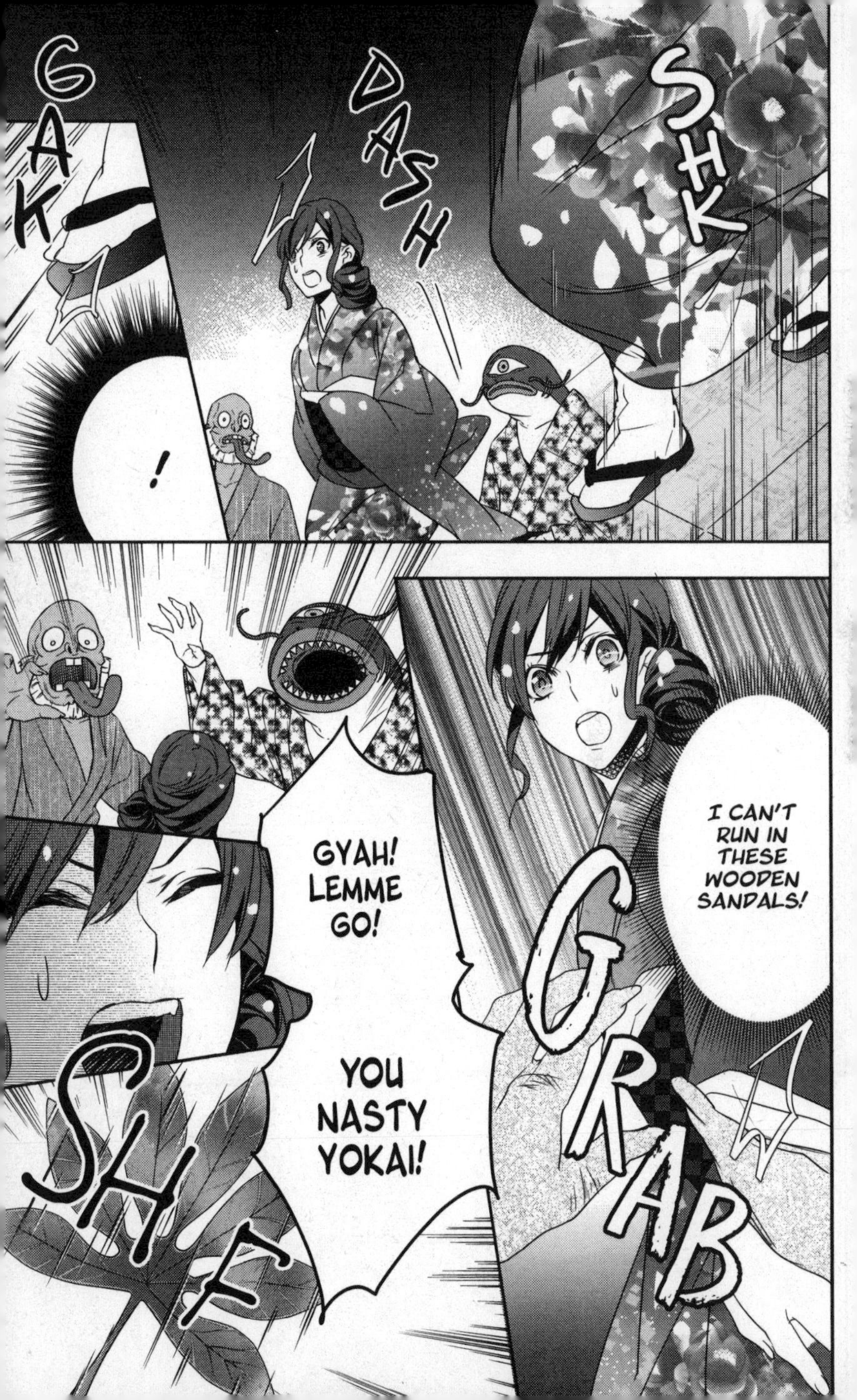
SHHK
DASH
GAK
!
I CAN'T RUN IN THESE WOODEN SANDALS!
GRAB
GYAH! LEMME GO!
YOU NASTY YOKAI!
SHFF

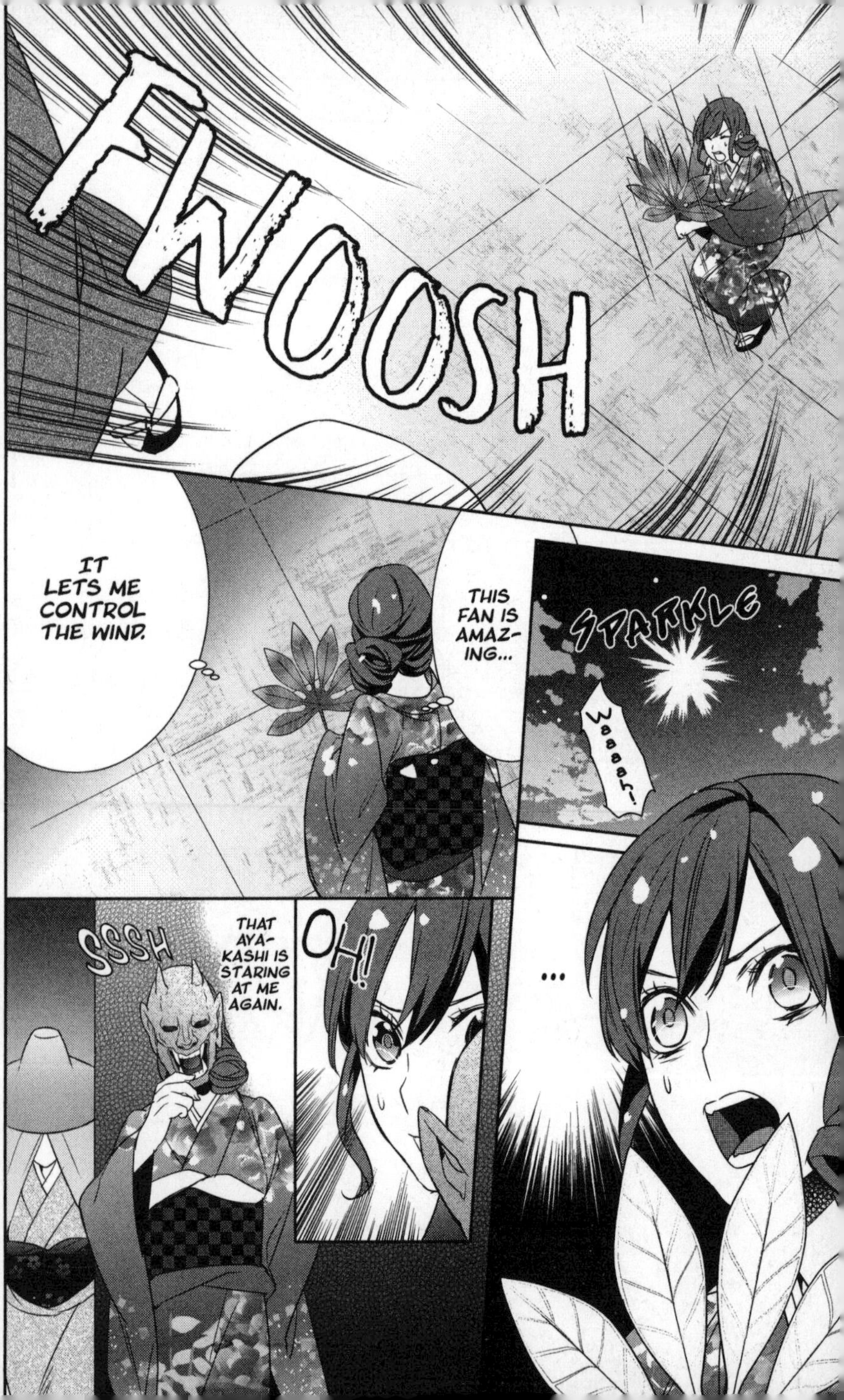
FWOOSH
THIS FAN IS AMAZING...
IT LETS ME CONTROL THE WIND.
SPARKLE
Waaaah!
...
OH!
THAT AYAKASHI IS STARING AT ME AGAIN.
SSSH

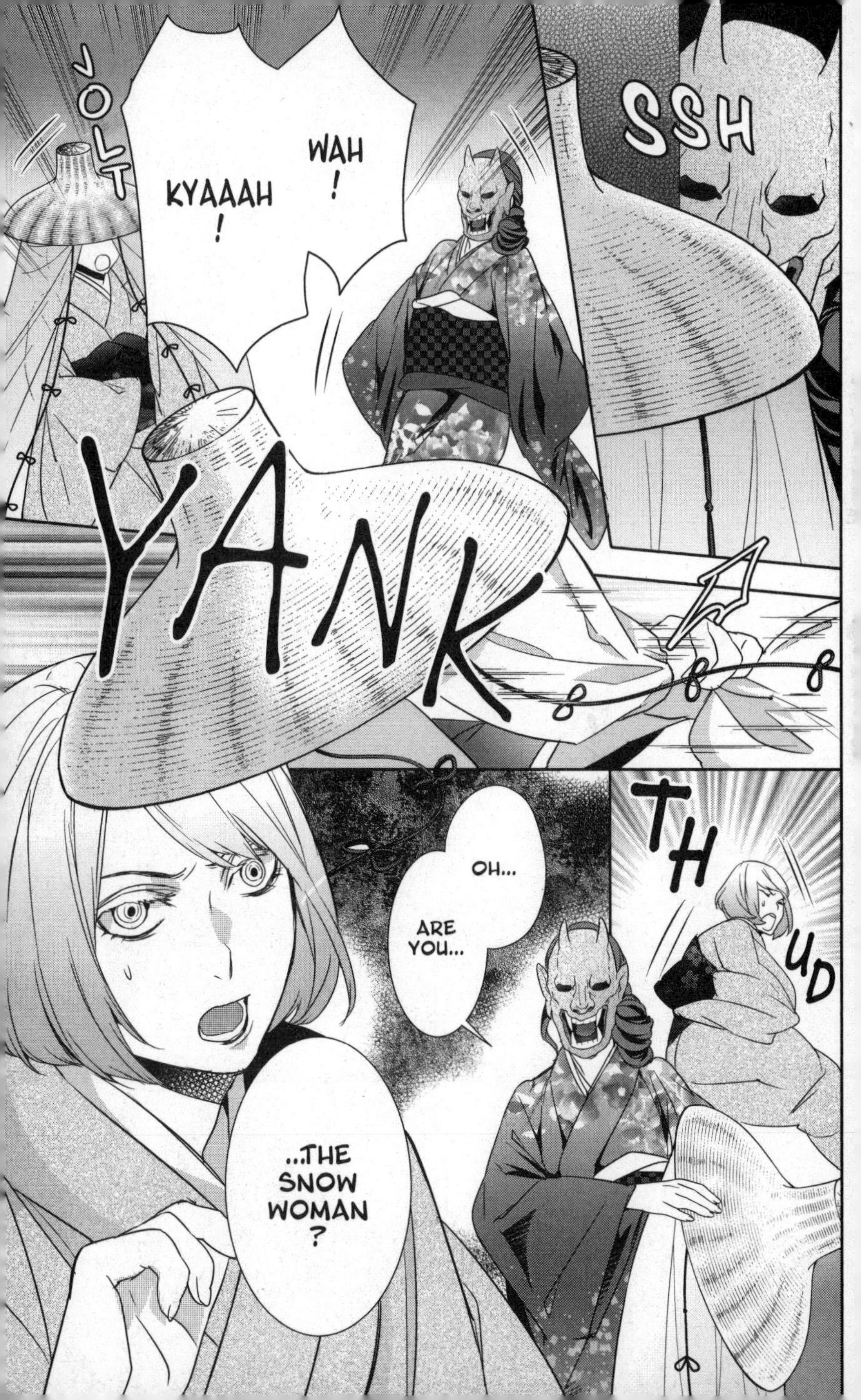
SSH
WAH!
KYAAAH!
VOLT
YANK
THUD
OH...
ARE YOU...
...THE SNOW WOMAN?

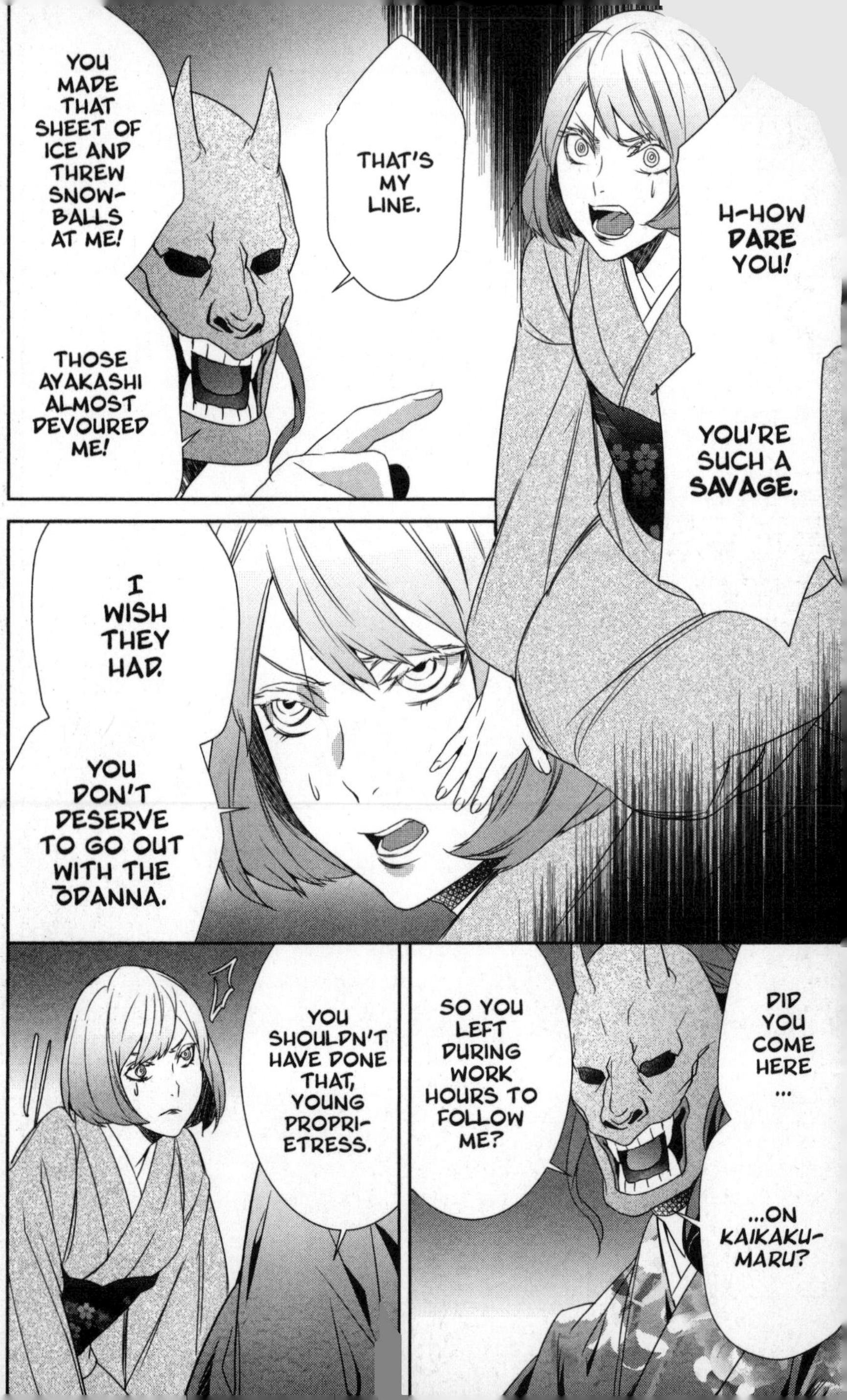
H-HOW DARE YOU!
YOU'RE SUCH A SAVAGE.
THAT'S MY LINE.
YOU MADE THAT SHEET OF ICE AND THREW SNOW-BALLS AT ME!
THOSE AYAKASHI ALMOST DEVOURED ME!
I WISH THEY HAD.
YOU DON'T DESERVE TO GO OUT WITH THE ŌDANNA.
DID YOU COME HERE...
...ON KAIKAKU-MARU?
SO YOU LEFT DURING WORK HOURS TO FOLLOW ME?
YOU SHOULDN'T HAVE DONE THAT, YOUNG PROPRI-ETRESS.

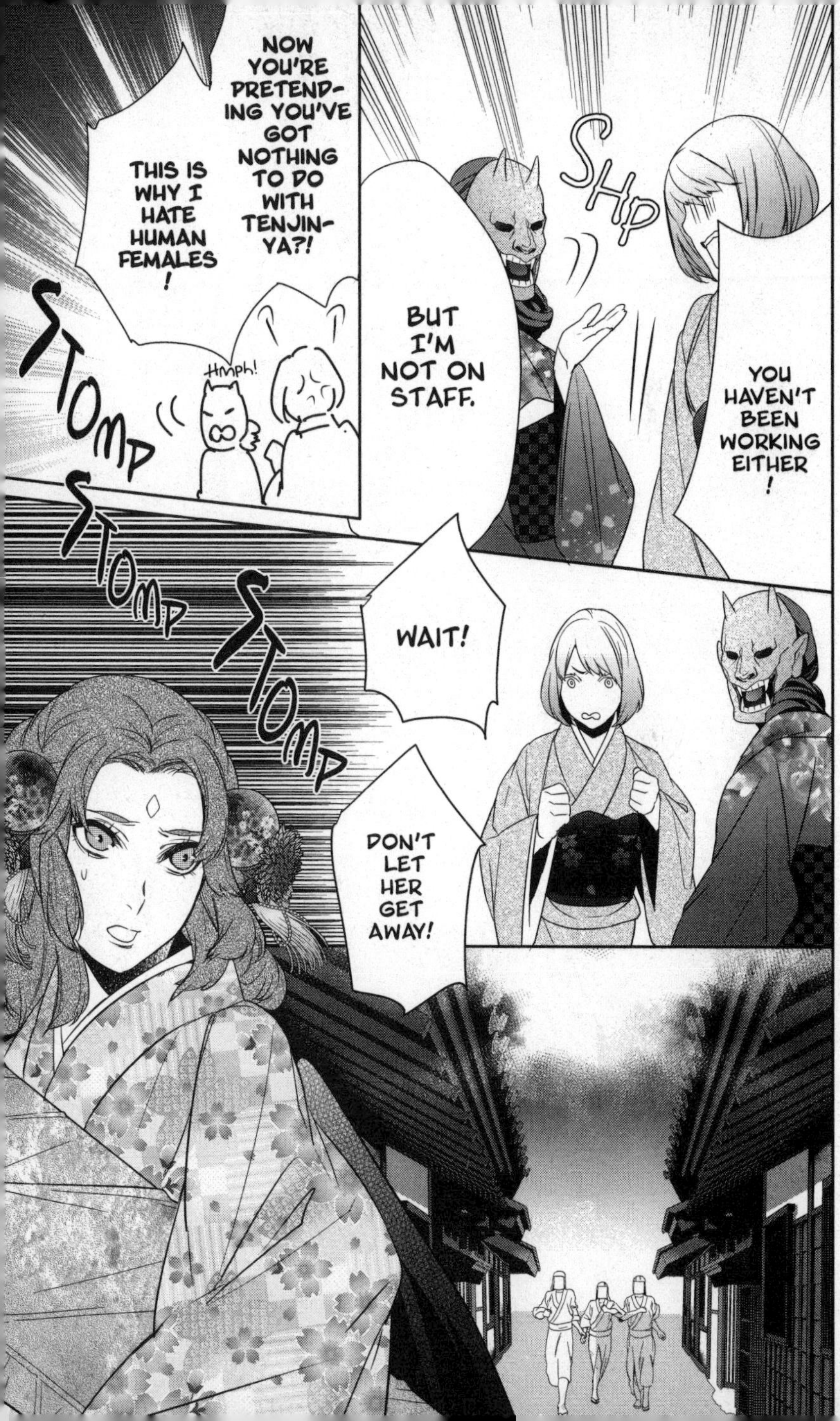
SHp
YOU HAVEN'T BEEN WORKING EITHER!
BUT I'M NOT ON STAFF.
NOW YOU'RE PRETENDING YOU'VE GOT NOTHING TO DO WITH TENJIN-YA?!
THIS IS WHY I HATE HUMAN FEMALES!
Hmph!
STOMP
STOMP
STOMP
STOMP
WAIT!
DON'T LET HER GET AWAY!

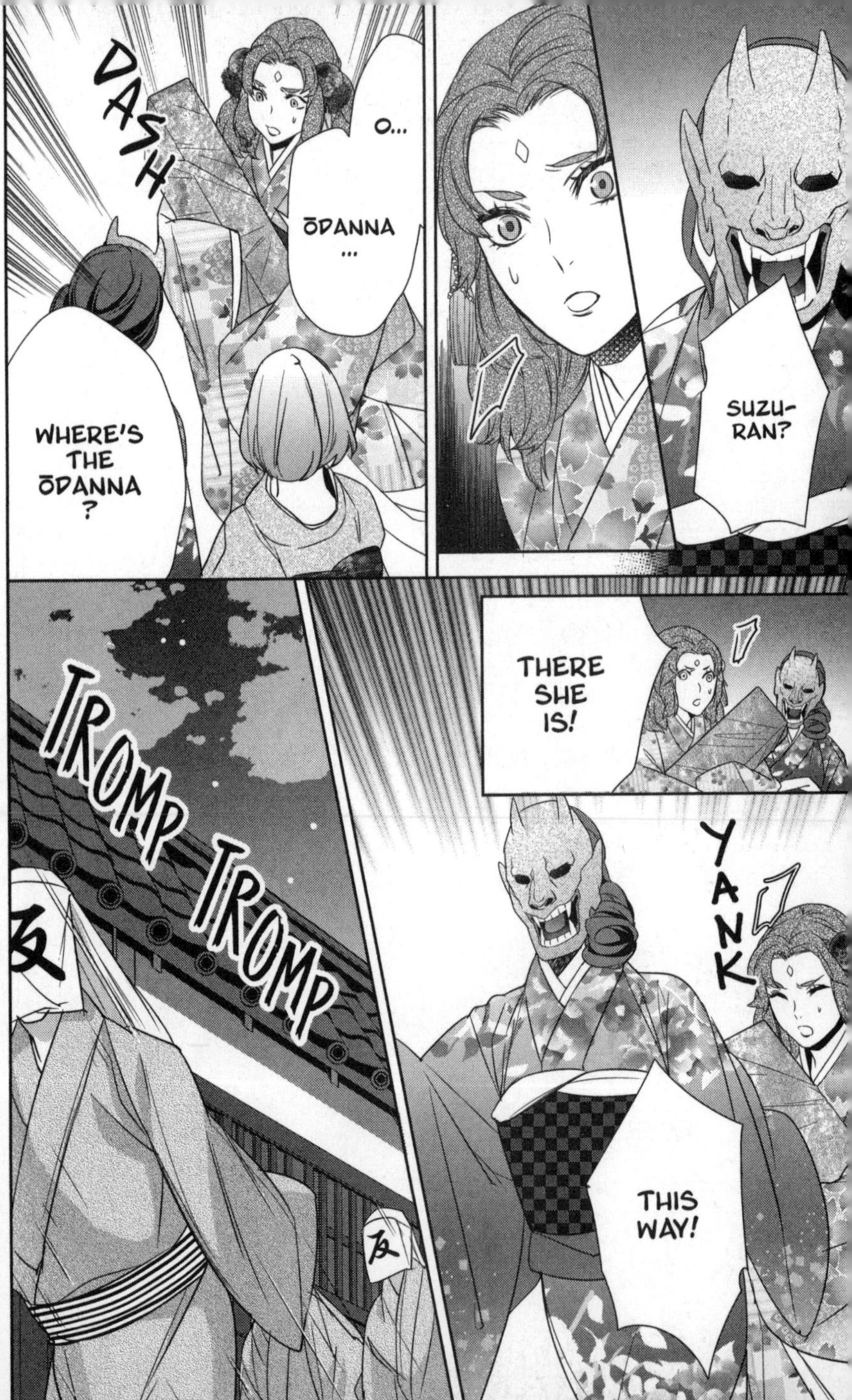
SUZU-RAN?
O...
ŌDANNA ...
DASH
WHERE'S THE ŌDANNA ?
THERE SHE IS!
YANK
THIS WAY!
TROMP TROMP TROMP

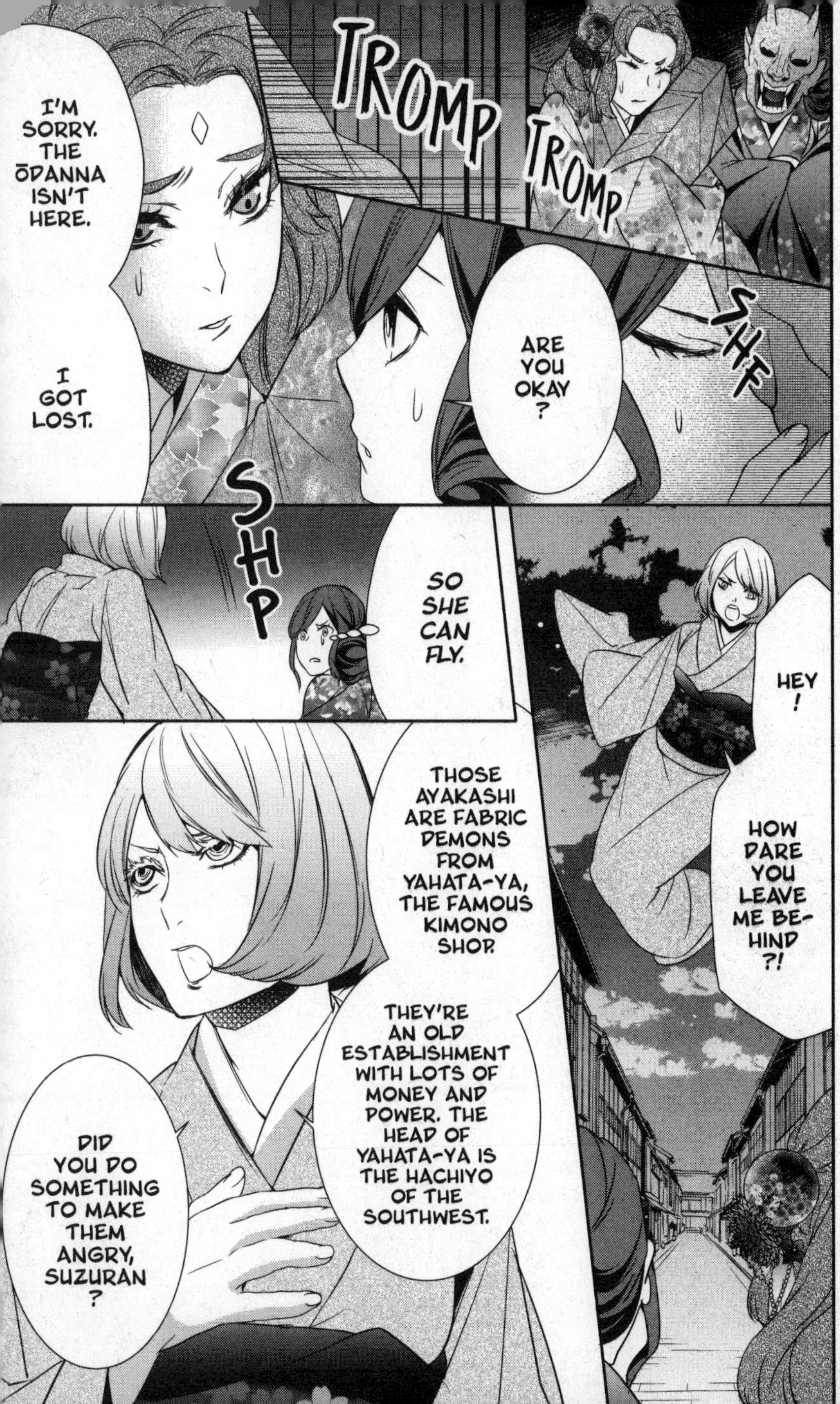
TROMP TROMP
ARE YOU OKAY?
SHF
I'M SORRY. THE ŌDANNA ISN'T HERE.
I GOT LOST.
SHP
HEY! HOW DARE YOU LEAVE ME BE-HIND?!
SHP
SO SHE CAN FLY.
THOSE AYAKASHI ARE FABRIC DEMONS FROM YAHATA-YA, THE FAMOUS KIMONO SHOP.
THEY'RE AN OLD ESTABLISHMENT WITH LOTS OF MONEY AND POWER. THE HEAD OF YAHATA-YA IS THE HACHIYO OF THE SOUTHWEST.
DID YOU DO SOMETHING TO MAKE THEM ANGRY, SUZURAN?

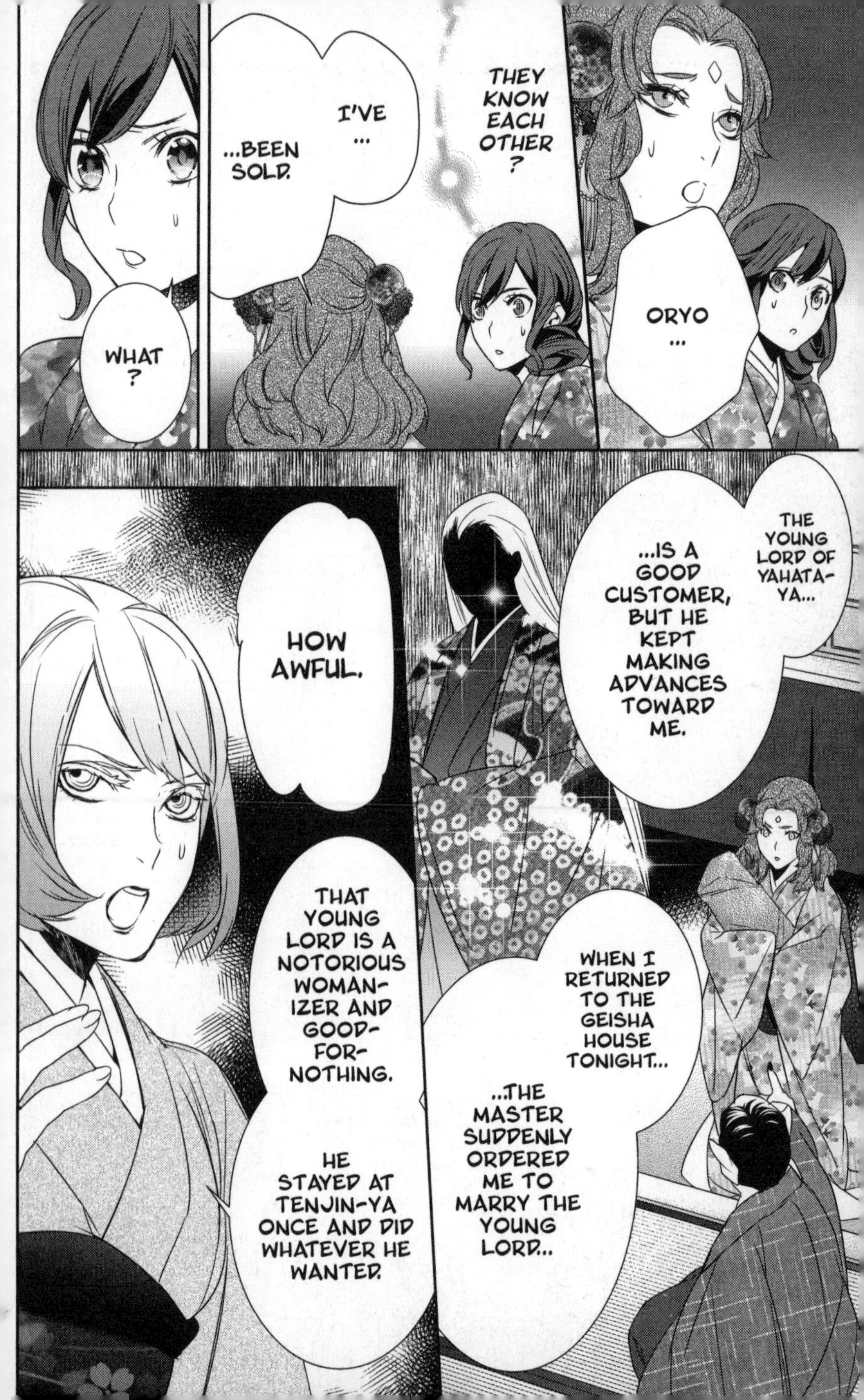
ORYO ...
THEY KNOW EACH OTHER ?
I'VE ...
...BEEN SOLD.
WHAT ?
THE YOUNG LORD OF YAHATA-YA...
...IS A GOOD CUSTOMER, BUT HE KEPT MAKING ADVANCES TOWARD ME.
WHEN I RETURNED TO THE GEISHA HOUSE TONIGHT...
...THE MASTER SUDDENLY ORDERED ME TO MARRY THE YOUNG LORD...
HOW AWFUL.
THAT YOUNG LORD IS A NOTORIOUS WOMAN-IZER AND GOOD-FOR-NOTHING.
HE STAYED AT TENJIN-YA ONCE AND DID WHATEVER HE WANTED.

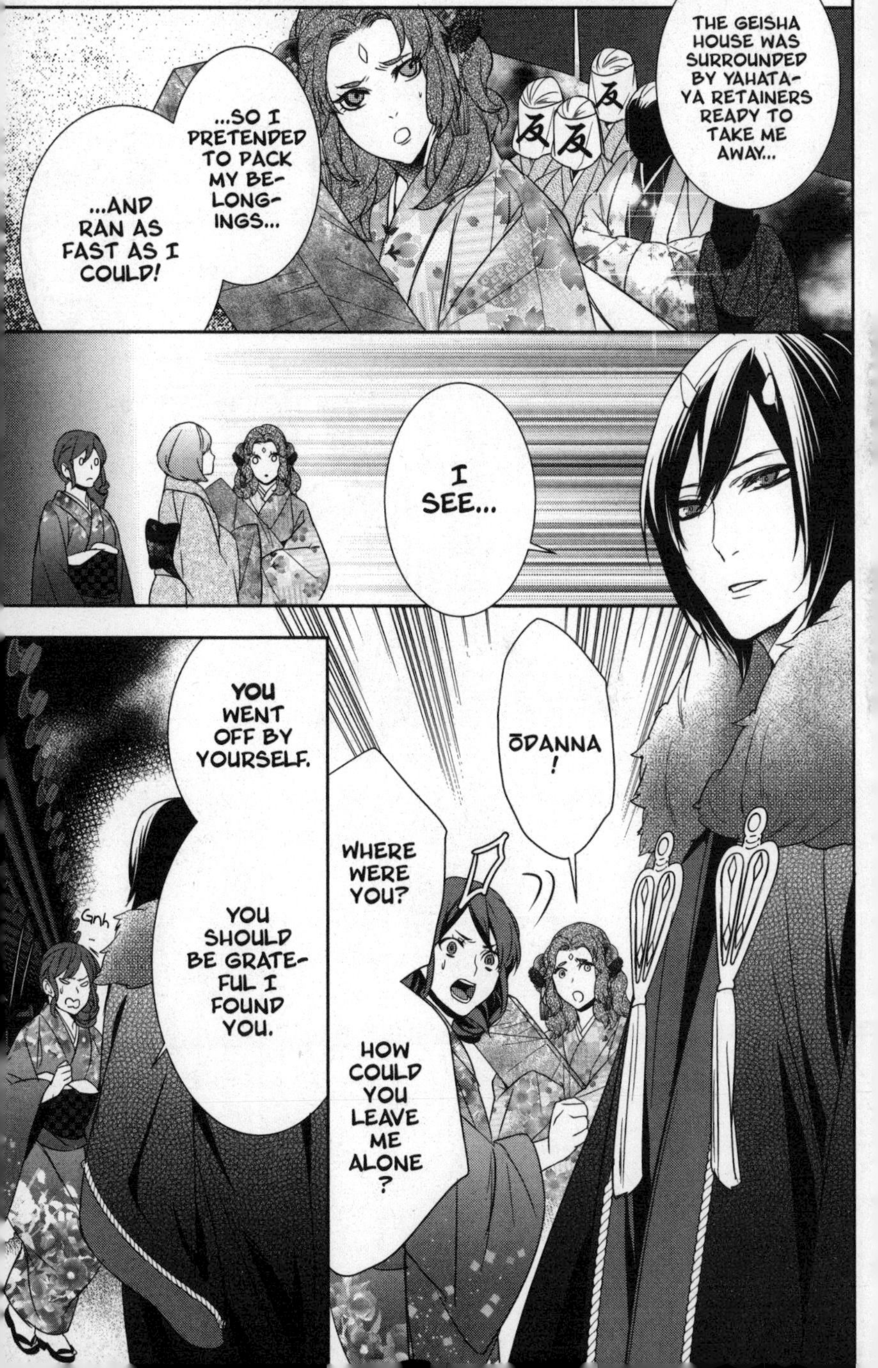
THE GEISHA HOUSE WAS SURROUNDED BY YAHATA-YA RETAINERS READY TO TAKE ME AWAY...
...SO I PRETENDED TO PACK MY BE-LONG-INGS...
...AND RAN AS FAST AS I COULD!
反
反
反
I SEE...
ŌDANNA!
WHERE WERE YOU?
HOW COULD YOU LEAVE ME ALONE?
YOU WENT OFF BY YOURSELF.
YOU SHOULD BE GRATE-FUL I FOUND YOU.
Gnh

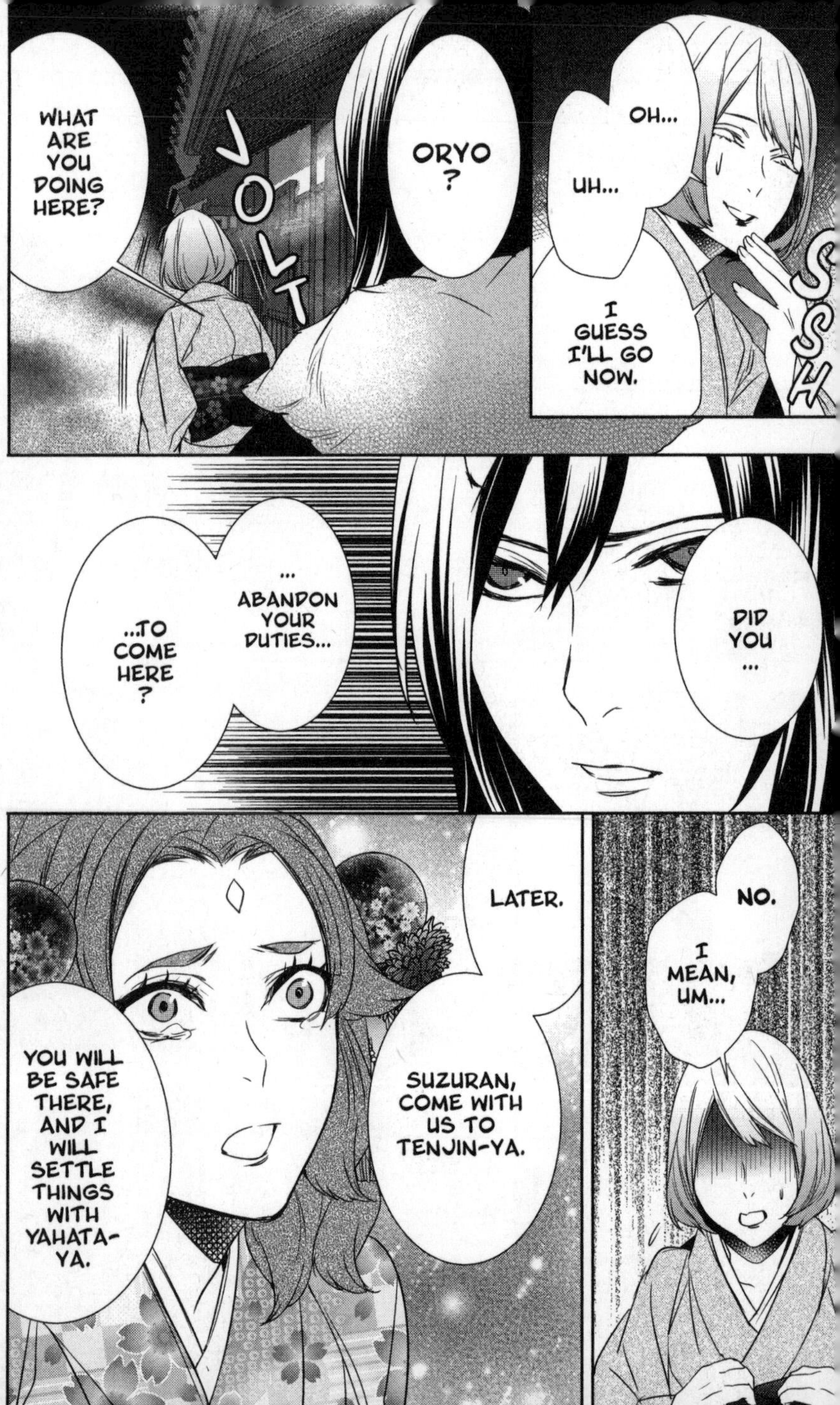
OH...
UH...
I GUESS I'LL GO NOW.
SSH
ORYO?
VOLT
WHAT ARE YOU DOING HERE?
DID YOU...
...ABANDON YOUR DUTIES...
...TO COME HERE?
NO.
I MEAN, UM...
LATER.
SUZURAN, COME WITH US TO TENJIN-YA.
YOU WILL BE SAFE THERE, AND I WILL SETTLE THINGS WITH YAHATA-YA.

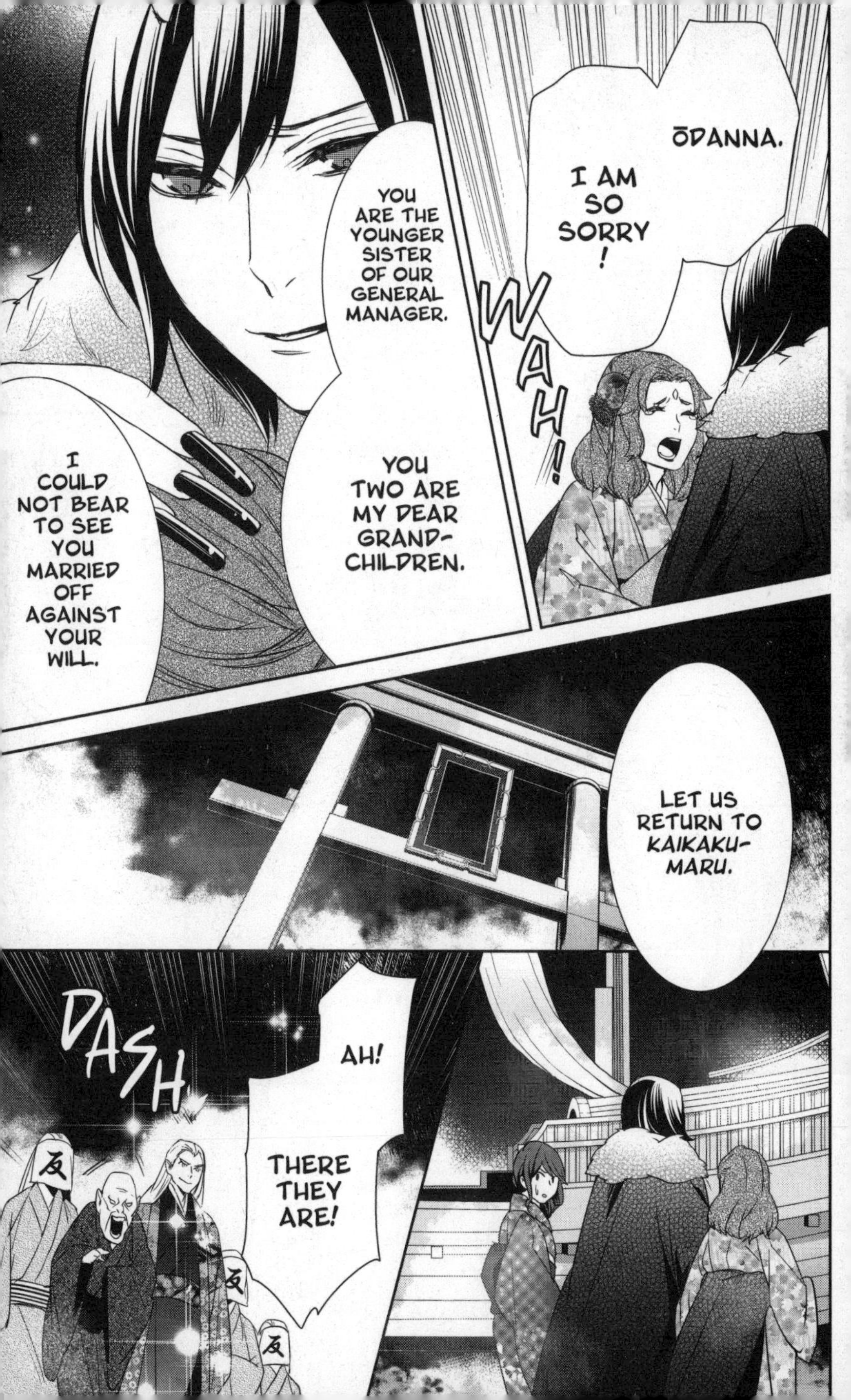
ŌDANNA.
I AM SO SORRY!
WAH!
YOU ARE THE YOUNGER SISTER OF OUR GENERAL MANAGER.
YOU TWO ARE MY DEAR GRAND-CHILDREN.
I COULD NOT BEAR TO SEE YOU MARRIED OFF AGAINST YOUR WILL.
LET US RETURN TO KAIKAKU-MARU.
AH!
THERE THEY ARE!
DASH

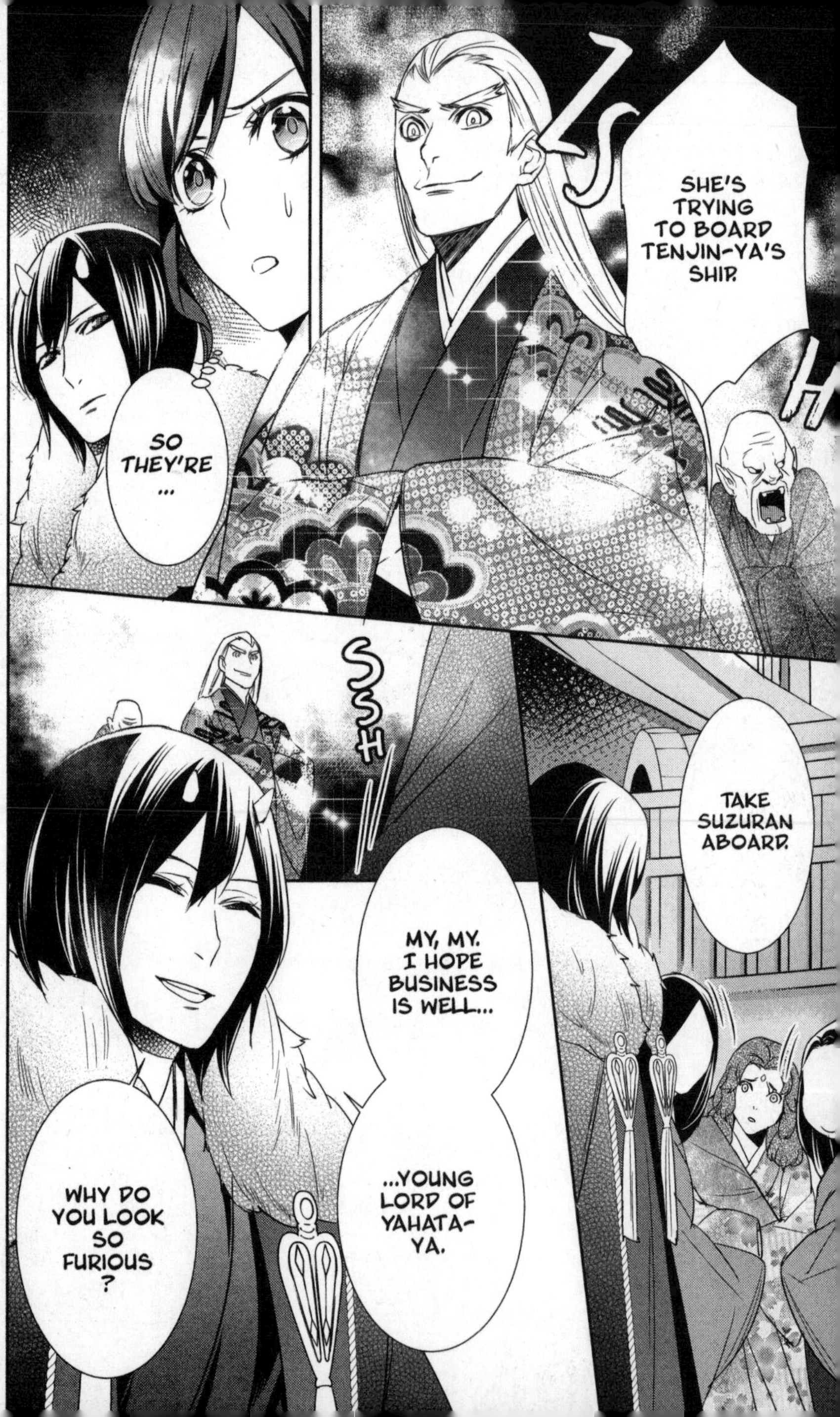
SHE'S TRYING TO BOARD TENJIN-YA'S SHIP.
SO THEY'RE ...
TAKE SUZURAN ABOARD.
SSSH
MY, MY. I HOPE BUSINESS IS WELL...
...YOUNG LORD OF YAHATA-YA.
WHY DO YOU LOOK SO FURIOUS?

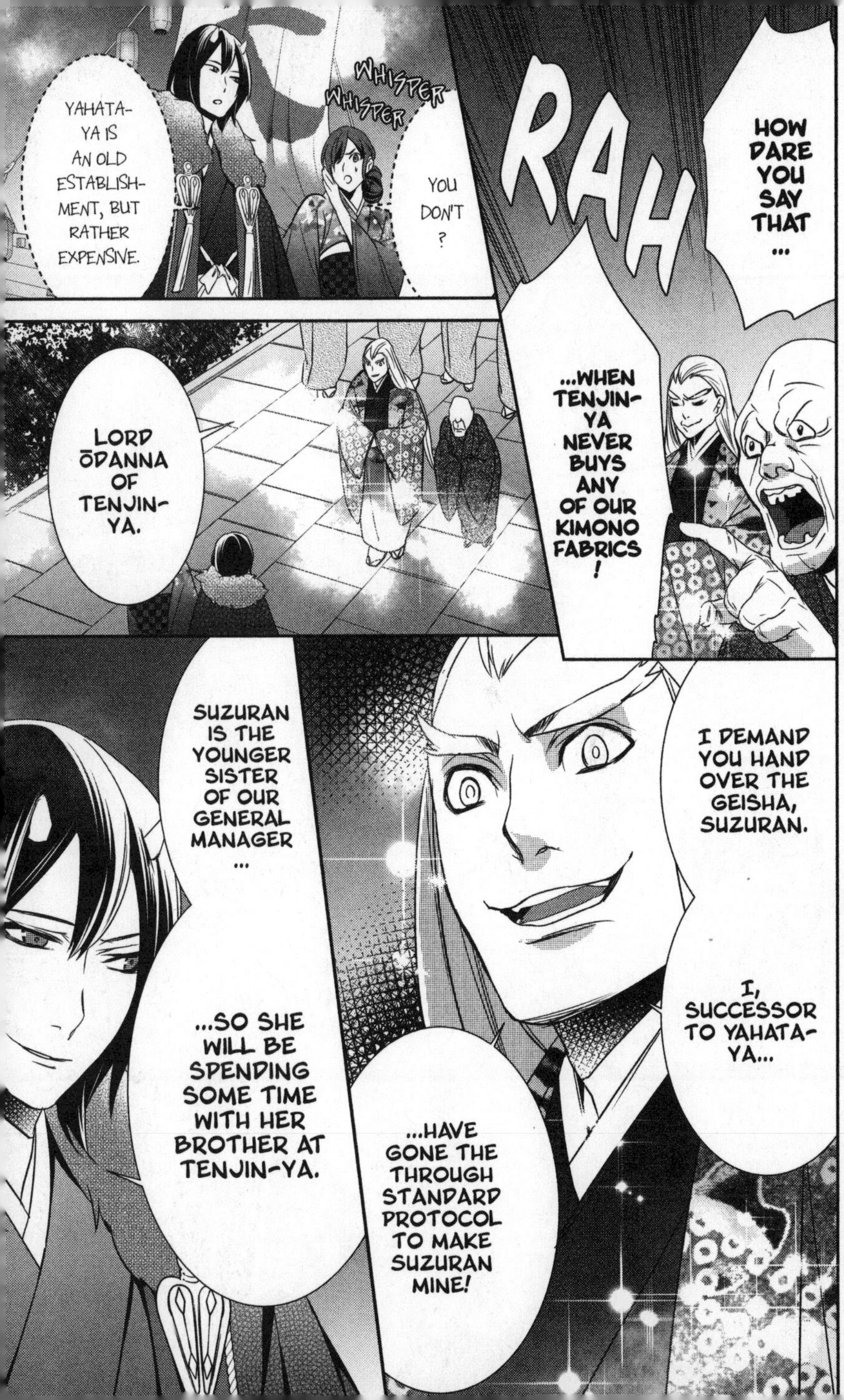
WHISPER WHISPER
YOU DON'T ?
YAHATA-YA IS AN OLD ESTABLISHMENT, BUT RATHER EXPENSIVE.
RAH
HOW DARE YOU SAY THAT...
...WHEN TENJIN-YA NEVER BUYS ANY OF OUR KIMONO FABRICS!
LORD ŌDANNA OF TENJIN-YA.
I DEMAND YOU HAND OVER THE GEISHA, SUZURAN.
I, SUCCESSOR TO YAHATA-YA...
...HAVE GONE THE THROUGH STANDARD PROTOCOL TO MAKE SUZURAN MINE!
SUZURAN IS THE YOUNGER SISTER OF OUR GENERAL MANAGER...
...SO SHE WILL BE SPENDING SOME TIME WITH HER BROTHER AT TENJIN-YA.

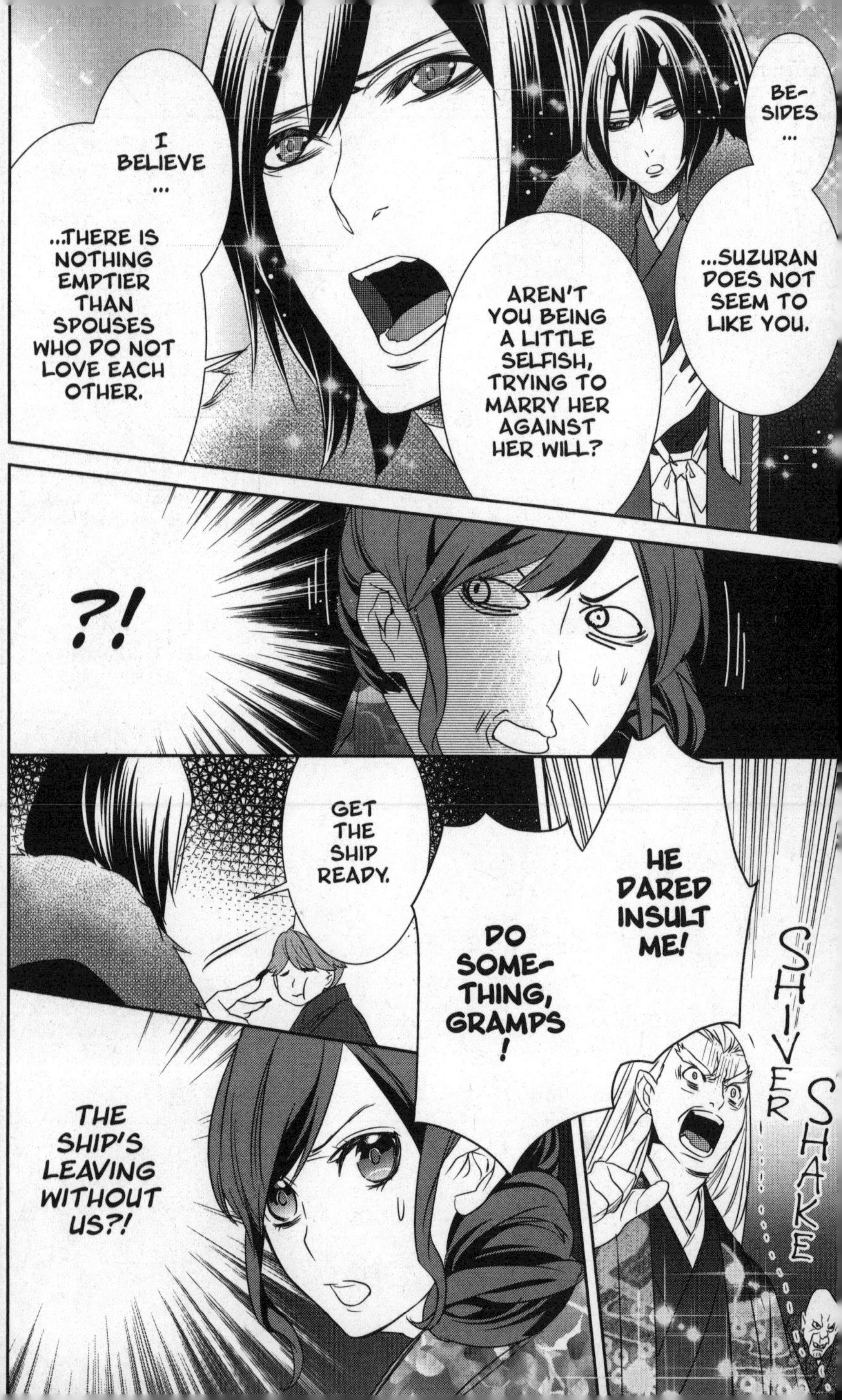
BE-SIDES ...
...SUZURAN DOES NOT SEEM TO LIKE YOU.
AREN'T YOU BEING A LITTLE SELFISH, TRYING TO MARRY HER AGAINST HER WILL?
I BELIEVE ...
...THERE IS NOTHING EMPTIER THAN SPOUSES WHO DO NOT LOVE EACH OTHER.
?!
SHIVER
SHAKE
HE DARED INSULT ME!
DO SOME-THING, GRAMPS!
GET THE SHIP READY.
THE SHIP'S LEAVING WITHOUT US?!

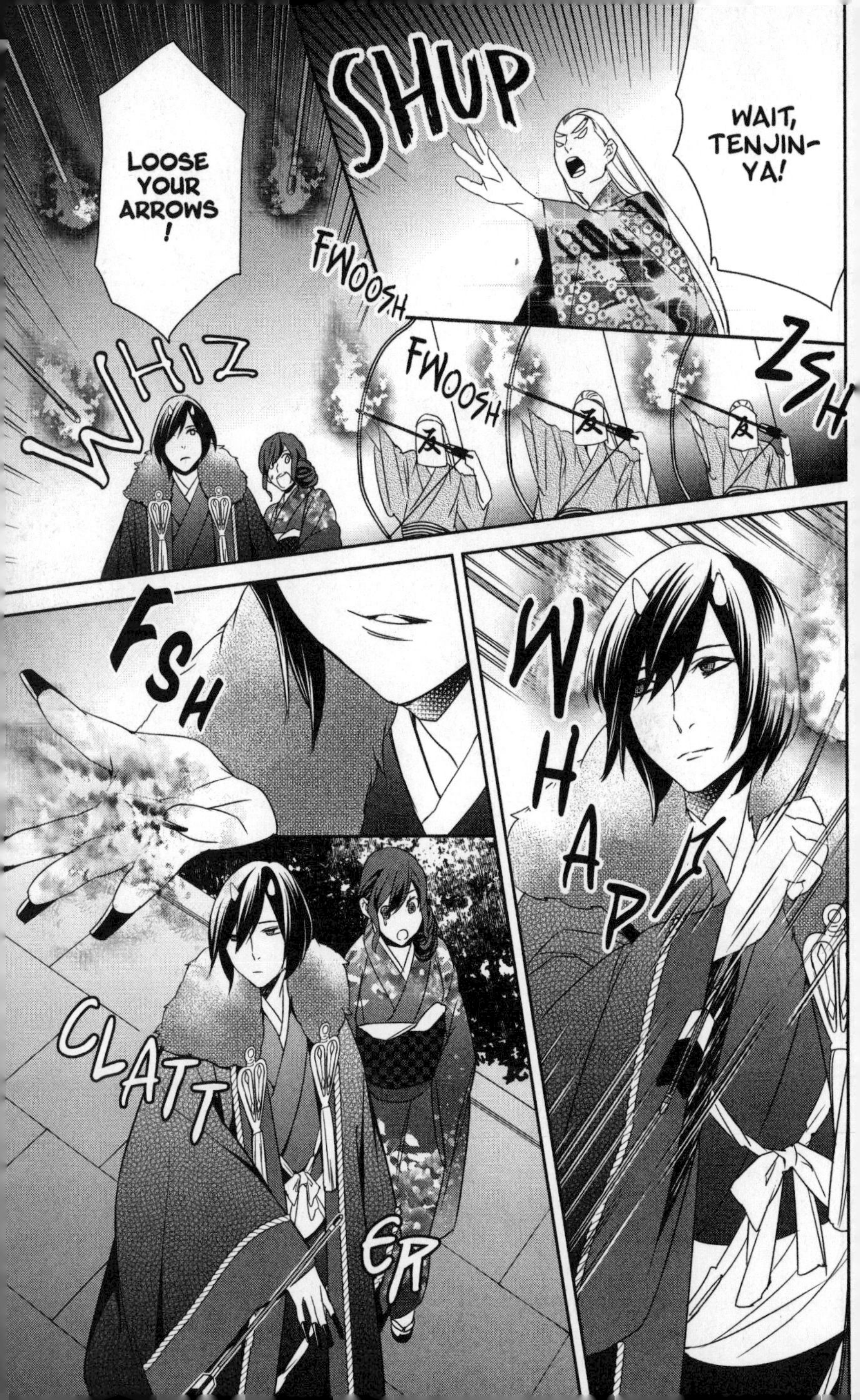
WAIT, TENJIN-YA!
SHUP
FWOOSH
LOOSE YOUR ARROWS!
ZSH
FWOOSH
WHIZ
WHAP!
FSH
CLATTER

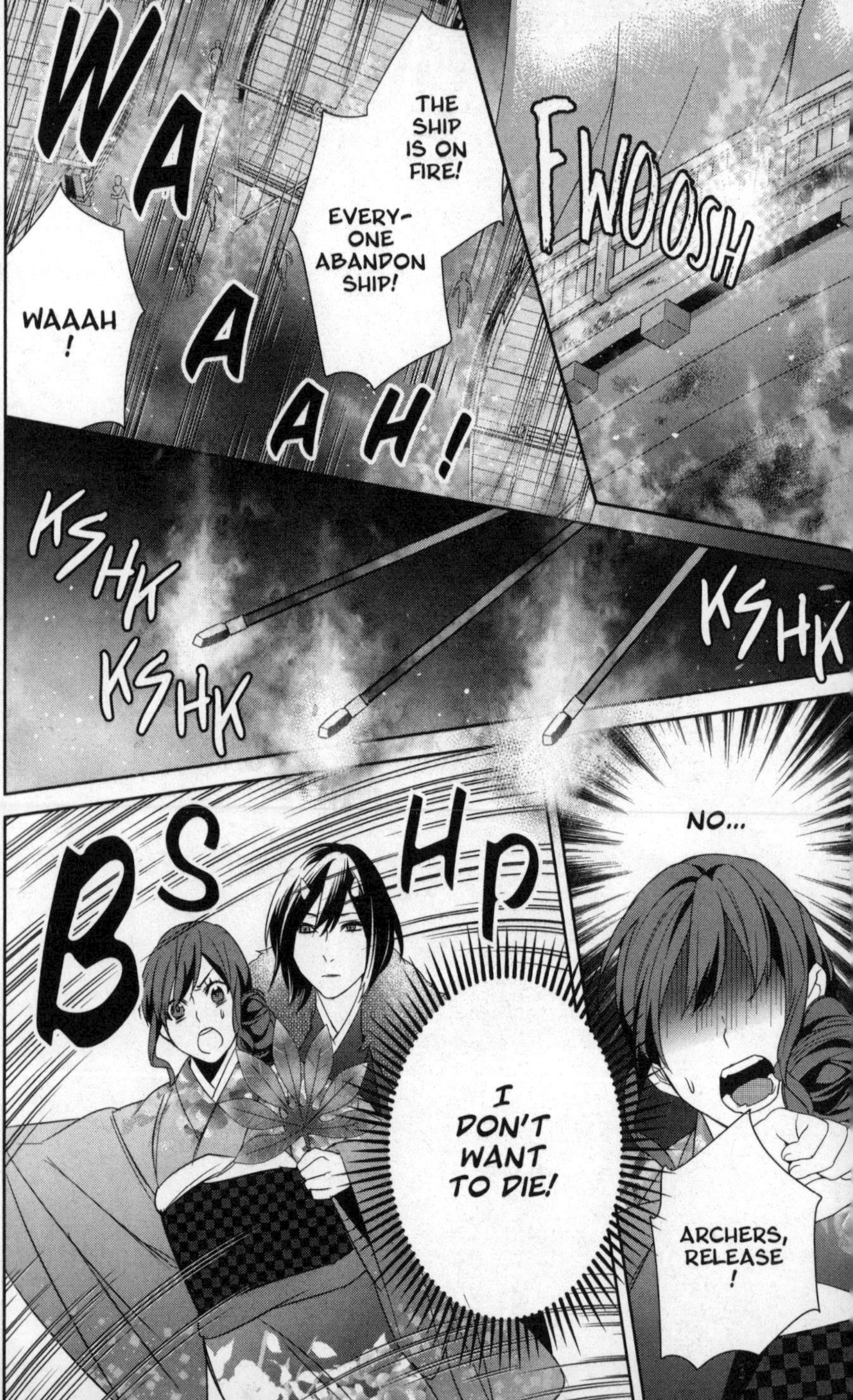
FWOOSH
THE SHIP IS ON FIRE!
EVERYONE ABANDON SHIP!
WAAAH!
WAAAH!
KSHK
KSHK KSHK
NO...
ARCHERS, RELEASE!
BSHP
I DON'T WANT TO DIE!

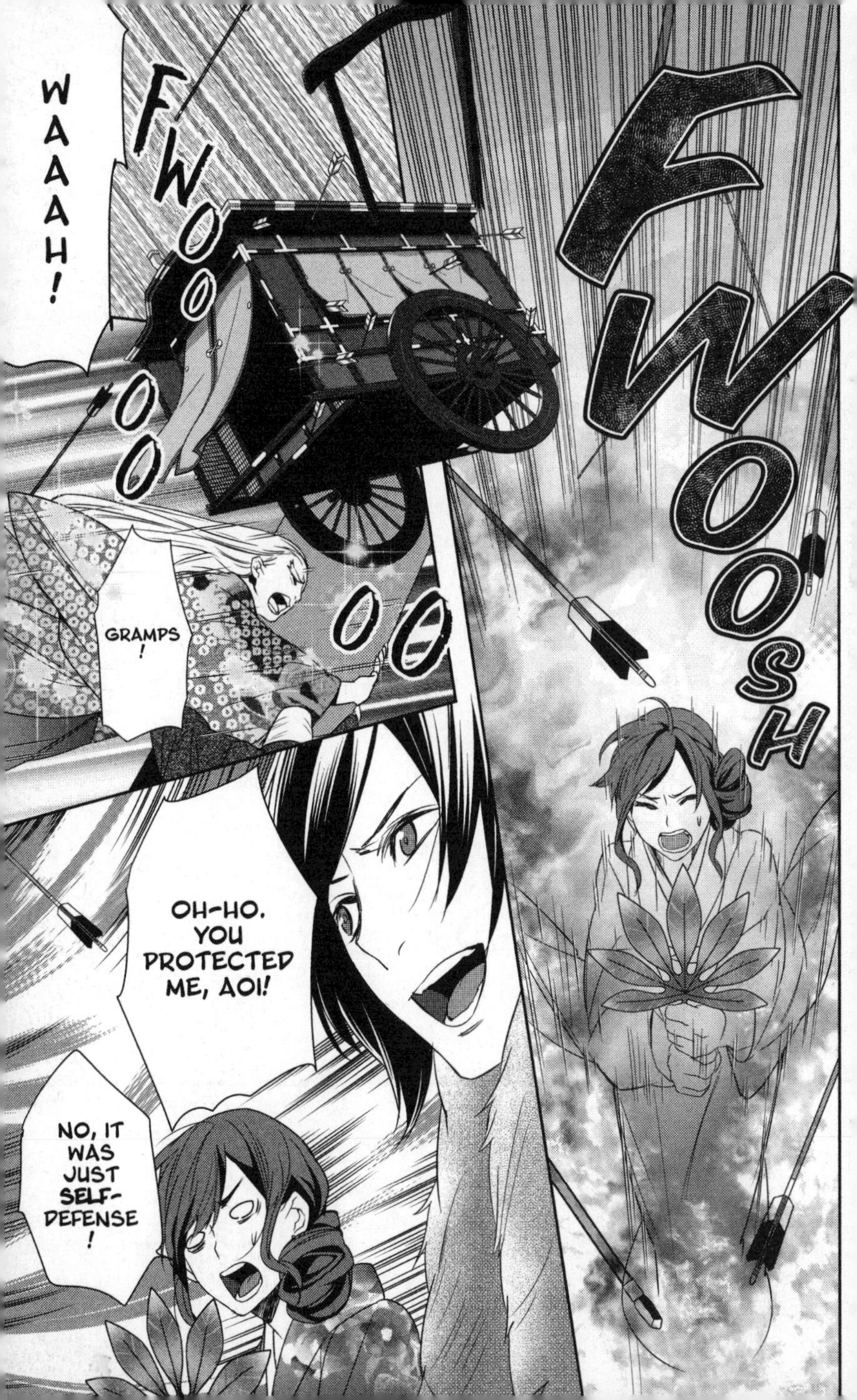
FWOOOSH
WAAAAH!
FWOOOOOOOOO
GRAMPS!
OH-HO. YOU PROTECTED ME, AOI!
NO, IT WAS JUST SELF-DEFENSE!

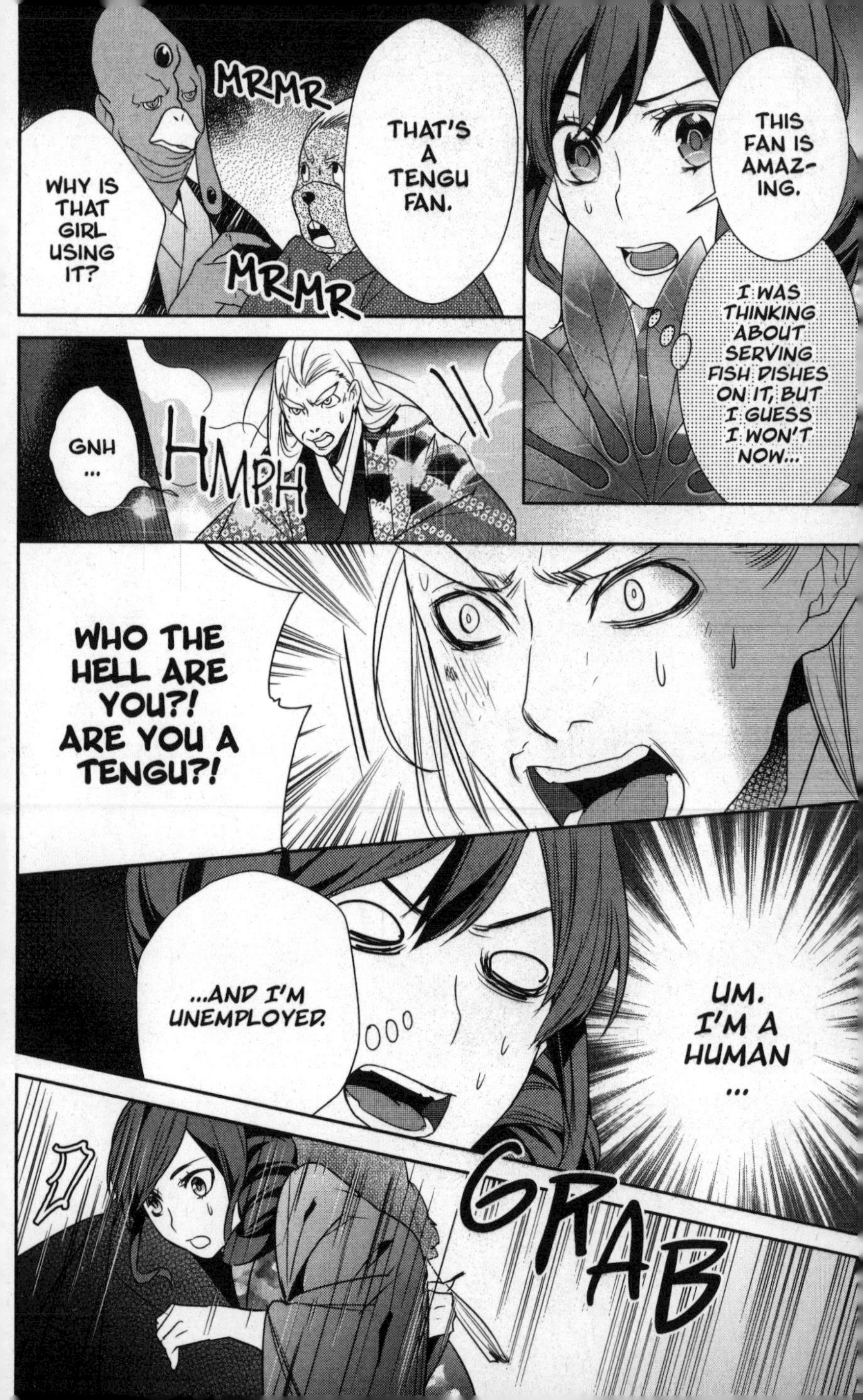
THIS FAN IS AMAZ-ING.
I WAS THINKING ABOUT SERVING FISH DISHES ON IT, BUT I GUESS I WON'T NOW...
MRMR
THAT'S A TENGU FAN.
WHY IS THAT GIRL USING IT?
MRMR
HMPH
GNH...
WHO THE HELL ARE YOU?! ARE YOU A TENGU?!
UM. I'M A HUMAN...
...AND I'M UNEMPLOYED.
GRAB

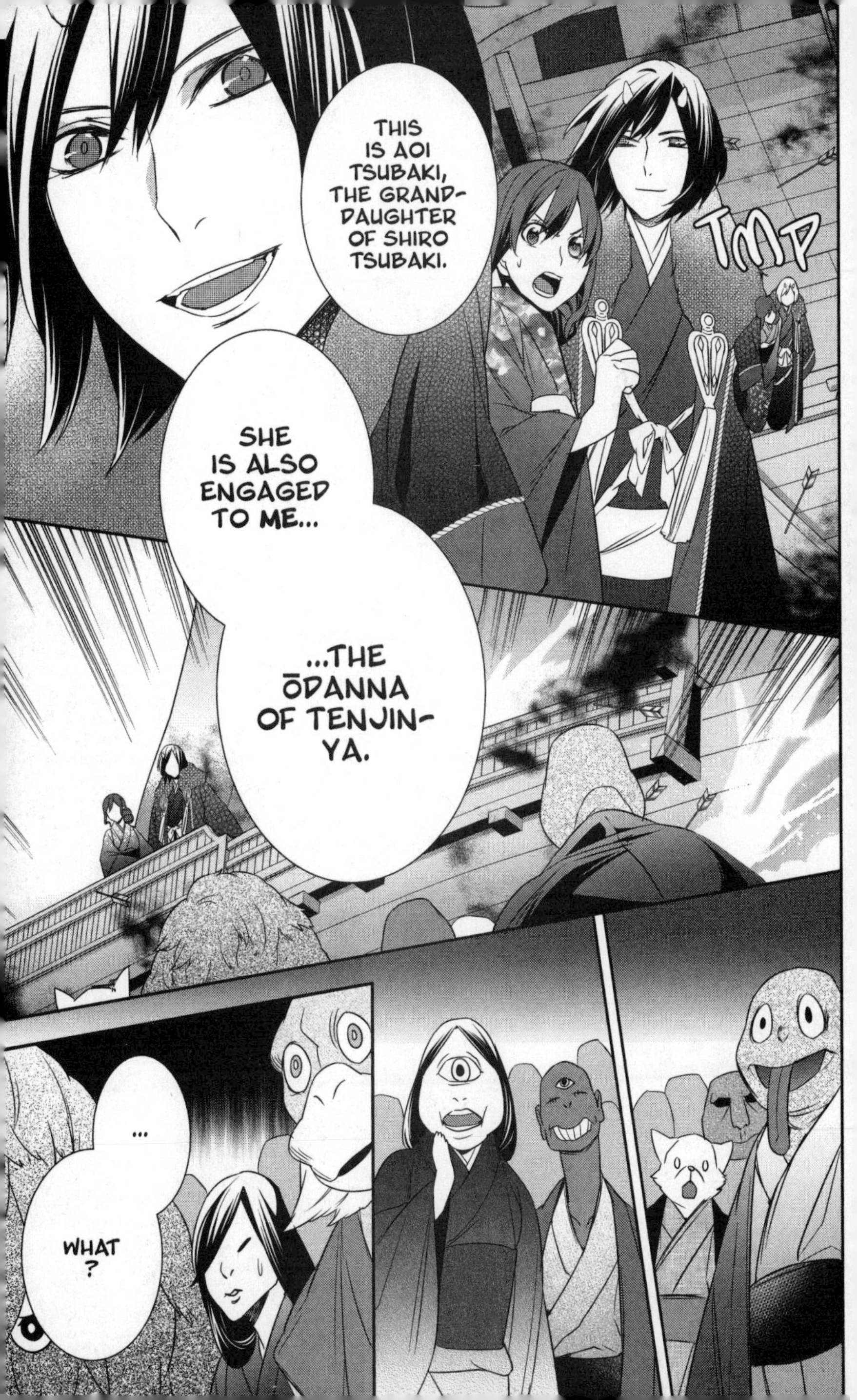
TMP
THIS IS AOI TSUBAKI, THE GRAND-DAUGHTER OF SHIRO TSUBAKI.
SHE IS ALSO ENGAGED TO ME...
...THE ŌDANNA OF TENJIN-YA.
...
WHAT?

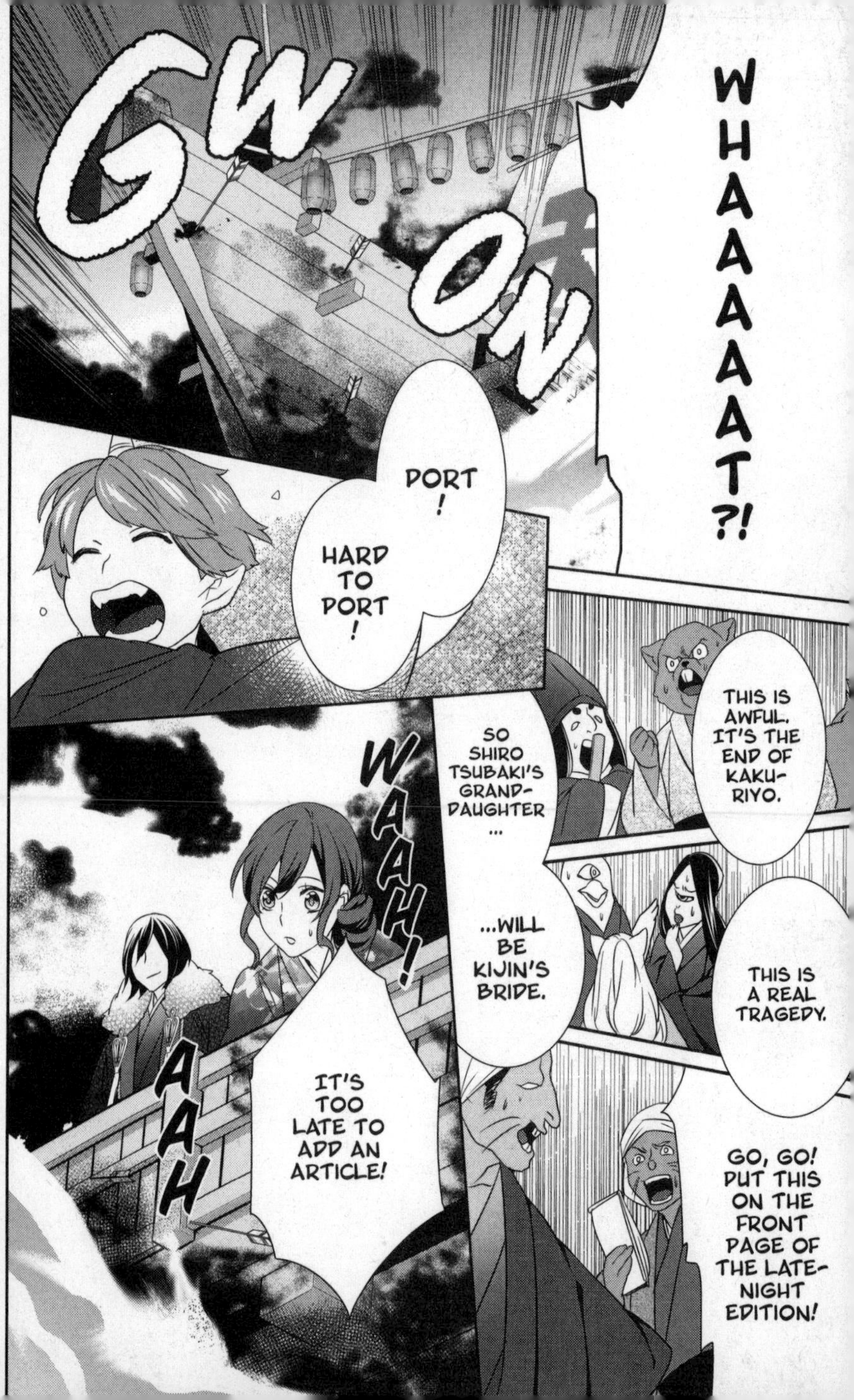
WHAAAAAT?!
GWOON
PORT!
HARD TO PORT!
THIS IS AWFUL. IT'S THE END OF KAKURIYO.
SO SHIRO TSUBAKI'S GRANDDAUGHTER...
...WILL BE KIJIN'S BRIDE.
THIS IS A REAL TRAGEDY.
GO, GO! PUT THIS ON THE FRONT PAGE OF THE LATE-NIGHT EDITION!
WAAAH!
AAAH
IT'S TOO LATE TO ADD AN ARTICLE!

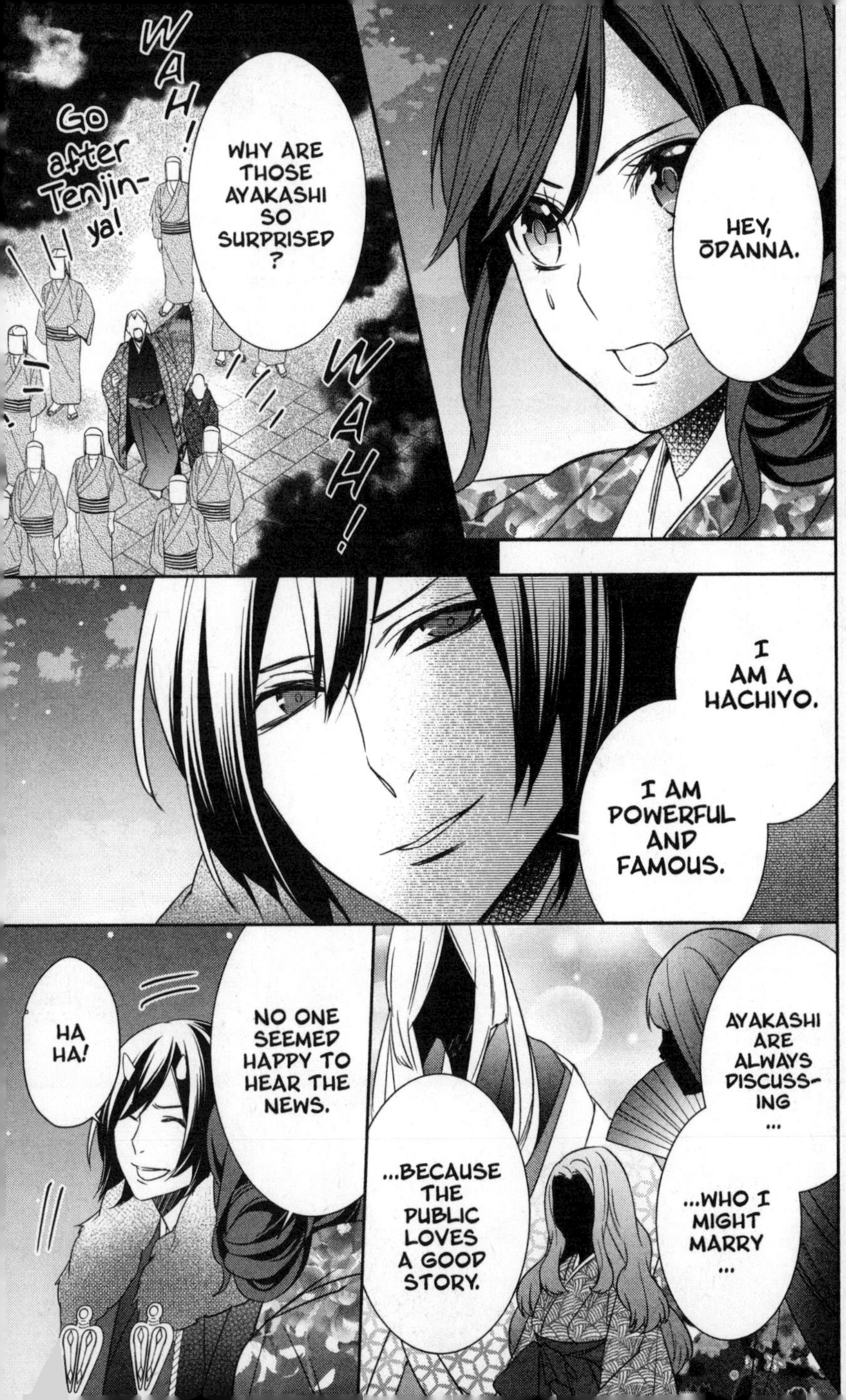
HEY, ŌDANNA.
WAH!
WAH!
WHY ARE THOSE AYAKASHI SO SURPRISED?
Go after Tenjin-ya!
I AM A HACHIYO.
I AM POWERFUL AND FAMOUS.
AYAKASHI ARE ALWAYS DISCUSSING...
...WHO I MIGHT MARRY...
...BECAUSE THE PUBLIC LOVES A GOOD STORY.
NO ONE SEEMED HAPPY TO HEAR THE NEWS.
HA HA!

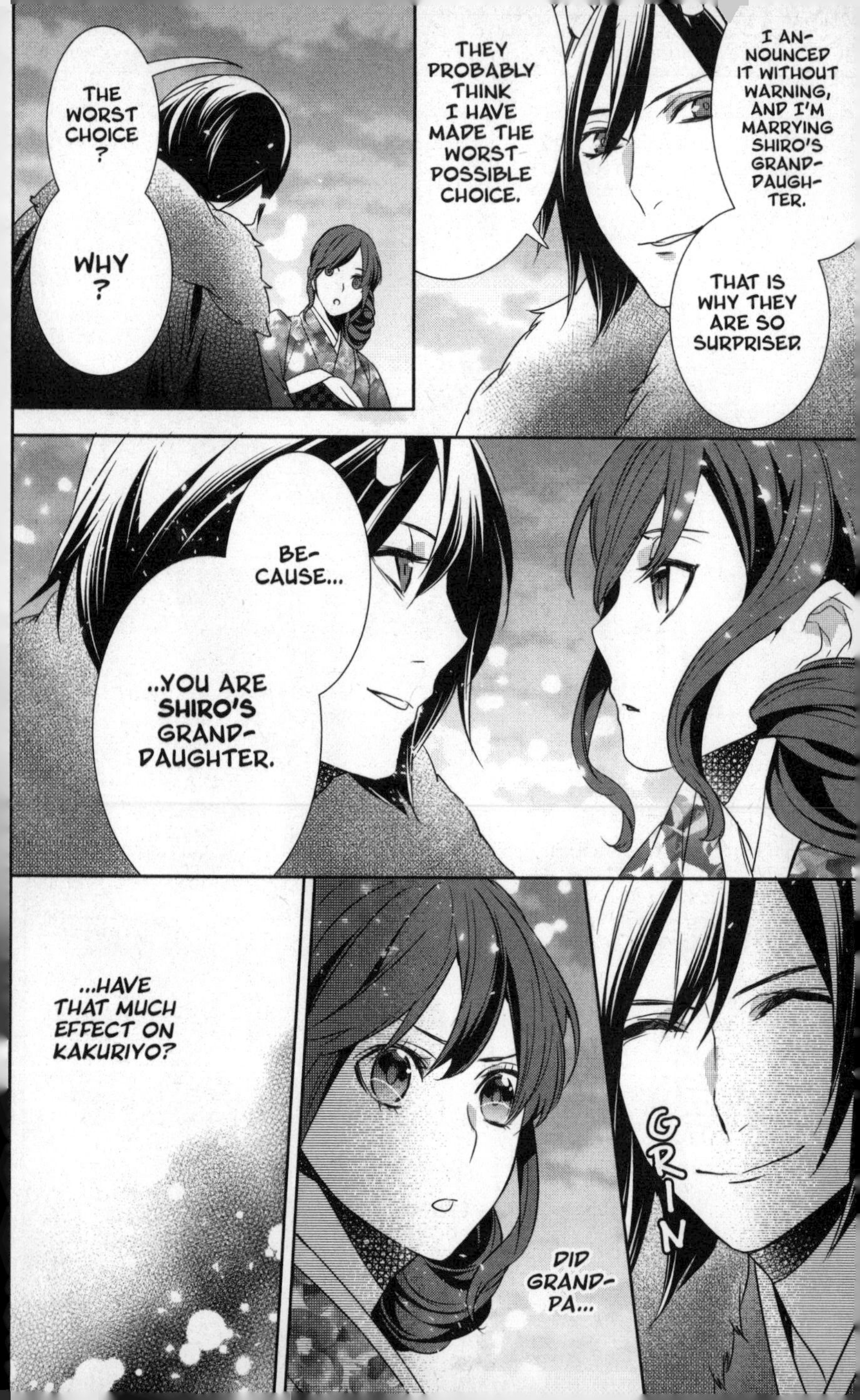
I ANNOUNCED IT WITHOUT WARNING, AND I'M MARRYING SHIRO'S GRANDDAUGHTER.
THAT IS WHY THEY ARE SO SURPRISED.
THEY PROBABLY THINK I HAVE MADE THE WORST POSSIBLE CHOICE.
THE WORST CHOICE?
WHY?
BECAUSE...
...YOU ARE SHIRO'S GRANDDAUGHTER.
GRIN
DID GRANDPA...
...HAVE THAT MUCH EFFECT ON KAKURIYO?

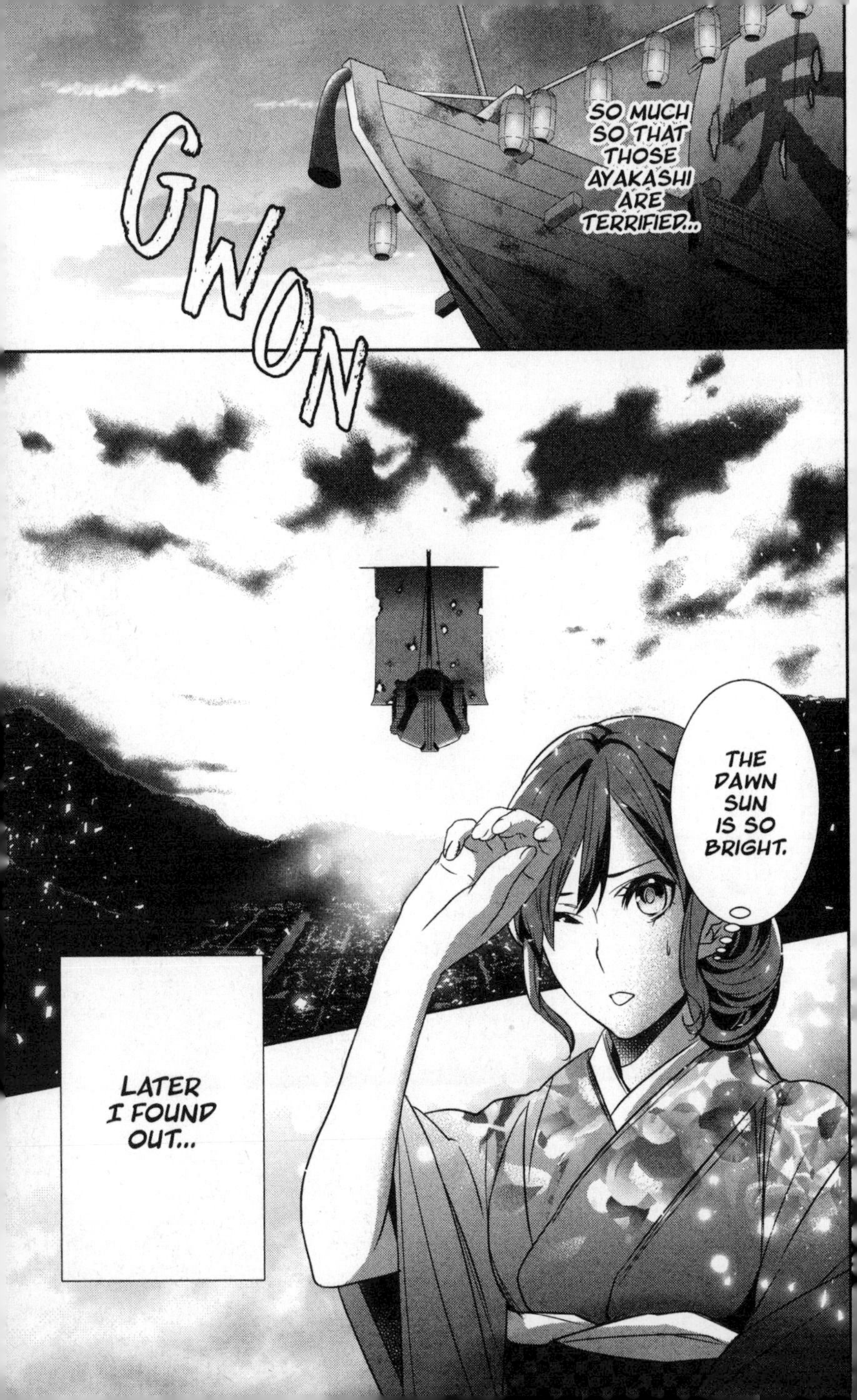
SO MUCH SO THAT THOSE AYAKASHI ARE TERRIFIED...
GWON
THE DAWN SUN IS SO BRIGHT.
LATER I FOUND OUT...

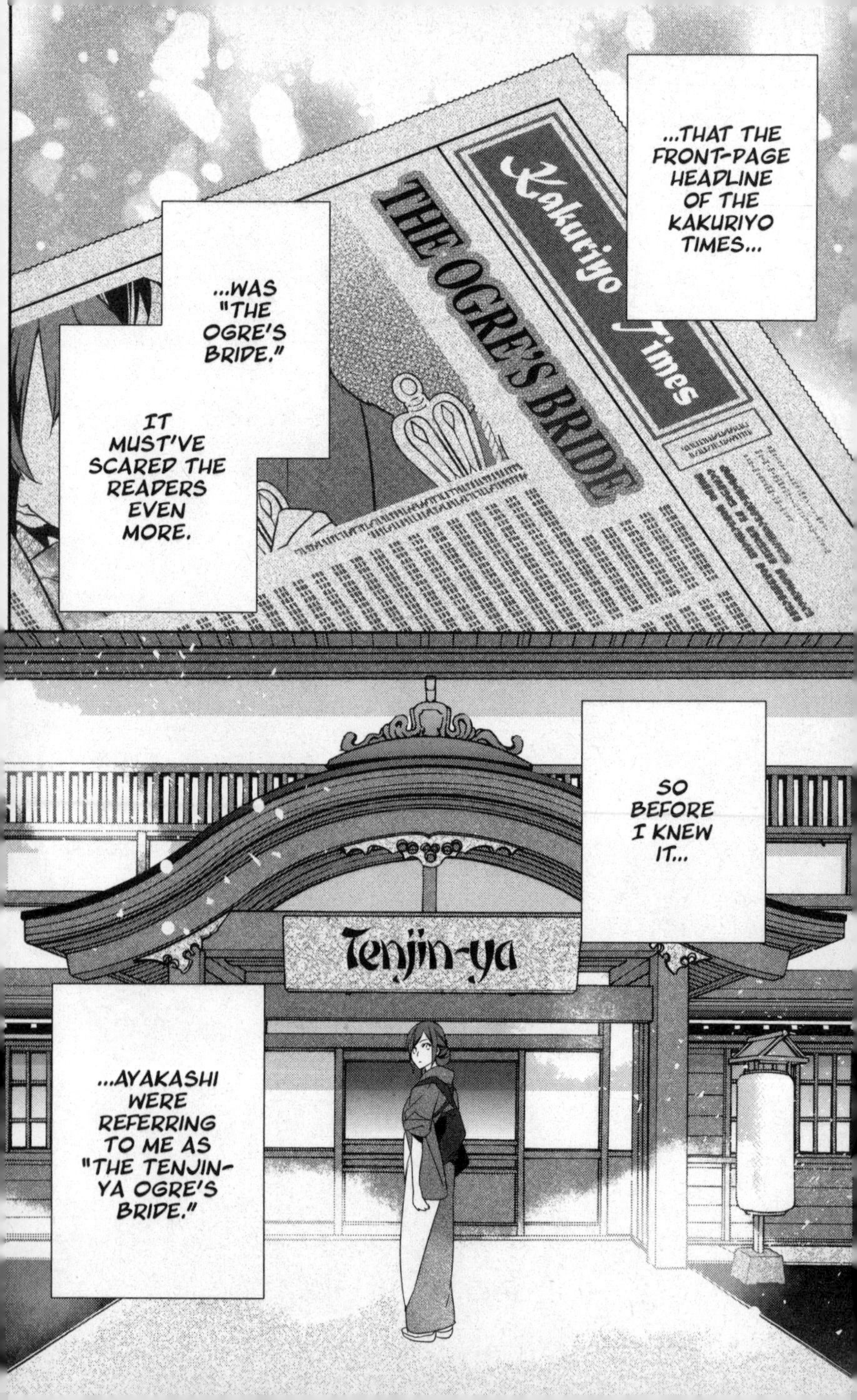
...THAT THE FRONT-PAGE HEADLINE OF THE KAKURIYO TIMES...
Kakuriyo Times
THE OGRE'S BRIDE
...WAS "THE OGRE'S BRIDE."
IT MUST'VE SCARED THE READERS EVEN MORE.
SO BEFORE I KNEW IT...
Tenjin-ya
...AYAKASHI WERE REFERRING TO ME AS "THE TENJIN-YA OGRE'S BRIDE."

Kakuriyo
Bed & Breakfast
for Spirits

Kakuriyo
Bed & Breakfast
for Spirits

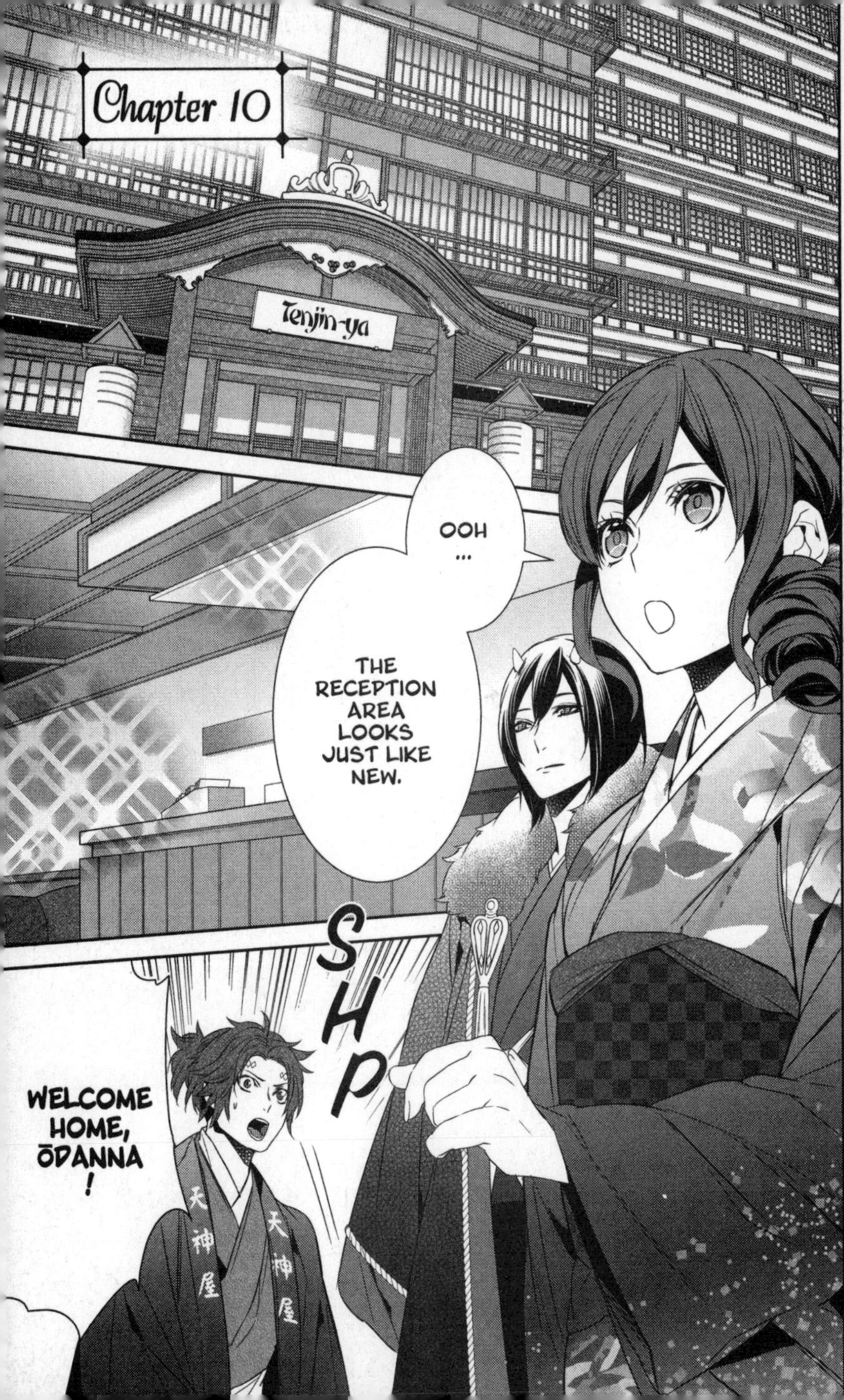
Chapter 10
Tenjin-ya
OOH ...
THE RECEPTION AREA LOOKS JUST LIKE NEW.
SHP
WELCOME HOME, ŌDANNA!
天神屋
天神屋

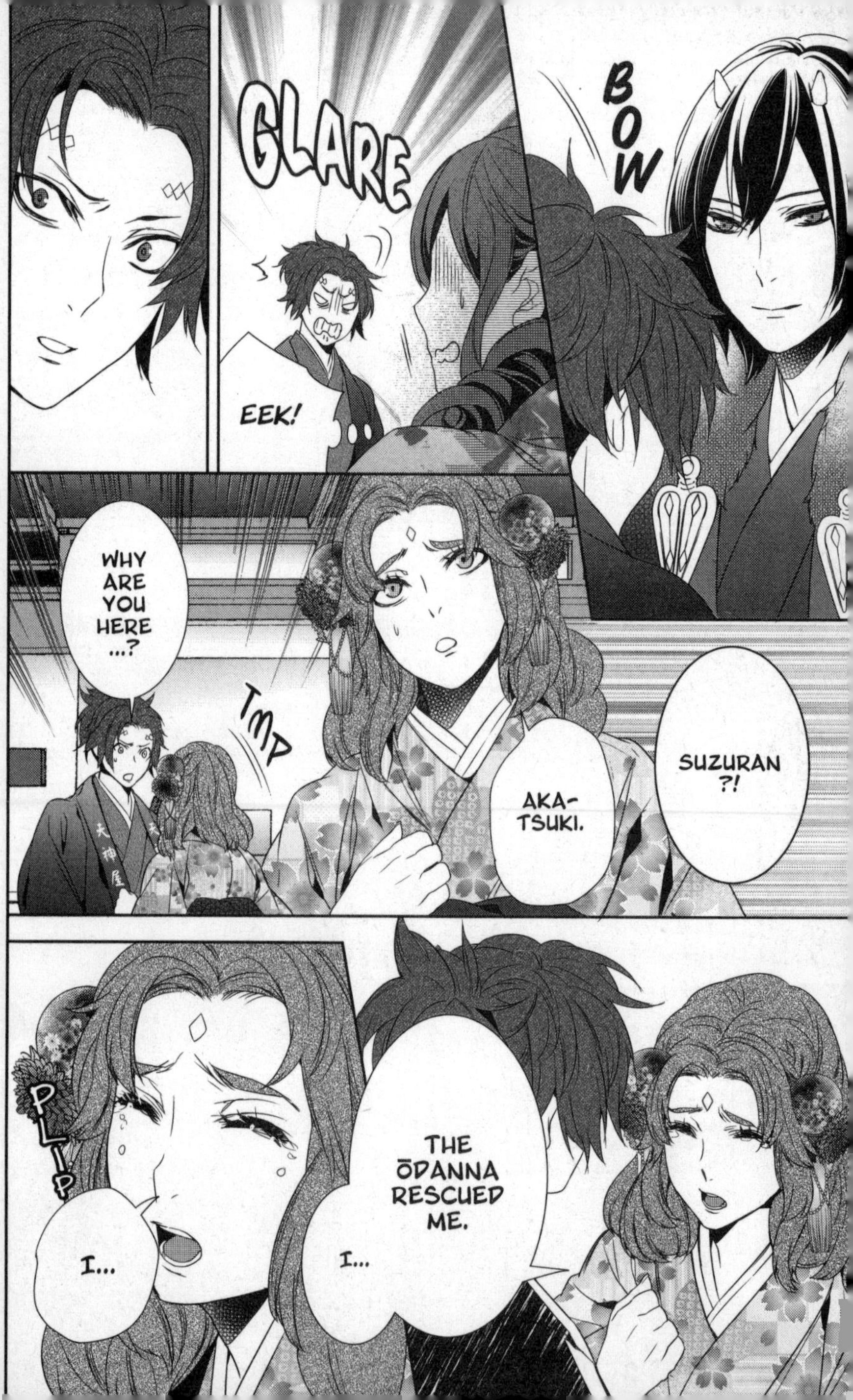
BOW
GLARE
EEK!
SUZURAN ?!
AKA-TSUKI.
TMP
WHY ARE YOU HERE ...?
THE ŌDANNA RESCUED ME.
I...
PLIP
I...

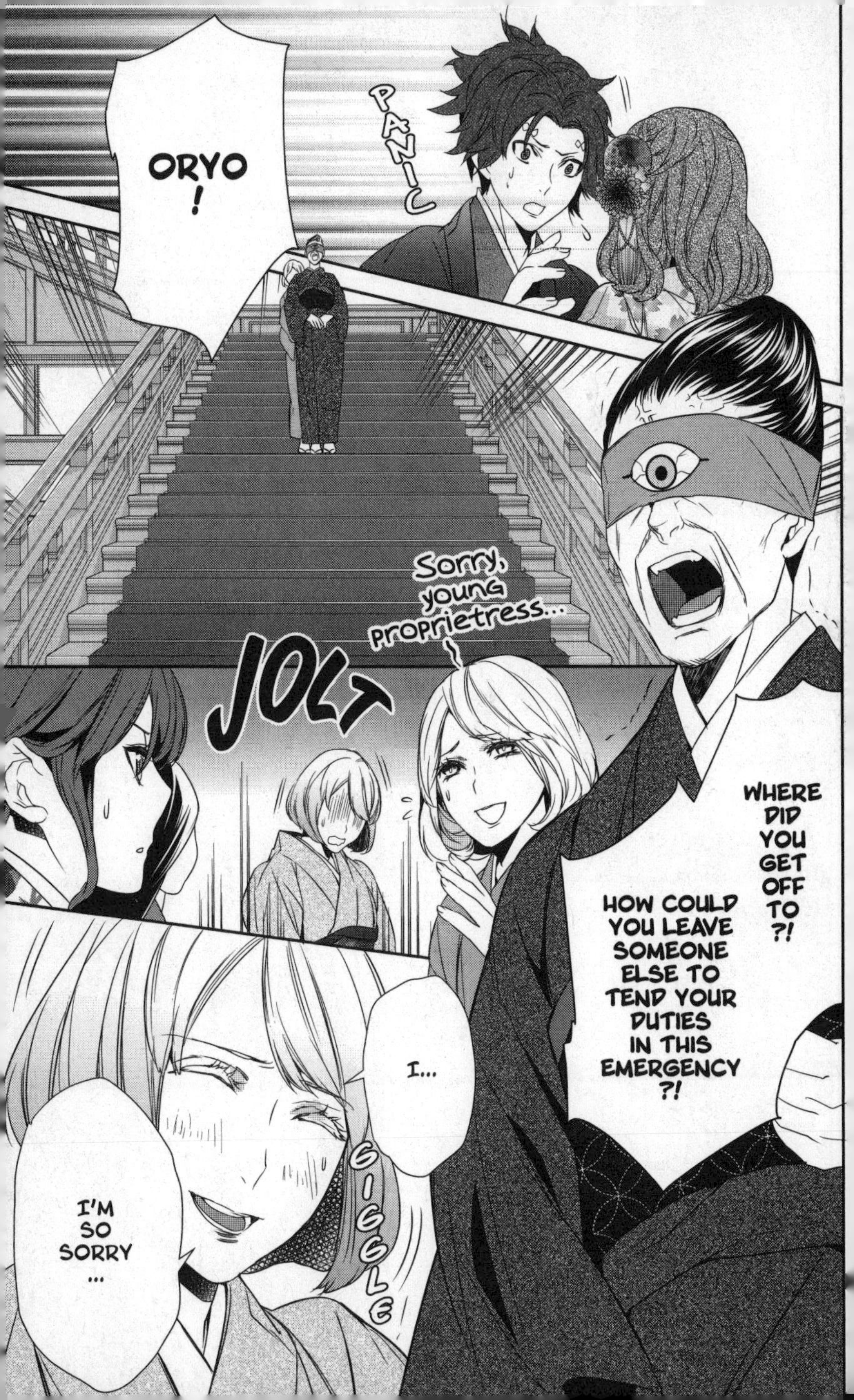
PANIC
ORYO!
WHERE DID YOU GET OFF TO?!
HOW COULD YOU LEAVE SOMEONE ELSE TO TEND YOUR DUTIES IN THIS EMERGENCY?!
Sorry, young proprietress...
JOLT
I...
GIGGLE
I'M SO SORRY...

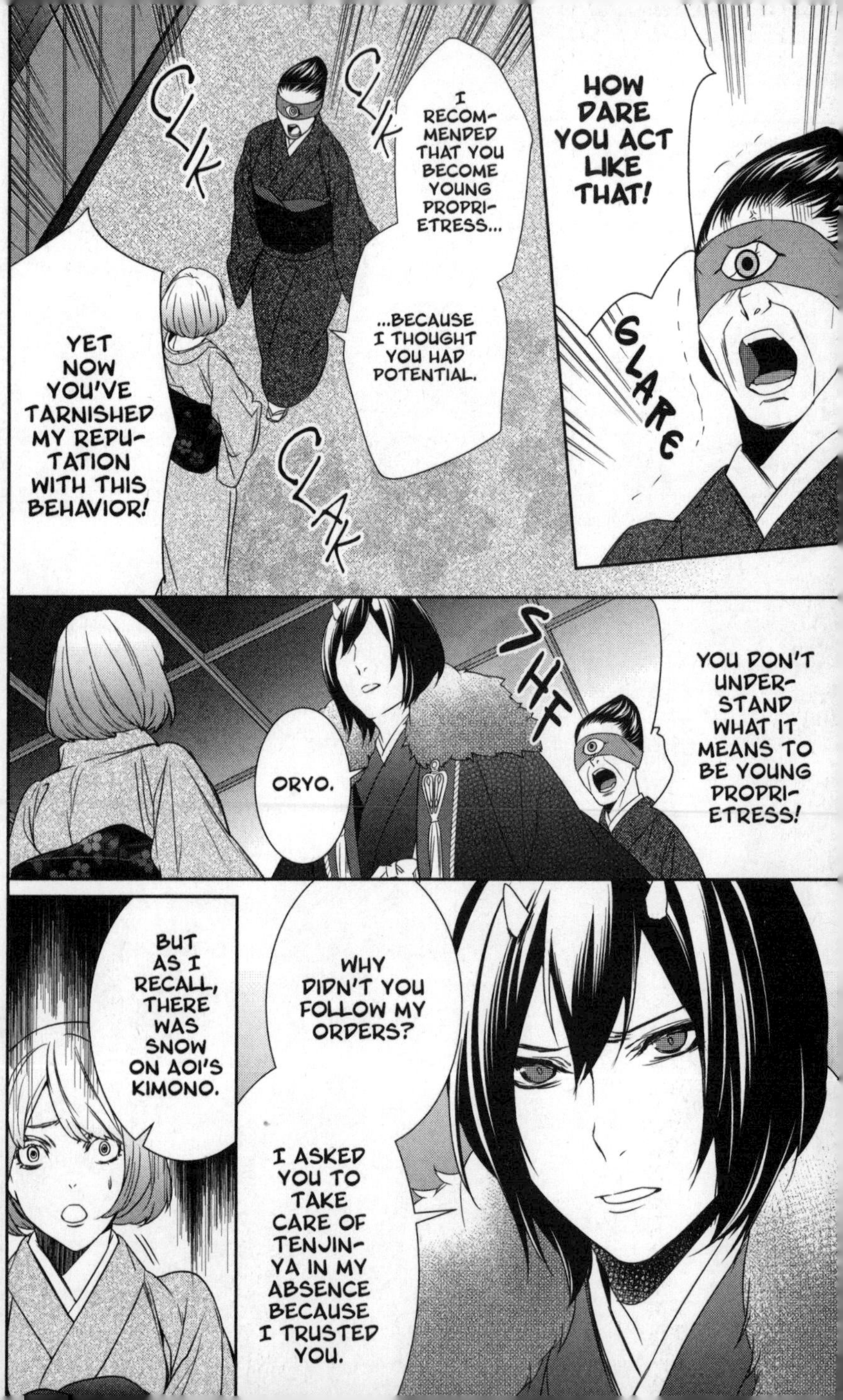
HOW DARE YOU ACT LIKE THAT!
GLARE
CLIK
CLIK
I RECOMMENDED THAT YOU BECOME YOUNG PROPRIETRESS...
...BECAUSE I THOUGHT YOU HAD POTENTIAL.
YET NOW YOU'VE TARNISHED MY REPUTATION WITH THIS BEHAVIOR!
CLAK
SHF
YOU DON'T UNDERSTAND WHAT IT MEANS TO BE YOUNG PROPRIETRESS!
ORYO.
WHY DIDN'T YOU FOLLOW MY ORDERS?
I ASKED YOU TO TAKE CARE OF TENJIN-YA IN MY ABSENCE BECAUSE I TRUSTED YOU.
BUT AS I RECALL, THERE WAS SNOW ON AOI'S KIMONO.

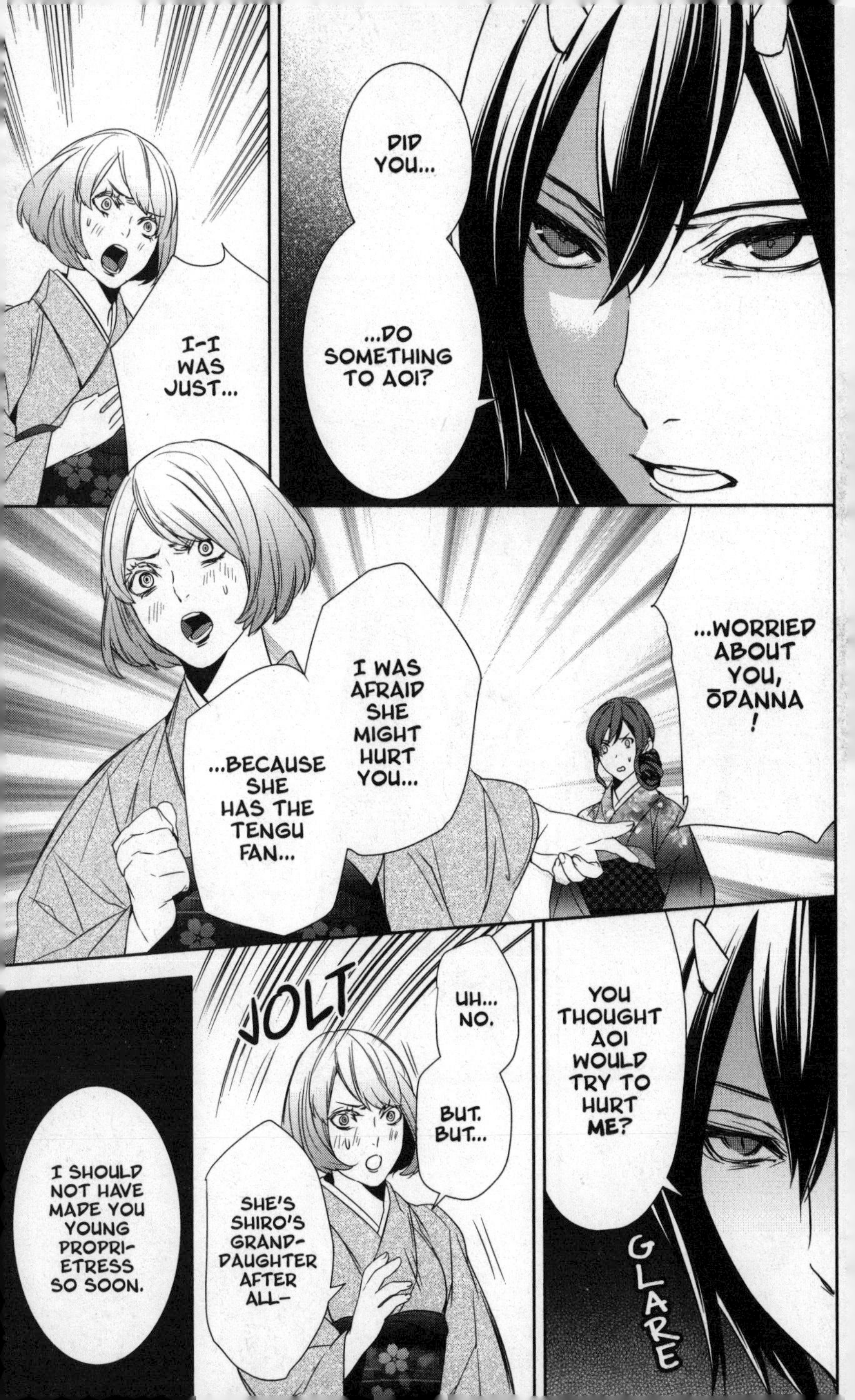
DID YOU...
...DO SOMETHING TO AOI?
I-I WAS JUST...
...WORRIED ABOUT YOU, ŌDANNA!
I WAS AFRAID SHE MIGHT HURT YOU...
...BECAUSE SHE HAS THE TENGU FAN...
YOU THOUGHT AOI WOULD TRY TO HURT ME?
GLARE
JOLT
UH... NO.
BUT. BUT...
SHE'S SHIRO'S GRANDDAUGHTER AFTER ALL-
I SHOULD NOT HAVE MADE YOU YOUNG PROPRIETRESS SO SOON.

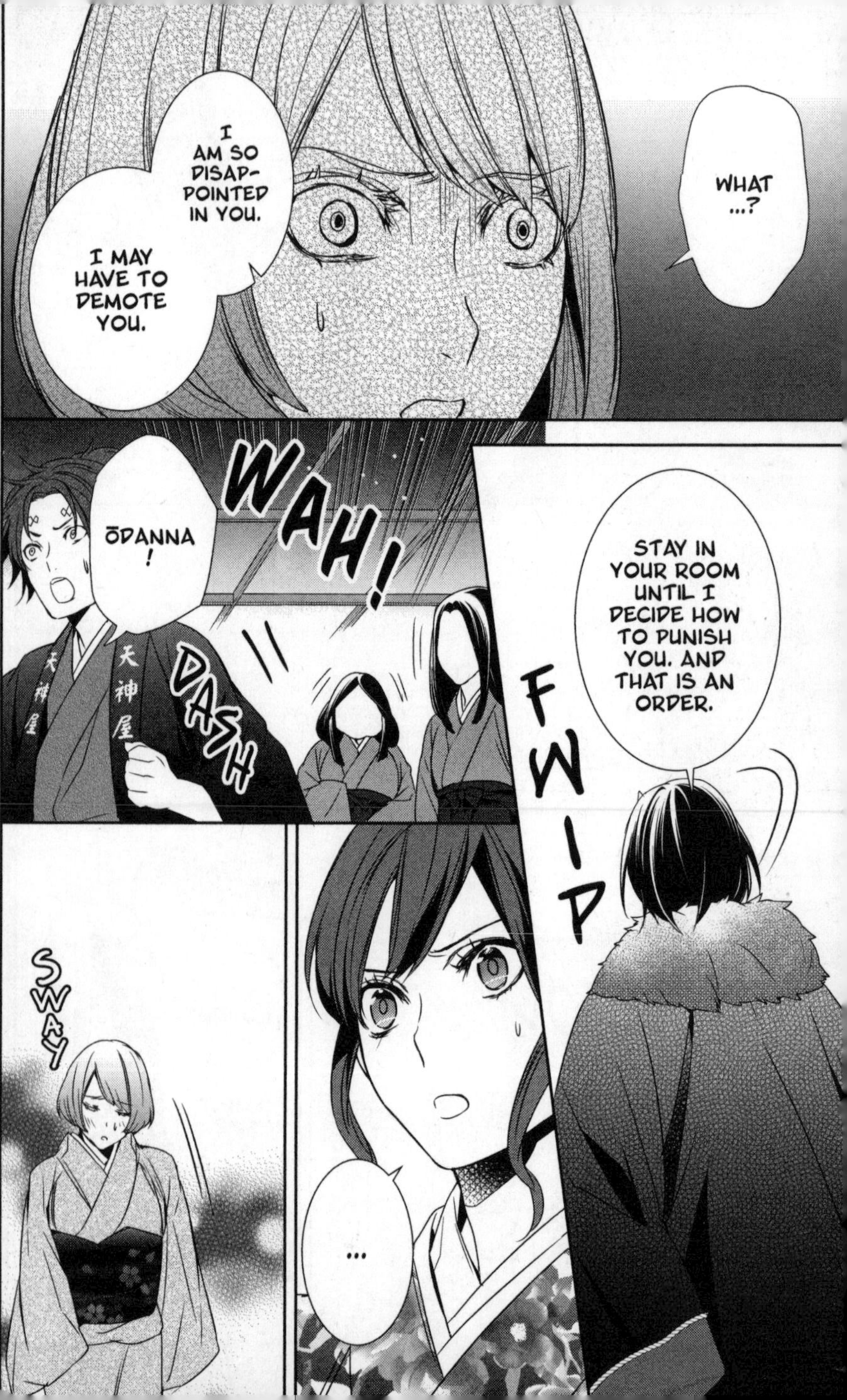

WHAT ...?
I AM SO DISAPPOINTED IN YOU.
I MAY HAVE TO DEMOTE YOU.
STAY IN YOUR ROOM UNTIL I DECIDE HOW TO PUNISH YOU. AND THAT IS AN ORDER.
FWIP
WAH!
ŌDANNA!
天神屋
DASH
...
SWAY

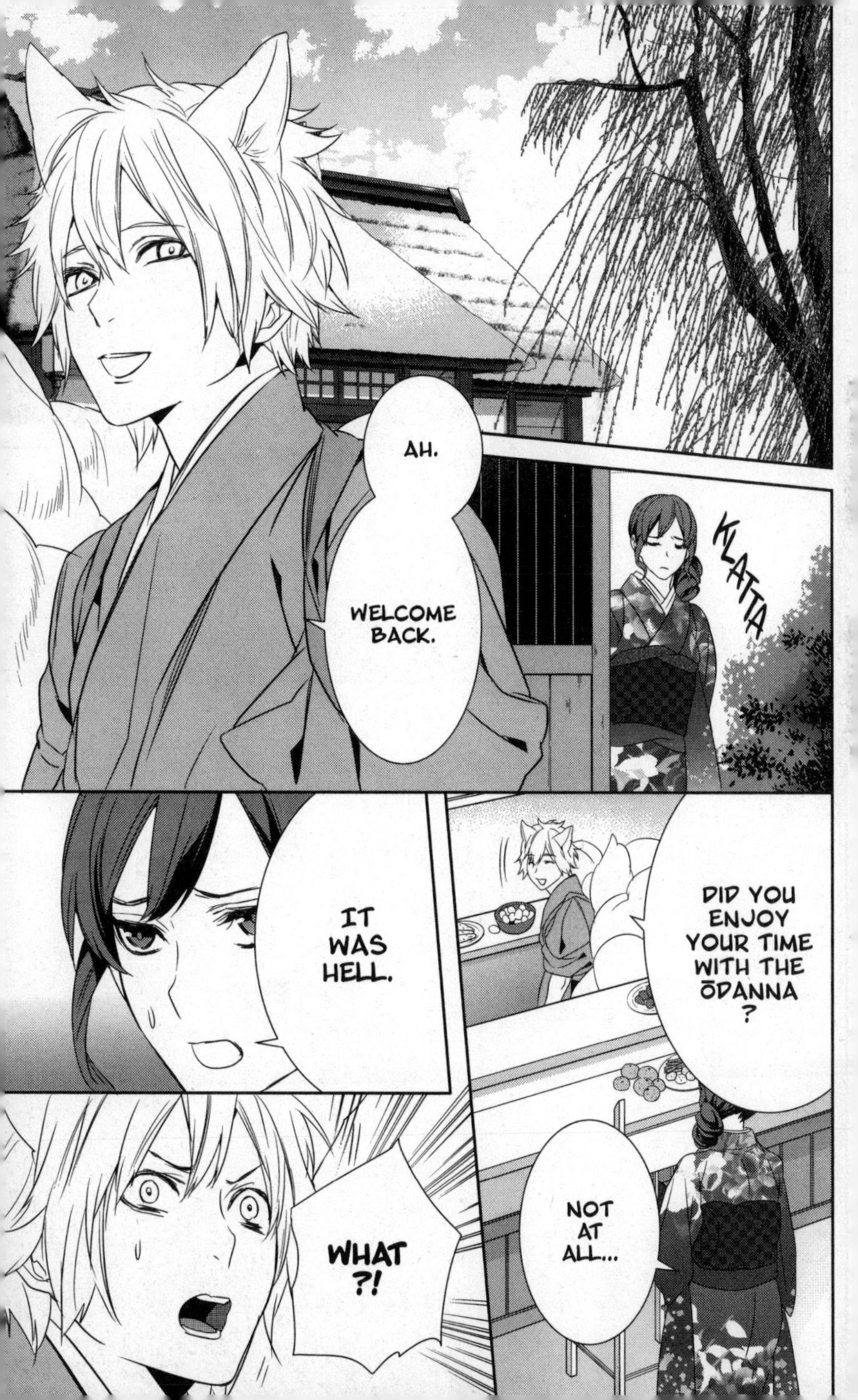
KLATTA
AH.
WELCOME BACK.
DID YOU ENJOY YOUR TIME WITH THE ŌDANNA?
NOT AT ALL...
IT WAS HELL.
WHAT?!

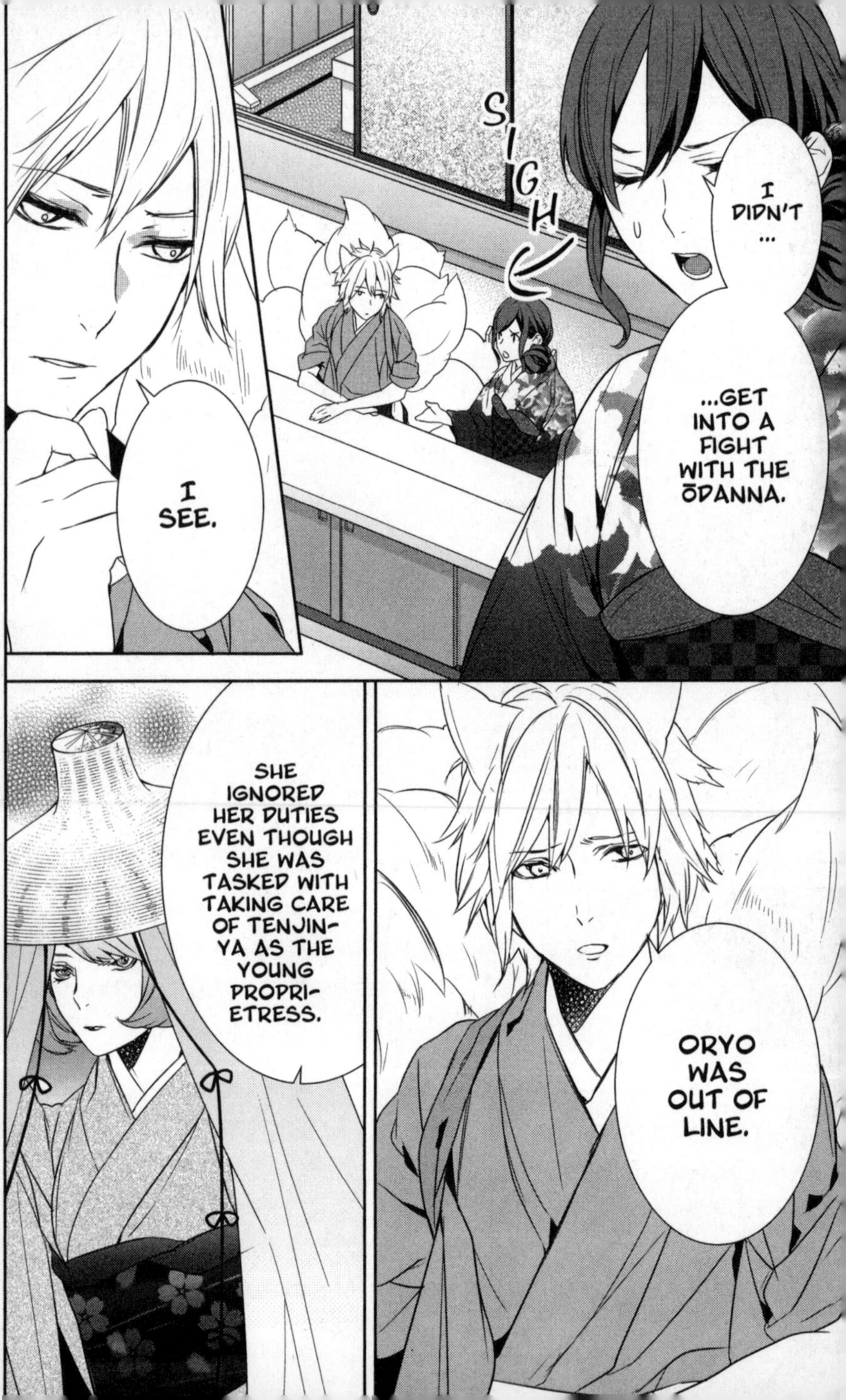
SIGH
I DIDN'T ...
...GET INTO A FIGHT WITH THE ŌDANNA.
I SEE.
ORYO WAS OUT OF LINE.
SHE IGNORED HER DUTIES EVEN THOUGH SHE WAS TASKED WITH TAKING CARE OF TENJIN-YA AS THE YOUNG PROPRIETRESS.

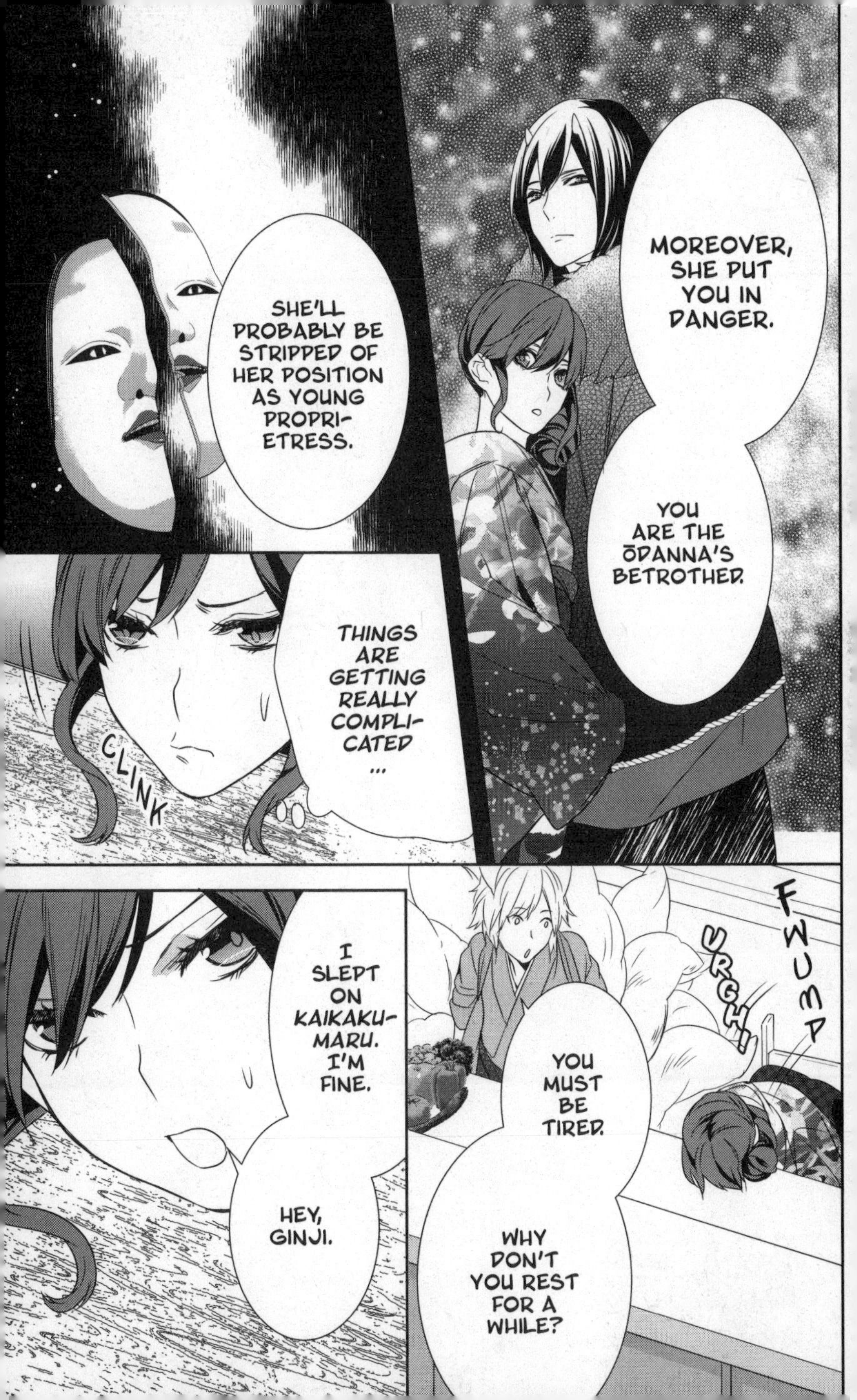
MOREOVER, SHE PUT YOU IN DANGER.
YOU ARE THE ŌDANNA'S BETROTHED.
SHE'LL PROBABLY BE STRIPPED OF HER POSITION AS YOUNG PROPRI-ETRESS.
THINGS ARE GETTING REALLY COMPLI-CATED ...
CLINK
FWUMP
URGH!
YOU MUST BE TIRED.
WHY DON'T YOU REST FOR A WHILE?
I SLEPT ON KAIKAKU-MARU. I'M FINE.
HEY, GINJI.

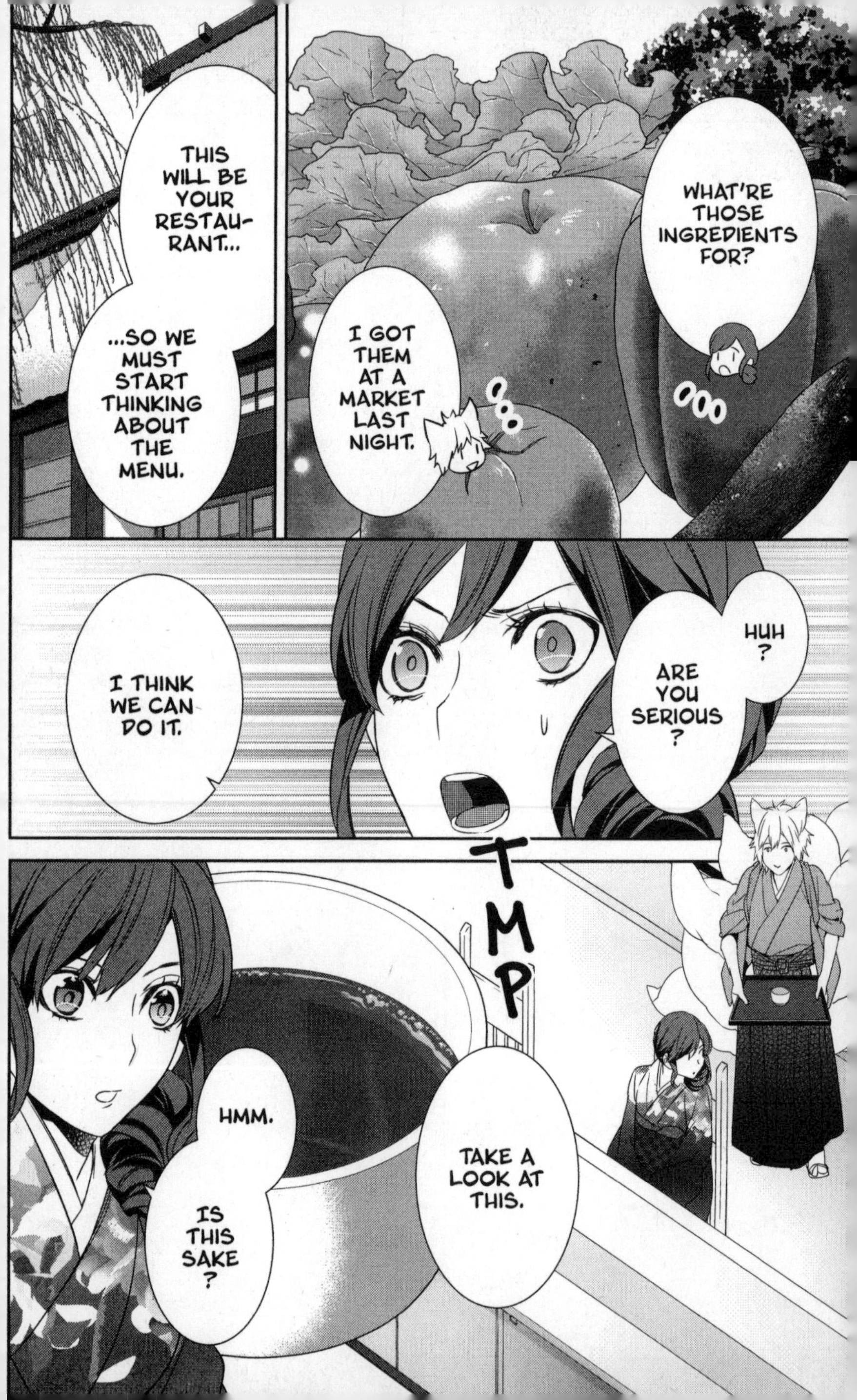
WHAT'RE THOSE INGREDIENTS FOR?
I GOT THEM AT A MARKET LAST NIGHT.
THIS WILL BE YOUR RESTAU-RANT...
...SO WE MUST START THINKING ABOUT THE MENU.
HUH?
ARE YOU SERIOUS?
I THINK WE CAN DO IT.
TMP
TAKE A LOOK AT THIS.
HMM.
IS THIS SAKE?

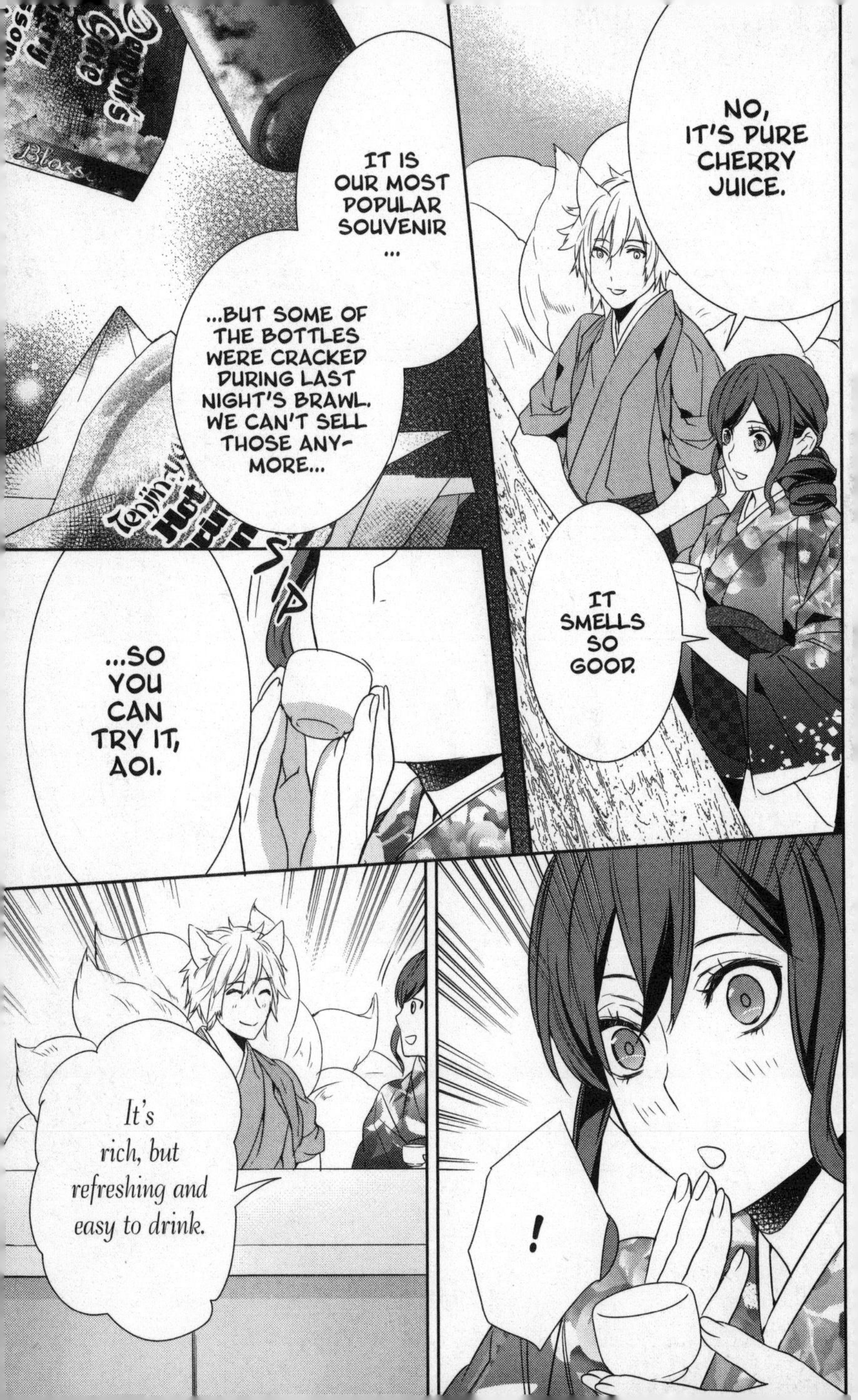
NO, IT'S PURE CHERRY JUICE.
IT SMELLS SO GOOD.
IT IS OUR MOST POPULAR SOUVENIR ...
...BUT SOME OF THE BOTTLES WERE CRACKED DURING LAST NIGHT'S BRAWL. WE CAN'T SELL THOSE ANY-MORE...
SIP
...SO YOU CAN TRY IT, AOI.
!
It's rich, but refreshing and easy to drink.

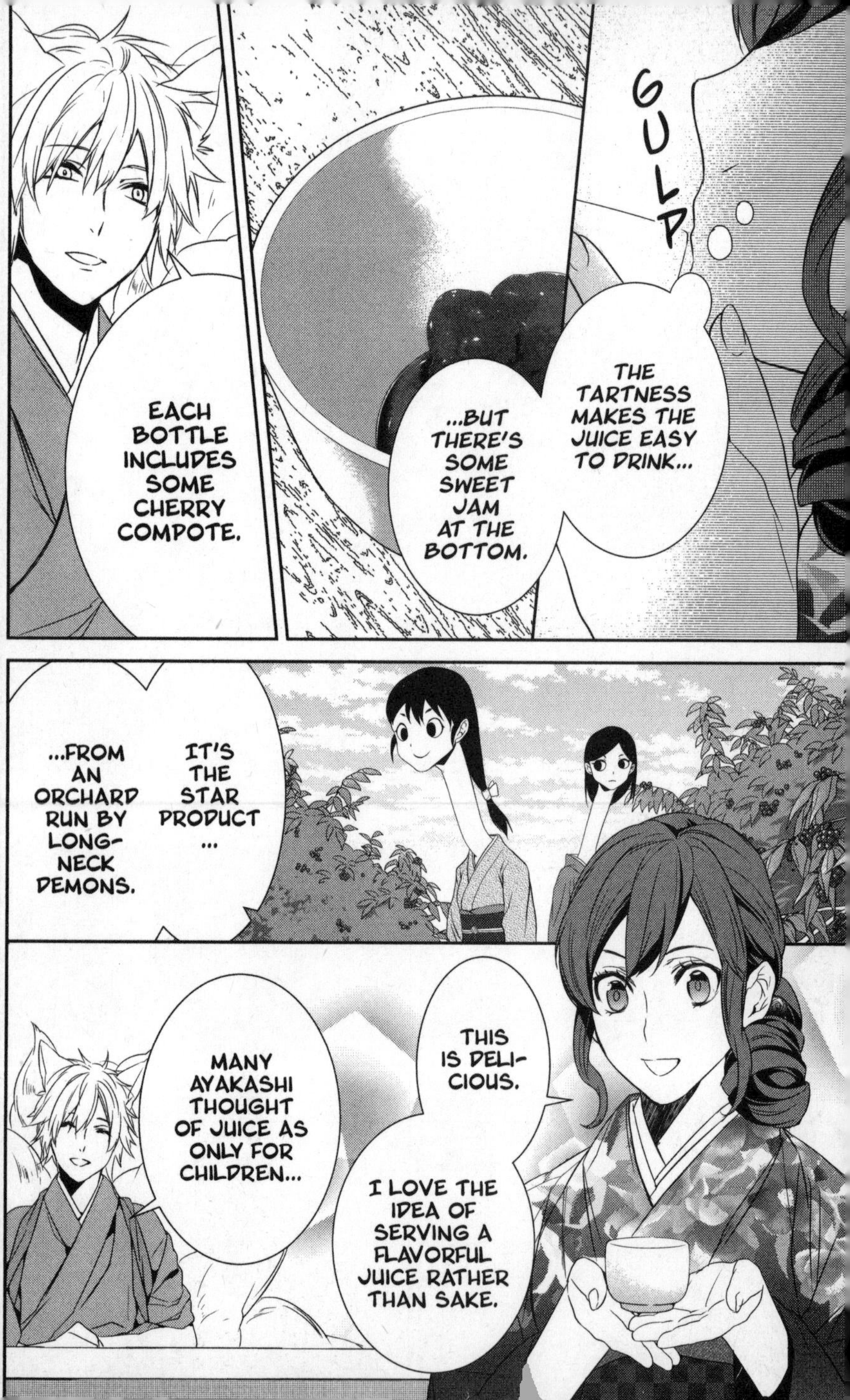
GULP
THE TARTNESS MAKES THE JUICE EASY TO DRINK...
...BUT THERE'S SOME SWEET JAM AT THE BOTTOM.
EACH BOTTLE INCLUDES SOME CHERRY COMPOTE.
IT'S THE STAR PRODUCT...
...FROM AN ORCHARD RUN BY LONG-NECK DEMONS.
THIS IS DELICIOUS.
I LOVE THE IDEA OF SERVING A FLAVORFUL JUICE RATHER THAN SAKE.
MANY AYAKASHI THOUGHT OF JUICE AS ONLY FOR CHILDREN...

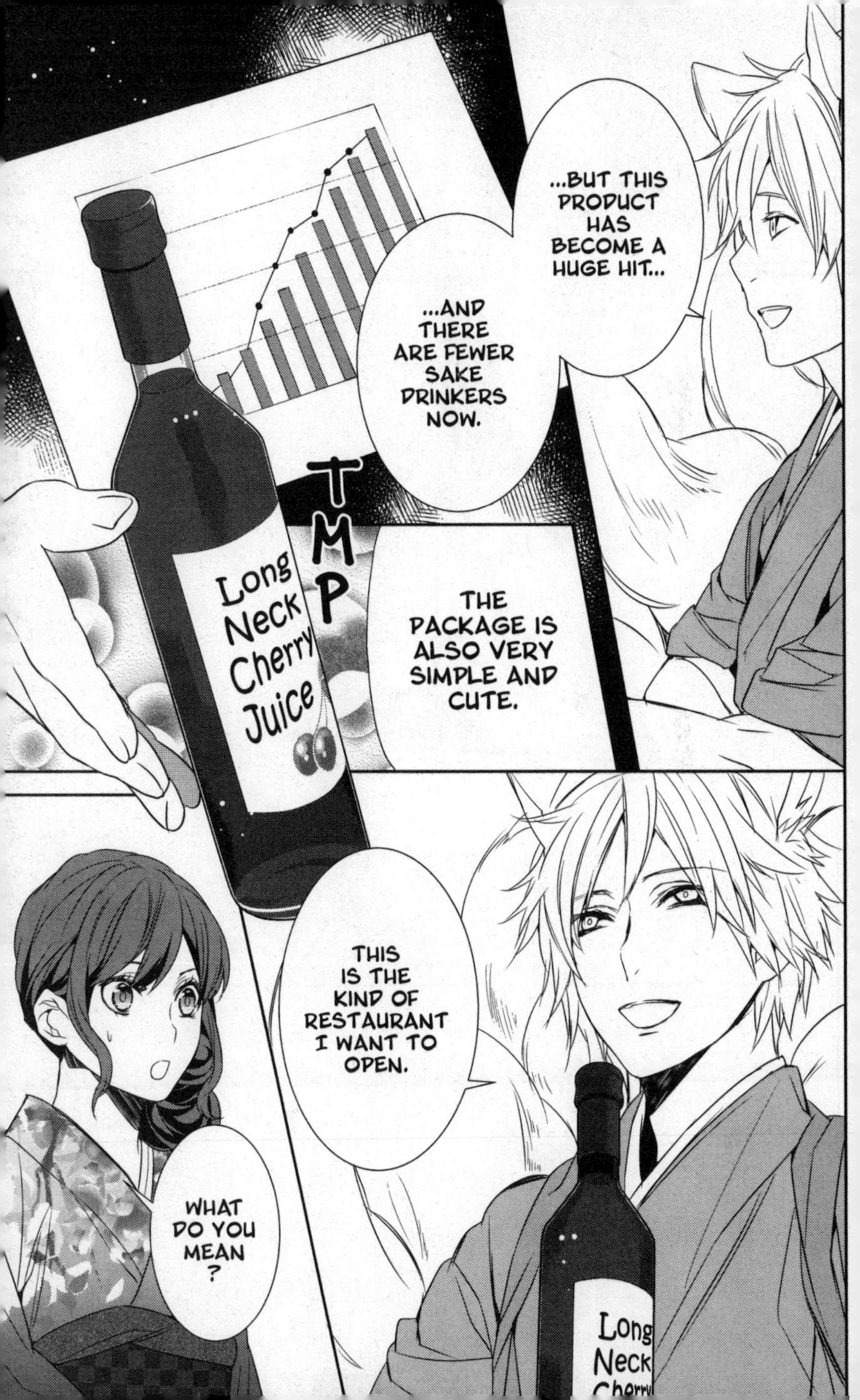
...BUT THIS PRODUCT HAS BECOME A HUGE HIT...
...AND THERE ARE FEWER SAKE DRINKERS NOW.
TMP
Long Neck Cherry Juice
THE PACKAGE IS ALSO VERY SIMPLE AND CUTE.
THIS IS THE KIND OF RESTAURANT I WANT TO OPEN.
Long Neck
WHAT DO YOU MEAN?

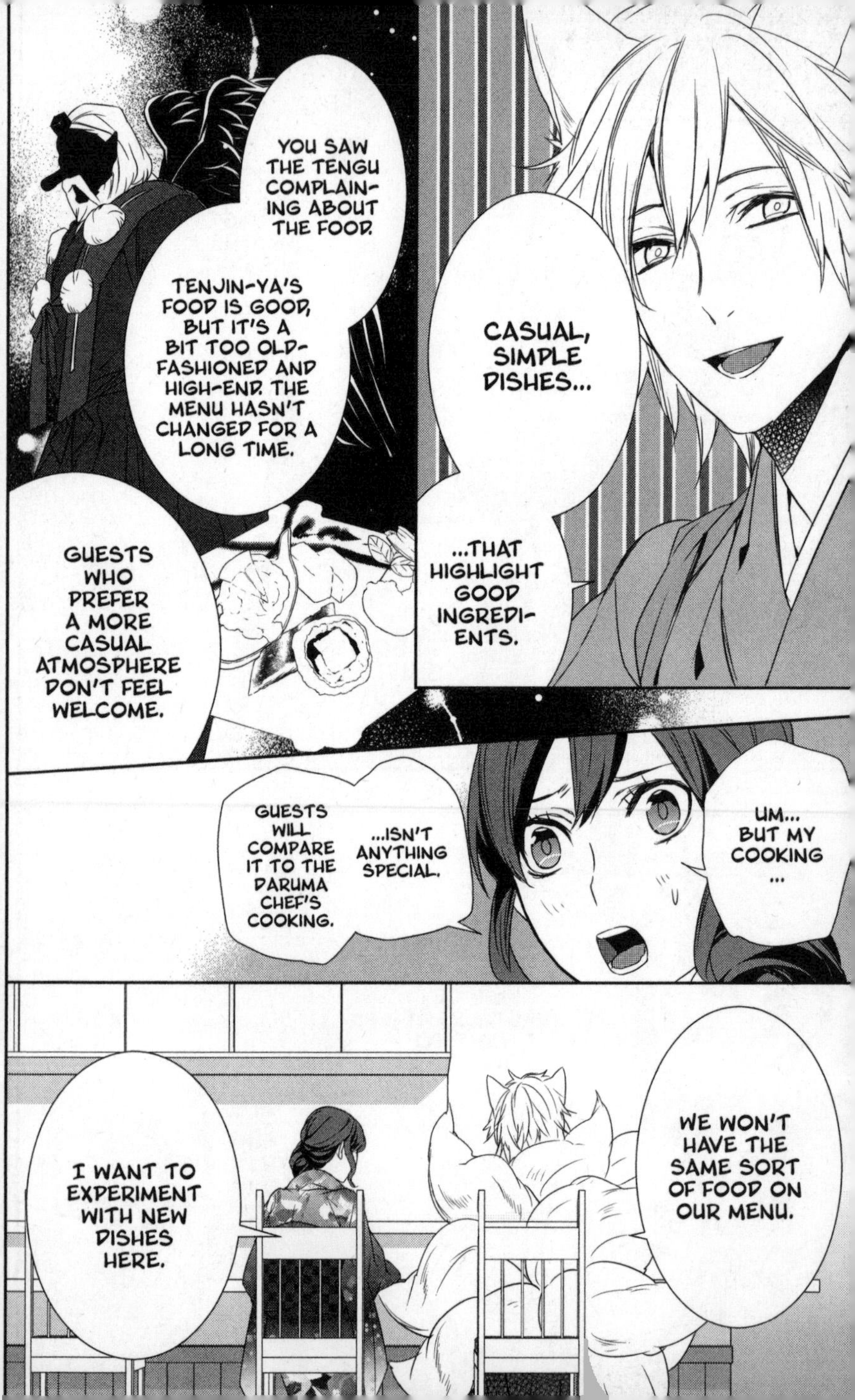
CASUAL, SIMPLE DISHES...
...THAT HIGHLIGHT GOOD INGREDIENTS.
YOU SAW THE TENGU COMPLAINING ABOUT THE FOOD.
TENJIN-YA'S FOOD IS GOOD, BUT IT'S A BIT TOO OLD-FASHIONED AND HIGH-END. THE MENU HASN'T CHANGED FOR A LONG TIME.
GUESTS WHO PREFER A MORE CASUAL ATMOSPHERE DON'T FEEL WELCOME.
UM... BUT MY COOKING ...
...ISN'T ANYTHING SPECIAL.
GUESTS WILL COMPARE IT TO THE DARUMA CHEF'S COOKING.
WE WON'T HAVE THE SAME SORT OF FOOD ON OUR MENU.
I WANT TO EXPERIMENT WITH NEW DISHES HERE.

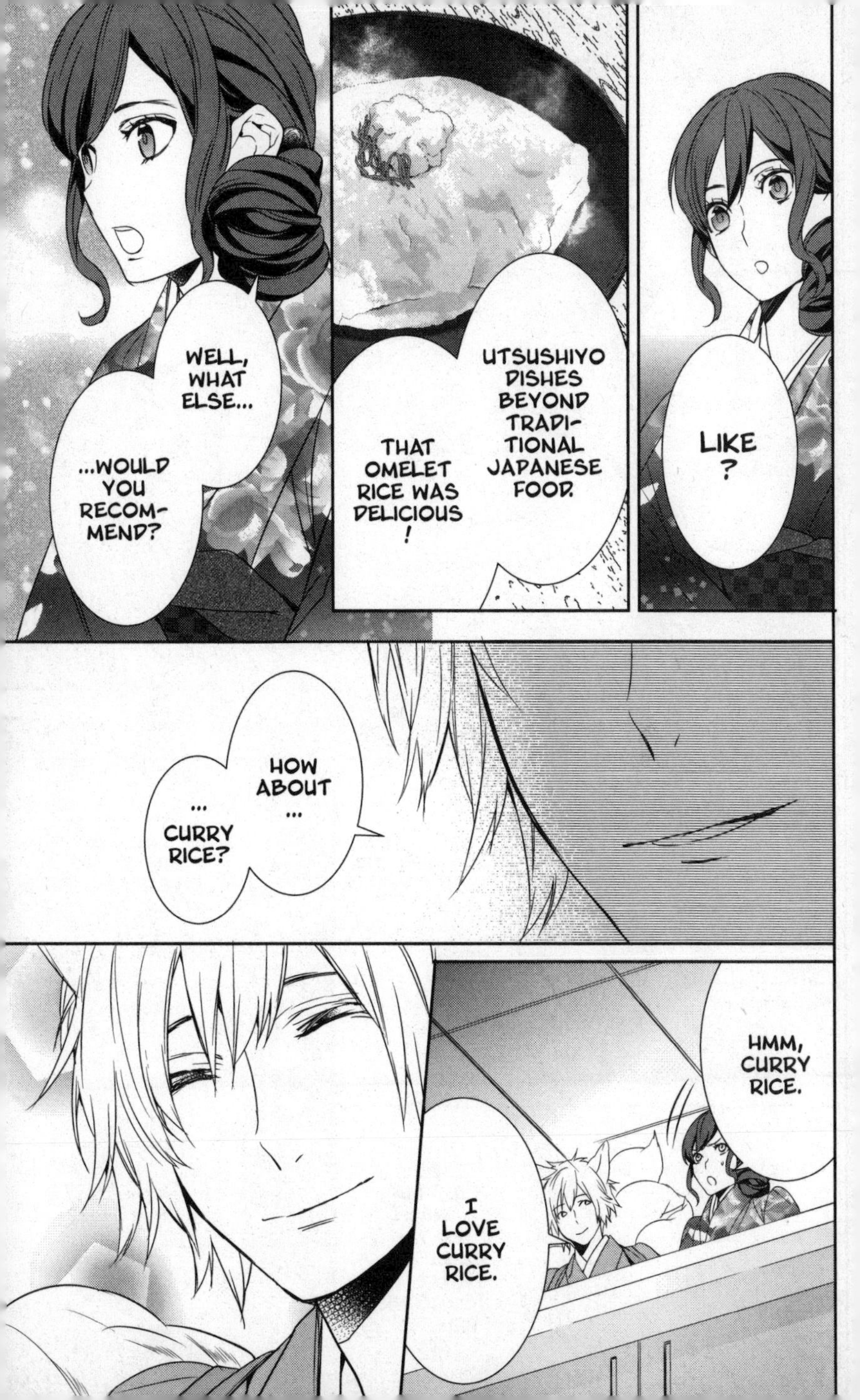
LIKE?
UTSUSHIYO DISHES BEYOND TRADITIONAL JAPANESE FOOD.
THAT OMELET RICE WAS DELICIOUS!
WELL, WHAT ELSE...
...WOULD YOU RECOMMEND?
HOW ABOUT...
...CURRY RICE?
HMM, CURRY RICE.
I LOVE CURRY RICE.

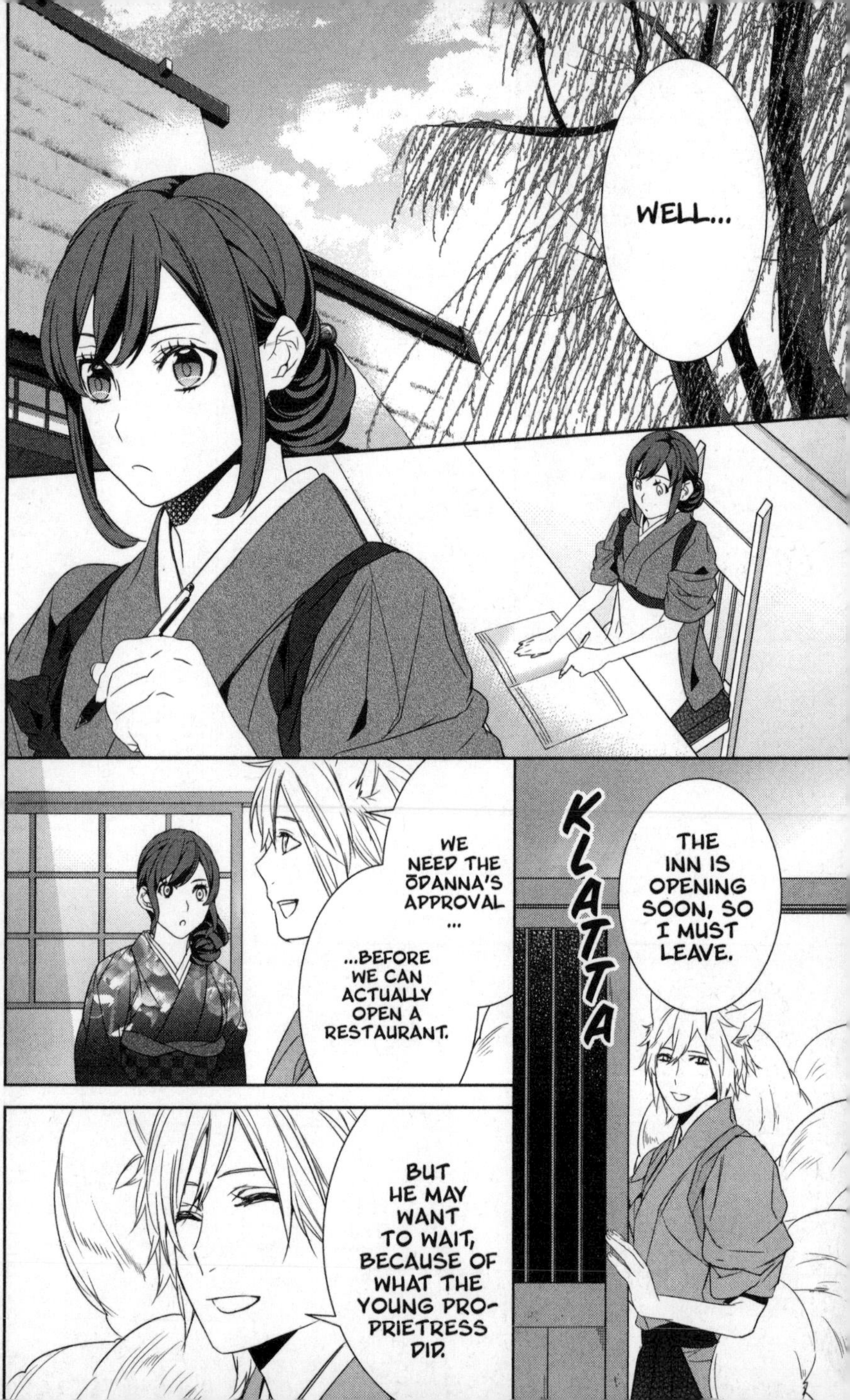
WELL...
KLATTA
THE INN IS OPENING SOON, SO I MUST LEAVE.
WE NEED THE ŌDANNA'S APPROVAL ...
...BEFORE WE CAN ACTUALLY OPEN A RESTAURANT.
BUT HE MAY WANT TO WAIT, BECAUSE OF WHAT THE YOUNG PRO-PRIETRESS DID.

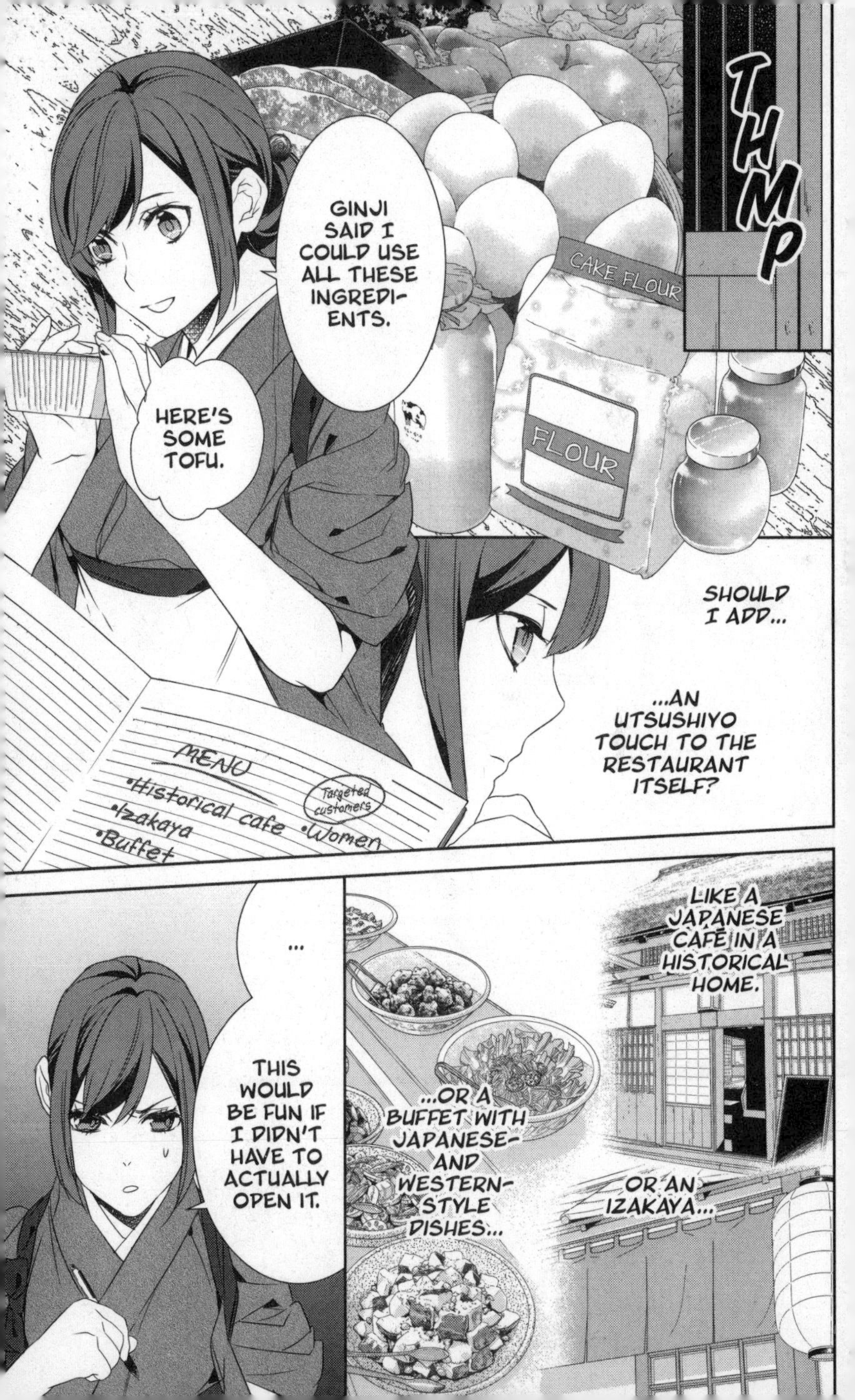
THUMP
GINJI SAID I COULD USE ALL THESE INGREDI-ENTS.
CAKE FLOUR
FLOUR
HERE'S SOME TOFU.
SHOULD I ADD...
...AN UTSUSHIYO TOUCH TO THE RESTAURANT ITSELF?
MENU
•Historical cafe
•Izakaya
•Buffet
Targeted customers
•Women
LIKE A JAPANESE CAFÉ IN A HISTORICAL HOME.
...OR A BUFFET WITH JAPANESE- AND WESTERN-STYLE DISHES...
OR AN IZAKAYA...
...
THIS WOULD BE FUN IF I DIDN'T HAVE TO ACTUALLY OPEN IT.

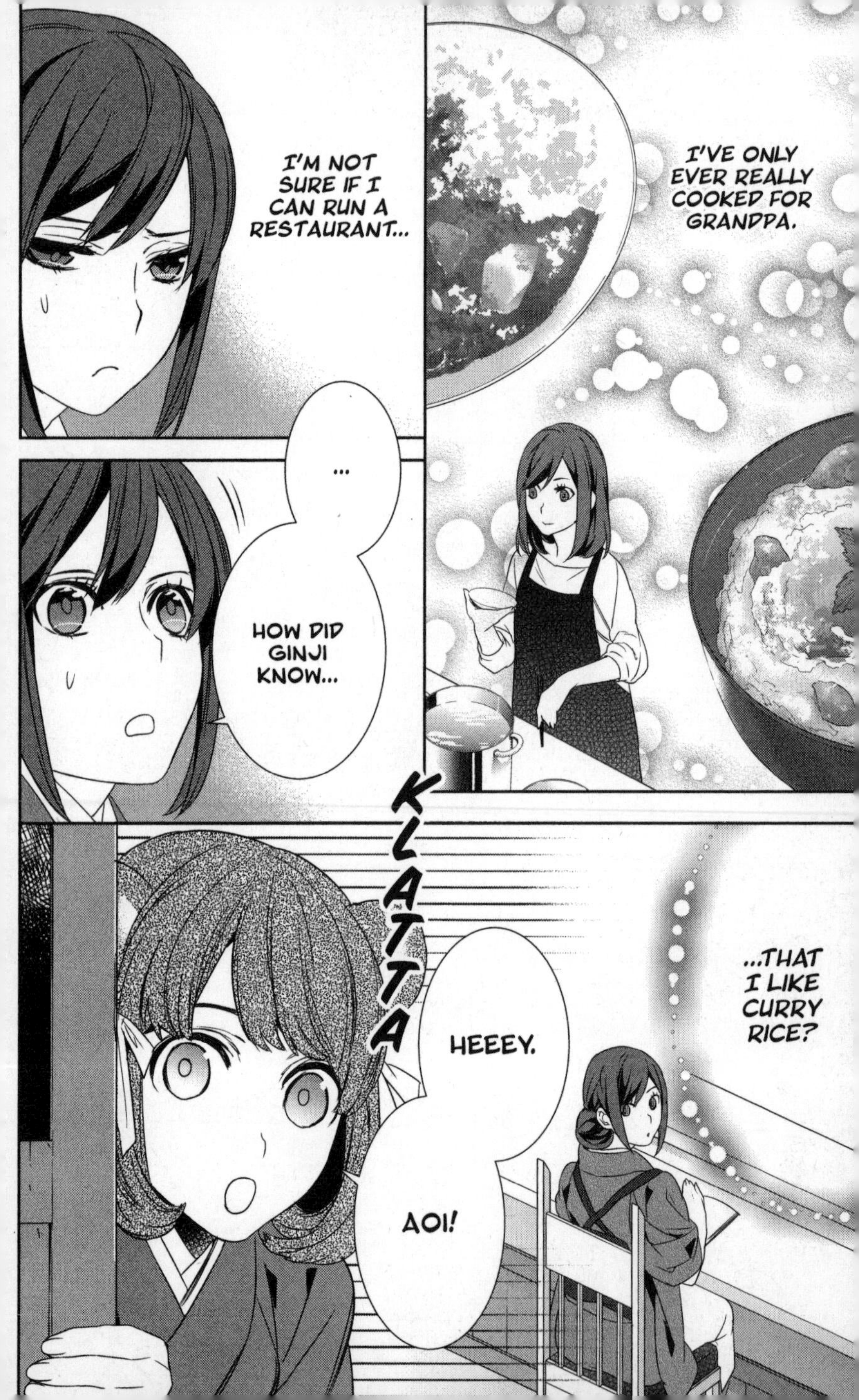
I'VE ONLY EVER REALLY COOKED FOR GRANDPA.
I'M NOT SURE IF I CAN RUN A RESTAURANT...
...
HOW DID GINJI KNOW...
...THAT I LIKE CURRY RICE?
KLATTA
HEEEY.
AOI!

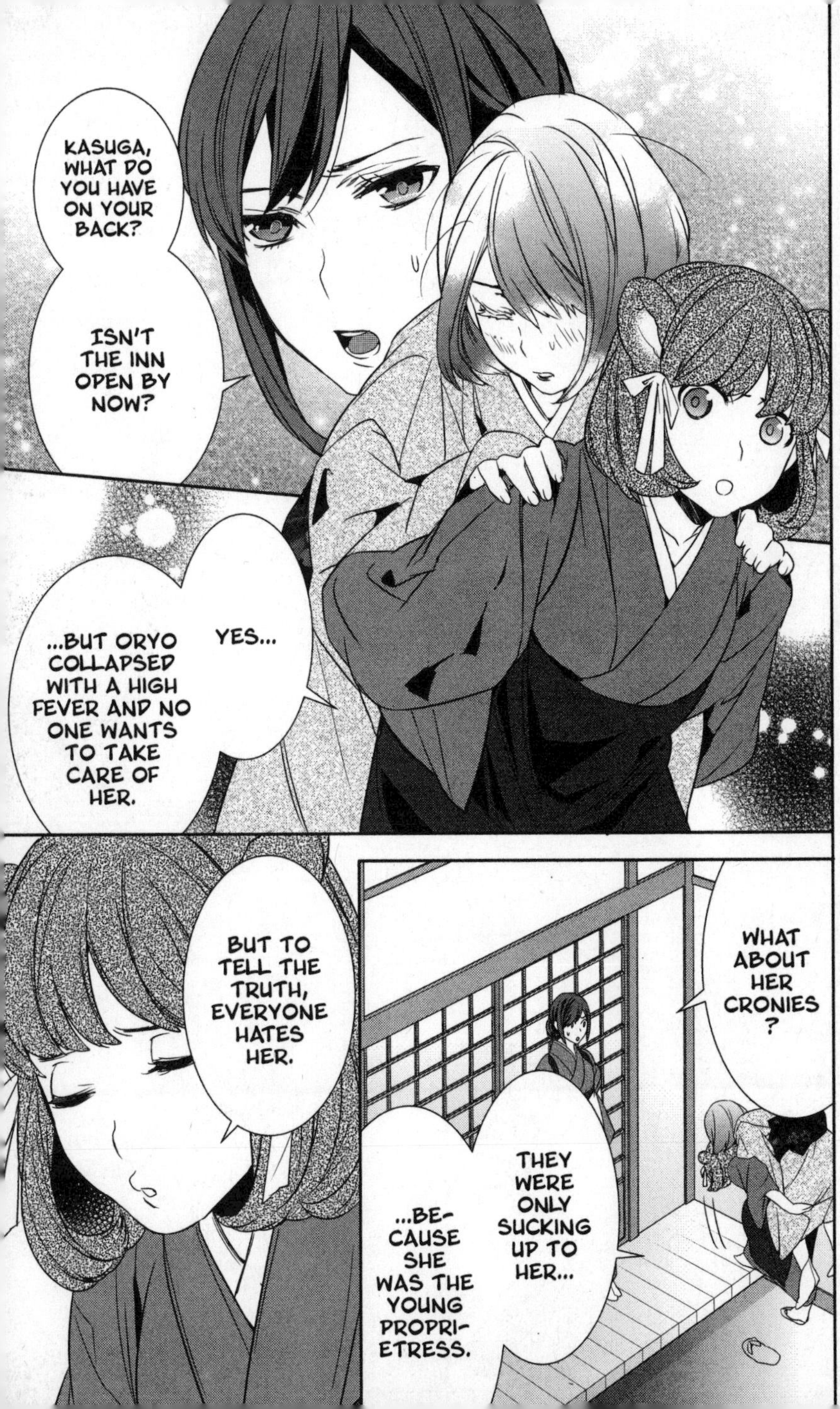
KASUGA, WHAT DO YOU HAVE ON YOUR BACK?
ISN'T THE INN OPEN BY NOW?
YES...
...BUT ORYO COLLAPSED WITH A HIGH FEVER AND NO ONE WANTS TO TAKE CARE OF HER.
WHAT ABOUT HER CRONIES?
THEY WERE ONLY SUCKING UP TO HER...
...BE-CAUSE SHE WAS THE YOUNG PROPRI-ETRESS.
BUT TO TELL THE TRUTH, EVERYONE HATES HER.

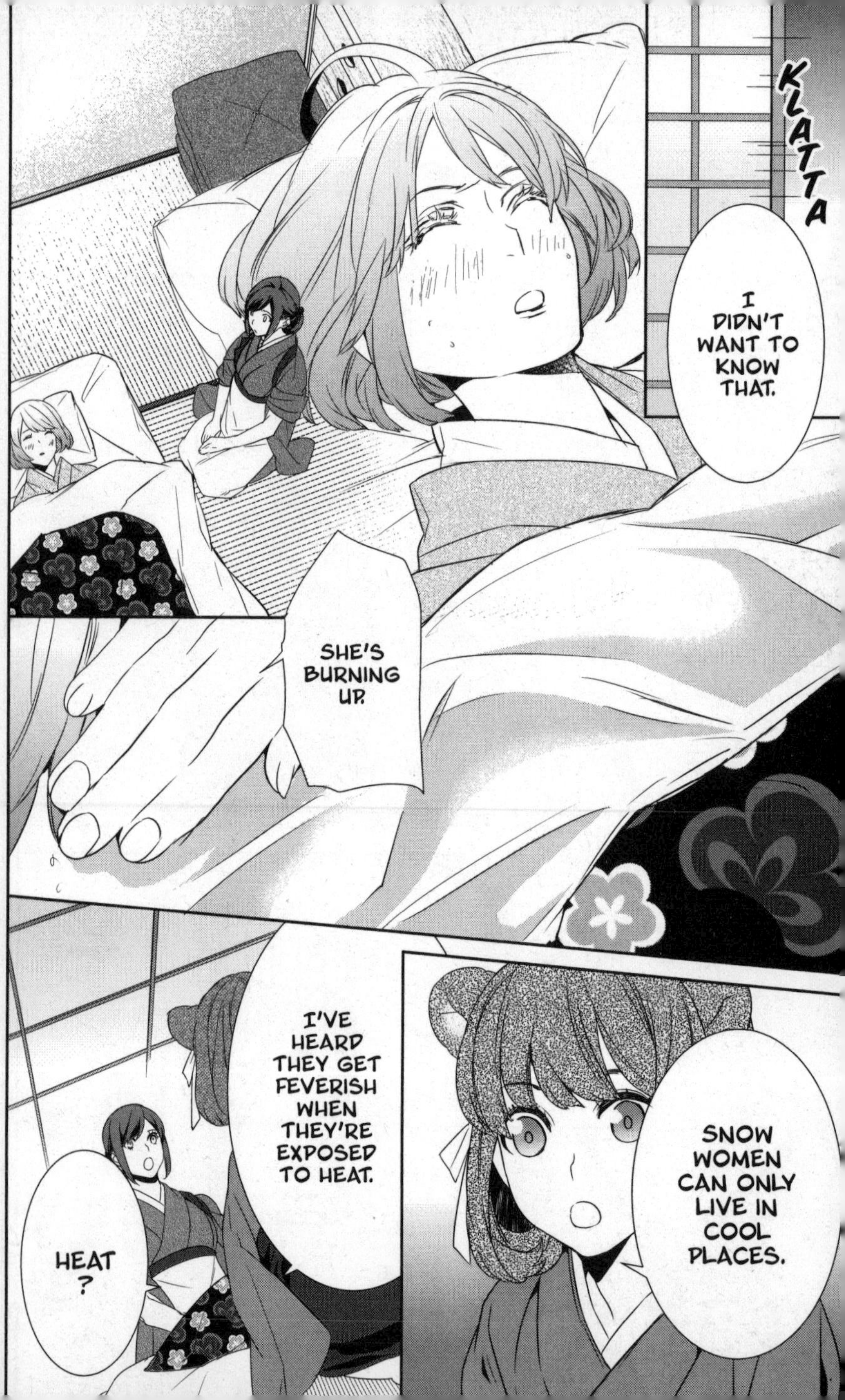
KLATTA
I DIDN'T WANT TO KNOW THAT.
SHE'S BURNING UP.
SNOW WOMEN CAN ONLY LIVE IN COOL PLACES.
I'VE HEARD THEY GET FEVERISH WHEN THEY'RE EXPOSED TO HEAT.
HEAT?

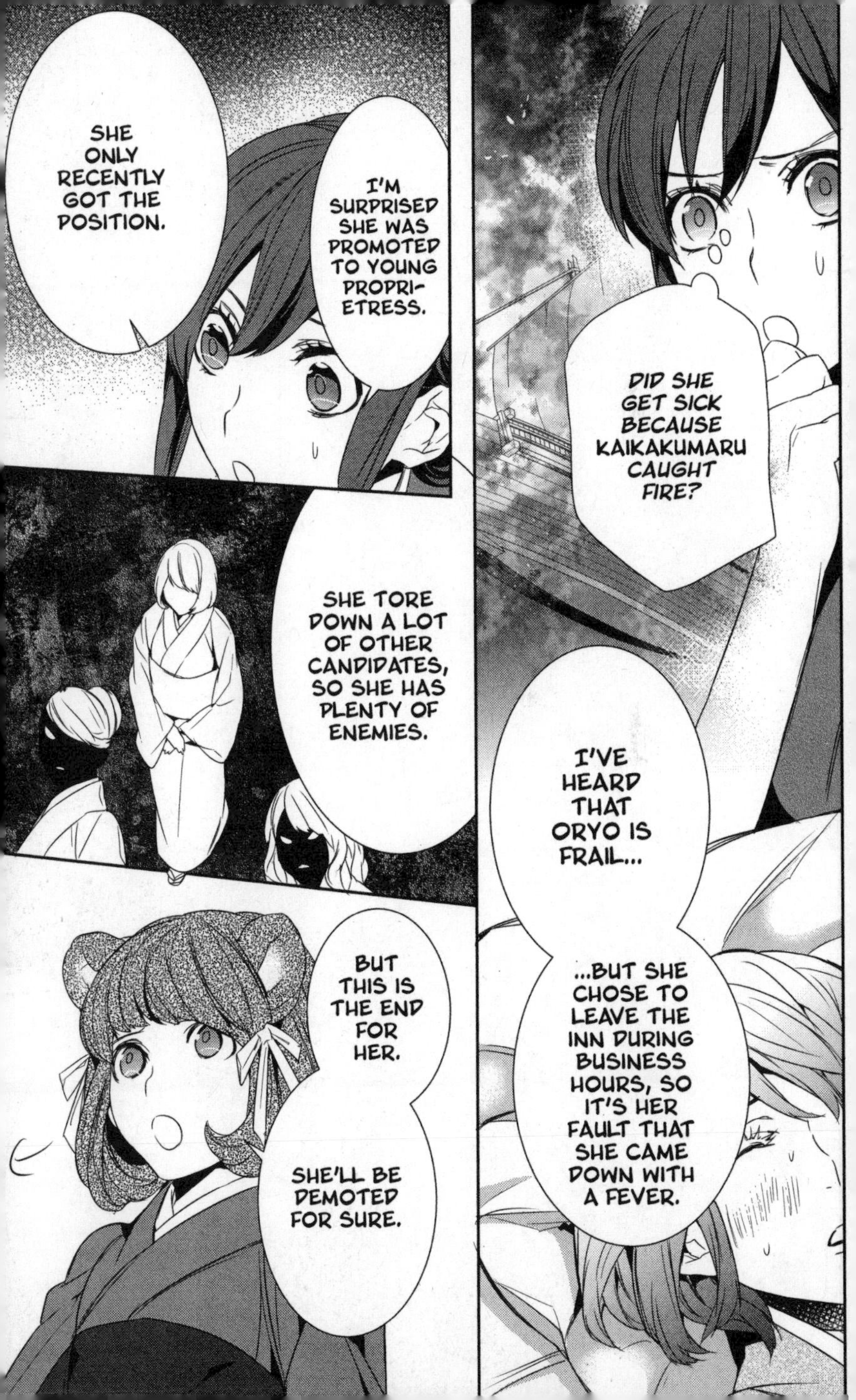
DID SHE GET SICK BECAUSE KAIKAKUMARU CAUGHT FIRE?
I'VE HEARD THAT ORYO IS FRAIL...
...BUT SHE CHOSE TO LEAVE THE INN DURING BUSINESS HOURS, SO IT'S HER FAULT THAT SHE CAME DOWN WITH A FEVER.
I'M SURPRISED SHE WAS PROMOTED TO YOUNG PROPRI-ETRESS.
SHE ONLY RECENTLY GOT THE POSITION.
SHE TORE DOWN A LOT OF OTHER CANDIDATES, SO SHE HAS PLENTY OF ENEMIES.
BUT THIS IS THE END FOR HER.
SHE'LL BE DEMOTED FOR SURE.

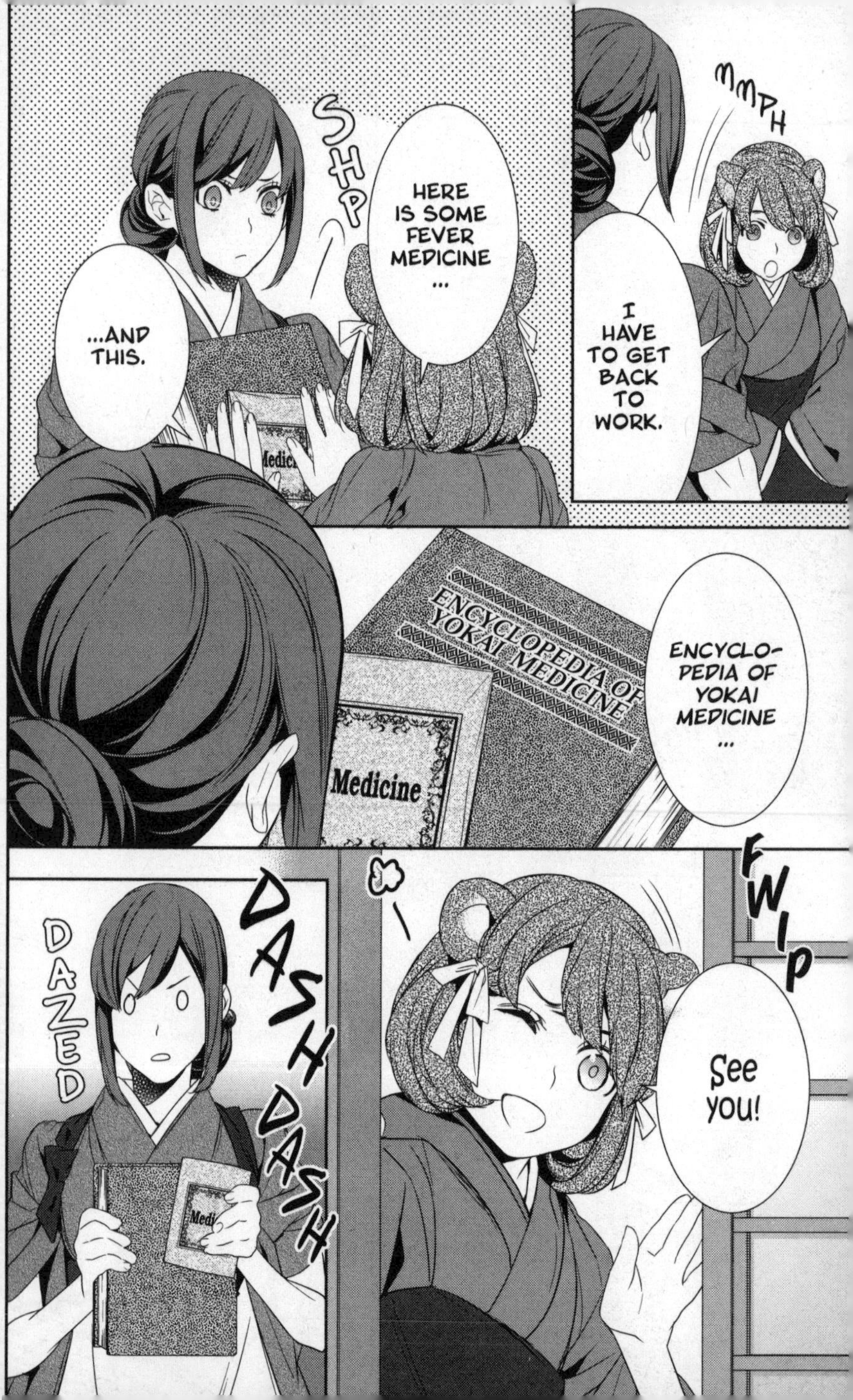
MMPH
I HAVE TO GET BACK TO WORK.
SHP
HERE IS SOME FEVER MEDICINE...
...AND THIS.
Medici
ENCYCLOPEDIA OF YOKAI MEDICINE
ENCYCLO-PEDIA OF YOKAI MEDICINE...
Medicine
FWIP
See you!
DASH DASH
DAZED
Medi

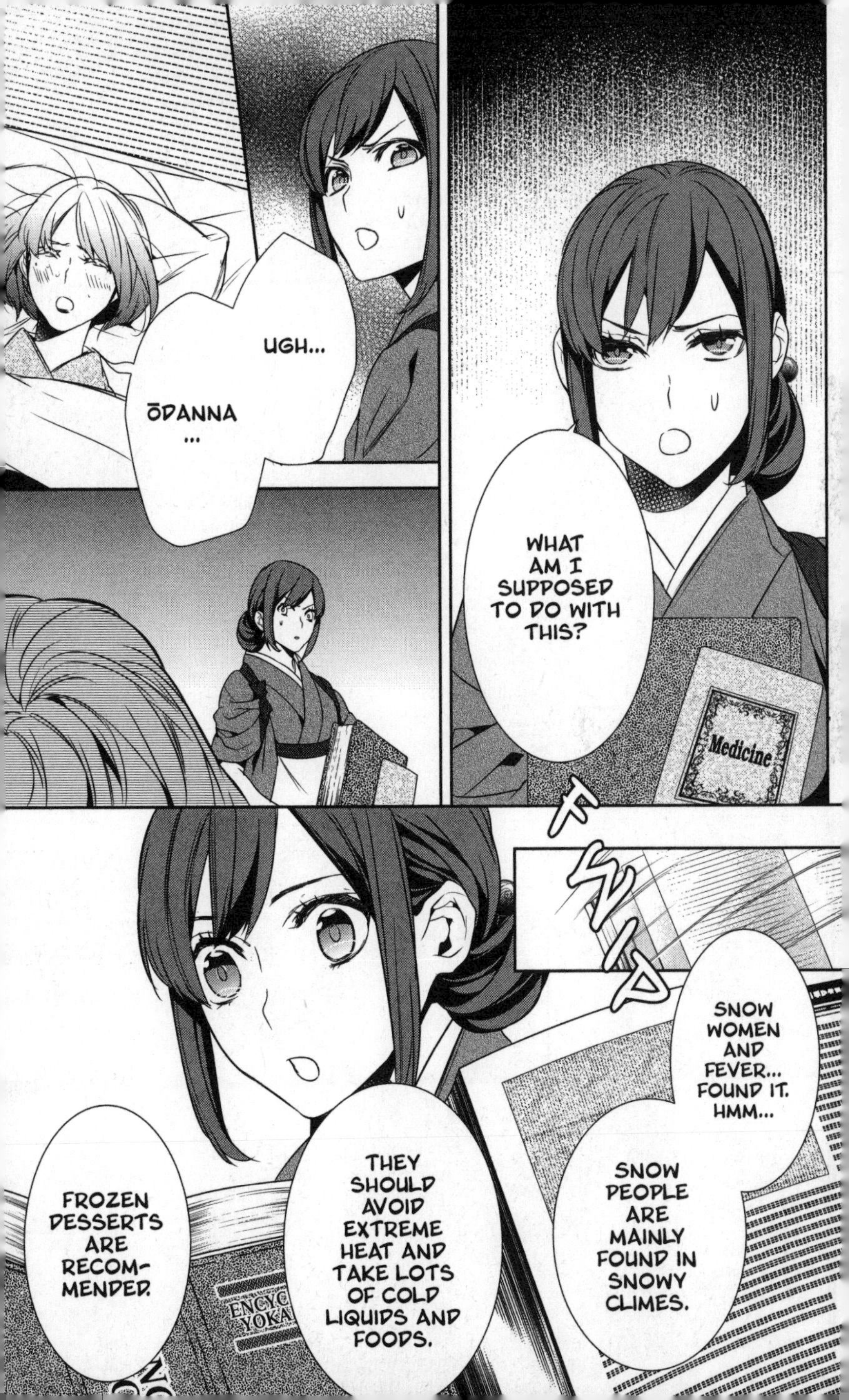
WHAT AM I SUPPOSED TO DO WITH THIS?
Medicine
UGH...
ŌDANNA...
FWIP
SNOW WOMEN AND FEVER... FOUND IT. HMM...
SNOW PEOPLE ARE MAINLY FOUND IN SNOWY CLIMES.
THEY SHOULD AVOID EXTREME HEAT AND TAKE LOTS OF COLD LIQUIDS AND FOODS.
FROZEN DESSERTS ARE RECOMMENDED.

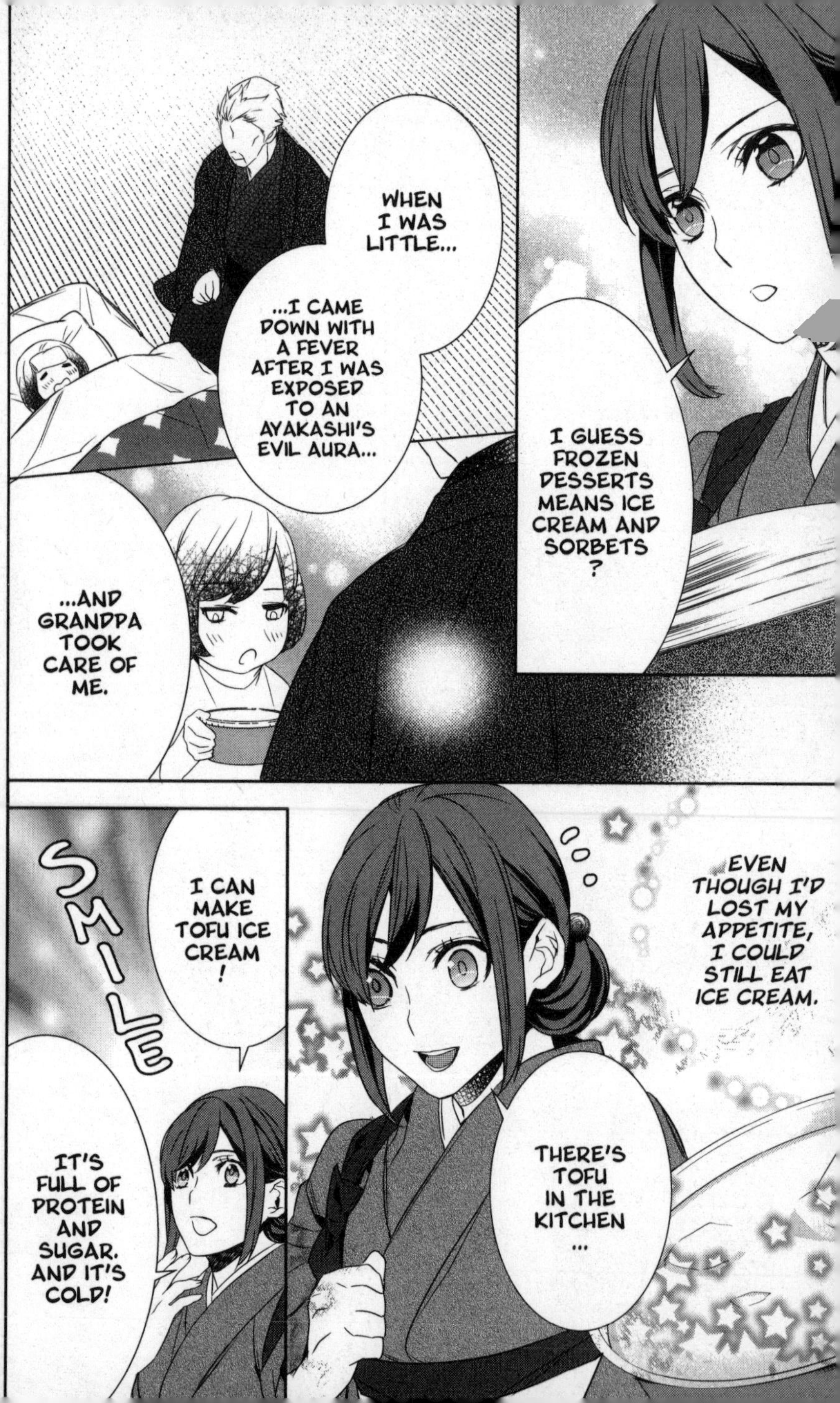
I GUESS FROZEN DESSERTS MEANS ICE CREAM AND SORBETS?
WHEN I WAS LITTLE...
...I CAME DOWN WITH A FEVER AFTER I WAS EXPOSED TO AN AYAKASHI'S EVIL AURA...
...AND GRANDPA TOOK CARE OF ME.
EVEN THOUGH I'D LOST MY APPETITE, I COULD STILL EAT ICE CREAM.
THERE'S TOFU IN THE KITCHEN...
SMILE
I CAN MAKE TOFU ICE CREAM!
IT'S FULL OF PROTEIN AND SUGAR. AND IT'S COLD!

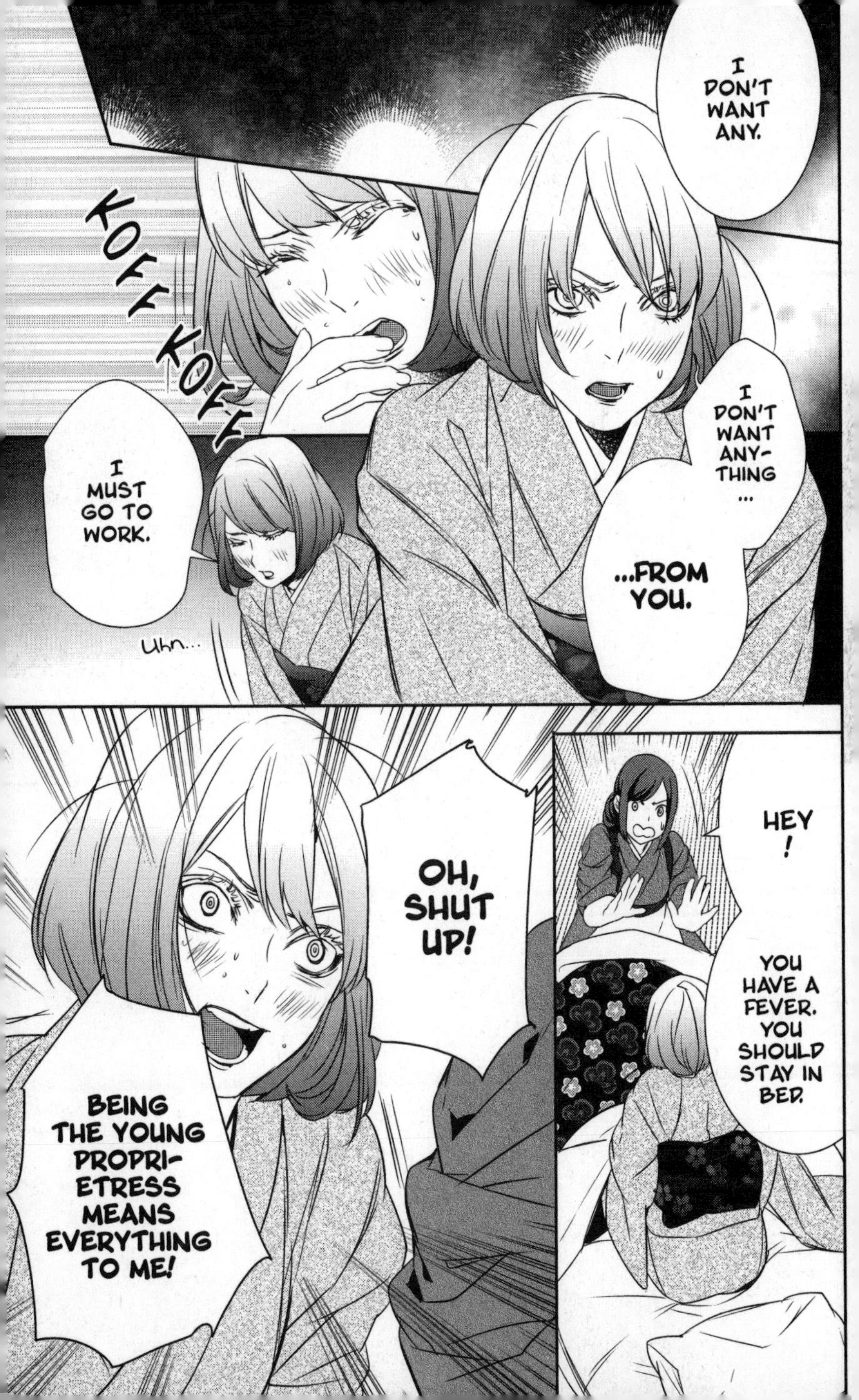
I DON'T WANT ANY.
KOFF KOFF
I DON'T WANT ANY-THING...
...FROM YOU.
I MUST GO TO WORK.
Uhn...
HEY!
YOU HAVE A FEVER. YOU SHOULD STAY IN BED.
OH, SHUT UP!
BEING THE YOUNG PROPRI-ETRESS MEANS EVERYTHING TO ME!

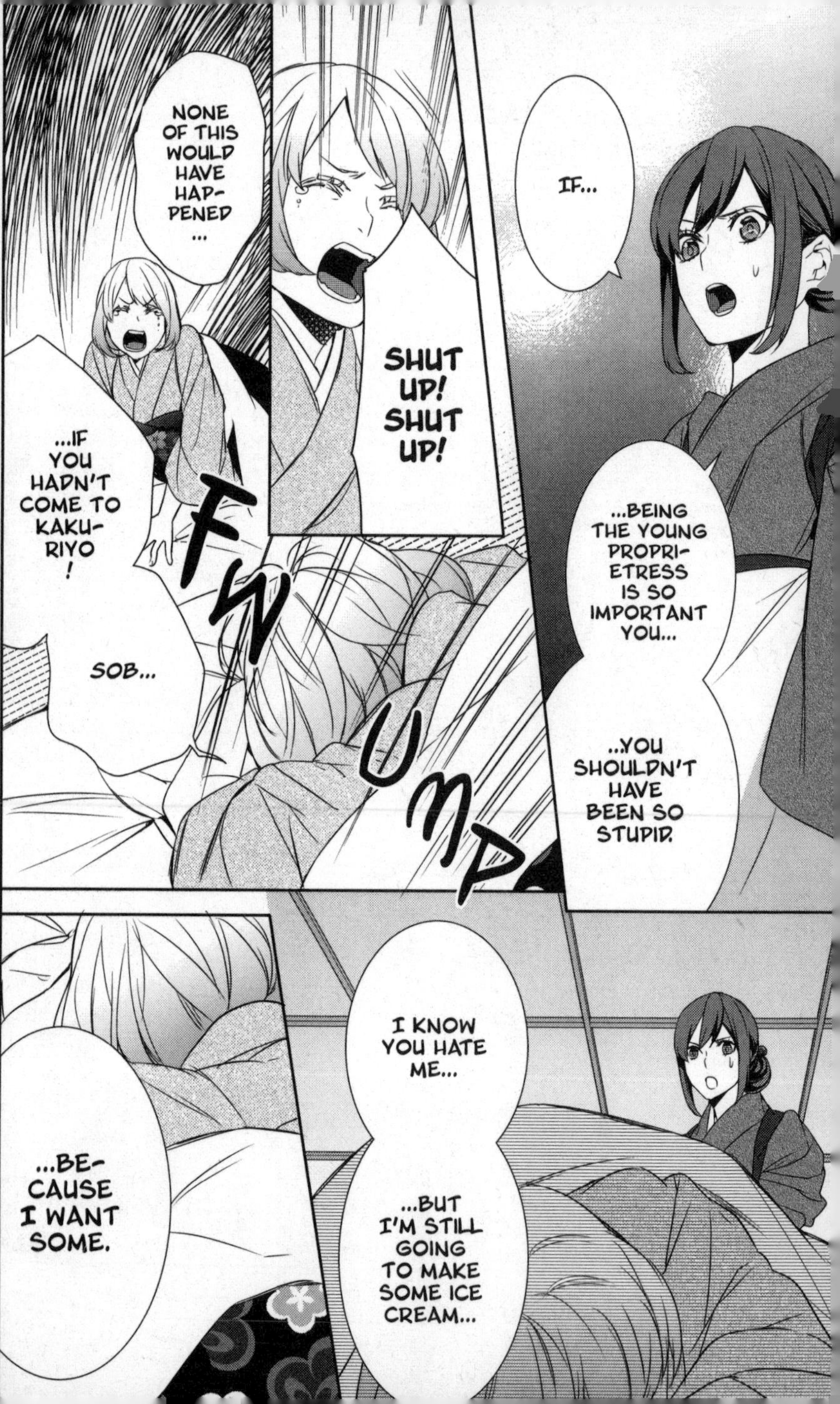
IF...
...BEING THE YOUNG PROPRI-ETRESS IS SO IMPORTANT YOU...
...YOU SHOULDN'T HAVE BEEN SO STUPID.
SHUT UP! SHUT UP!
NONE OF THIS WOULD HAVE HAP-PENED ...
...IF YOU HADN'T COME TO KAKU-RIYO !
SOB...
FWUMP
I KNOW YOU HATE ME...
...BUT I'M STILL GOING TO MAKE SOME ICE CREAM...
...BE-CAUSE I WANT SOME.

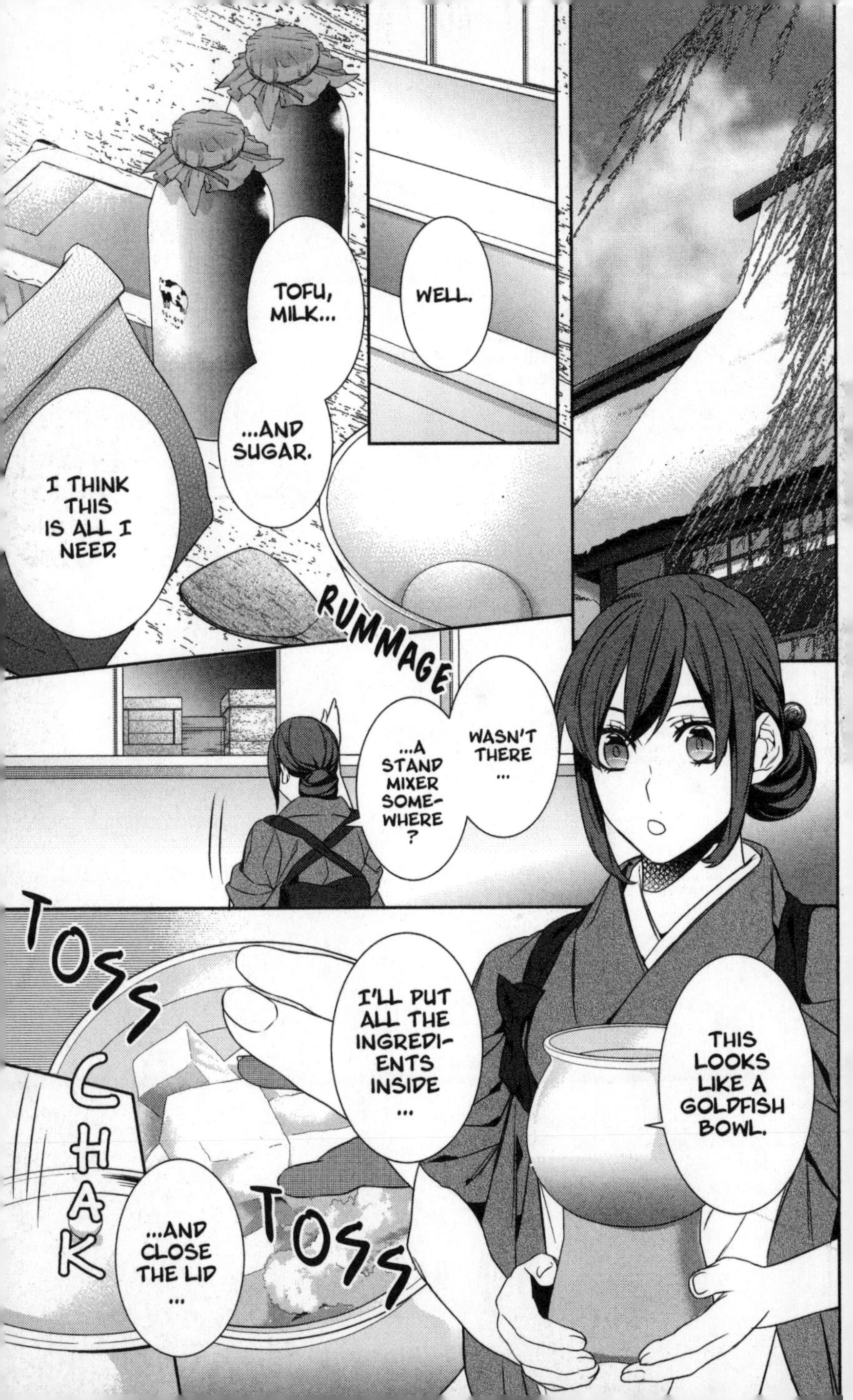
WELL.
TOFU, MILK...
...AND SUGAR.
I THINK THIS IS ALL I NEED.
RUMMAGE
WASN'T THERE ...
...A STAND MIXER SOME-WHERE ?
THIS LOOKS LIKE A GOLDFISH BOWL.
I'LL PUT ALL THE INGREDI-ENTS INSIDE ...
TOSS
TOSS
CHAK
...AND CLOSE THE LID ...

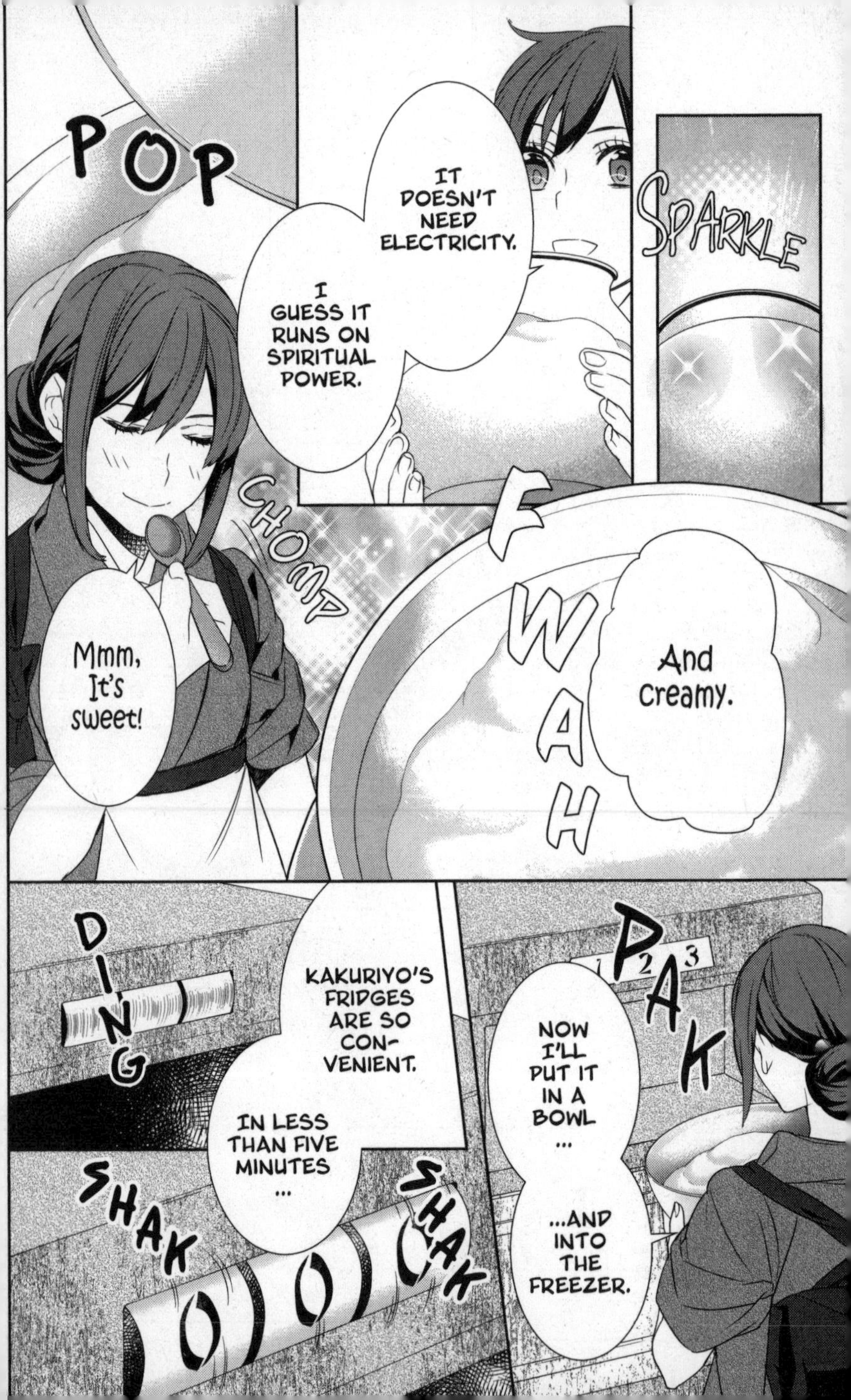
SPARKLE
IT DOESN'T NEED ELECTRICITY.
I GUESS IT RUNS ON SPIRITUAL POWER.
FWAH
And creamy.
POP
CHOMP
Mmm, It's sweet!
PAK
NOW I'LL PUT IT IN A BOWL ...
...AND INTO THE FREEZER.
KAKURIYO'S FRIDGES ARE SO CON-VENIENT.
IN LESS THAN FIVE MINUTES ...
DING
SHAK
SHAK

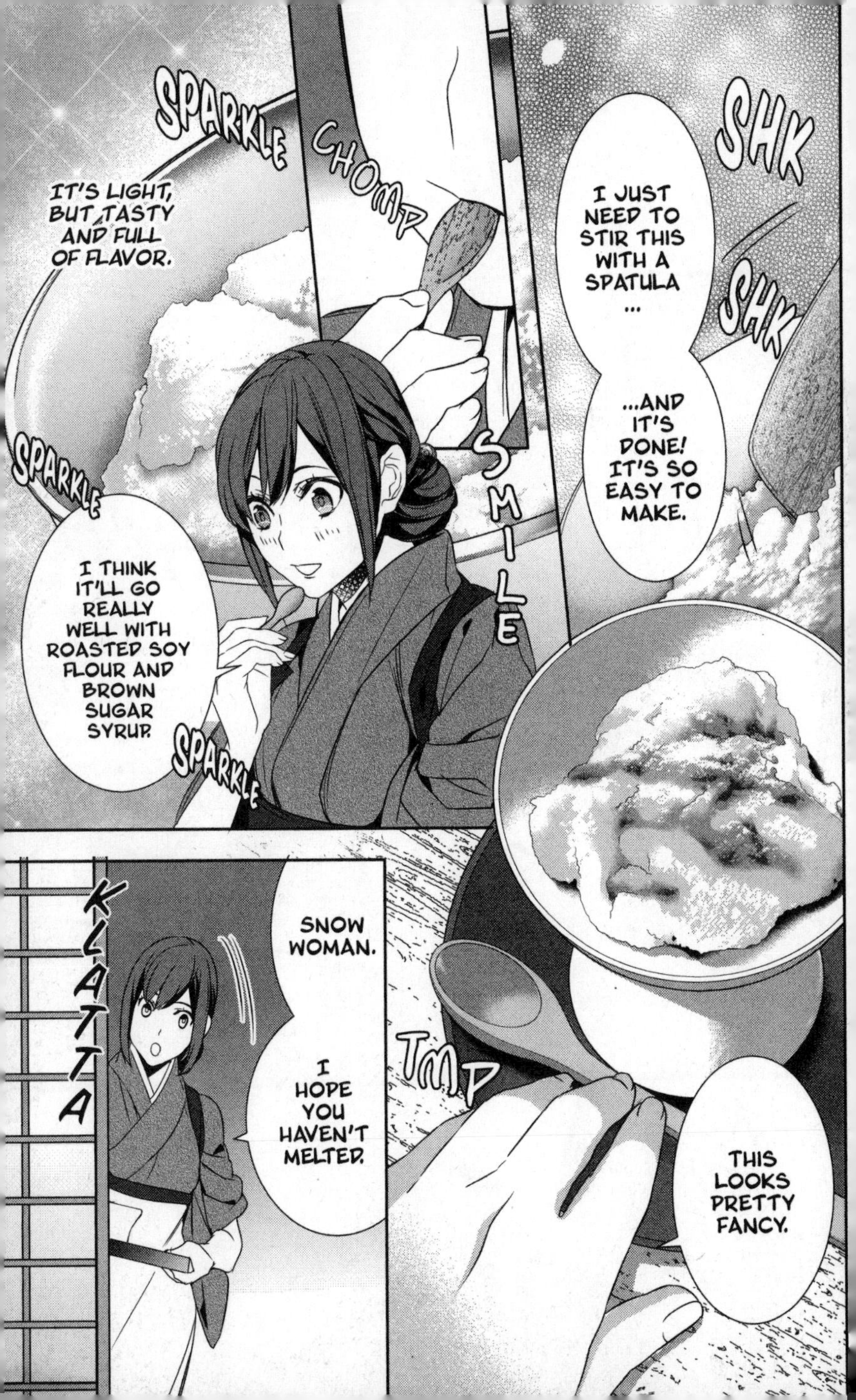
SHK
SHK
I JUST NEED TO STIR THIS WITH A SPATULA...
...AND IT'S DONE! IT'S SO EASY TO MAKE.
CHOMP
SPARKLE
IT'S LIGHT, BUT TASTY AND FULL OF FLAVOR.
SMILE
SPARKLE
I THINK IT'LL GO REALLY WELL WITH ROASTED SOY FLOUR AND BROWN SUGAR SYRUP.
SPARKLE
TMP
THIS LOOKS PRETTY FANCY.
KLATTA
SNOW WOMAN.
I HOPE YOU HAVEN'T MELTED.

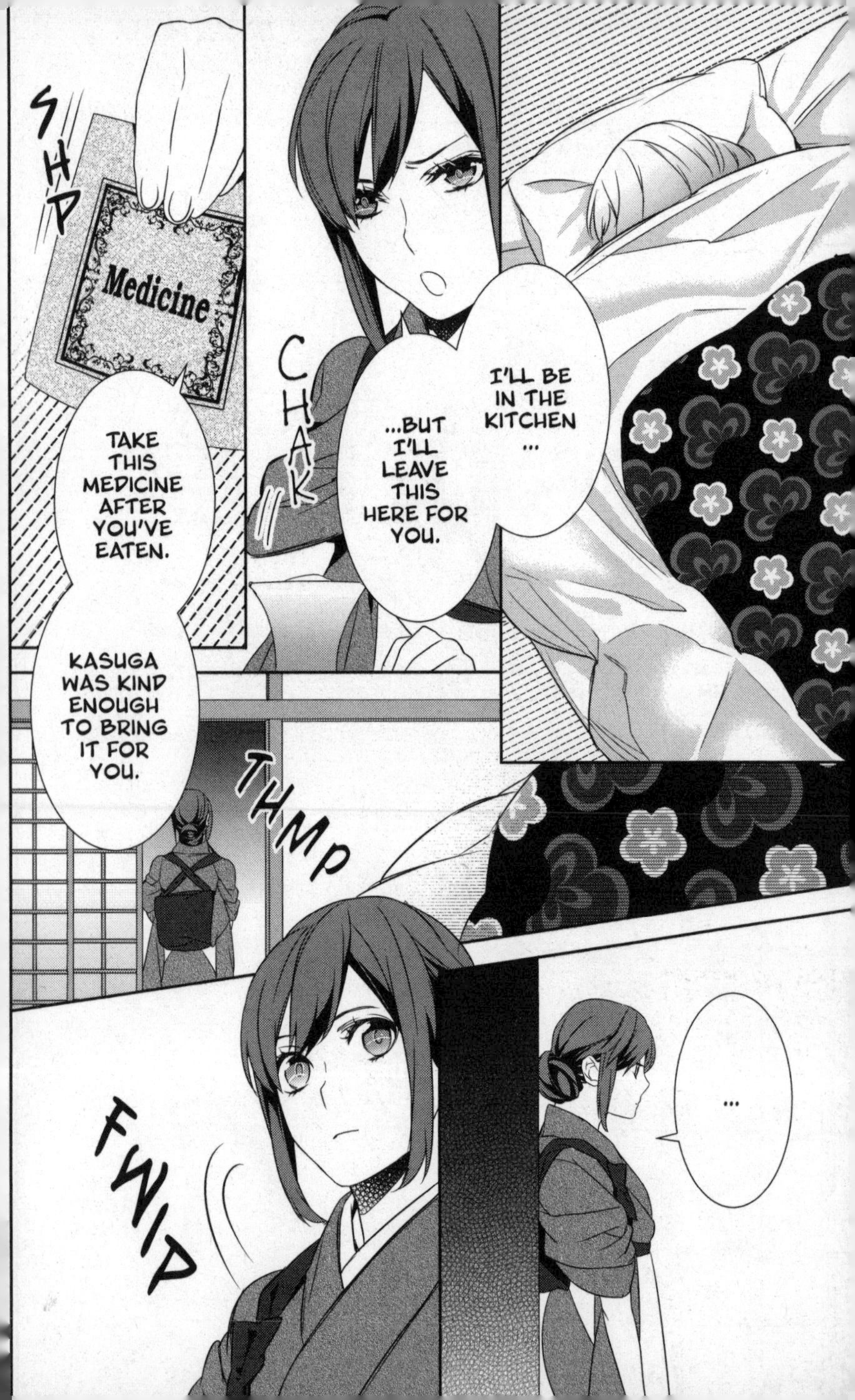
I'LL BE IN THE KITCHEN ...
...BUT I'LL LEAVE THIS HERE FOR YOU.
CHAK
SHP
Medicine
TAKE THIS MEDICINE AFTER YOU'VE EATEN.
KASUGA WAS KIND ENOUGH TO BRING IT FOR YOU.
THMP
...
FWIP

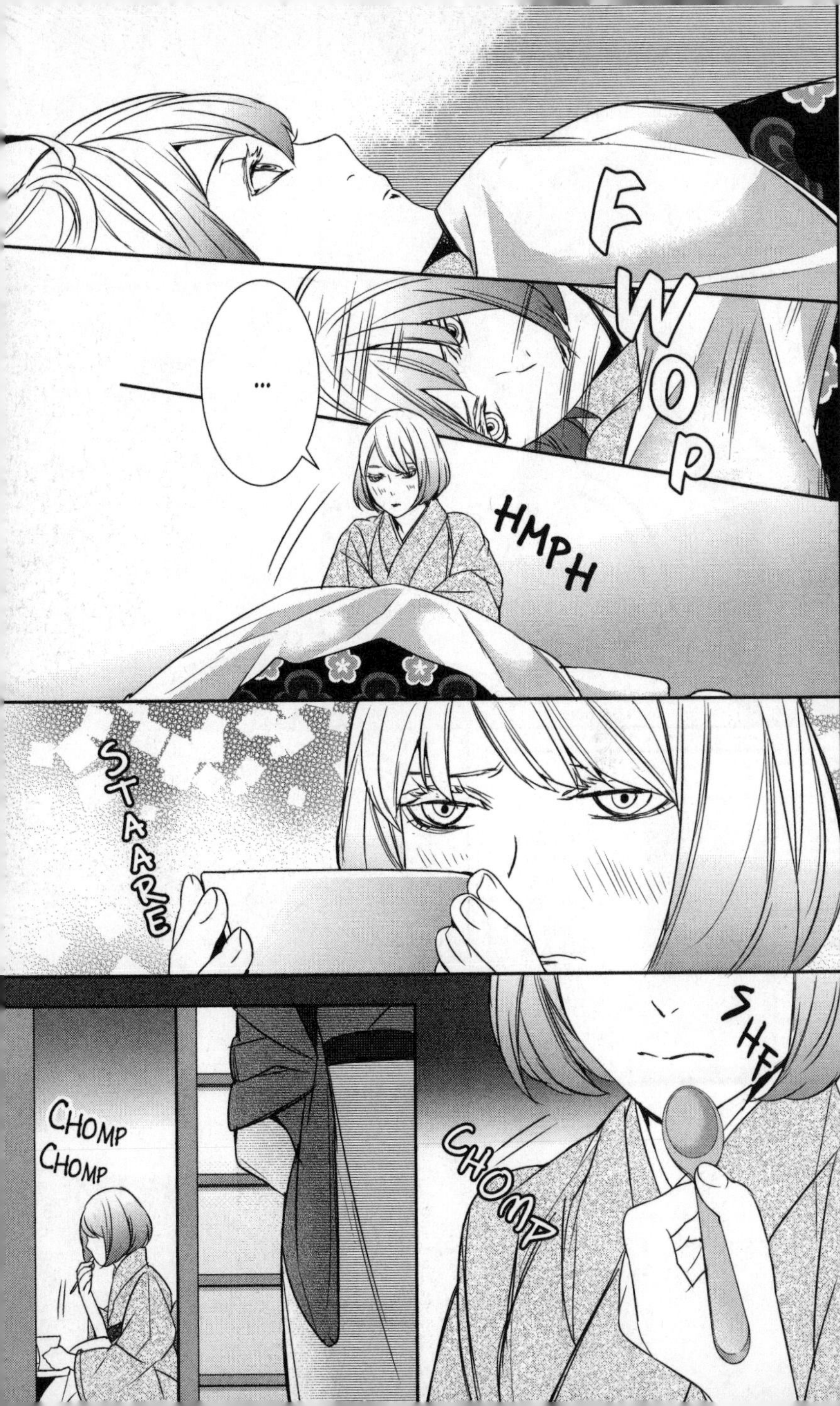
FWOP
...
HMPH
STAARE
SHF
CHOMP
CHOMP
CHOMP

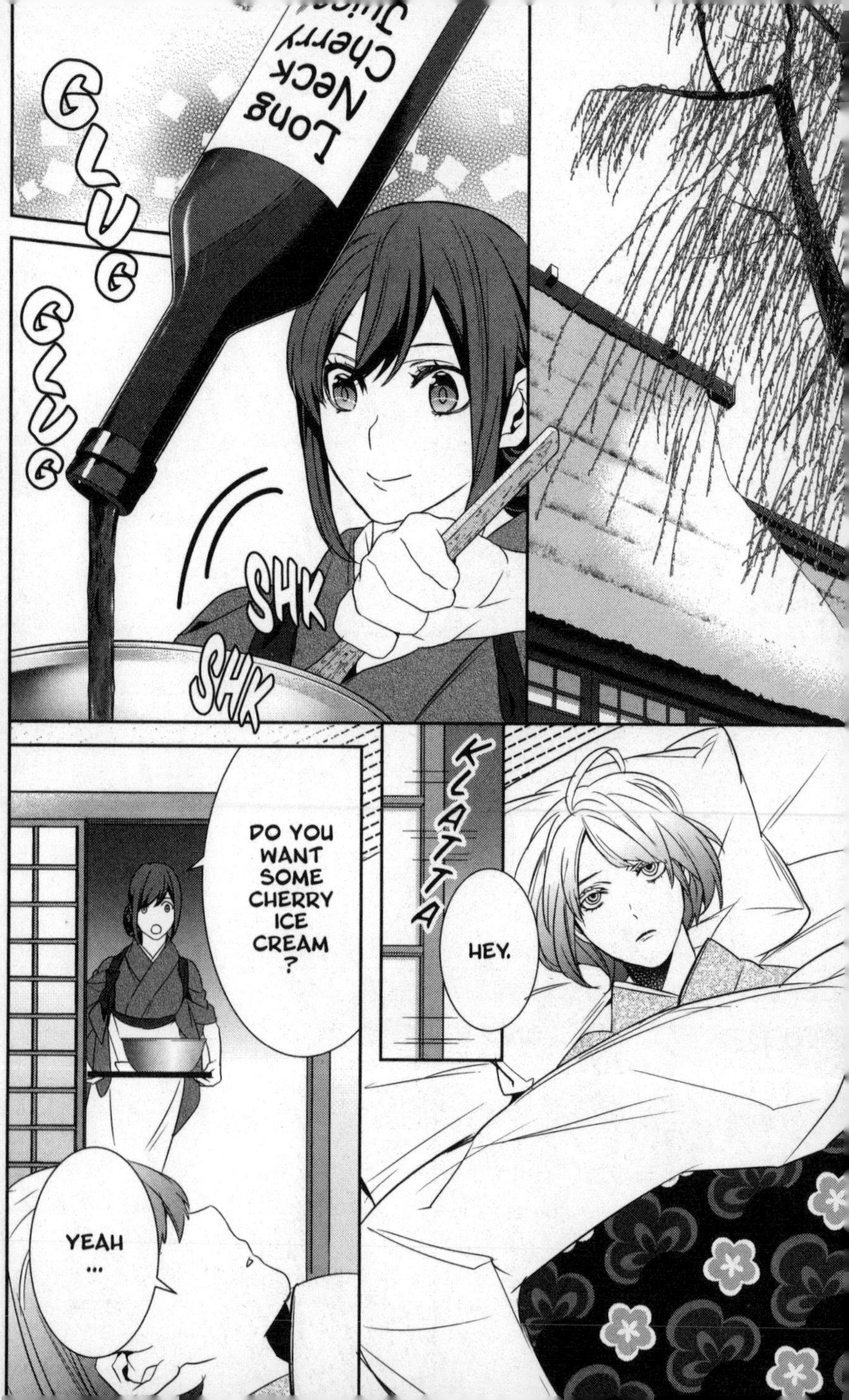
Long Neck Cherry Juice
GLUG
GLUG
SHK
SHK
KLATTA
HEY.
DO YOU WANT SOME CHERRY ICE CREAM?
YEAH ...

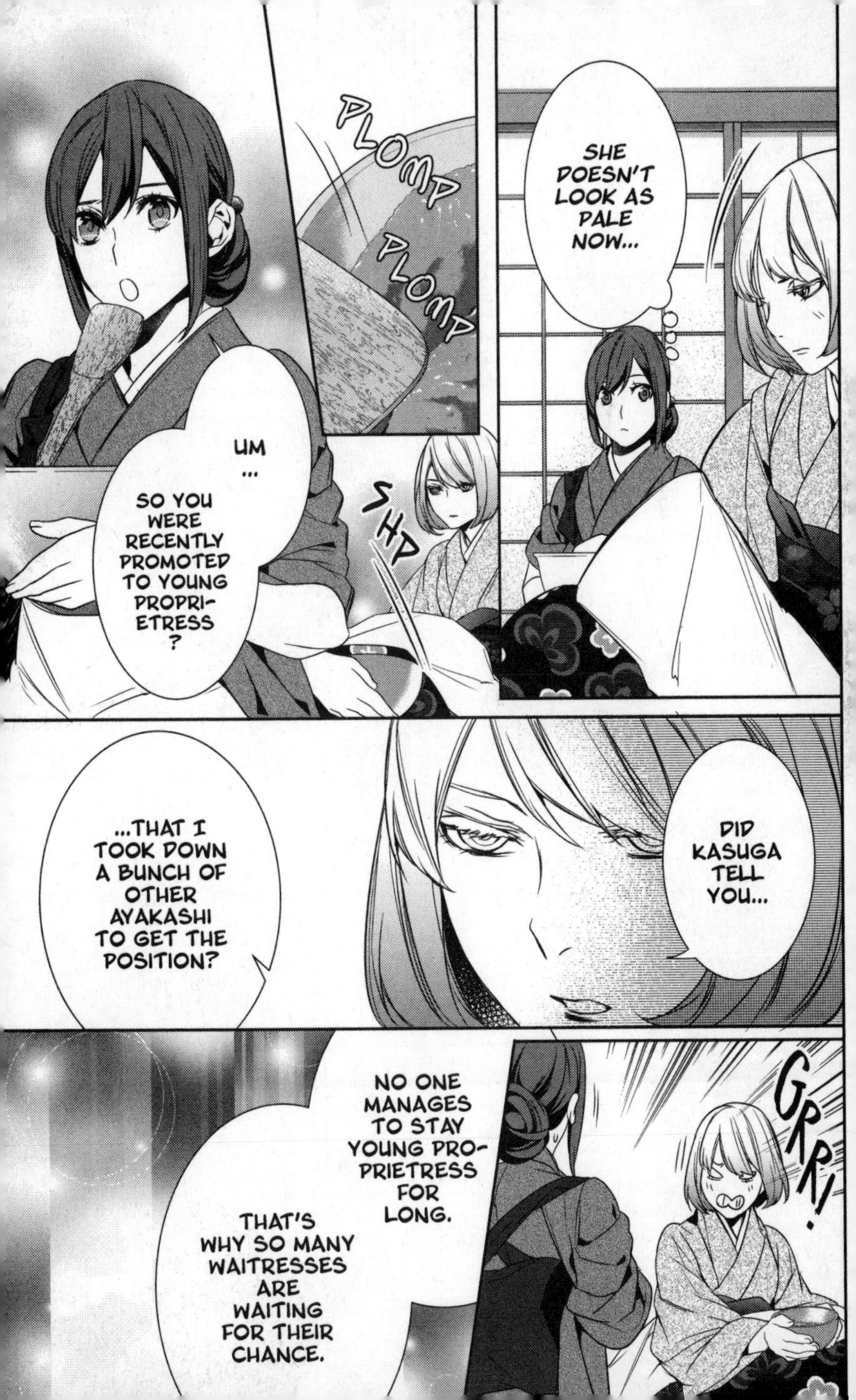
SHE DOESN'T LOOK AS PALE NOW...
PLOMP
PLOMP
UM... SO YOU WERE RECENTLY PROMOTED TO YOUNG PROPRIETRESS?
SHP
DID KASUGA TELL YOU...
...THAT I TOOK DOWN A BUNCH OF OTHER AYAKASHI TO GET THE POSITION?
GRR!
NO ONE MANAGES TO STAY YOUNG PROPRIETRESS FOR LONG.
THAT'S WHY SO MANY WAITRESSES ARE WAITING FOR THEIR CHANCE.

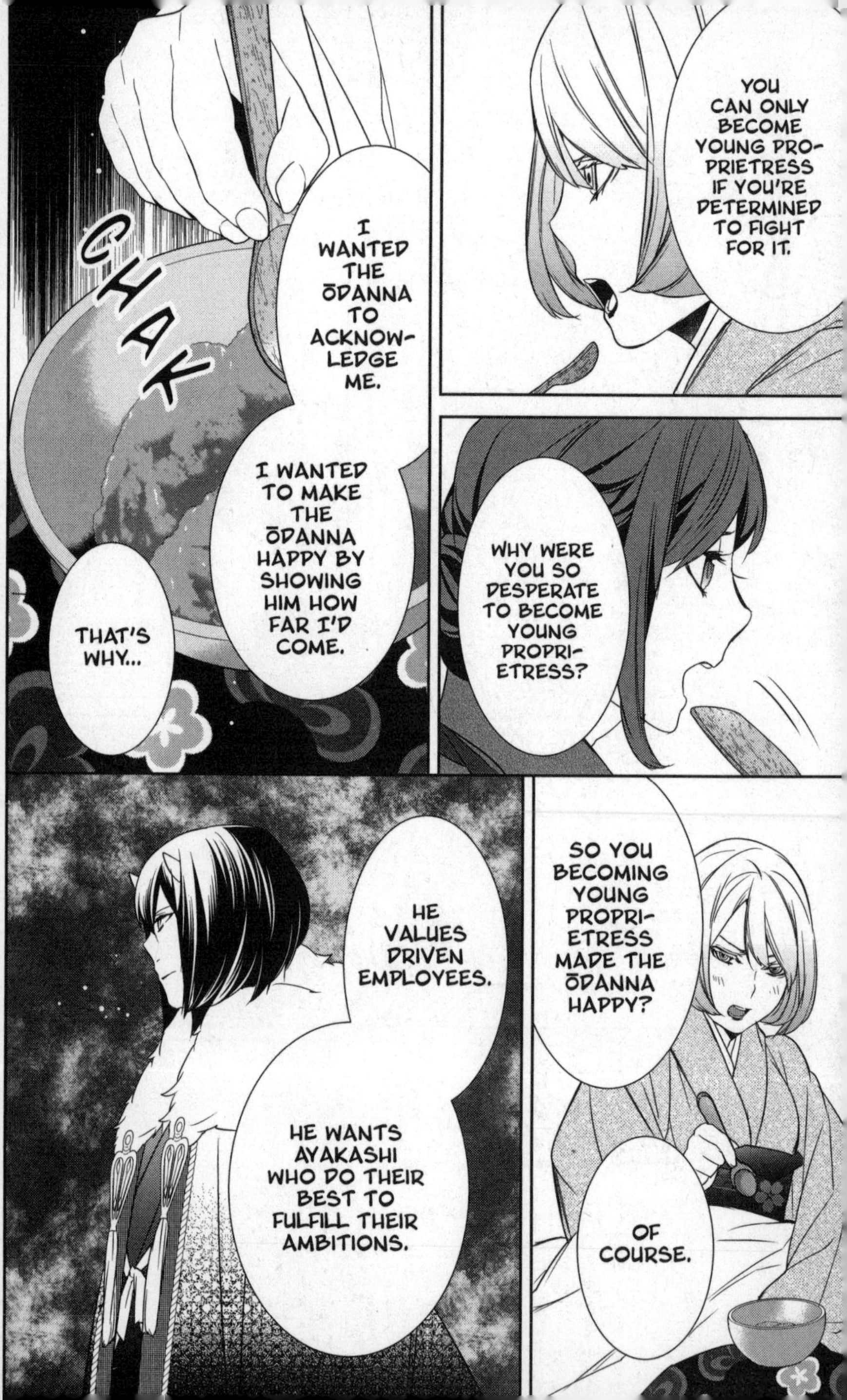
YOU CAN ONLY BECOME YOUNG PROPRIETRESS IF YOU'RE DETERMINED TO FIGHT FOR IT.
WHY WERE YOU SO DESPERATE TO BECOME YOUNG PROPRIETRESS?
CHAK
I WANTED THE ŌDANNA TO ACKNOWLEDGE ME.
I WANTED TO MAKE THE ŌDANNA HAPPY BY SHOWING HIM HOW FAR I'D COME.
THAT'S WHY...
SO YOU BECOMING YOUNG PROPRIETRESS MADE THE ŌDANNA HAPPY?
OF COURSE.
HE VALUES DRIVEN EMPLOYEES.
HE WANTS AYAKASHI WHO DO THEIR BEST TO FULFILL THEIR AMBITIONS.

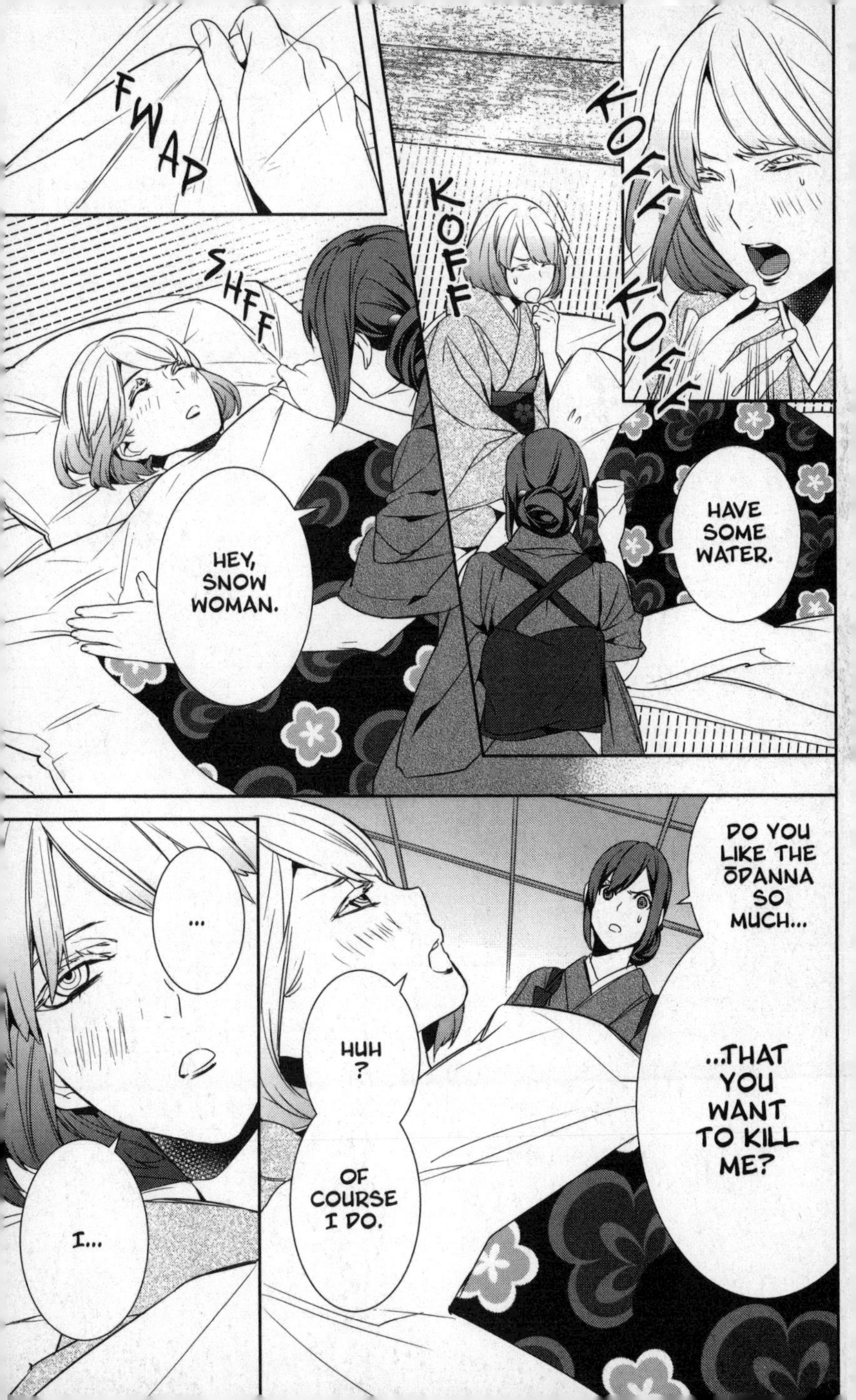
KOFF KOFF
KOFF KOFF
HAVE SOME WATER.
FWAP
SHFF
HEY, SNOW WOMAN.
DO YOU LIKE THE ŌDANNA SO MUCH...
...THAT YOU WANT TO KILL ME?
HUH?
OF COURSE I DO.
...
I...

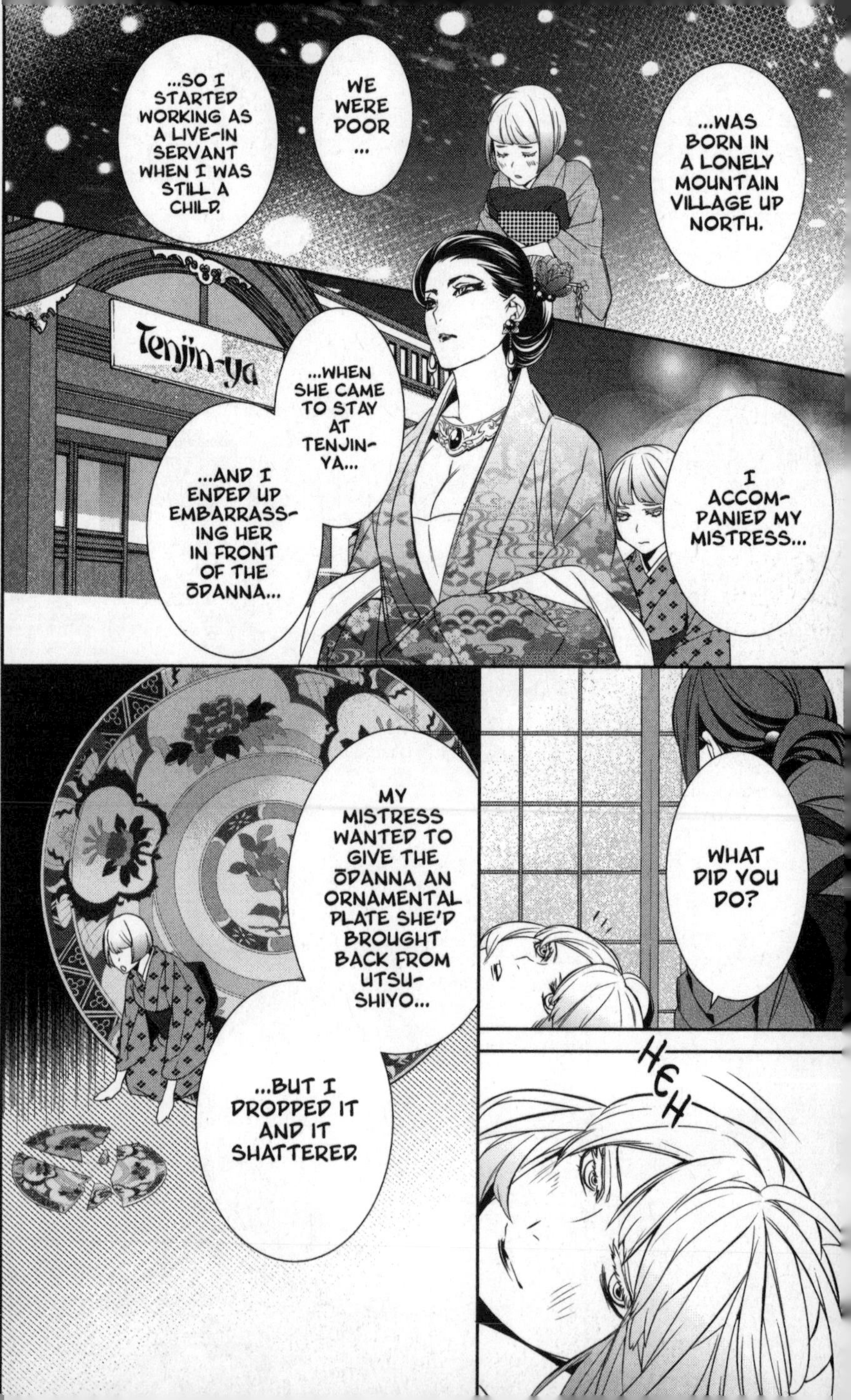
...WAS BORN IN A LONELY MOUNTAIN VILLAGE UP NORTH.
WE WERE POOR...
...SO I STARTED WORKING AS A LIVE-IN SERVANT WHEN I WAS STILL A CHILD.
I ACCOMPANIED MY MISTRESS...
Tenjin-ya
...WHEN SHE CAME TO STAY AT TENJIN-YA...
...AND I ENDED UP EMBARRASSING HER IN FRONT OF THE ŌDANNA...
WHAT DID YOU DO?
HEH
MY MISTRESS WANTED TO GIVE THE ŌDANNA AN ORNAMENTAL PLATE SHE'D BROUGHT BACK FROM UTSUSHIYO...
...BUT I DROPPED IT AND IT SHATTERED.

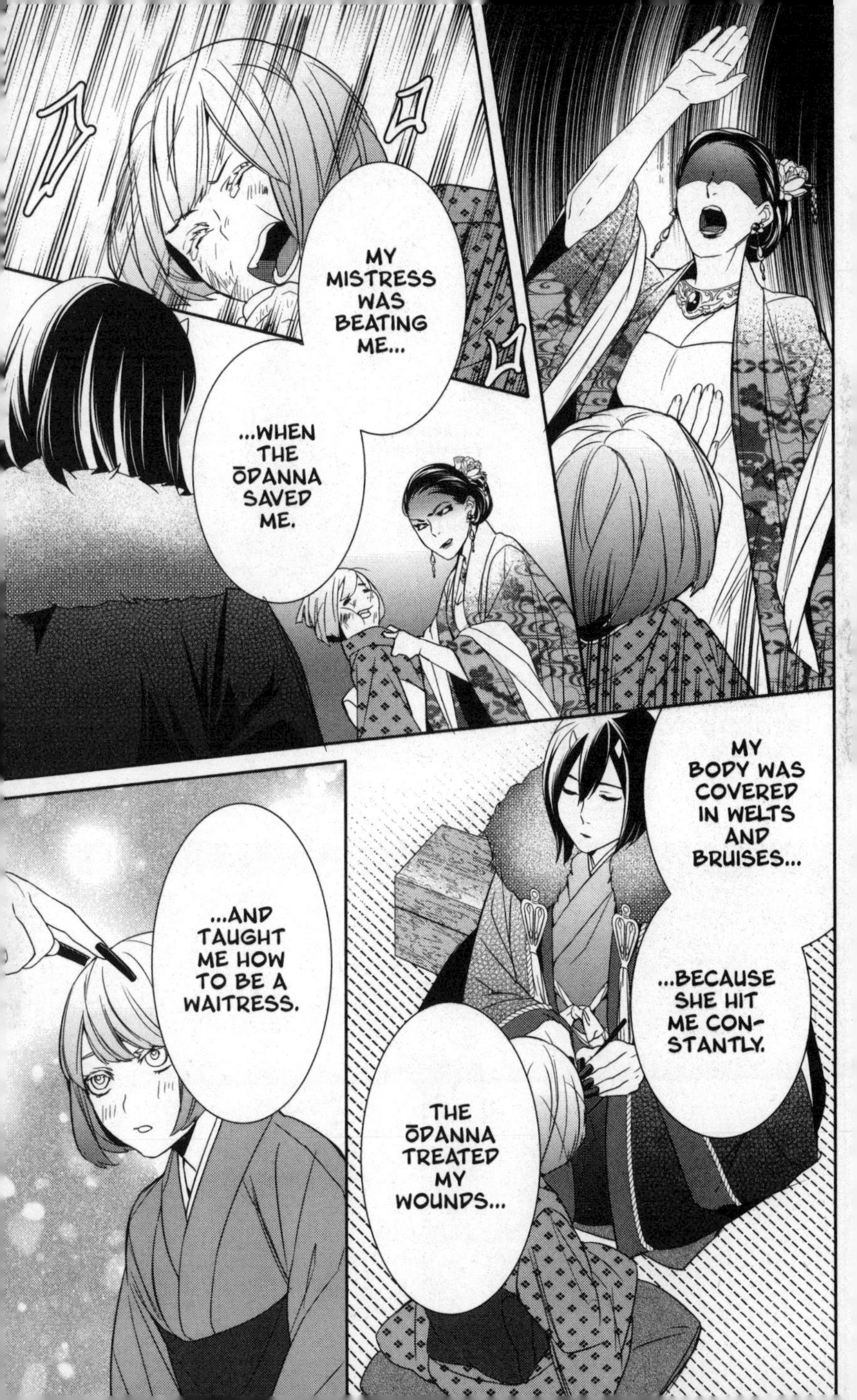
MY MISTRESS WAS BEATING ME...
...WHEN THE ŌDANNA SAVED ME.
MY BODY WAS COVERED IN WELTS AND BRUISES...
...BECAUSE SHE HIT ME CON-STANTLY.
THE ŌDANNA TREATED MY WOUNDS...
...AND TAUGHT ME HOW TO BE A WAITRESS.

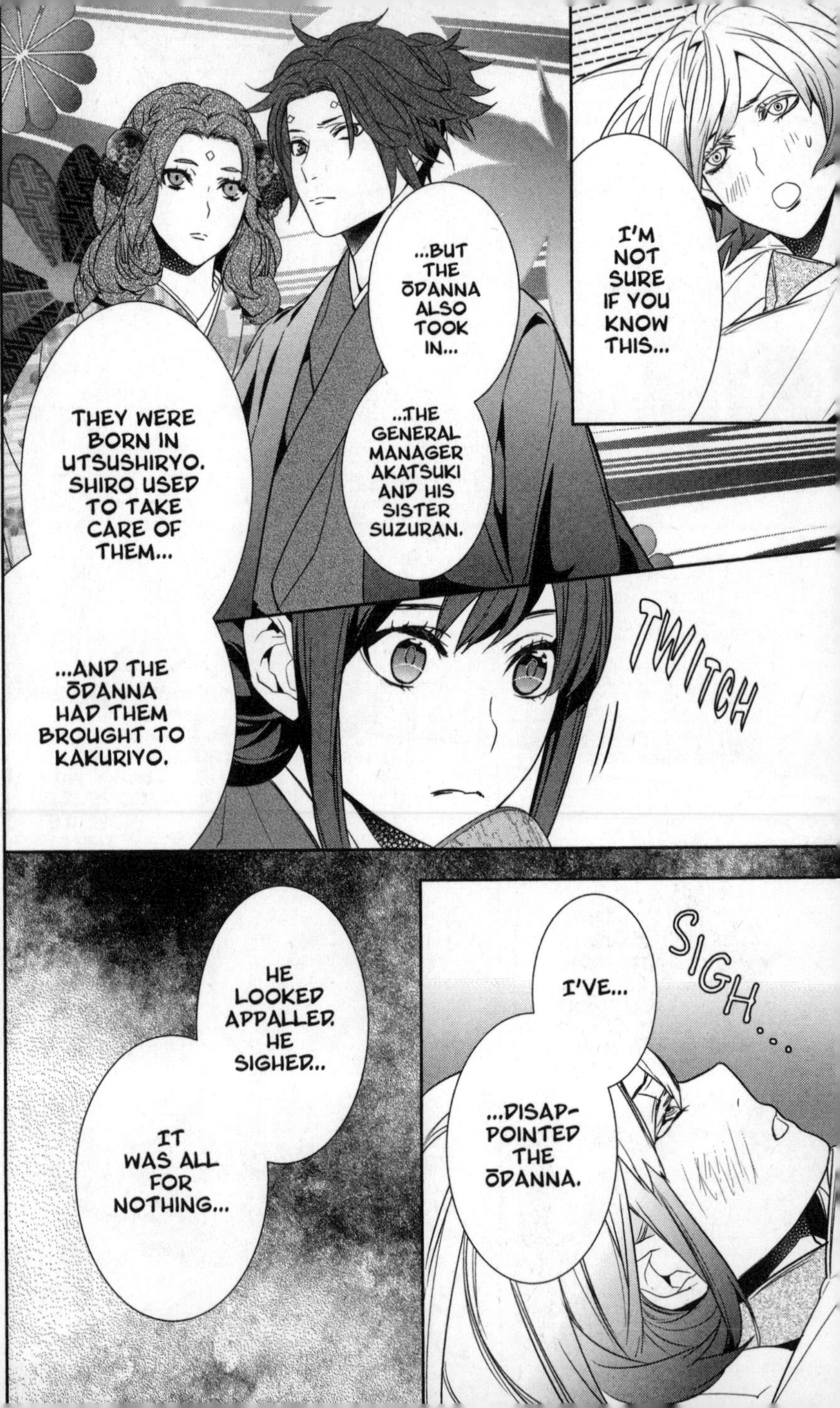
I'M NOT SURE IF YOU KNOW THIS...
...BUT THE ŌDANNA ALSO TOOK IN...
...THE GENERAL MANAGER AKATSUKI AND HIS SISTER SUZURAN.
THEY WERE BORN IN UTSUSHIRYO. SHIRO USED TO TAKE CARE OF THEM...
TWITCH
...AND THE ŌDANNA HAD THEM BROUGHT TO KAKURIYO.
SIGH...
I'VE...
...DISAP-POINTED THE ŌDANNA.
HE LOOKED APPALLED. HE SIGHED...
IT WAS ALL FOR NOTHING...

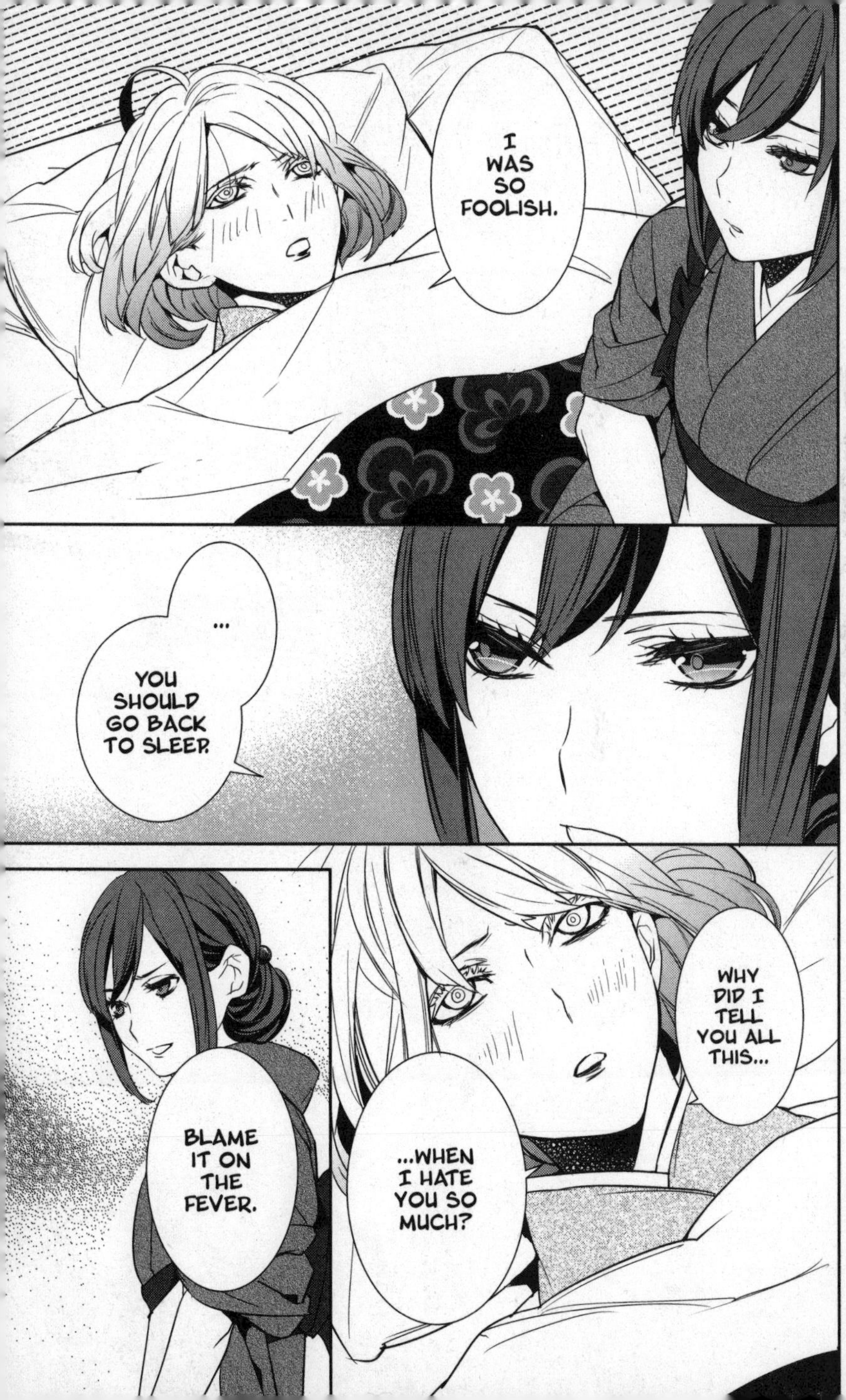
I WAS SO FOOLISH.
...
YOU SHOULD GO BACK TO SLEEP.
WHY DID I TELL YOU ALL THIS...
...WHEN I HATE YOU SO MUCH?
BLAME IT ON THE FEVER.

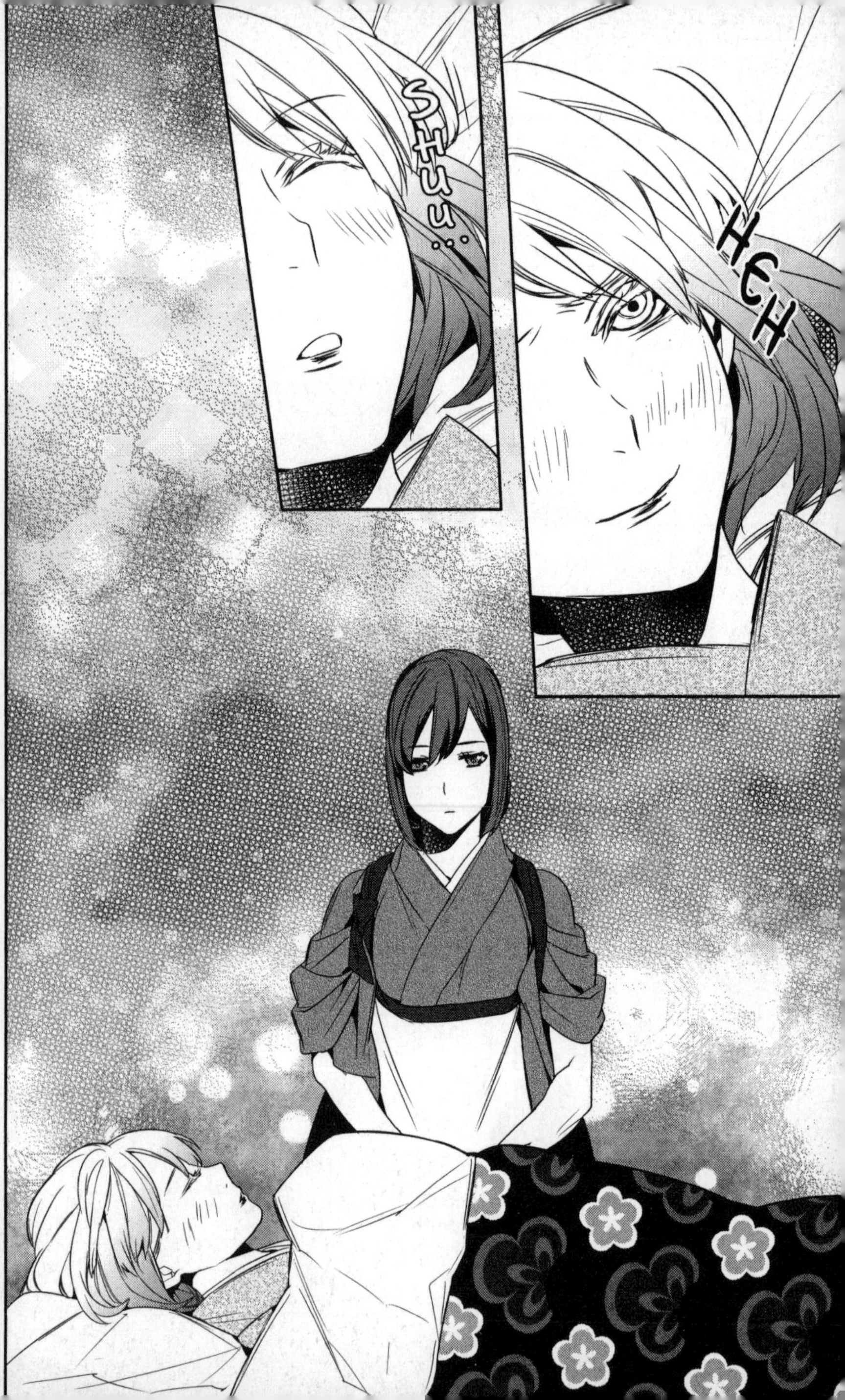
HEH
Shuu...

Kakuriyo
Bed & Breakfast
for Spirits

Kakuriyo
Bed & Breakfast
for Spirits

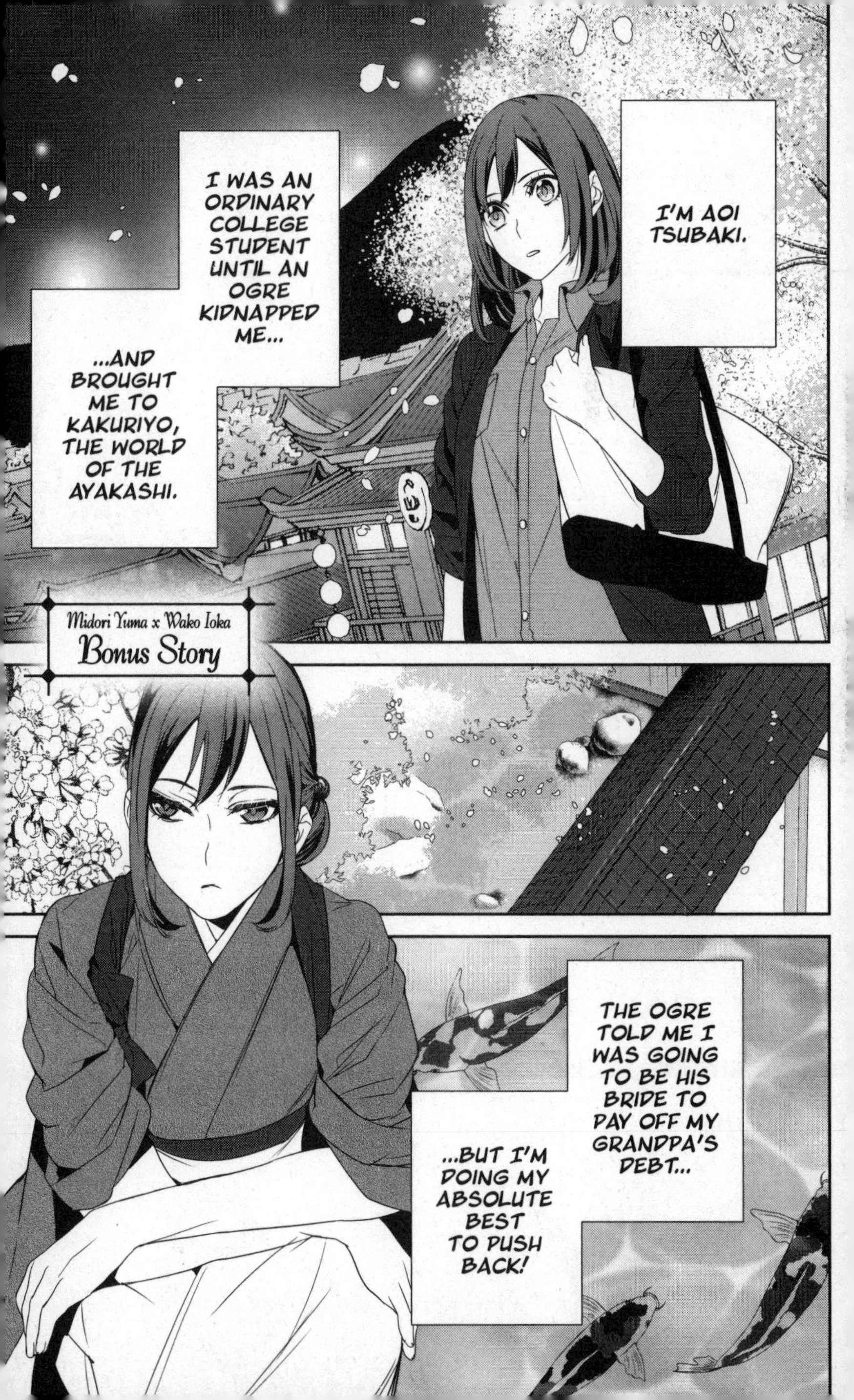
I'M AOI TSUBAKI.
I WAS AN ORDINARY COLLEGE STUDENT UNTIL AN OGRE KIDNAPPED ME...
...AND BROUGHT ME TO KAKURIYO, THE WORLD OF THE AYAKASHI.
Midori Yuma x Wako Ioka
Bonus Story
THE OGRE TOLD ME I WAS GOING TO BE HIS BRIDE TO PAY OFF MY GRANDPA'S DEBT...
...BUT I'M DOING MY ABSOLUTE BEST TO PUSH BACK!

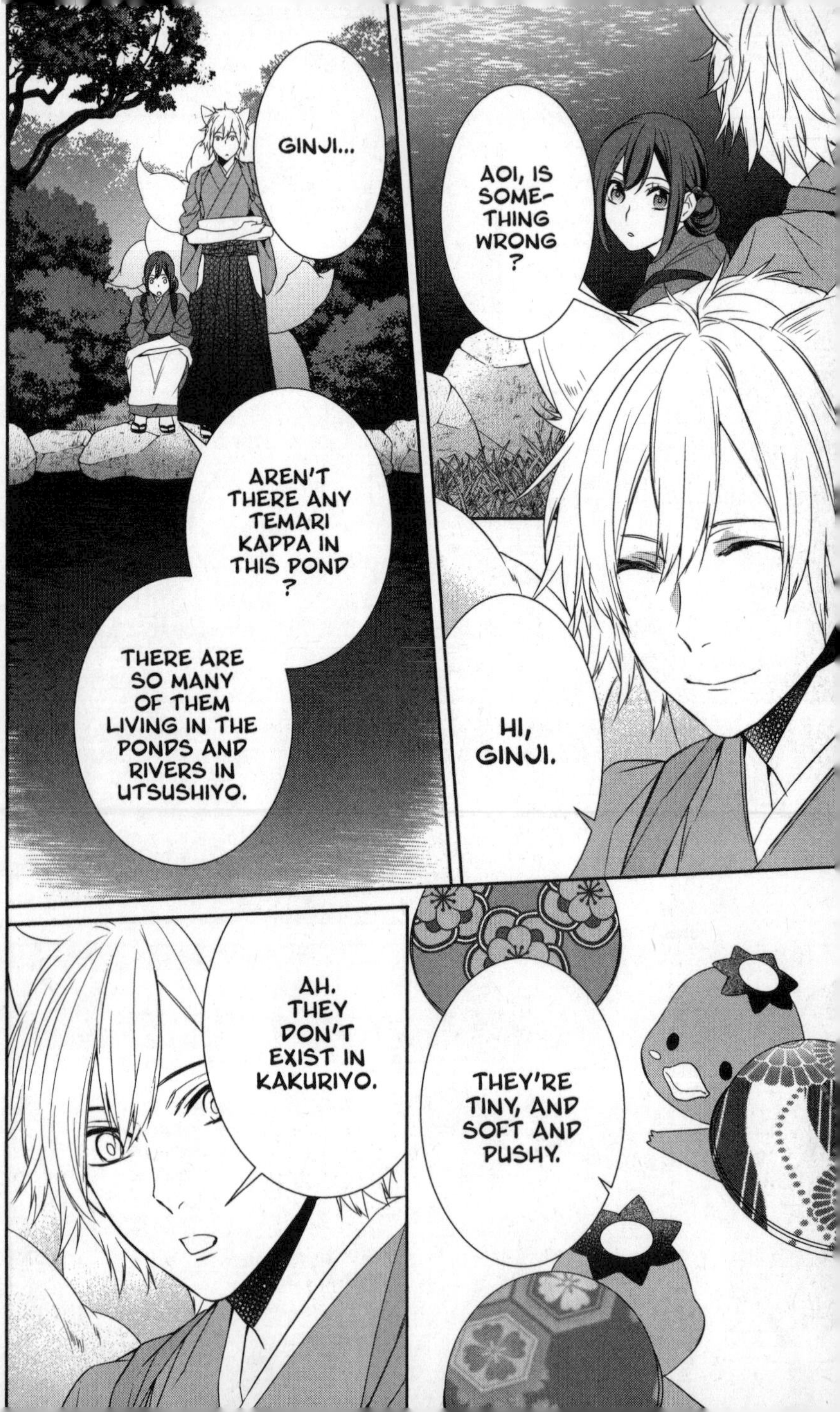
AOI, IS SOME-THING WRONG?
HI, GINJI.
GINJI...
AREN'T THERE ANY TEMARI KAPPA IN THIS POND?
THERE ARE SO MANY OF THEM LIVING IN THE PONDS AND RIVERS IN UTSUSHIYO.
THEY'RE TINY, AND SOFT AND PUSHY.
AH. THEY DON'T EXIST IN KAKURIYO.

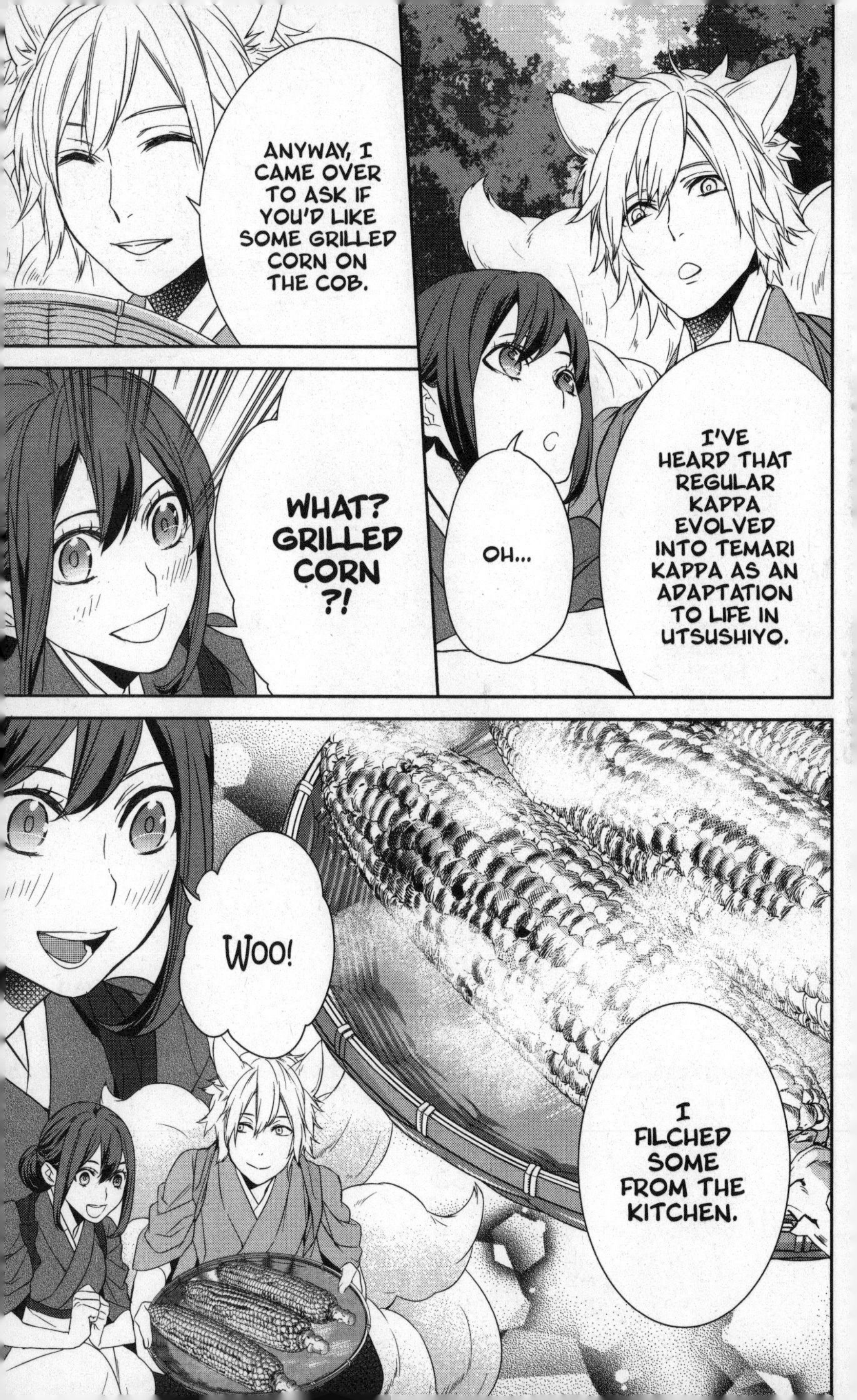
I'VE HEARD THAT REGULAR KAPPA EVOLVED INTO TEMARI KAPPA AS AN ADAPTATION TO LIFE IN UTSUSHIYO.
OH...
ANYWAY, I CAME OVER TO ASK IF YOU'D LIKE SOME GRILLED CORN ON THE COB.
WHAT? GRILLED CORN ?!
I FILCHED SOME FROM THE KITCHEN.
Woo!

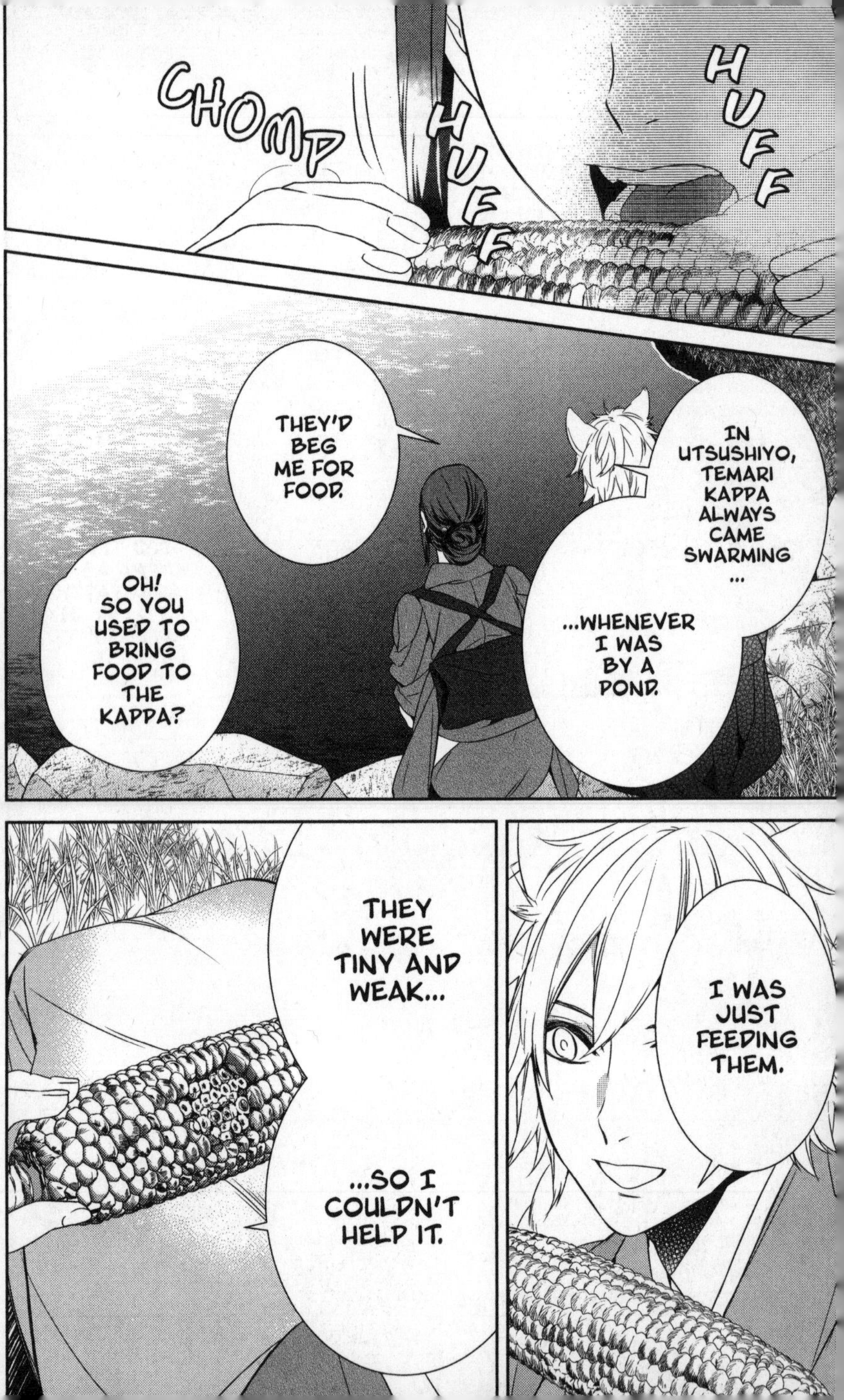
HUFF HUFF
HUFF HUFF
CHOMP
IN UTSUSHIYO, TEMARI KAPPA ALWAYS CAME SWARMING...
...WHENEVER I WAS BY A POND.
THEY'D BEG ME FOR FOOD.
OH! SO YOU USED TO BRING FOOD TO THE KAPPA?
I WAS JUST FEEDING THEM.
THEY WERE TINY AND WEAK...
...SO I COULDN'T HELP IT.

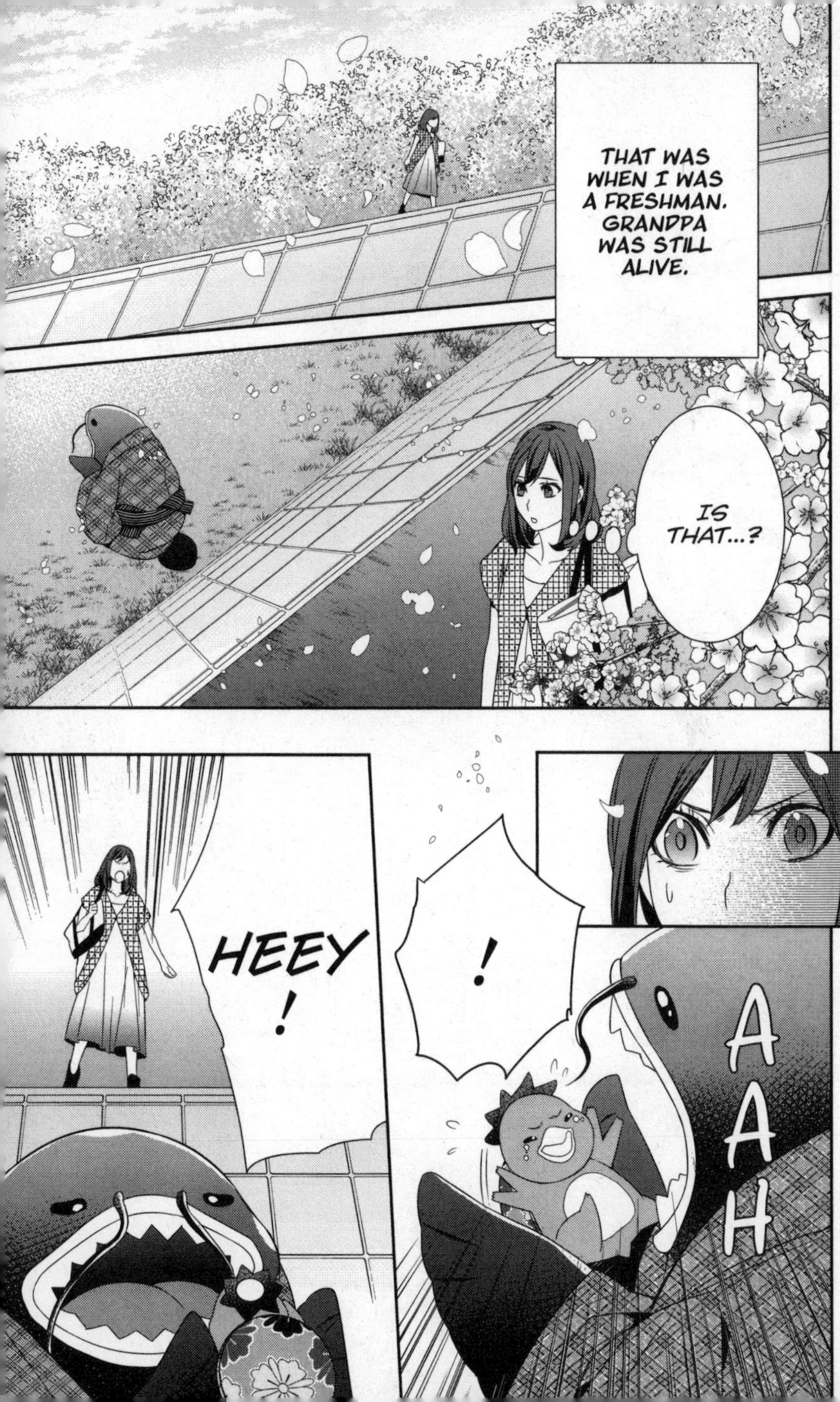
THAT WAS WHEN I WAS A FRESHMAN. GRANDPA WAS STILL ALIVE.
IS THAT...?
!
AAH
HEEY!

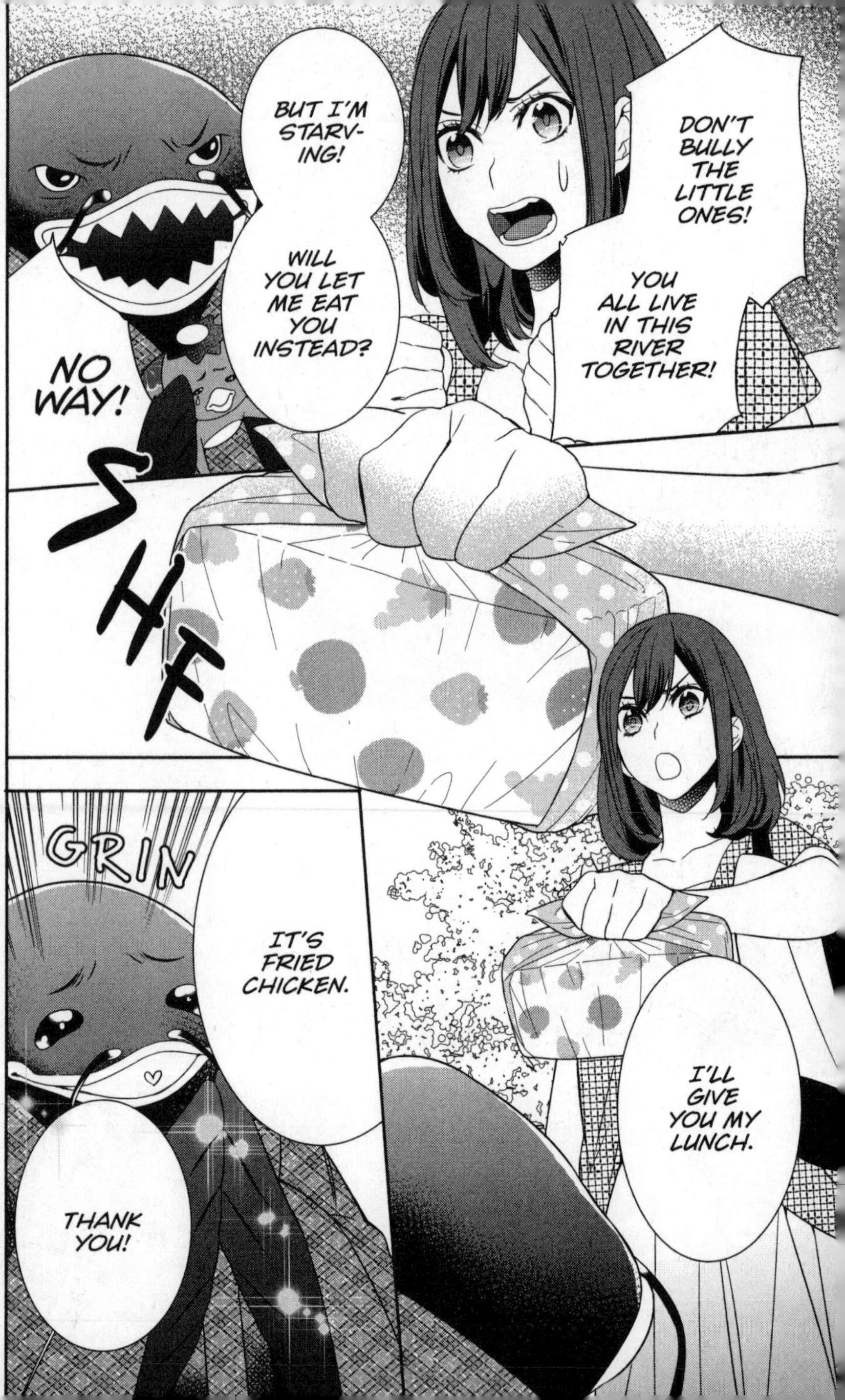
DON'T BULLY THE LITTLE ONES!
YOU ALL LIVE IN THIS RIVER TOGETHER!
BUT I'M STARV-ING!
WILL YOU LET ME EAT YOU INSTEAD?
NO WAY!
SHF
I'LL GIVE YOU MY LUNCH.
GRIN
IT'S FRIED CHICKEN.
THANK YOU!

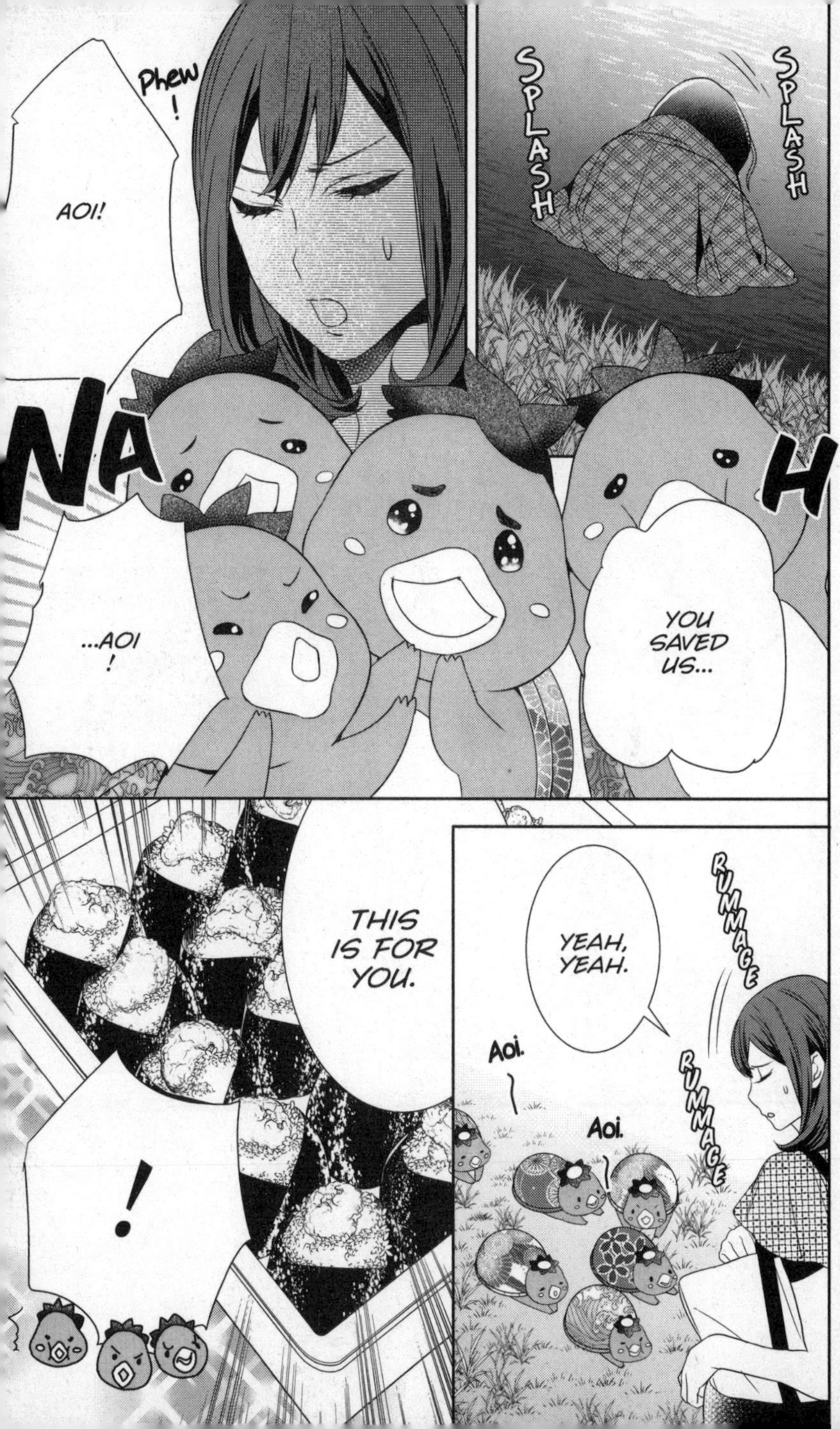
SPLASH
SPLASH
Phew!
AOI!
NAAH
YOU SAVED US...
...AOI!
RUMMAGE
RUMMAGE
YEAH, YEAH.
Aoi.
Aoi.
THIS IS FOR YOU.
!

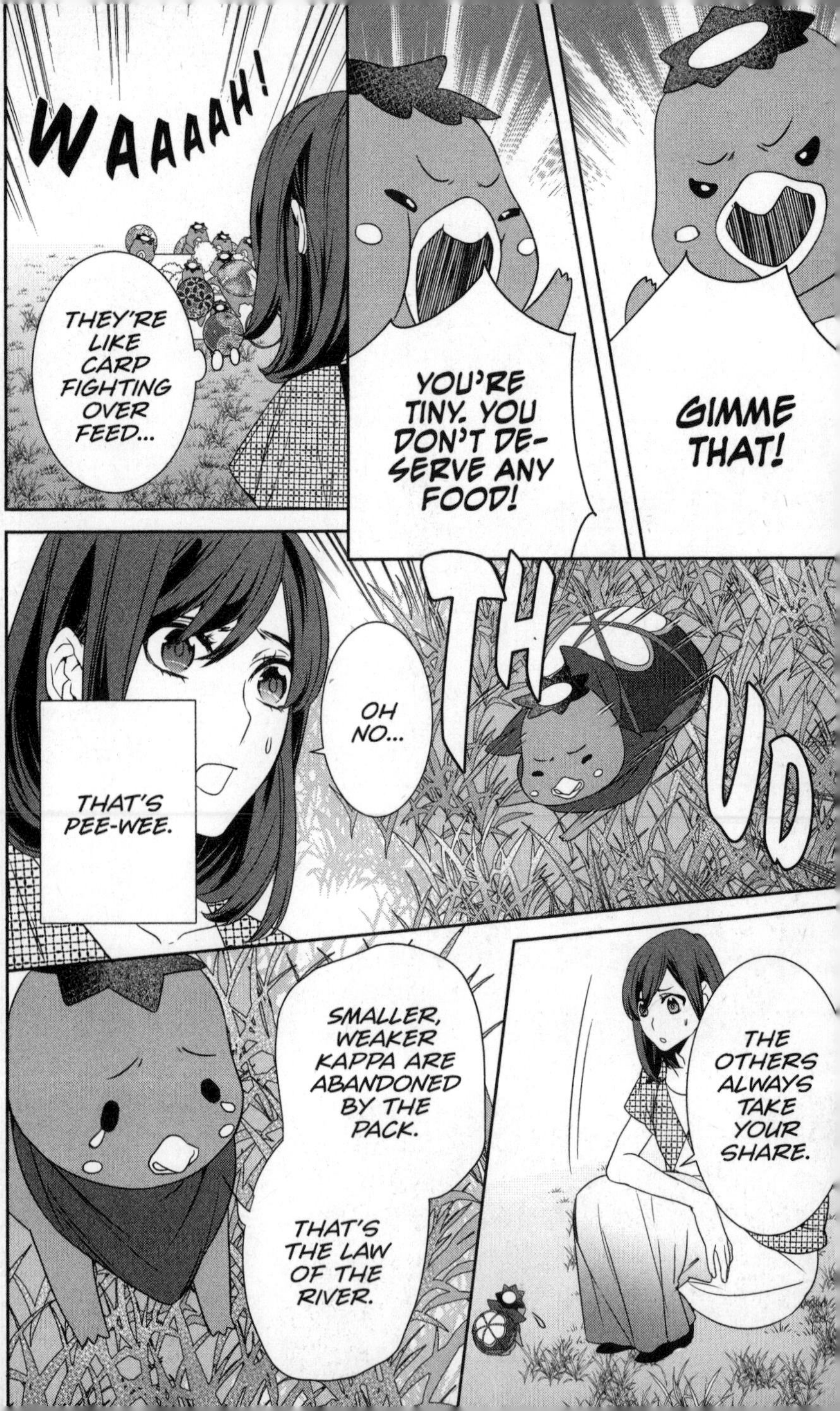
GIMME THAT!
YOU'RE TINY. YOU DON'T DE-SERVE ANY FOOD!
WAAAAH!
THEY'RE LIKE CARP FIGHTING OVER FEED...
THUD
OH NO...
THAT'S PEE-WEE.
THE OTHERS ALWAYS TAKE YOUR SHARE.
SMALLER, WEAKER KAPPA ARE ABANDONED BY THE PACK.
THAT'S THE LAW OF THE RIVER.

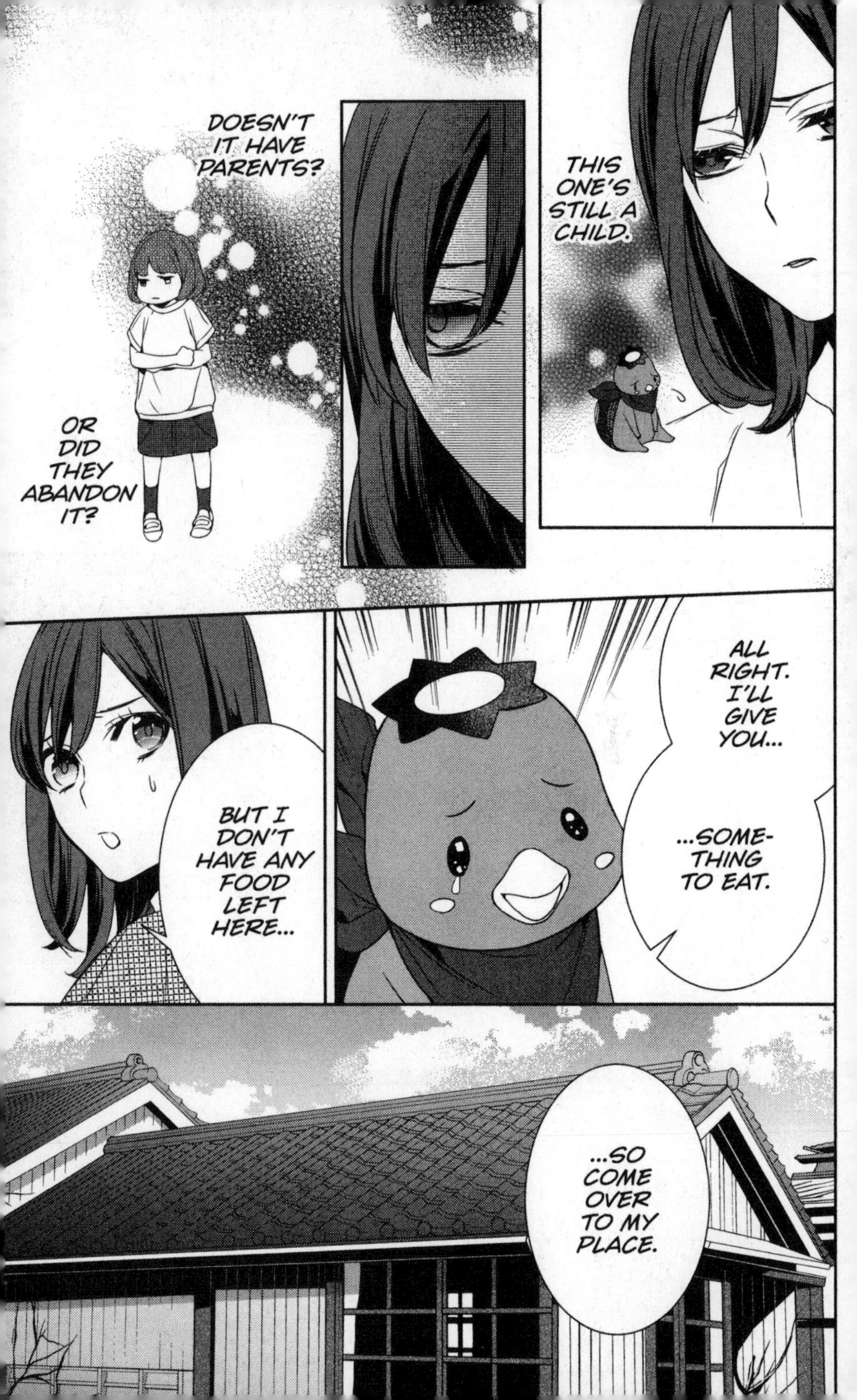
THIS ONE'S STILL A CHILD.
DOESN'T IT HAVE PARENTS?
OR DID THEY ABANDON IT?
ALL RIGHT. I'LL GIVE YOU...
...SOME-THING TO EAT.
BUT I DON'T HAVE ANY FOOD LEFT HERE...
...SO COME OVER TO MY PLACE.

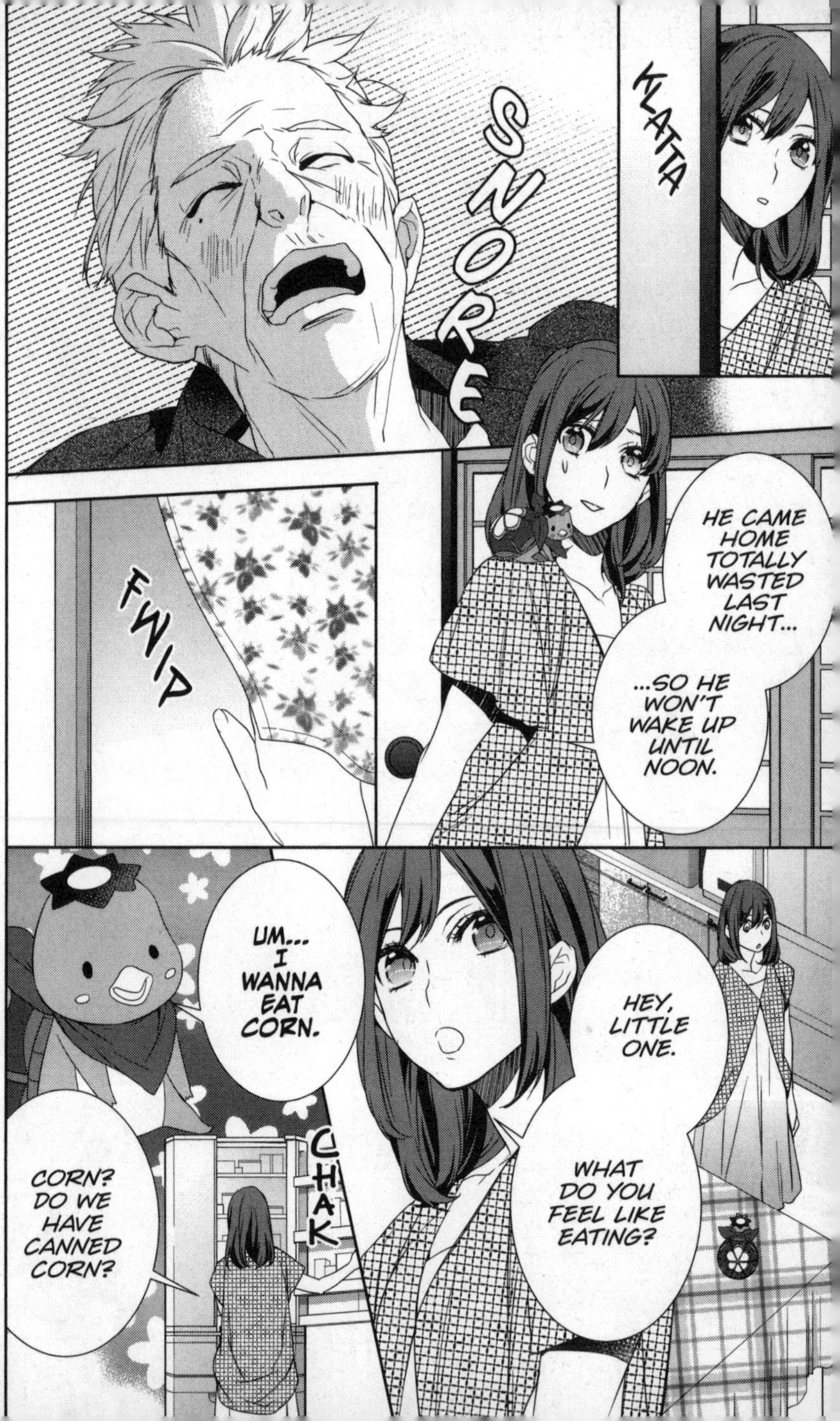
KLATTA
SNORE
HE CAME HOME TOTALLY WASTED LAST NIGHT...
...SO HE WON'T WAKE UP UNTIL NOON.
FWIP
HEY, LITTLE ONE.
WHAT DO YOU FEEL LIKE EATING?
UM... I WANNA EAT CORN.
CHAK
CORN? DO WE HAVE CANNED CORN?

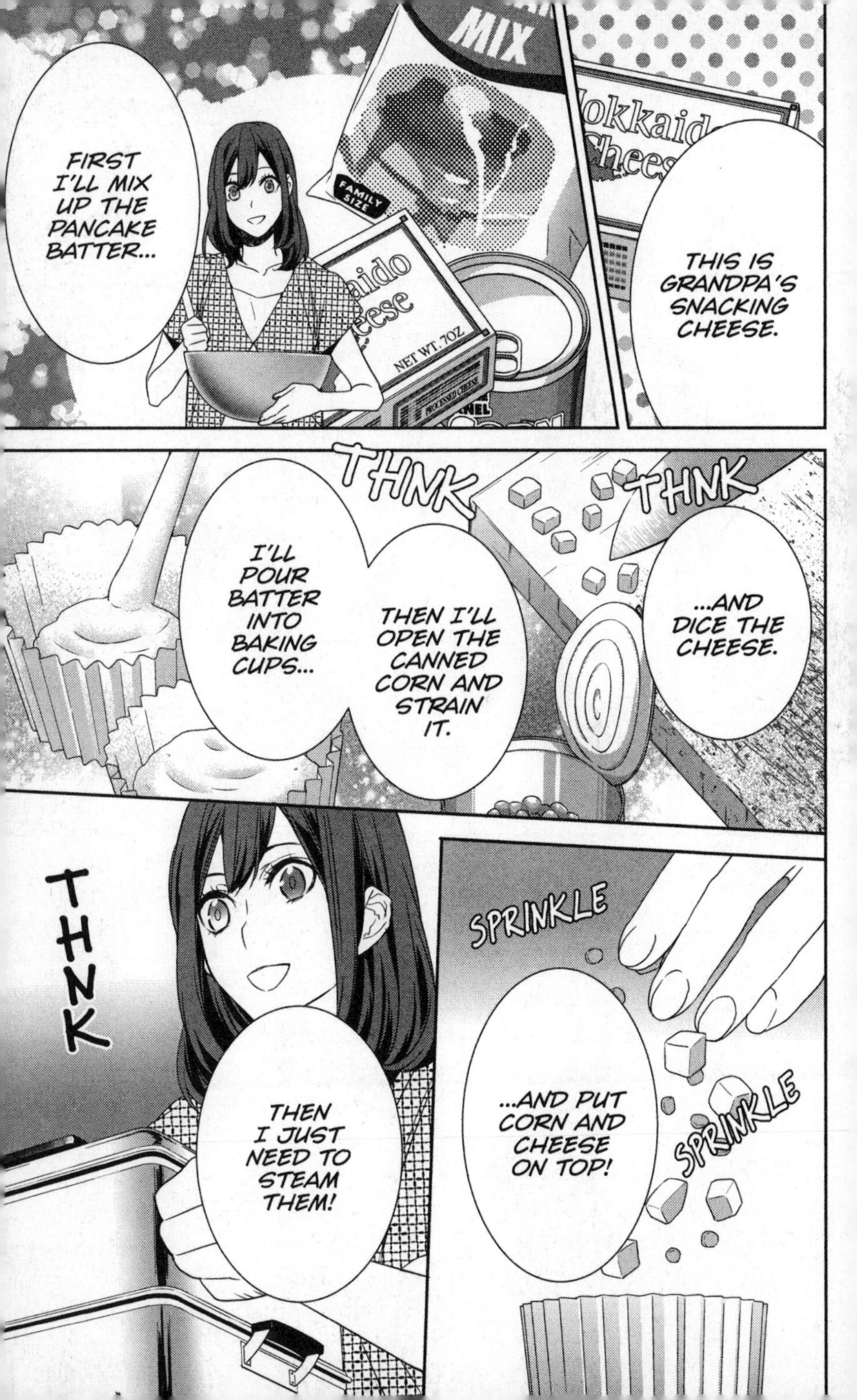
THIS IS GRANDPA'S SNACKING CHEESE.
FIRST I'LL MIX UP THE PANCAKE BATTER...
THNK
THNK
...AND DICE THE CHEESE.
THEN I'LL OPEN THE CANNED CORN AND STRAIN IT.
I'LL POUR BATTER INTO BAKING CUPS...
SPRINKLE
SPRINKLE
...AND PUT CORN AND CHEESE ON TOP!
THEN I JUST NEED TO STEAM THEM!
THNK

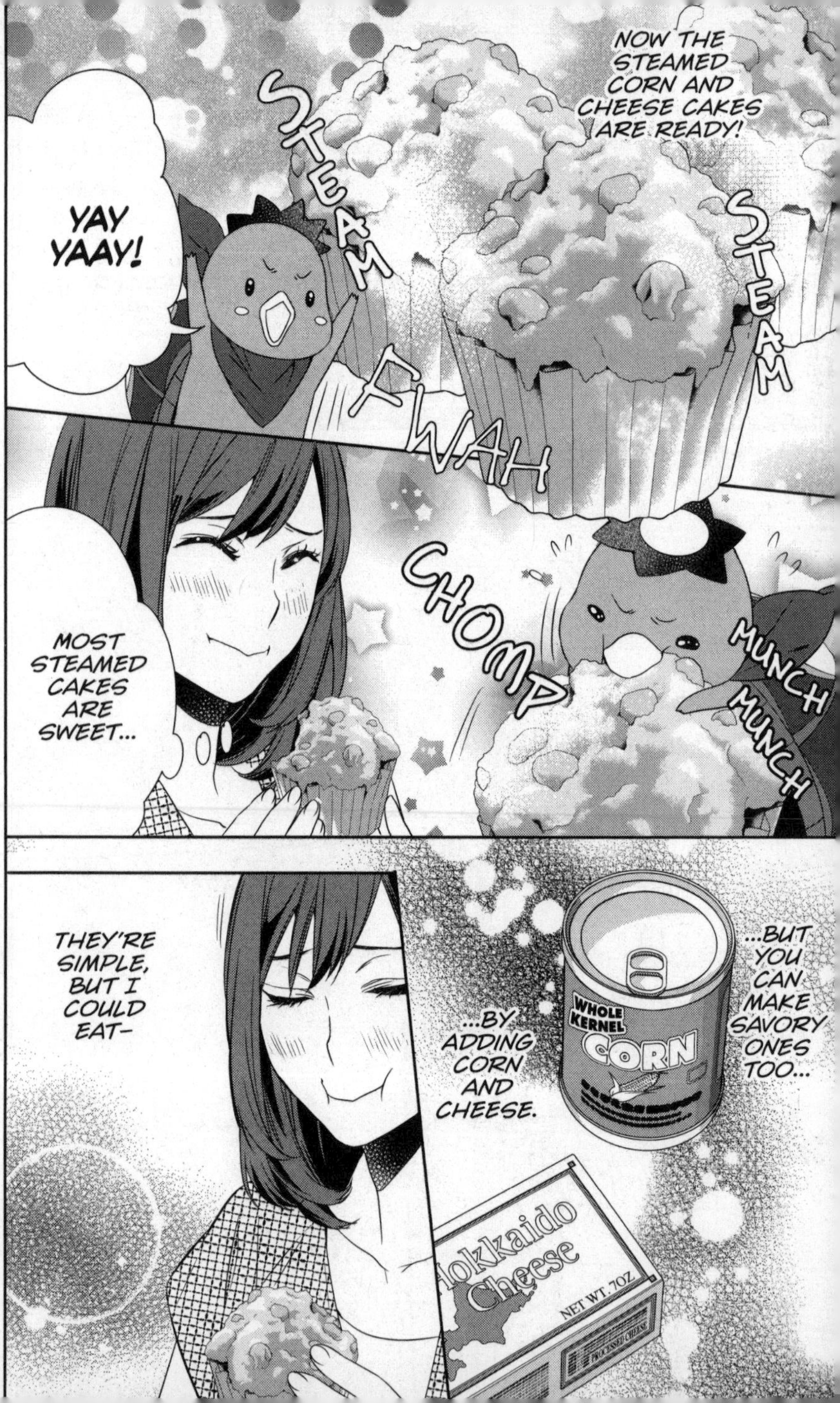
NOW THE STEAMED CORN AND CHEESE CAKES ARE READY!
STEAM
STEAM
YAY YAAY!
FWAH
MUNCH MUNCH
CHOMP
MOST STEAMED CAKES ARE SWEET...
...BUT YOU CAN MAKE SAVORY ONES TOO...
WHOLE KERNEL CORN
...BY ADDING CORN AND CHEESE.
THEY'RE SIMPLE, BUT I COULD EAT-
Hokkaido Cheese
NET WT. 7OZ
PROCESSED CHEESE

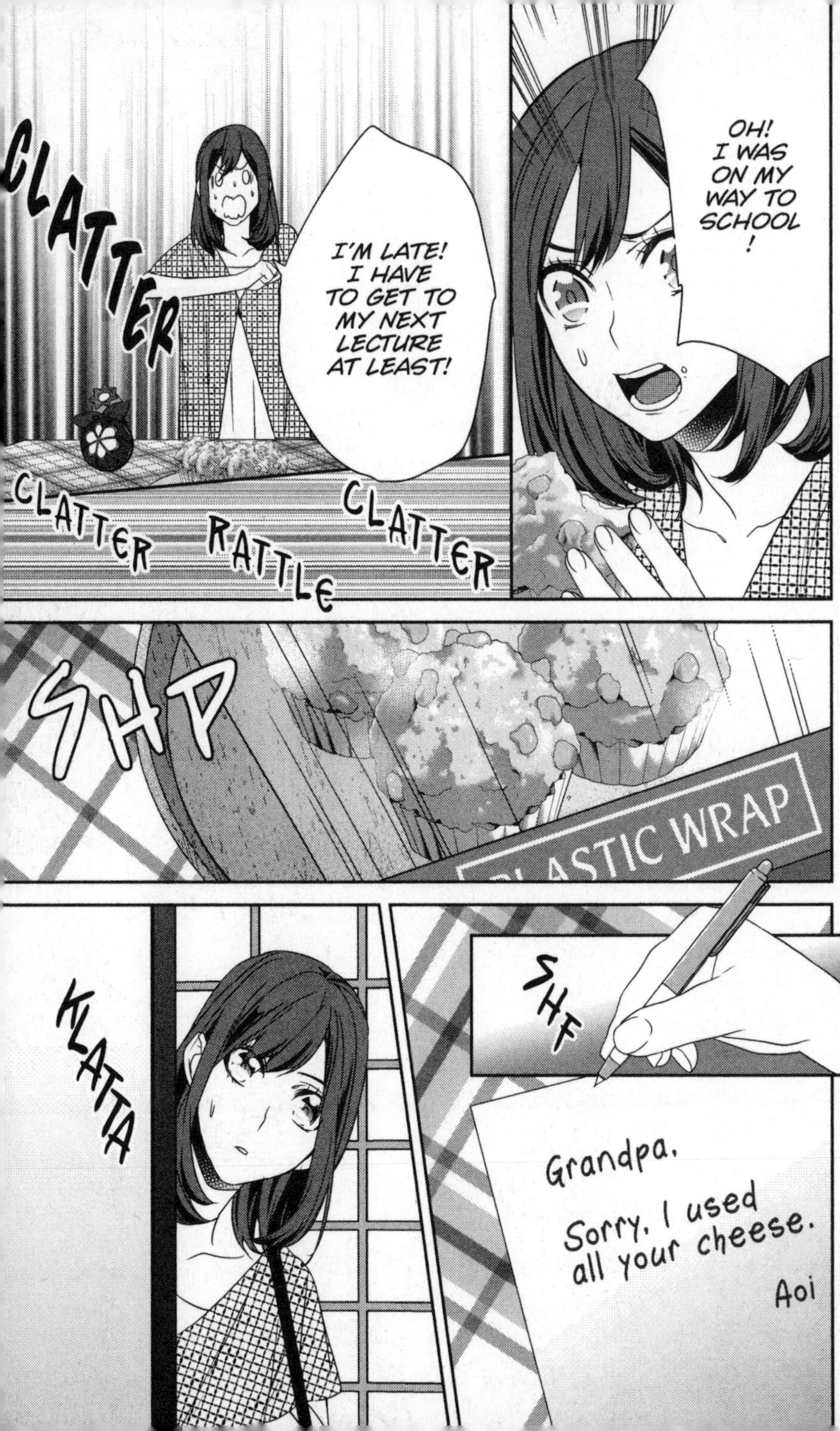
OH! I WAS ON MY WAY TO SCHOOL!
I'M LATE! I HAVE TO GET TO MY NEXT LECTURE AT LEAST!
CLATTER
CLATTER
RATTLE
CLATTER
SHP
PLASTIC WRAP
SHF
Grandpa,
Sorry, I used all your cheese.
Aoi
KLATTA

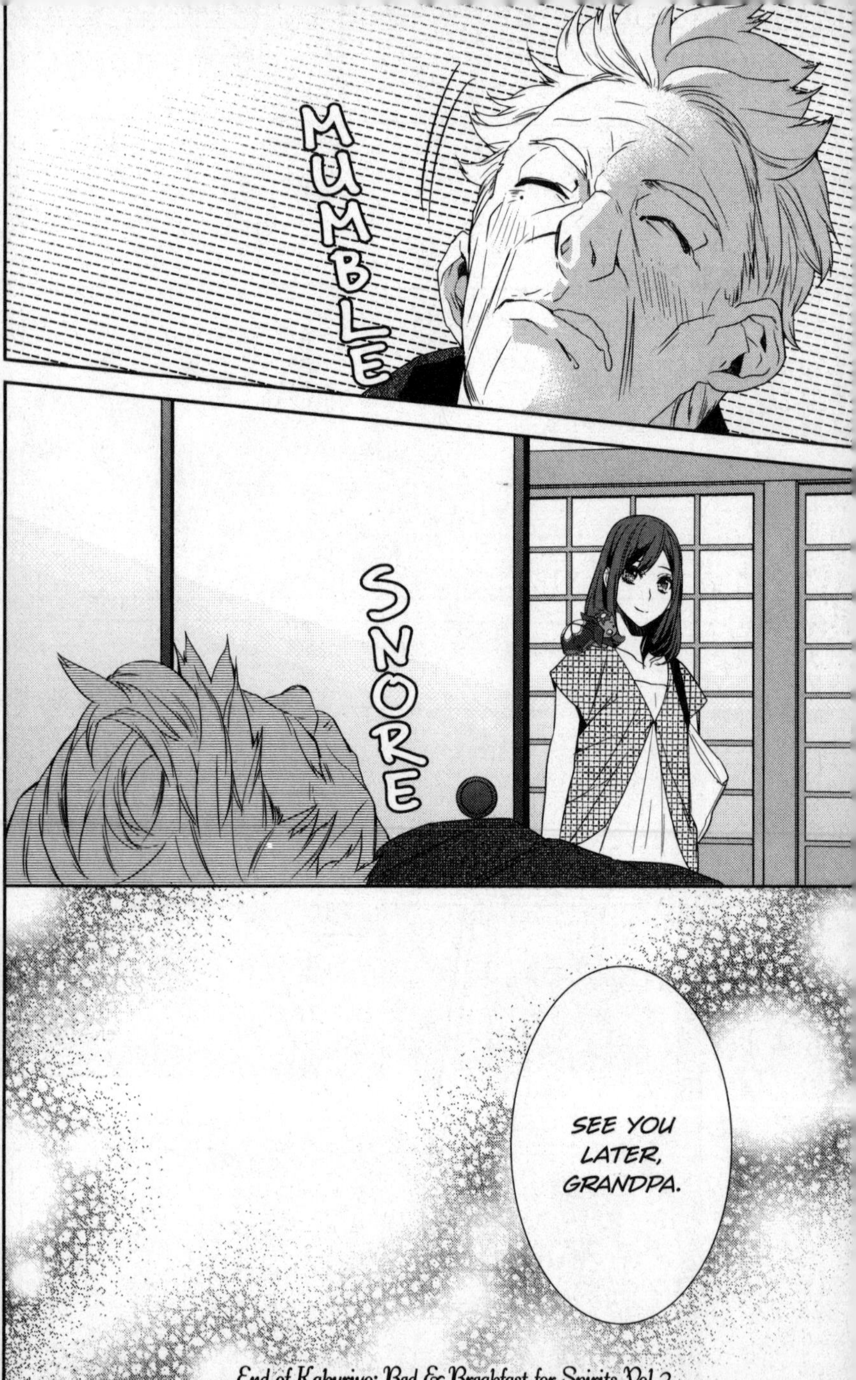
MUMBLE
SNORE
SEE YOU LATER, GRANDPA.

End of Kakuriyo: Bed & Breakfast for Spirits Vol 2

Kakuriyo
Bed & Breakfast
for Spirits

END NOTES

PAGE 93, PANEL 2
Konpira funefune
An old Japanese folk song that accompanies a game of the same name that geisha use to entertain customers.

PAGE 107, PANEL 5
Fabric demons
Ittan-momen in Japanese, which literally means "a bolt of cotton fabric." They look like long pieces of cloth and fly around at dusk choking or killing humans. The demons in this manga have the character for "tan" in ittan -momen on their face cloths.

PAGE 138, PANEL 4
Long-neck demons
Rokurokubi in Japanese. Yokai with long, flexible retractable necks or heads that detach from their bodies.

PAGE 143, PANEL 2
Izakaya
Something like a pub or tapas bar that provides a casual place to drink with a little bites-style menu.

PAGE 155, PANEL 3
Roasted soy flour
Kinako in Japanese. Often used to coat rice flour dumplings (dango, mochi) and has a nutty, malty flavor.

PAGE 170, PANEL 2
Kappa
A type of water ayakashi that mainly haunts rivers. Kappa look like children, are green or red, have plates on their heads, tortoise shells on their backs, webbed hands and a beak.

PAGE 5, PANEL 5
Tengu
Winged mythical beings thought to be either gods or ayakashi. They are usually dressed as mountain priests and have prominent noses.

PAGE 14, PANEL 3
Utsushiyo
The human realm. A Shinto term for the actual or unconcealed world, as opposed to the hidden world, Kakuriyo.

PAGE 42, PANEL 5
Raccoon ayakashi
They can transform into other living creatures or inanimate objects.

PAGE 74, PANEL 1
Yohto cut class
Probably derived from Edo cut class, a traditional craft in Tokyo where patterns are cut on either colored or transparent glass.

PAGE 77, PANEL 1
The Ogre and the Spiked Club
A play on the Japanese expression "like an ogre with a metal club," with means to make something strong even stronger.

PAGE 90, PANEL 4
Shamisen
The traditional three-stringed instrument that geisha are accompanied by when they sing.

Kakuriyo
Bed & Breakfast for Spirits

SHOJO BEAT EDITION

Art by **Waco Ioka**
Original story by **Midori Yuma**
Character design by **Laruha**

English Translation & Adaptation **Tomo Kimura**
Touch-up Art & Lettering **Joanna Estep**
Design **Alice Lewis**
Editor **Pancha Diaz**

KAKURIYO NO YADOMESHI AYAKASHIOYADO NI YOMEIRI SHIMASU, Vol. 2
©Waco Ioka 2017
©Midori Yuma 2017
©Laruha 2017
First published in Japan in 2017 by KADOKAWA CORPORATION, Tokyo.
English translation rights arranged with KADOKAWA CORPORATION, Tokyo.

Printed in the U.S.A.

Published by VIZ Media, LLC.
P.O. Box 77010
San Francisco, CA 94107

10 9 8 7 6 5 4 3 2 1
First printing, March 2019

viz.com

shojobeat.com

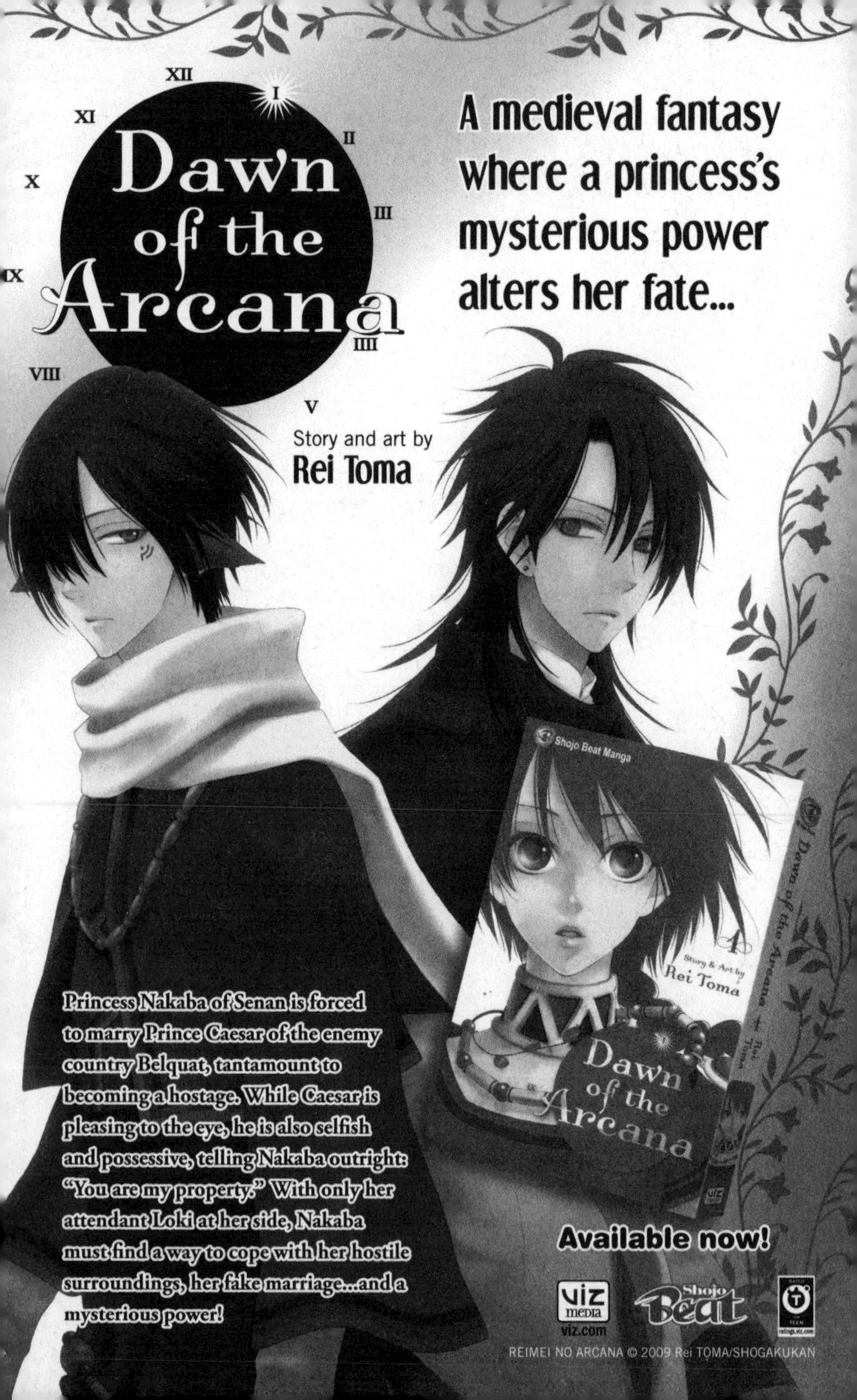
Dawn of the Arcana
A medieval fantasy where a princess's mysterious power alters her fate...
Story and art by
Rei Toma
Shojo Beat Manga
Story & Art by
Rei Toma
Dawn of the Arcana
Princess Nakaba of Senan is forced to marry Prince Caesar of the enemy country Belquat, tantamount to becoming a hostage. While Caesar is pleasing to the eye, he is also selfish and possessive, telling Nakaba outright: "You are my property." With only her attendant Loki at her side, Nakaba must find a way to cope with her hostile surroundings, her fake marriage...and a mysterious power!
Available now!
viz media
viz.com
REIMEI NO ARCANA © 2009 Rei TOMA/SHOGAKUKAN

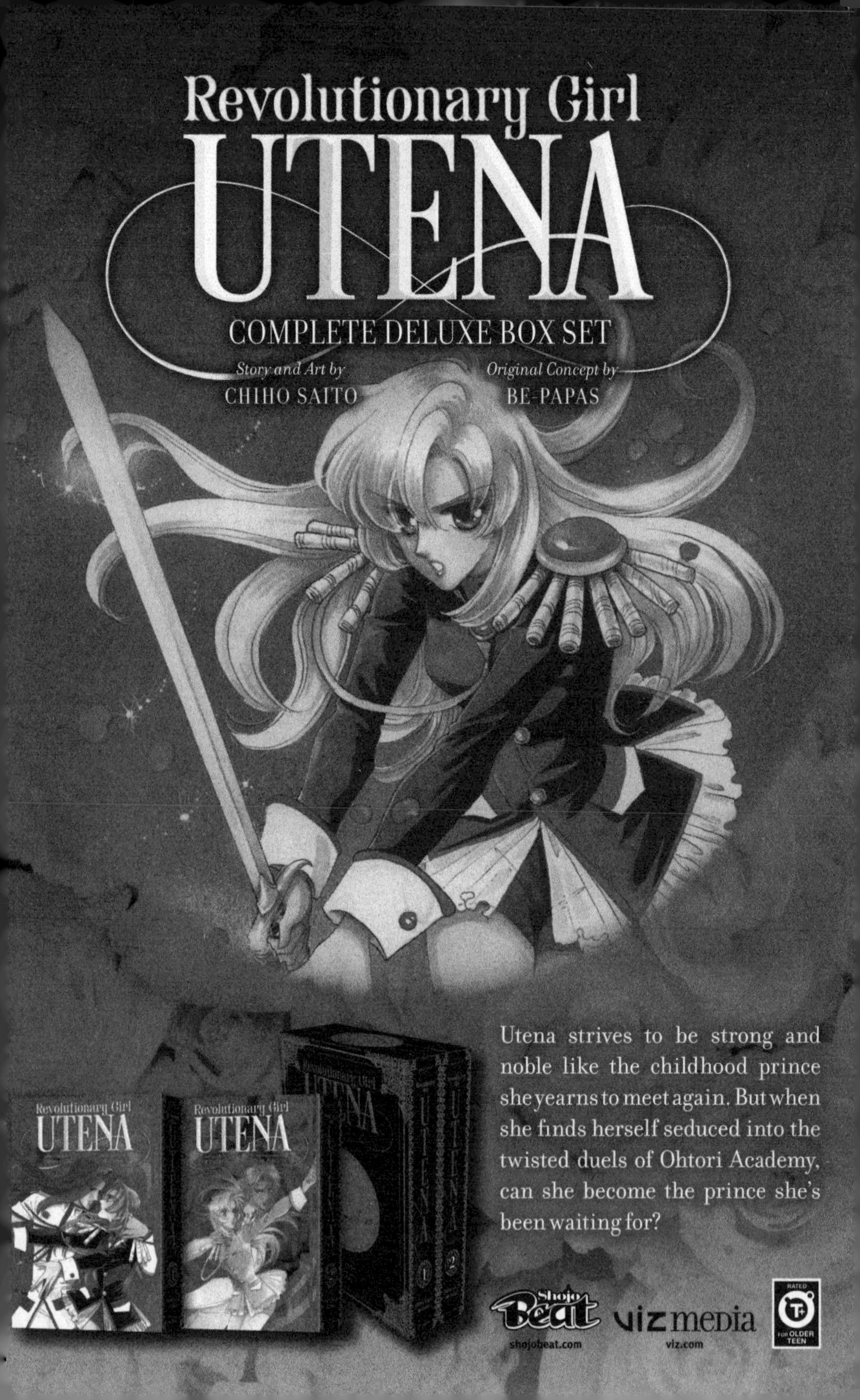
Revolutionary Girl
UTENA
COMPLETE DELUXE BOX SET
Story and Art by
CHIHO SAITO
Original Concept by
BE-PAPAS
Revolutionary Girl
UTENA
Revolutionary Girl
UTENA
Utena strives to be strong and noble like the childhood prince she yearns to meet again. But when she finds herself seduced into the twisted duels of Ohtori Academy, can she become the prince she's been waiting for?
Shojo Beat
shojobeat.com
viz media
viz.com
RATED
T+
FOR OLDER TEEN

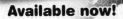

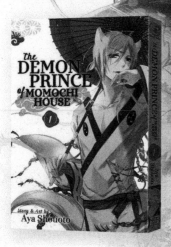
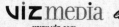

"Bloody" Mary, a vampire with a death wish, has spent the past 400 years chasing down a modern-day exorcist named Maria who is thought to have inherited "The Blood of Maria" and is the only one who can kill Mary. To Mary's dismay, Maria doesn't know how to kill vampires. Desperate to die, Mary agrees to become Maria's bodyguard until Maria can find a way to kill him.

Bloody + Mary

Story and Art by
akaza samamiya

This is the last page.

Kakuriyo: Bed & Breakfast for Spirits has been printed in the original Japanese format to preserve the orientation of the artwork.

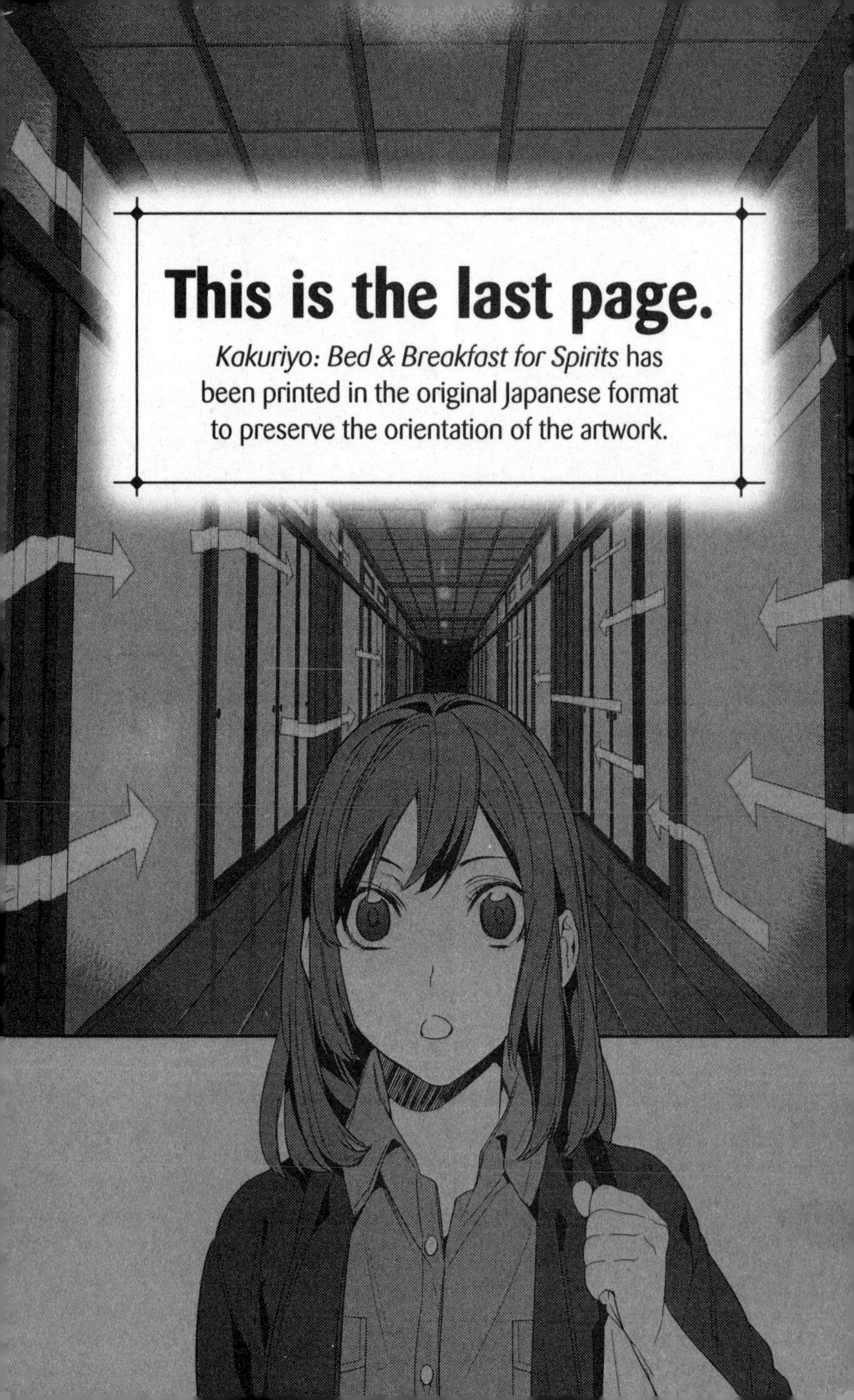